# Incomparable worth

Equal pay for comparable worth, or pay equity, is now an established policy in some states such as Minnesota and in England and Australia. Yet Steven Rhoads's research on those jurisdictions indicates there is no consensus on how to compare the value of dissimilar jobs involving "comparable" amounts of effort, skill, and responsibility. Consultants whose job evaluation systems are used in states adopting comparable-worth policies do not agree on the factors to be included or how they should be weighed.

Arbitrary results produced by comparable-worth policies have led to inefficient functioning of the labor markets Professor Rhoads has studied. By holding down wages despite labor shortages, Minnesota localities have been unable to hire needed computer specialists and nurses. Qantas must have its planes serviced by other companies because the Australian airline cannot attract enough mechanics to work at wages authorities deem fair. These policies have generated ill will among the workers who lose in pay-equity decisions, with political as well as economic consequences.

This is the first book to look at the implementation of pay equity from a critical perspective. It argues that jobs are truly incomparable using the methods comparable worth relies on and that the principles of comparable worth are not reconcilable with those of a market economy.

# *Incomparable worth*

*Pay equity meets the market*

STEVEN E. RHOADS
*University of Virginia*

Published by the Press Syndicate of the University of Cambridge
The Pitt Building, Trumpington Street, Cambridge CB2 1RP
40 West 20th Street, New York, NY 10011-4211, USA
10 Stamford Road, Oakleigh, Victoria 3166, Australia



First published 1993

Printed in the United States of America

*Library of Congress Cataloging-in-Publication Data*
Rhoads, Steven E.
Incomparable worth : pay equity meets the market / Steven E. Rhoads.
p. cm.
Includes index.
ISBN 0-521-44187-0 (hc)
1. Pay equity – Minnesota. 2. Pay equity – Australia. I. Title.

HD6061.2.U6M637 1993 92-39227
331.2′153′09776 – dc20 CIP

A catalog record for this book is available from the British Library.

ISBN 0-521-44187-0 hardback

To my talented and loving wife Diana, and to her family
To our marvelous children, Chris, Nick, and John
To my admirable brothers and sister, Jay, Mike, Deirdre, and to their families
And to all the other Rhoadses, near and far

# Contents

# Acknowledgments

Much of this book draws heavily on information developed in interviews, and thus it is dependent on the goodwill of hundreds of people who gave freely of their time. I spoke with more supporters of equal pay for comparable worth than opponents, and I am most grateful to them for their invariable cordiality and helpfulness.

I regret that I have been unable to support the policies advocated by intelligent and public-spirited proponents of comparable worth, such as Heidi Hartmann, Christopher McCrudden, Nina Rothchild, and Michael Rubenstein. I am pleased, however, to be able to help give voice to less well known arguments of dedicated public servants who have long had doubts about comparable worth. To all those I interviewed on both sides of the issue I offer thanks for their time and concern.

During the five years I have been working on this book, I have enjoyed the research support of a number of talented graduate students. Mary Sue McShea's excellent master's thesis helped convince me that a major research project on comparable worth might be fruitful. Andy Busch, Steve Camarota, John Dinan, and Steve Teles read the entire manuscript, and all offered important advice on style and substance. Busch, in particular, will find many instances where his words, rather than mine, have survived the editorial process. Kari Davidson, assisted by Angela Barbee, provided superb help of many kinds during the busy time when most of the research was done. Jackie Rejman, Bob Stacey, and Tracey Warren helped check my footnotes and quotations. Stacey helped as well with his critique of Chapter 2 and with his skill at finding elusive data. Finally, thanks go to Toby Bryce, Anne Burgeson, Cathy Crawford, Cary Federman, Andrew Hall, Bruce Larson, Mike McElroy, and Jackie O'Reilly for significant help at various stages.

Among my faculty colleagues special thanks go to my friends from economics, Bill Johnson and Ed Olsen. Both have given generously of their time to read not only the entire manuscript, but other economists' commentary on it. Since they performed similar tasks on my earlier *The Economist's View of the World,* Bill and Ed make me wonder if there may be such a thing as a free lunch after all. In any case it is a tasty one. I am most grateful for their friendly counsel through the years.

In the midst of his typically frantic schedule, my colleague and friend Jim Ceaser also read all of this manuscript in its early, ugly form and all of my earlier manuscripts as well. As his many graduate students know, Jim's counsel is always valuable, but even more so is the joie de vivre he brings to most corners of old Cabell Hall.

A friend and old colleague, Gary Marks, read the entire manuscript, and his comments on the European Community and United Kingdom chapters were especially helpful. James Alvey and Mark Killingsworth gave such detailed and helpful comments that one could have imagined they must be old friends.

In 1987 I knew little about comparable worth and little more about the politics of Minnesota, the United Kingdom, and Australia. The faculty and staff of Nuffield College, Oxford University, generously provided a research home during the first six months of 1988 while I conducted research on the United Kingdom's approach to equal pay for equal value. At a later stage Michael O'Connor, Hjalte Rasmussen, Benjamin Roberts, Ann Robinson, Michael Rubenstein, and Geoffrey Wood offered critical remarks on drafts of Chapters 5 and 6. Merry Beckmann and Dick Brainerd performed a similar task for the Minnesota chapters, as did Michael Angwin, Elise Callander, Paul McGavin, and my friends and colleagues James Savage and Herman Schwartz for the one on Australia.

I am most grateful for all my readers' time and judgment. I have not always taken their advice, and they are of course blameless for errors of fact or interpretation that may remain.

A magnificent grant from the Lynde and Harry Bradley Foundation enabled me to go to the United Kingdom, Australia, and Minnesota and to support myself while researching and writing the first draft. At a later stage substantial grants from the Earhart and John M. Olin foundations enabled me to bring the project to a more expeditious conclusion. Significant support for the project was also provided by the University of Virginia's Center for Advanced Studies and its Bankard Fund.

At later stages of the project, Steve Finkel provided help with a translation of European Community treaty language, and Larry Sabato shared relevant experiences from his store of successful publishing ventures. Word processing whizzes Donna Packard, Barbara McCauley, and Judy

Birckhead made my life much easier, as did the skill and enthusiasm of my Cambridge editors, Emily Loose, Scott Parris, Mary Racine, and Robert Racine.

Finally, as always, my wife Diana was my most important editor of more versions than either of us cares to remember. As we start our second twenty-five years together, I am pleased to be able to thank her here for the fond memories of the first twenty-five.

# 1

# Introduction

The comparable-worth movement gets its fuel from a number – $.71. This is the amount that women working full time in 1990 earned for every dollar earned by men working full time.[1] Supporters of comparable worth believe that at least half of the wage gap reflects discrimination and that women in many predominantly female occupations are paid substantially less than their work is actually worth. Comparable worth would require employers to pay employees equal salaries for dissimilar jobs requiring "comparable" amounts of factors such as know-how, problem solving, accountability, and undesirable working conditions. The Hay Associates job evaluation system, for example, used these four factors to rate delivery van drivers and "clerk typists 2" working for the state of Minnesota. The jobs were found to be of equal worth, but the maximum monthly salary for the delivery van driver was more than $200 higher.[2] Under Minnesota's 1982 pay-equity law this disparity was remedied by means of a substantial raise for clerk typists.

Sometimes comparable worth is seen as a way to eliminate racial discrimination in pay, but it is everywhere aimed at eliminating gender discrimination in pay. The women's movement as well as some unions with large numbers of women members have kept the issue alive in the public arena. Their goal is a substantial reduction in the female–male wage gap.

The effort to establish equal pay for comparable worth is worldwide, though in most of the world it goes by the title "equal pay for work of equal value." For over fifteen years, Australia and the countries of the European Community (EC) have legally required both public and private employers to base salaries on comparable-worth/equal-value criteria.[3] For well over a decade, various Canadian political jurisdictions have also mandated equal value for public employees, and in 1988 the application of the concept was extended into the private sector in Ontario. In that province all public and private organizations with more than nine employees are required to assess occupations according to comparable-worth criteria and to pay accordingly.[4]

In the United States comparable worth is less pervasive, but a number of state and local governments have passed pay equity legislation that applies to their public employees. The National Committee on Pay Equity, a coalition of labor, women's, civil rights, religious, and other organizations working to achieve pay equity, reports that twenty states and over seventeen hundred local governments, school districts, and universities have begun to make comparable-worth pay adjustments for their employees.[5] Many other jurisdictions are studying the issue, and national conferences of both mayors and governors have passed resolutions supporting comparable worth.[6]

States in the East and Midwest, states with a unionized public sector, and states controlled by the Democratic party have been the most likely to institute comparable worth, often called "pay equity."[7] At the national level partisan divisions have been particularly marked, with Democrats generally supportive and Republicans generally opposed.[8]

Democratic support for the idea began with the Kennedy administration's 1963 proposal to have an equal-pay act applying to comparable as well as to equal work. Congress strongly resisted the idea, and the bill that passed prohibited discrimination only for wages paid for equal work.[9] Democratic presidential candidates Carter, Mondale, and Dukakis all supported comparable worth or pay equity. Bill Clinton has not taken an explicit position on the subject, although pay equity is in the 1992 Democratic platform, as it was in 1984 and 1988.

Toward the end of his term in office President Carter proposed an executive order that would have required federal contractors to set pay rates according to comparable-worth criteria. President Reagan, however, killed the proposal shortly after taking office,[10] and his chairman of the Commission on Civil Rights – Clarence Pendleton, Jr. – later called comparable worth "the looniest idea since Looney Tunes."[11] President Bush and the Republican leaders in Congress have also been opposed to comparable worth.

During the years of the Reagan and Bush presidencies, comparable-worth supporters did not, however, give up the cause. Senator Alan

Cranston introduced a bill that would have required the executive branch to eliminate "discriminatory wage differentials" throughout the economy.[12] Three times the House passed bills that would ask a commission to determine whether the U.S. government's position-classification scheme allows sex or race to influence pay rates. The House debates on these measures have sometimes been vitriolic. In 1988 after a Republican's characterization of comparable worth as "sexist socialism" was called "insulting, outrageous and frankly sickening" by a Democratic representative, another Republican suggested that Democratic representatives might want to "step outside."[13] The federal pay study bill then under consideration passed 302 to 98. In the Senate it failed because, in the crush of end of the term business, fourteen senators promised a filibuster on the bill, and according to a National Committee on Pay Equity staff member, there were only fifty-seven senators who could be counted on to vote to break a filibuster. In these circumstances the Democratic leader, Senator Byrd, refused to proceed with the measure.

Abandoning attempts to pass a congressional bill funding the federal pay commission, comparable-worth congressional supporters have asked the General Accounting Office (GAO) to study the question. The GAO has treated comparable worth sympathetically in the past, and proponents expect its report, due in the fall of 1993, to be helpful.

Advocates think equal pay for comparable worth a matter of elemental justice. As their "Looney Tunes" and "sexist socialism" statements suggest, opponents strongly disagree. When I decided to begin researching this contentious issue, I was skeptical and puzzled: skeptical because I did not see how comparable worth could be reconciled with a market economy in which wages, like other prices, are meant to be influenced powerfully by supply and demand; puzzled because I saw that a number of economists and a National Academy of Sciences committee were numbered among the many knowledgeable people supporting comparable worth.

I decided to investigate what was actually happening in three areas often cited as success stories by proponents of comparable worth: Minnesota, the United Kingdom, and Australia. Minnesota is an obvious choice. It is the only state requiring all its localities to develop and implement a comparable-worth/pay equity plan for their employees. Of the more than seventeen hundred local bodies that have implemented pay equity plans nationwide, more than thirteen hundred are in Minnesota.[14] Moreover, most reports from Minnesota are quite favorable, and advocates see the state as "the shining example of how to do pay equity right."[15] Proponents use the favorable reports on Minnesota in Congress and elsewhere to refute critics who predict intolerable repercussions if comparable worth is made the law of the land.

To find cases where comparable worth had been legally mandated for the private sector, I had to go abroad. The ambitious Ontario law had only just been passed, and it would be years before results on its implementation would be available. The obvious foreign choices were the United Kingdom, which – in its domestic courts – has provided most of the litigation under EC law, and Australia, frequently used by proponents to show that one can achieve dramatic improvements in women's wages without incurring serious economic costs.[16]

As a result of my travels, interviews, and reading, my initial skepticism about comparable worth has turned to firm opposition. Although the author of a book that adopts such a position might seem hostile to the aspirations of working women, I hope that readers will not assume that this author is. I expect many readers who support the *idea* of comparable worth or pay equity to be surprised at how inequitable it can be in *practice*. In Minnesota utility and library directors have come out of the comparable-worth process with higher pay than their city managers, and workers previously paid equally for equal work have been assigned unequal pay for doing equal work. In the United Kingdom a cook who won her case was awarded a higher salary than her supervisor was paid. U.K. experts assigned to different firms and given the relatively narrow task of deciding whether female machinists are as valuable as male upholsterers have been unable to agree. As a result, some firms must pay their women not only more than the market dictates, but also more than their competitors do.

Even from the point of view of those who defend higher pay for jobs traditionally performed by women, comparable-worth evaluation results are sometimes quite unsatisfactory. In St. Paul, for example, predominantly male police officers received large comparable-worth pay raises, and in many Minnesota localities public-sector nurses' salaries are being held below private-sector levels because of the results of comparable-worth studies. In Australia government secretaries are similarly disadvantaged compared to many of their private-sector counterparts, and the Australian wage-fixing system is responsible.

Comparable worth is dependent on finding a reliable way to compare the value of predominantly male and predominantly female jobs. Proponents of the concept in the United States publicly state that job evaluation provides "objective criteria to value the content and requirements of jobs."[17] But in none of the areas studied have I found "objective" job evaluations. There is no agreement among experts on factors to be included, on how they should be weighed, or even on how factors (such as working conditions) should be measured once decided on. Further, as the book's final chapter illustrates, comparable-worth advocates in private or at conferences among the initiated often stress the political, not the objective nature of job evaluation. Politics clearly played an important role in Minnesota, where the route to higher pay was often a rhetorically effective presentation of job duties on questionnaires or in job evaluation committees.

As a nation we cannot agree about whether welfare, education, or law enforcement is the higher good, so it should perhaps not surprise us that pay experts have found no objective way to determine the relative worth of social workers, teachers, and police officers. As the title of this book suggests, jobs are truly "incomparable" using the methods comparable worth relies on. But in all three places studied the attempt to assume otherwise brought considerable ill will among workers. This effect might also be expected once the political nature of the comparable-worth process is unveiled. One can succeed in politics by advertising one's virtues or by criticizing the competition. Similarly, one can promote the merits of one's job either by embellishing its requirements or by running down the importance of jobs currently paying more. The latter method was applied in all three areas studied with predictable results on employee morale.

As fatal to comparable worth as the incomparable nature of job "worth" is the inability to reconcile the principles of "pay equity" with those of a market economy. In a well-functioning market economy a sudden rise in a job's wage signals a shortage of labor, thus inducing more people to train or apply for the work in question. Yet in Minnesota the vagaries of the process were such that numerous libraries that had forty to sixty applicants for every opening were compelled to give librarians raises of 20–60 percent. This occurred at the same time that nurses, in short supply but found to be "worth" much less than they were being paid in the private sector, could not be offered a wage high enough to induce them to apply for government jobs. By holding down wages despite shortages Minnesota localities have been unable to get the nurses they need, and Qantas in Australia must get other countries' airlines to service their planes because they cannot attract enough mechanics at the pay level the administrative authorities have deemed fair. Similarly, by raising wages in the face of surpluses, Minnesota localities and the United Kingdom have caused cooks, among others, to lose jobs.

In Australia I found that the wage-setting system became increasingly rigid, centralized, and politicized through time. With their pay in the balance, members of predominantly male unions engaged in veiled threats and sometimes coercion and sabotage to get the attention of the Industrial Relations Commission, which set their pay. The commission has openly acknowledged that it has felt compelled to grant larger wage increases than it has thought wise from the point of view of inflation, unemployment, investment, and economic growth.

Spurred by economic troubles far greater than any we face, Australia is now in the process of abandoning the wage-fixing system that made possible the reduction in the pay gap advertised by U.S. proponents. At the same time, the United States debates the adoption of comparable worth because some believe that the reduction in the U.S. female–male pay gap (from 60 percent in 1980 to 71 percent in 1990) is occurring too slowly.[18] My investigations suggest that it would be an enormous mistake to move toward what Australia flees. The stakes for our economy and our polity are as grave as comparable-worth critics suggest.

# 2

## The debate over equal pay for comparable worth

As explained in Chapter 1, full-time working women get only $.71 for every dollar received by full-time working men. Supporters of comparable worth know that few years have passed since separate want ads for men and women restricted options for working women.[1] They also know that surveys show that many managers think men more likely than women to have the traits thought to be associated with managerial effectiveness.[2] They cite court cases showing that some major firms continue to restrict women's access to jobs and promotions.[3] And they endorse and publicize an influential report of the National Academy of Science's National Research Council which concludes that a substantial portion of the wage gap results from sex discrimination.[4]

Comparable-worth advocates are outraged that male animal-care attendants get paid more than female child-care workers, and male high school graduates more than female college graduates. They argue that remedying such discrimination is efficient as well as fair since "resources aren't reasonably allocated when some people are underpaid and others are overpaid, relative to their contribution to the employer."[5] Moreover, at a time when so many families are dependent on women's income, underpaying women is considered a cause of poverty and other social ills.

The heart of the problem is seen as job segregation. Employers can no longer legally pay women less for doing the same work, but if they can shuffle them into a limited number of job categories, they can pay women in those jobs less than they pay for comparable jobs dominated by men: "In 1981 more than 60 percent of the female (or male) labor force would have had to change jobs for the two sex groups to have the same detailed occupational distribution."[6] In an era when occupational segregation by race has declined substantially, segregation by sex, at least among whites, has decreased very little, and it is now much more pronounced than segregation by race.

When comparable-worth proponents look at the labor market, they do not see what the neoclassical economist sees: pervasive competition with wage outcomes affected mightily by the supply of and demand for labor. Instead, they see what institutional economists and many sociologists see: labor markets that are inherently rigid and balkanized. Large firms promote from within based on rules and customs that have little to do with external labor market forces. Union agreements determine hiring rules and pay rates in uncompetitive ways. And segmented labor markets sort individuals into noncompeting groups largely on the basis of sex and to some extent race.

How is it that the segregation of women into certain jobs leads to the wage gap? The crowding theory argues that by excluding women from "men's work" such as truck driving and the building trades and by shuffling women into a limited number of jobs, employers increase the supply of labor for these "women's" jobs and thus drive down the going wage. However, there has been a large increase in employment in many "women's jobs" in recent decades. This would tend to mitigate any crowding effect.[7] Most comparable-worth proponents thus rely on another theory to explain how job segregation leads to the wage gap. This explanation is more loosely developed than the crowding theory and draws more on sociology than on economics. It is a cultural theory that emphasizes concepts such as socialization.

According to this theory, our society has a pervasive tendency to undervalue women and the work they typically perform. Women's traditional nurturing role in the family goes unpaid and underappreciated. Thus, when women take up the nurturing and helping jobs in the work force – e.g., nurse, teacher, child-care worker, secretary – the jobs are seen as natural to women and requiring less skill than comparable male-dominated jobs, for instance, police officer, electrician, administrator. Because women and women's work have been historically devalued, the jobs women hold are undervalued and underpaid. Worse yet, many women themselves begin to accept society's judgments. Through a long process of socialization they come to believe that they are meant to help and support, not to lead and exercise authority. The result is that "women are paid less because they are in women's jobs, and women's jobs are paid less because they are done by women."[8]

Supporters of comparable worth usually acknowledge that a part of the wage gap reflects not market discrimination, but differences in productivity or "human capital," such as education and training, work experience, continuity of work history, and the like. But they are quick to add that statistical studies which try to use such human capital variables to explain the differences in average earnings between the sexes leave more than one-half the wage gap still unexplained.

The more technically oriented proponents of comparable worth acknowledge that the remaining unexplained "residual" in the wage gap could be caused by unmeasured factors that influence earnings or by measurement errors instead of by discrimination. But the proponents tend to agree with the National Research Council's *Women, Work and Wages,* which concludes that the unexplained differences indicate "the probability of discriminatory processes, unless the contrary can be shown."[9]

Another kind of statistical study used by proponents asks if the proportion of female workers in an occupation explains a significant portion of the wage gap after controlling for human capital variables. Some such studies show that the sex composition of an occupation explains 10–30 percent of the variation.[10] Comparable-worth proponents see this finding as a sign that the market undervalues "women's work" in a discriminatory way.

## COMPARABLE-WORTH OPPONENTS

Opponents of comparable worth first challenge proponents on the size of the wage gap itself. They point out that the $.71 on the dollar ratio used by proponents refers to the ratio of full-time female *annual* earnings to full-time male *annual* earnings. But "full-time" women workers, on average, work fewer weeks and fewer hours per week than males. The weekly female–male earning ratio after adjusting for hours worked is about 78 percent, not 71 percent. Opponents also argue that the favorable trends in all the ratios are evidence that the wage gap will close considerably without comparable worth. When campaigning for the Equal Rights Amendment in the 1970s, the National Organization for Women featured a campaign button saying "59 cents." It represented the unadjusted full-time annual earnings ratio that has since closed to \$.71. The ratio based on full-time weekly earnings has been closing still faster. Even more encouraging for the future is the fact that the wage gap for working women aged twenty to twenty-four had closed to 90 percent by 1990. (It was 78 percent in 1980.)[11]

Opponents also disagree about the role of discrimination in wage differences. They often distinguish between current labor market discrimination and premarket disadvantages – for example, less training or experience – that may result from broader discrimination of various kinds. Current labor market discrimination can be defined as "the valuation in the labor market of personal characteristics of the worker that are unrelated to productivity."[12] Current labor market discrimination concerns especially the discriminatory tastes of employers – discrimination that shows up in their demand for labor – and it ignores societal or familial discrimination that may affect the "supply-side" tastes or educational credentials that women bring to the labor market.

Opponents of comparable worth grant that instances of current labor market discrimination still occur, but many of them doubt that they are pervasive enough to be an important cause of either occupational segregation or the wage gap. Regarding occupational segregation, the Stanford economist Victor Fuchs argues that prejudice against blacks is at least as great as prejudice against women, yet the occupational segregation indexes by race are much lower than by sex. Moreover, sex segregation is *lowest* for workers with higher degrees – precisely the workers most likely to intrude on the domain of prejudiced male employers.[13] With respect to the wage gap, Fuchs notes that millions of workers' wages are not determined by employers, prejudiced or not. Instead:

> Their earnings depend upon self-employment income, commissions, tips, piece rates, and other forms of compensation closely tied to individual performance. The sex difference in hourly earnings of such workers is just as large as among regular wage and salary employees. . . . Indeed, among the self-employed, the gap in hourly earnings is slightly larger than among the employed.[14]

When trying to explain wage levels, most economists and most comparable-worth opponents look first to supply and demand. They argue that the relative demand for one's labor depends on the demand for the product or service one helps make. If the demand for what a person helps produce is high and the supply of those who share the skill or interest in making it is relatively low, that person will probably command a high wage. Competitive pressures push wages toward levels that reflect the marginal (last-hired) laborer's additional contribution to output – what that laborer adds by working here rather than elsewhere or not at all. To be sure, many in business would like to pay their women only half of what they add to their firm's profitability. But they would no doubt like to pay their men only half as much as well. And in any case, employers who adopted either course of action would face pressure from other employers who could make extra profits for themselves if they were to hire the first firm's employees and pay them a little more but still less than their productivity warrants. And the new employers in turn would face pressure from firms willing to pay a little more still.

Most proponents of comparable worth argue that this elementary theory so frequently offered by opponents neglects the real world of segmented and union-dominated labor markets and is instead based on unrealistic assumptions such as perfect competition.[15] Opponents in turn say the theory is the best we have and far better than the theory of insulated, segmented labor markets relied on by proponents. Indeed, opponents point out that increased international competition has left labor markets less rigid and balkanized than they have been for a long time. For example, in recent years even the powerful steel and auto workers unions have had to grant substantial wage concessions because they have realized that making their companies' prices competitive with those abroad required reducing costs of production.[16] One can imagine cases where workers might be vulnerable to exploitation, say hospital nurses in a town with only one hospital. But as Victor Fuchs notes:

> As a practical matter, . . . this issue of employer control of labor markets does not have much force. In most markets there are numerous employers who must, within reasonable limits, pay the going wage in order to attract and hold their share of well-qualified employees.[17]

Child-care workers, argue opponents of comparable worth, surely perform important work, and they are not very well paid. But the same could be said of certain male-dominated professions such as farming or the ministry. Why assume that child-care workers are paid less than animal keepers because of discrimination? Opponents argue that they may be paid less because there are so many more people who know how to take care of young children than there are people who know how to look after wild animals. Or maybe they are paid less because taking care of children is less risky and, for many, more enjoyable.[18]

In higher education, the engineering and scientific faculty, which are dominated by men, are paid more than faculty in the humanities, which have far more women. But one study found the differences in pay were not the result of discrimination but of the greater employment opportunities available to engineering and scientific faculty outside of the academy. Given high-paying opportunities elsewhere, faculty in the hard sciences will not supply their labor in sufficient numbers at the pay rates that are adequate to attract faculty in the humanities.[19]

Opponents offer still other reasons for the wage gap, and few of them can be linked very directly to employer discrimination against female occupations. Studies show that 15–40 percent of the wage gap can be explained by the disproportionate number of women in industries such as banking and retail trade that pay lower wages to women *and* men (after controlling for human capital) as compared with industries where men are disproportionately represented, such as mining, construction, transport, communications, and public utilities. The latter industries pay higher wages both because they are more heavily unionized and because they are more capital intensive.[20]

Comparable-worth critics think that another large portion of the wage gap reflects the different roles of men and women in the typical family. Single women between the ages of twenty-five and sixty-four earn 91 percent of the income of men who are single, and never-married women have complete wage parity with never-married men.[21] Proponents counter by arguing that never-married men are atypical in that they are more likely than most men to be economic losers. But something more must be going on because not just marriage, but the presence of children in the family seems to affect earnings. The addition of each child enhances the married man's earnings by another 3 percent while depressing that of the married woman by 7–10 percent.[22]

Marriage itself decreases promotion seeking among women as it increases it among men. Women are far more likely than their husbands to say that their spouse's job is the more important in terms of family income. They are also far more likely to express willingness to give up their jobs to follow a spouse who has obtained a better job in another city.[23] When couples do move, the wage gap between them increases substantially. One study of husband–wife families that moved across state lines in 1971–2 found that, in the succeeding four years, the value of the husband's earnings went up $4,254 while the wives' went down $1,716.[24]

Women are also more likely than men to drop out of the labor force for a time to care for children, and some surveys show that dropping out of the labor force has a profound effect by lowering future wages. A worker who drops out of the labor force for five years earns one-third less on returning than an identical worker who has been employed continuously. Even five years after reentering the work force the returning worker earns 15 percent less.[25]

Opponents argue that a significant number of women, realizing that they may wish to drop out of the work force for a period, choose occupations that have relatively light penalties for intermittent employment. Thus, one study finds that college major subjects chosen by women with high parenting expectations "are those that are less subject to the obsolescence that would occur during periods of labor force withdrawal."[26] Teaching, nursing, clerical work, and child care are occupations that are relatively easy to reenter in either one's old or a new location.

Still other factors not involving current market discrimination by employers are said to contribute to the wage gap. Women, for example, may have less time for their jobs than their spouses because wives employed full time do much more housework including child care than husbands employed full time. In the mid-1970s, wives employed full time averaged 25 hours of work in the home and 39 hours of work in the market each week, while husbands employed full time averaged 13 hours of work in the home and 47 hours of work in the market.[27] Less complete data show that, by the 1980s, these differentials had narrowed only slightly.

Gary Becker has noted that child care and other housework are tiring and "demand relatively large quantities of energy compared to leisure and other nonmarket uses of time by men." Becker argues that married women who do most of the housework thus have less energy available for the market than do most husbands. When women spend less energy per hour of work, they earn less, and their "household responsibilities also induce occupational segregation because married women seek occupations and jobs that are less effort intensive and otherwise are more compatible with the demands of their home responsibilities."[28]

Because women assume more family responsibilities than men, they take jobs that require less overtime and commuting time.[29] Moreover, both men and women in predominantly female jobs report that it is relatively easy to take time off for personal reasons. There is evidence that women choose branches of medicine and law that permit them more time with their families and that women in federal employment choose less demanding and absorbing jobs "because of their greater involvement in – and responsibility for – their children."[30]

Part of the wage differential between men and women may be explained by the former's relatively greater interest in obtaining high pay or in taking a leadership role, which generally commands a high salary. In planning for and seeking jobs, men put more emphasis on wages and leadership opportunities. Women selecting jobs, on the other hand, are more apt to stress nonmonetary benefits, such as good physical conditions, convenient hours, or rewarding interpersonal aspects of the job – relations with co-workers and supervisors, the opportunity to help others, and the like.[31] Patients of self-employed female physicians must wait longer to get an appointment; moreover, female physicians charge higher fees, and yet they see 37 percent fewer patients per hour (after controlling for specialty, experience, etc.).[32] Women doctors apparently put relatively more of a premium on attention to their patients than on earnings. That both men and women in predominantly female jobs report better supervisors and better relations with co-workers than do men and women in predominantly male jobs corroborates the statistics suggesting that women selecting jobs give greater priority to positive social interaction.[33] Women's interest in good physical conditions is supported by studies indicating that men and women in predominantly female jobs report fewer illnesses and accidents and by other data confirming their subjective opinions.[34]

Better supervisors, fewer risks, shorter commutes, easier time off for personal reasons – all these are nonmonetary benefits disproportionately available to predominantly female jobs. Opponents of comparable worth argue that by ignoring these aspects of jobs, most studies inflate the size of the real wage gap.

Opponents also argue that the studies that seek to explain earnings in terms of differences in human capital use very inadequate measures of economically relevant human capital such as years of schooling completed and years of experience. Economist Robert Rector has argued:

> This approach leads to absurd conclusions. Example: A male worker, Bill, has four years of college and a BS in electrical engineering; a female worker, Anne, has four years of college and a BA in English. Both have been employed for four years; Bill works as an engineer and Anne works as a secretary. Since both workers have identical years of education and work, wage gap models would expect them to be paid equally. Any difference in pay would be attributed to "discrimination" or held to be "unexplained" (and thus suspect).[35]

Opponents see no reason at all to think that the portion of the wage gap unexplained by human capital, experience, and the like is probably the result of discrimination. They point out that studies that attempt to explain differences in earnings among white males have an unexplained residual greater than that of the studies that attempt to explain differences between men and women. Yet no one thinks this residual is the result of discrimination.

Opponents also criticize the statistical studies that control for human capital variables and then ask how much of the wage gap is explained by the proportion of female workers in an occupation. They argue that so long as men make more than women for *any* reason, the percentage of females in an occupation will be an indicator of lower wages. Economist James Smith points out that these job segregation studies also find that an increasing proportion of Asians in an occupation raises wages. He notes that no one argues that occupations pay more because they have more Asians in them, and he worries about the asymmetric interpretation of similar findings: "If a protected minority group has a positive coefficient on a comparable worth variable, is it unobserved components of skill? And if it is a negative one, is it discrimination?"[36] In any case the opponents argue that if a large number of controls are used, the percentage of women in an occupation in fact explains little or nothing, and unexplained residuals become so small as to seem trivial given all the plausible nondiscriminatory contributors to a wage gap that remain unmeasured and perhaps unmeasurable.[37]

Many economists who believe that market discrimination is not a significant cause of the wage gap simultaneously believe that there is a substantial amount of market discrimination in the U.S. economy.[38] They think these beliefs are reconcilable if we reflect on the nature of a private enterprise system with a large number of employers with differing tastes.

The point can best be understood by reference to a recent study of race discrimination done by the Urban Institute. The institute matched black and white males, aged nineteen to twenty-four, according to education, experience, and intangibles such as openness, apparent energy levels, and articulateness. Ten pairs of auditors looked for entry-level jobs in the retail and service trades. The study found that blacks "were denied a job that was offered to an equally qualified white 15 percent of the time; white testers were denied a job when their black counterparts received an offer in 5 percent of the audits."[39] In 13 percent of the cases both candidates received an offer. Overall, 28 percent of the white testers got offers whereas only 18 percent of the black testers did.

Richard Epstein argues that, even given these disparities, there is reason to think that the real-world salaries of applicants such as these will be very close. "While testers apply for jobs in matched pairs, real job seekers look for those employers who will offer them the most favorable deals. Black workers gravitate to firms that afford them a preference or to those that are indifferent to matters of race."[40] In the Urban Institute study a majority of the firms that hired any tester either favored the black applicant or were indifferent to race. For the reasons already discussed (pp. 10–11), those who doubt that discrimination has a significant effect on the wage gap think that competition among this majority of firms will usually be adequate to ensure a nondiscriminatory wage.

One cannot be sure whether women face more or less discrimination than blacks and whether the pattern would be different in other industries or for applicants for promotion rather than for entry-level positions. Still, the general point remains. Because of competition among firms, pervasive discrimination need not necessarily mean a large wage gap. In 1992 the State Farm Insurance Company settled for $157 million a lawsuit brought by 814 California women who were not given an opportunity to become insurance agents. The suit was initiated by a woman who, in the 1970s, was an $8,000-a-year secretary. When turned down by State Farm, this woman was hired immediately as an agent by a rival insurance company, and at the time she received her settlement her salary was "in the six figures."[41]

There were no doubt other State Farm women who "settled" for the lower positions they occupied and did not seek opportunities elsewhere when State Farm discriminated against them. Thus, though Epstein's point seems relevant and important, it is surely not conclusive.

## REFLECTIONS ON THE DEBATE

To one coming afresh to this literature what is perhaps most surprising is the huge difference between the typical proponent and the typical opponent on the question of how much of the female–male wage gap has been satisfactorily explained by differences in variables that do not reflect discrimination. The proponents often say that no more than 50 percent of the wage gap can be explained by differences in nondiscriminatory variables. The opponents frequently say that less than 10 percent of the wage gap remains unexplained by differences in a range of nondiscriminatory variables.

I have interviewed a number of the academics doing this research, and it is clear that the differences are conceptual as well as technical. Proponents argue that many of the explanatory variables used by opponents are just "proxies for gender itself rather than indicators of substantive factors that could reasonably be linked to productivity differences."[42] For example, "percent part time" is used by some analysts as a factor that presumably has some effect on productivity. Some proponents wonder why having lots of part-timers should reduce productivity. They also say that this variable is so correlated with "percent female" that, by including it, the analyst cannot distinguish between the explanatory effect on the wage gap of the two variables.

Proponents also quarrel with the way opponents interpret results. An opponent will assume that marital status may affect productivity and lead to a lower wage for married women because of differences in male and female family roles. A proponent may wonder if the results obtained when a marital status variable is included may not reflect the greater discrimination faced by married women as compared with single women.[43] Similarly, proponents will say that perhaps "percent part time" is not a "fair" variable because many of the women are stuck in part-time jobs and would prefer full-time ones, but discrimination prevents their obtaining them. Finally, that women are not in the risky, dirty, relatively well-paid blue collar jobs like construction and mining may reflect their free choices, but it may also reflect the hostility that women feel on such male-dominated work sites.[44] The opponents, even the academic ones, often do not acknowledge these alternative possibilities in their work.

At the same time academic proponents, in their analysis of occupational segregation, rarely mention, much less discuss, the possibility that because of different family roles or other reasons, women on average may have different occupational tastes than do men. There was usually tension in the air after I raised this subject with proponents of comparable worth. When I asked the top aide to a leading congressional supporter of comparable worth if the issue of women's differing tastes ever arose in the Washington debate, he said no, "it never comes up. It would be embarrassing. It's a myth. The people [who raised it] would be hooted down."[45] I was also told that arguments claiming women's jobs pay less because time off is easier to get are met by women's groups with disbelieving cries: "Where are all these flexible jobs? I'd like to have one."

It seems that, for some proponents, the source of this anger is a sense that the different family roles/different tastes arguments have force but that, in a larger sense, they do not begin to dispose of the injustices to which women are subjected. Toward the end of a long interview with Nina Rothchild, the head of the Minnesota Department of Employee Relations (DOER) and the principal architect of Minnesota's comparable-worth policies, I raised with her the hypothesis that different job preferences explain lower women's wages. As a part of her answer she commented on the view that women take more sick leave than men. Rothchild said there was "no difference in sick leave usage" except that "women with sick children" are more likely to take time off to care for the children than are their husbands. This was because of their homemaking/child-care responsibilities. She saw no reason "to penalize women with a low wage" as their reward.

The stated goal of comparable worth in the United States is pay based either on the worth of work to the employer or on other unbiased, gender-neutral criteria such as skill, effort, and responsibility.[46] While taking time off to attend to sick children seems desirable from the perspective of society as a whole, employees who take more sick leave for whatever reason are less productive, and on either worth to the employer or job factor-based criteria they could be seen as deserving less pay. One reason advocates resist this argument is that they know that the women who seek flexible jobs, where it is relatively easy to get time off, do not want the extra time to goof off. The women want it to attend to their other, unpaid job at home. The advocates also know that full-time working women who are married work *more* hours, not fewer, than men if you compare the total work of each in the workplace *and* at home. And they may know of polls that show that 60 percent of working fathers, but only 36 percent of working mothers feel that they have enough time to themselves.[47]

Though the convention is to assume that differences in the wage gap resulting from differences in human capital are justified, proponents of comparable worth do not really believe that even these differences are unconnected to discrimination. Women may have less human capital because employers who expect them to drop out of the labor market give them fewer opportunities for on-the-job training[48] or because many parents are still willing to spend more money on a son's education than on a daughter's. And if women face a competitive disadvantage because of their greater family responsibilities, proponents see these responsibilities as foisted upon women, not as freely chosen.

At the heart of the comparable-worth philosophy is the belief that our culture teaches us that women are more naturally suited to nurturing and helping roles than to others. On the surface it seems odd for people who insist that women are socialized differently to refuse to consider seriously the possibility that job segregation may reflect different tastes or preferences about occupations. The explanation, I think, is that comparable-worth proponents do not believe that these differences in taste are authentic and free of coercion.

From one point of view the debate over the importance of discrimination in explaining the wage gap between men and women is not particularly relevant to the related debate over the merits of comparable worth. One sign of this is the existence of people who strongly agree with proponents about the significance of employer discrimination in explaining the wage gap, but strongly oppose comparable worth (see Chapter 8, pp. 231–2). Such people base their opposition on the costs of comparable worth, on its inability to identify the effect that employer discrimination has on pay for particular occupations, and on the existence of better, alternative ways to combat discrimination.

There are, however, proponents who would argue that the costs of comparable worth are irrelevant. Such proponents are convinced that employer discrimination is an important reason for the wage gap, that comparable worth is one remedy, and that both legally and morally, the high cost of not discriminating is no defense.[49]

Many opponents of comparable worth think, however, that the case for employer discrimination as a significant cause of the wage gap has not been persuasively made. If these opponents are themselves persuasive, the need for a comparable-worth remedy is called into question even without considering the costs of comparable worth.

## THE CONTROVERSIAL REMEDY: JOB EVALUATION SYSTEMS

The human capital studies use economywide data and relate the characteristics of individuals to their pay. At most they can suggest that something may be amiss if pay differentials are not explained by education, experience, and similar variables. Since employers pay for *jobs* performed, not the jobholders' education, experience, and the like, the broad economic studies give "little guidance as to whether and, if so, to what extent the pay for any particular job ought to be adjusted" to remedy inequities.[50] The method almost always used to spot particular inequities and indicate remedies is a job evaluation study (JES) conducted at the firm level.

One occasionally finds a city such as Los Angeles that, without doing a study, deals with charges of inequitable pay by simply increasing the pay of female-dominated occupations by some fixed percentage. And aware of the controversial nature of job evaluations, the National Committee on Pay Equity (NCPE) takes care to emphasize that it has not supported requiring them of all employers.[51] Still, NCPE's explanatory literature states that the underlying premise of pay equity is that "pay should be based on job-related factors such as skill, effort, responsibility and working conditions." In organizations of any size such a goal requires some sort of JES. Moreover, pay equity or comparable worth has been inextricably linked with job evaluation in all the states of the United States and throughout the world. Some definitions of comparable worth even center on "the application of a single, bias-free point factor job evaluation system."[52] And in the debate it is the proponents who defend comparable-worth job evaluation studies and the opponents who attack them.

Comparable-worth proponents note that job evaluation systems were well established in both the public and private sectors decades before the birth of the pay equity movement. Job evaluation has been used to set pay in the federal government for over a hundred years. Though good data do not exist, it is thought that a majority of large, private U.S. firms have formal job evaluation procedures.[53] Supporters of comparable worth thus ask why the evaluation systems suddenly become controversial when they are used to spot long-standing inequities.

There are two main types of job evaluation systems: policy capturing and a priori. The policy-capturing method, popular in the private sector, uses models that attempt to capture statistically the relationship between the wages paid for benchmark jobs and the job's contents (e.g., skill, responsibility). The regression coefficients show which job content factors are important in predicting wages. The coefficients are then used "to create the weights necessary to 'capture' the firm's implicitly valued wage criteria and apply them to all the jobs within that firm."[54]

The policy-capturing systems pick up factors valued by current employers in the market. Thus, if there is discrimination in the market wage hierarchy, the policy-capturing systems will include discriminatory factors in the job evaluation weighing model. For example, comparable-worth proponents argue that firms in the market discriminate by rewarding more highly responsibility for financial resources (likely to be male-dominated) than responsibility for human resources (likely to be female-dominated). Thus, proponents do not support policy-capturing systems,[55] though a heavily modified version that did not make comparisons with market wages was used for state employees in New York.[56]

The alternative a priori system is the type used for comparable-worth purposes in all state systems except New York as well as in Canada and the United Kingdom. With this approach a predetermined system of factors and factor weights is used to evaluate jobs within any given organization. For example, the popular Hay system uses know-how, problem solving, accountability, and where appropriate, working conditions. Other common systems replace problem solving with effort, and accountability with responsibility. Some have many more than four factors. The decision band method of Arthur Young Co., used widely by local jurisdictions in Minnesota, assumes that the value of a job is directly related to its decision-making requirements. Higher-banded decision-making jobs deal with more uncertainty and are seen as requiring more skill and effort.

Factors are usually broken down into multiple subfactors. Jobs receive points for their worth in terms of all subfactors. Factors and subfactors are then weighted, usually in terms of their importance to the organization. For example, in almost all systems knowledge and skills required count more heavily than do working conditions. Thus, a job with a medium numerical ranking on knowledge and a low ranking on working conditions (i.e., conditions are good) will usually be assigned a higher pay rate than a job with a low ranking on knowledge and a high ranking for (bad) working conditions.

Each job is assigned a total number of points and then plotted on a scattergram with job evaluation points on one axis and pay on the other axis. For comparable-worth purposes one also wants to identify separately the female- and male-dominated jobs. When one does so, proponents say, one invariably finds a pattern like that for Minnesota state employees, which is shown in Figure 1. Female-dominated jobs regularly pay less than male-dominated jobs for the same point value. A line that "fits" the male jobs data best is then drawn. An illustrative diagram from a Minnesota publication, Figure 2, shows the likely result. All the female-dominated jobs fall below the line. Comparable worth seeks to bring all the female-dominated jobs up to the male line or at least to have female jobs scattered above and below the line in the same way as for male jobs.

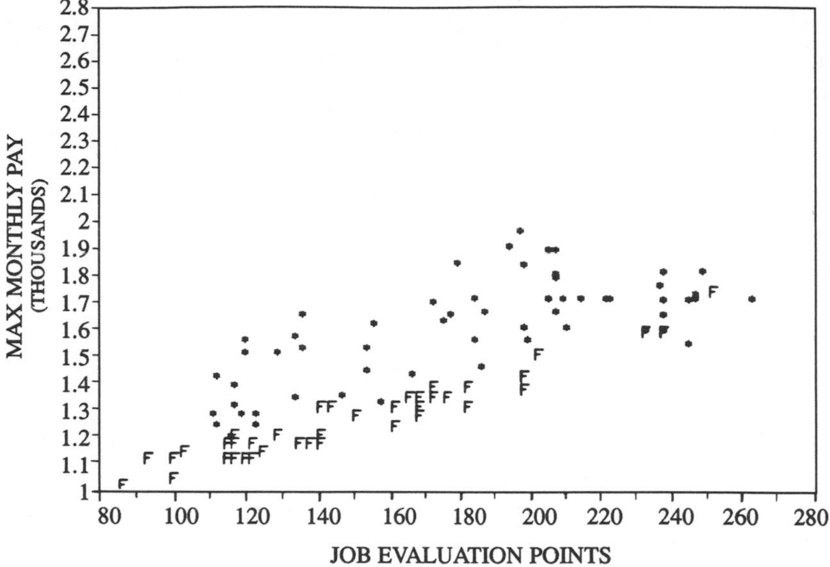


Figure 1. Each asterisk on the scattergram represents one male job class, and each "F" represents one female job class, in the Minnesota state government before pay equity. *Source:* "Pay Equity: The Minnesota Experience," Commission on the Economic Status of Women, 1986, p. 12.

As discussed later, critics of comparable worth charge that the job evaluations necessary to implement it are subjective, arbitrary, and capricious. Politicians who support pay equity are thus at pains to emphasize the objective nature of the enterprise. The 1988 U.S. House bill "to promote equitable pay practices," HR387, called for an "objective, quantitative" analysis of positions so as to establish "composite values . . . based on factors such as the skill, effort, responsibilities, qualification requirements, and working conditions involved." Similarly, a bill introduced in the state of Connecticut legislature, and circulated at NCPE's 1989 tenth anniversary conference, was entitled "An Act Concerning Objective Job Evaluations for Municipal Employees." In debate in congressional committees and on the floor, political supporters note that job evaluation, "born in the private sector," is not "some new and strange device, untried and untested."[57] They defend the need for a new objective study of the federal government's position classification system that seeks

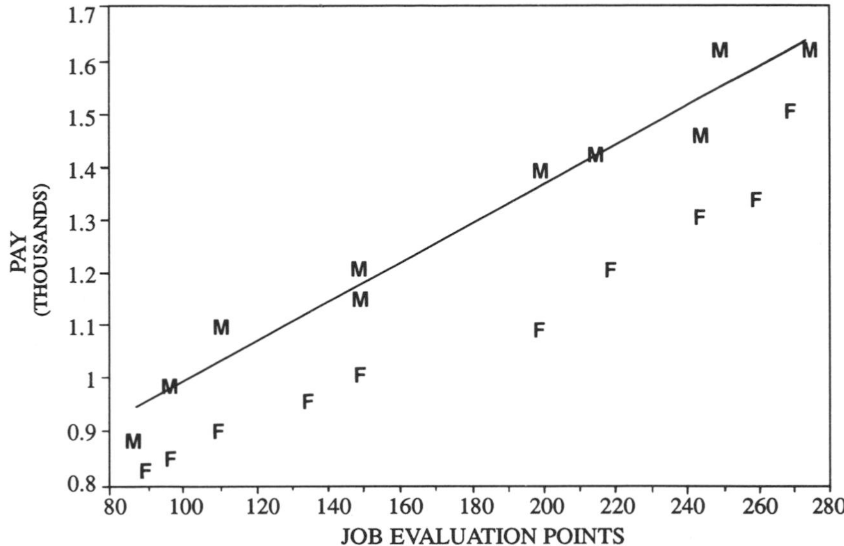


Figure 2. Schematic scattergram with the central tendency for male-dominated jobs shown by the diagonal line and all female-dominated jobs falling below that line. *Source:* "Pay Equity: The Minnesota Experience," Commission on the Economic Status of Women, 1986, p. 13.

to determine "exactly how much sex discrimination and race discrimination there is in each G.S. [general schedule] scale."[58]

In support of their views, politicians lean heavily on the conclusion of the General Accounting Office (GAO) that a pay equity study of the federal work force is feasible. The GAO says that steering committees can "facilitate . . . objectivity,"[59] and it discusses in a very general way methods to test for "bias" and ensure "reliability and validity," but it never actually says that job evaluation studies are objective. Instead, it notes that many criticisms of job evaluation have focused on "the way the evaluation process has been used, not as it is theoretically possible to use." It then cites suggestions that have been made to improve systems.

Most of the suggestions are too general to be very helpful. For example, they include using "compensable factors that are not redundant and represent the value of jobs to the organization" and also reviewing and updating job descriptions periodically "to ensure accuracy."[60] A more specific suggestion for improvement is to use "only one evaluation plan for all employees," a suggestion seemingly called into question later in the report by the statement that "the broader the coverage of the study (e.g., all federal pay systems) the more difficult it will be to select and weight factors which will evaluate all jobs accurately."[61]

Just as many congressional supporters defer to the expertise of the GAO, at the crucial stage the GAO's pivotal report in turn defers to another source of expertise, the ubiquitous report *Women, Work and Wages* of the National Academy of Sciences' National Research Council (NRC). The GAO says:

> Despite [the] possible shortcomings, the National Academy and other analysts have cautiously endorsed the use of job evaluations to study wage differentials based on sex. The National Academy noted that job evaluation plans "do provide a systematic method of comparing jobs to determine whether they are fairly compensated," and the use of job evaluation scores to determine pay rates "will generally go some way toward reducing discriminatory differences in pay when they exist."[62]

If, in turn, one looks closely at *Women, Work and Wages,* one finds a committee report whose endorsement of job evaluation is so tentative that opponents as well as proponents have quoted from it. Thus, for example, the Reagan administration's Department of Justice's "briefing book" on House bill HR387 quotes a section that says, "In our judgment no universal standard of job worth exists, both because any definition of the 'relative worth' of jobs is in part a matter of values and because, even for a particular definition, problems of measurement are likely."[63]

The middle ground that *Women, Work and Wages* seems to seek is that though no universal across-firms standard of job worth is possible, job evaluation systems can nonetheless be used objectively to spot discrimination within a firm. This view, however, is explicitly rejected by a dissenter from the committee who says, "If there is no available hierarchy of worth, there is no objective basis upon which to make claims of bias."[64] Moreover, parts of the majority's report also appear to reject this view. For example, the report says that job evaluation is "an inherently subjective method," that sex stereotyping and undervaluation of jobs held mainly by women may influence evaluations, and that the use of market weights to establish factor weights in most job evaluation plans injects "bias." The report concludes that it is "impossible at the present time to recommend without reservation the use of job evaluation procedures to establish the relative worth of jobs for the resolution of disputes over pay discrimination."[65] Indeed, *Women, Work and Wages* comes out firmly against requiring "the installation of a job evaluation plan in a firm not using one in an attempt to ensure that the firm's pay system is nondiscriminatory. At present we know of no method that would guarantee a 'fair' pay system."[66]

Still, on the whole, the advocates are right in saying that the at times contradictory report is nonetheless on their side. In the midst of a political debate in which one side subjects comparable-worth job evaluation to ridicule, the NRC report suggests in places that it can be used to determine fair compensation. Moreover, in its final sentence, the report says that job evaluation plans "have a potential that deserves further experimentation and development."[67]

As University of Minnesota professors Barbara Nelson and Sara Evans have noted, comparable-worth proponents are "in the strategically awkward position of defending *a priori* job [evaluation] systems while also correcting them."[68] Like the authors of *Women, Work and Wages,* the proponents believe that many job evaluation systems are biased against women. For example, the charge is made that the working conditions factor ignores or deemphasizes negative features of predominantly female jobs such as the health effects on video display operators and "inside dirt" such as feces or vomit in the nursing profession. Still, an academic proponent such as Ronnie Steinberg has written that consultants are now producing packages that are substantially improved in terms of the elimination of culturally based sex bias.[69]

On the whole, advocates who are academics and practitioners stress the need for good judgment a little more and the objectivity of job evaluation a little less than do their politician allies. However, in their most public statements there is not much difference. The assumption is that job evaluation systems are or can fairly easily be made to be up to the task comparable-worth proponents assign them. In the latest NRC volume, comparable-worth strategies are seen as relying "on the use of objective criteria to value the content and requirements of jobs (job evaluation) in a way that eliminates gender as a compensable factor."[70] Similarly, Nina Rothchild, a prominent practitioner, says that job evaluation systems allow comparisons of different jobs so as "to determine to what extent persons in female-dominated jobs are unfairly underpaid."[71]

As for opponents, one of their main arguments is that comparable worth is fundamentally antagonistic to a market system. The proponents have been effective rhetorically in responding to this argument by noting that comparable worth cannot undermine the market because the central tool, job evaluation, is being used voluntarily by thousands of large, private companies. There is plenty of room for confusion here because not only is the term "job evaluation" used in both the commercial and the comparable-worth governmental settings, but often the same consulting firms conduct both types of studies using similar evaluation factors. Nevertheless, the opponents question the analogy between commercial and governmental job evaluation on the grounds that they are fundamentally different. Job evaluations by private firms do not interfere with the market determination of wages, whereas job evaluations under comparable worth do.

As a leading industrial relations specialist has noted:

> The actual criterion of job evaluation [in the private sector] is not worth in a job content sense, but market wages....
>
> ...the developmental steps of job evaluation practice are specifically aimed at generating a correspondence between job evaluation results and wages. Samples of jobs and perhaps factors are juggled about (often statistically) until an equation is obtained which satisfactorily correlates evaluations with actual wages. The criterion is an existing wage distribution, not worth.[72]

Firms almost always classify jobs in several separate job families for job evaluation, and thus comparisons are made only within job categories with similar characteristics, such as blue collar, clerical, or managerial. As *Women, Work and Wages* notes, such categorization makes it much easier to accurately evaluate jobs, but as it also notes, many reformers want to "improve" this practice by having a single evaluation plan for all employees. They seek this reform because only such an ambitious expansion of the scope of job evaluation would make it possible for an organization to compare all of its male-dominated jobs to all of its female-dominated ones. Moreover, as *Women, Work and Wages* further mentions, reformers believe that using market values to establish job evaluation factor weights injects bias.

But to get rid of market weights is not to tidy up an existing process because market weights are the very heart of that process. To substitute for market-driven factors and weights others that reflect a conviction that responsibility for people, "caring" functions, "inside dirt," and various other characteristics of jobs held by women have been undervalued by consultants and by markets is to truly revolutionize job evaluation even if the name is unchanged.

In private-sector systems, experts in compensation seem to agree on the following:

When job evaluation results and market data are at odds, the market almost always takes precedence – on both the up and down side. Salary structures are typically revised annually to reflect market levels and changes in the market relationships between jobs. Jobs with high turnover rates are typically repriced sooner, if pay is thought to be a problem.[73]

Critics of comparable worth point out that there are a number of cases where gender is not an issue, but where there is nonetheless great disparity between pay and points. In large companies, for example, glamour product divisions such as electronic office equipment pay more per point than do low-tech divisions such as metal castings. For now, engineers get more per point than accountants, but relative pay could change – just as geologists' pay per point tumbled after the OPEC price cartel lost power in the 1980s.[74] This was presumably due to decreased demand for new sources of oil, which many geologists are hired to find. In the public sector, Illinois's study found that (mainly male) electricians were paid more than (mainly male) accountants though the latter's "points" were 889 as compared to the former's 578.[75] Critics say these differences reflect supply and demand, not discrimination, just as such differences usually do in comparisons of male-dominated and female-dominated occupations.

In addition to arguing that the traditional policy-capturing job evaluation systems used in the private sector are market driven, comparable-worth critics focus on the great differences in the individual rankings of jobs according to different a priori job evaluation systems. And these differences are important because comparable-worth implementation requires not just a finding that women's occupations are unfairly treated in general, but also a persuasive way of determining *which* occupations should have salaries raised (or cut) and by *how much*.

Robert Rector notes that "while Minnesota ranked a registered nurse, a chemist, and a social worker equally, Iowa found the nurse worth 29 percent more than the social worker, who in turn was worth 29 percent more than the chemist. Vermont reversed these ratings, paying the social worker 10 percent more than the nurse, who was paid 10 percent above the chemist."[76] When confronted with this evidence, proponents seem unconcerned, noting both that similarly *titled* jobs may in fact differ among the states and that, in any case, each state should be able to rank the occupations according to its own values.

Though both responses have some force, it is unlikely that the great differences found between adjoining states like Minnesota and Iowa can be adequately explained by simply assuming widely varying job duties and values among the states. Moreover, these responses fail to explain the large differences among studies within states such as Washington and Alaska, where more than one consultant has examined the *same* state's jobs. In Washington, the differences were so great that whereas the first firm found discrimination that would require millions of dollars to remedy, the second found *no* disparity in pay per point salaries between predominantly male and female jobs.[77] Opponents are so sure that embarrassing differences inevitably emerge that, in the House of Representatives, they (unsuccessfully) offered an amendment to require that three different consultants, rather than the one supported by proponents, study the federal pay system.[78]

If market wage rates are not used to test the validity of job evaluation, the systems are left without any obvious standard of validity. The consultants' systems – the number and substance of factors incorporated – all differ. Some states worry that their systems have several factors measuring the same aspects of jobs though the factors have different names.[79] Independent econometric studies have indeed found that results on three of the four Hay factors "are so highly correlated that it is unlikely they capture more than one dimension of a job."[80]

Critics charge that, in the comparable-worth process, arbitrary decisions about which factors to use are followed by arbitrary decisions about how to weigh them. With just one evaluation system for an entire organization, some factors will be more important in some classes of jobs and others in other classes, and the requisite composite weighting will be especially arbitrary. For example, one critic quarrels with a California public agency's decision to allow more maximum points for a subfactor of "contact" with department heads and the public (which may include routine contacts with the emotionally disturbed) than for working conditions described as "[c]ontinuous exposure to hazards involving a high possibility of loss of life."[81] The state studies include hundreds of other arbitrary decisions about weightings, usually set forth without any explanation at all.

Still another arbitrary element, critics charge, is the decision about the percentage of an occupation that must be males or females to make it "dominated" by one sex or the other. Many states use 70 percent as the definition of domination, but some states use other percentages, and as the GAO acknowledges, the 70 percent figure is "simply traditional."[82] Then there is the arbitrary decision about what line to draw through the male-dominated jobs (such as in Figure 2) so as to establish the degree of underpayment of the female jobs falling under it. In a study of one Washington state report, it was found that "equally defensible statistical analyses of job evaluation data can yield widely varying estimates of the amounts by which wages on particular jobs should be changed."[83]

Critics rarely look at the comparable-worth process in any detail, but they look at the studies that result and deduce that, far from being objective, the process is thoroughly politicized. Unions are heavily represented on the oversight task forces. As a result, pay increases for predominantly women's jobs (not decreases for the men's) are the only remedy ever considered. Advocates of women are also heavily represented on the task forces, and critics argue that they are predisposed toward seeing discrimination against women and toward hiring consultants with eyes as good as theirs.[84] A Wisconsin study, for example, ranked an entry-level secretarial position as high as an aircraft pilot for factors such as job complexity, knowledge required, judgment, and amount of discretion,[85] and the first Washington state study put clerical supervisors ahead of chemists. The Washington study also put nurses at the very top, ahead of chemists, computer systems analysts, and all other occupations. At the time, the market, however, paid computer systems analysts 56 percent more than nurses. Critics see very little remedying of inequities here, much less of inefficiencies. As economist June O'Neill has noted:

> You can imagine what goes on in the room when the head of the nurses' association sits on a panel that assigns points. You can be pretty sure that nurturing will be weighted very heavily indeed.[86]

Opponents wonder why anyone would ever expect agreement about the worth of jobs when we cannot agree about the relative worth of the ends those jobs seek to further.[87] Representative Richard Armey (R-Texas) points out the large number of suits that have resulted from comparable-worth studies, such as the Illinois case where the women prison guards sued the state when union-negotiated raises were set aside so as to allow greater increases for nurses.[88]

Critics do not believe that employers will be left free to devise their own evaluation systems to determine the worth of occupations to their firm. Some proponents promise such flexibility, but the catch always is that the systems must be "nondiscriminatory." As the critics see it, in a priori job evaluation, discrimination is in the eye of the beholder. It will be very easy for employers to produce a system that justifies the status quo. Indeed, competitive pressures will provide strong incentives for a low-cost option. Women employees then will complain to women's groups, who will want to know where women with complaints should go. The courts, the Equal Employment Opportunity Commission (EEOC), a wage board – someone will have to hear them.[89]

Proponents want to minimize the oversight dimension until comparable worth becomes law. When pressed, however, as economist proponent Heidi Hartmann was in a debate with June O'Neill, some say that the EEOC could issue guidelines on the fair use of job evaluation just as they did on the fair use of testing.[90] The question then is whether it would be substantially more difficult to second guess employers' opinions about the relative worth of librarians and computer analysts to their organizations than it is to second guess opinions about the connection between test results and employment qualifications for a particular occupation.

## ECONOMIC INEFFICIENCY

The first part of the chapter explained why most economists and most comparable-worth opponents think that the interaction of supply and demand plays an important part in the determination of wage levels (see pp. 10–12). One reason why economists are so prominent among opponents of comparable worth is that most of them think supply and demand not only do, but *should,* play the major role in determining wage levels and that comparable worth interferes with this economically efficient,[91] welfare-enhancing process. If wages for scarce male-dominated professions, say, computer scientists, are fixed at a level below the point where supply and demand are equated, there will be labor shortages. Employers will find it hard to attract the workers needed to meet the demands of consumers. A higher wage would attract more workers to the market and increase output. Thus, as Ronald Ehrenberg and Robert Smith conclude in their popular text on labor economics, "An increase [in the wage level] would benefit the people in society in *both* their consumer and worker roles."[92]

In response to this argument comparable-worth proponents say that their interest is in raising the pay of female-dominated occupations, not in reducing the pay of male-dominated occupations below some market equilibrium. Comparable-worth critics in turn argue that, at any given time, there is only so much real (as opposed to inflated) income that can be allocated among workers.[93] If predominantly female jobs are given real-wage increases, other occupations will suffer real-wage decreases. Opponents note that the federal pay system's long-standing overemphasis on nonmarket notions of equity helps explain the government's difficulties in recruiting in high-demand occupations like engineering and medicine where federal pay is below the market wage.[94] Robert Rector wonders if, at a time of heightened international competition, we should adopt a policy "designed to cut the salaries of 'overpaid' engineers, scientists, and skilled manufacturing workers to raise the pay of typists and retail clerks."[95]

From the point of view of maximizing societal well-being, wages can be too high as well as too low. Ehrenberg and Smith call workers overpaid, "if their wages are higher than the market equilibrium wage for the job," that is, the level at which employers can fill their job openings with competent employees and all such employees who want this type of job can obtain it.[96] Wages above equilibrium cause higher consumer prices because higher wages mean higher costs of production, which get passed on to consumers. (In the case of government jobs, higher salaries may lead to increases in taxes not prices.) Higher consumer prices lead to lower sales, which lead businesses to cut back production, increasing unemployment.

Thus, if comparable worth should raise the economywide wage of, say, secretaries, above the level dictated by markets, even those comparable-worth proponents who are economists agree with opponents that some added unemployment will result.[97] The only disagreement is about the extent and seriousness of the unemployment. Employers' labor costs will go up, and they will look for ways to economize on secretarial labor in particular. Mid-level managers may get word processors so they can do their own typing. Answering machines may also save on more expensive secretarial time. Though employers will want fewer secretaries, the higher pay makes the secretarial job more attractive than ever, so the newly unemployed and others will remain "attached" to the secretarial market longer, raising the unemployment rate as would-be secretaries hope that jobs will become available. Opponents say that with a larger pool of applicants for fewer jobs, employers will be choosy, and the most vulnerable, including displaced homemakers, are likely to figure prominently among the unemployed.[98]

Economists have long discussed the costs of overpaying public or other employees. Ehrenberg and Smith note that many occupations in New York City have been paid well above equilibrium wages in the recent past. For example, in 1974 sanitation workers received 60 percent higher wages than the average for laborers-material handlers in their area. At the time there were over 36,000 qualified applicants on a waiting list for this city job in which the total number of employees was under 11,000. Apparently realizing that they had a pretty good deal, very few current employees quit, so new hiring was about zero in this period.

In an attempt to show why this outcome is inefficient, Ehrenberg and Smith argue:

> Suppose in the case of sanitation workers that *only* the wages of *newly hired* sanitation workers were lowered – to $10,000. Current workers thus would not lose, but many laborers working at $9,200 per year (the prevailing wage for them in 1974) would jump at the chance to take a $10,000-a-year job. Taxpayers, knowing that garbage-collection services could now be expanded at lower cost than before, would increase their demand for such services, thus creating jobs for these new workers. Thus, some workers would gain while no one lost – and social well-being would be clearly enhanced.[99]

The sanitation workers were in a predominantly male, not a predominantly female occupation, and their unjustifiably high salary had nothing to do with comparable worth. But comparable-worth critics think the solution to this inequity is to reduce the inflated "male" wages in such situations, not to cause new problems like those in the sanitation workers market by raising above market equilibrium some "female" wages.

Occasionally an opponent of comparable worth will say of attempts to compare dissimilar jobs, "You can't compare apples and oranges." Proponents like to argue that you can compare apples and oranges. Indeed, at the NCPE tenth anniversary conference, there was a large chart literally comparing apples and oranges in terms of weight, calories, vitamins, fiber, and the like. Proponents argue that, in some of these ways, apples and oranges may be equivalent just as some jobs may be in terms of skill or responsibility. And despite the differences, the fruits may be comparable in providing energy just as jobs may be in worth to the employer.[100]

Comparable-worth opponents respond by noting that fruits providing equivalent energy do not necessarily sell for the same price in a market economy. If one energy-equivalent fruit is tastier, it will tend to have higher demand and a higher price, other things being equal. If another can be grown and brought to market at lower cost, it will tend to have greater supply and a lower price, other things being equal. The intrinsic "worth" of a food – whether in terms of energy produced, nutrition, or whatever – plays only a small part in market price. After all, water is more important to us than caviar, but a bucket of the latter brings considerably more.[101]

Similarly, as opponents frequently note, perfectly equivalent jobs may have to be paid differently if we want to maximize societal well-being. Imagine English–French and English–Spanish translators in the same firm. By job evaluation criteria they would almost certainly be ranked similarly. But in many U.S. cities the supply of Spanish translators will be much higher, and the demand may be as well. One cannot be sure which excess would control, but there is no reason to expect Spanish translators to have the same wage as French translators if we allow the market to find an equilibrium in an efficient manner.[102]

Opponents note that labor is the source of 73 percent of total business costs,[103] and they often make dire predictions about what comparable worth's revolutionary way of pricing labor could do to the functioning of the economy. There is talk of Soviet-style planning, "intellectual nightmare[s]," "disastrous" impacts, constant disruption, "creating havoc in the market," and proponents who deserve Fs in economics. Comparable worth is a "radical departure from the economic system we have," more like a $15 an hour minimum wage than the slightly above market minimums that we have known to date.[104]

For their part, proponents think this rhetoric is hysterical, and they wonder if it is driven more by fears about the decline of patriarchy than about the decline of capitalism.[105] Though economist proponents expect a minor amount of unemployment, activists wonder why requiring women to be paid according to the worth of their work to the employer should cause anyone to be fired. As for shortages, they argue that proposed and existing comparable-worth systems allow extra pay where there are "documented" cases of shortages and recruitment difficulties.[106]

Opponents are not assuaged. They think there are benign reasons for most of the pay gap, but they think that advocates will push for quick reductions in it. Companies used to raising pay quickly when market forces dictate will now first have to convince a bureaucrat, under pressure from interest groups, that, for example, though there were three applicants for the computer systems programmer opening, none of them had the qualifications needed for the job. In the wake of technological change, job descriptions will change, but any time that male-dominated jobs gain points or female-dominated ones lose them, suspicions will be aroused, and more "documentation" will be called for.[107]

Advocates who are politicians and activists are convinced that the market does not respond to female shortages as it does to male shortages. Even though both nurses and secretaries-typists have enjoyed above-average salary increases in recent years,[108] proponents believe salaries are still not high enough:

> Many male jobs are paid well despite an abundance of qualified applicants while female jobs – notably nursing and clerical work – continue to be low-paying even when applicants are in short supply.[109]

In Nina Rothchild's view, "maybe 10 percent of the jobs [in the market] are affected by supply and demand."[110] Elsewhere she and a coauthor say:

> Most employers find only a few specialized or highly technical occupations subject to upward wage changes because of supply and demand factors; wages never go down in accord with economic theory.
>
> For most jobs, there is little measurable relationship between availability of workers and wages for that job.[111]

Rothchild blames economic theorists for propagating a contrary view, though, as explained earlier (pp. 26–7), industrial relations specialists as well as economists would be numbered among those who would consider Rothchild's views here to be off base.

Some advocates further distinguish between prevailing wages and supply and demand. They believe that wages are usually set according to industry surveys, a practice that amounts to "wage fixing," not responding to supply and demand.[112] A lawyer and proponent, Winn Newman, has said:

> Giving somebody, as a result of a market survey, a 25 percent increase is hardly any more disruptive than giving them a 25 percent increase in order to eliminate sex-based wage discrimination.[113]

However, opponents would say, such a market survey is often precipitated by a concern with recruitment and retention. Therefore, meeting the prevailing wage in order to keep the people needed to run a business is congruent with efficiency, whereas raising pay 25 percent where no labor shortages exist is not.

Opponents think that predictable responses to the new market incentives that comparable worth provides will bring some results proponents will be unhappy with. First, since the relative monetary gains of aiming for predominantly male occupations will be lower, fewer women will be pioneers willing to turn from the psychologically safe, traditionally female occupations. Though proponents counter that higher salaries will attract men to the traditionally female jobs, opponents see few reverse pioneers since most predominantly male jobs will still pay more than most women's. Greater occupational segregation by gender is more likely than not.[114]

Second, there will be negative effects for women in firms not required to adhere to comparable-worth policies. Coverage would probably be limited to employers with at least a certain number of employees. But women are more likely to work in small firms, and those in small firms are paid less than those in large firms. This intragender inequality would be aggravated by comparable worth because at the higher comparable-worth-imposed wage the sector adhering to comparable worth would be able to hire fewer employees. The newly unemployed from this sector would increase supply and thus depress wages further in the sector not covered by comparable worth.[115]

The reduced wage for women in the sector not required to adhere to comparable worth may do as much to increase the overall wage gap as changes in the covered sector would do to close it. And, opponents argue, benefits for women in the covered sector are bound to be less than proponents suspect because it will be easy for employers to get around any regulations and because a concern for profit will tempt them to try. For example, employers could (1) reduce the "points" and pay for female jobs by reducing stated qualifications (e.g., a B.A. not an M.A. for librarians) while continuing to in fact hire "overqualified" people who will continue to be available in the market just as before; (2) add additional unofficial duties for the new higher-paid women who will be reluctant to complain, knowing of the large waiting list for jobs among the newly unemployed in their occupation; (3) reduce on-the-job training opportunities, thus depressing long-term female incomes; (4) hire more temporaries, thus reducing fringe benefit costs; (5) contract out, thus getting rid of a whole "underpaid" occupation (say cooks in the lunchroom).[116]

Even if comparable worth could accomplish half of what its advocates seek, opponents see it as a mixed bag for women. Wives who do not work or who work part time would find their family income reduced somewhat as the relative, real (inflation-adjusted) income of their husbands declined. Any narrowing of the wage gap would be countered by the money going to *men* in such "female-dominated" occupations as librarians. Moreover, women trailblazers in predominantly male jobs may feel unjustly penalized when their relative pay is reduced for the sake of improving the salaries of other women.[117]

## CONCLUSION

The arguments and evidence surveyed are sufficient to recommend caution toward, if not opposition to, the further implementation of comparable worth. Proponents cite statistical studies showing that differences in human capital between the sexes are not sufficient to explain the wage gap and that the proportion of female workers in an occupation explains a significant portion of that gap. Opponents of comparable worth, however, provide reasons and evidence showing women – many of whom have a second, child-centered, homebound job – on average have different preferences than do men about their workplace jobs, and thus segregation in jobs may be in large part voluntary. Moreover, the opponents show that even substantial discrimination need not lead to a wage gap if there are a large number of nondiscriminating employers. They further argue that there are nonmonetary benefits of the predominantly female jobs and thus that the wage gap itself is overstated. In sum, there remains great uncertainty about whether employer discrimination is a significant cause of the wage gap. Any comparable-worth policy is based on the assumption that employer discrimination *is* a significant cause of the wage gap. The very uncertainty about this assumption would seem to count against a policy that would price a major element of the economy (labor) through a government-determined rather than a market process at a time when so much of Eastern Europe, Latin America, and other parts of the world think efficiency requires moves in the opposite direction.

Even if a foolproof case could be made for the importance to women's incomes of pervasive employer discrimination, comparable worth also requires a defensible means of identifying the amount of discrimination suffered by the members of various female-dominated occupations so that appropriate remedies can be established. Proponents say that objective evaluation can find and correct discrimination, but their own complaints about the bias in existing evaluation systems, not to mention the views of opponents, raise doubts about whether objective job evaluation exists.

Suppose that the evaluation systems did produce identical job rankings. The studies could change things only if they disagreed with market outcomes. But opponents argue that, if they did so, implementation of the study results would cause economic efficiency losses. Shortages of labor in some places and surpluses (unemployment) in others would be likely to occur.

Even if the effects of discrimination were as pervasive as proponents think, if an objective firm-centered comparable-worth technique were available, and if problems with shortages and surpluses could be overcome, implementation of comparable worth might do little to overcome discrimination and the wage gap. Comparable worth could do nothing about the fact that women tend to work in relatively low-paying firms and industries. Nor could it do much to prevent profit-oriented businesses from adopting policies such as contracting out that would make comparable-worth policies much less effective. Decreases in the wage gap beyond those the market is already providing[118] might be small, especially if one considers the effect on working women in the uncovered sector.

Yet proponents of comparable worth have important arguments not yet considered. They think their most powerful arguments are based not on theory or statistical analysis, but on experience. In support of this view, they note that most reports on actual implementation are quite favorable.

There are exceptions to the pattern of favorable reports from the field. For example, comparable-worth critic June O'Neill has looked at some Washington state data and reported some potentially worrisome results. The economic return for human capital investments such as experience and high school graduation had fallen since comparable-worth implementation. Moreover, occupations that were receiving comparable-worth increases were losing employment share in state government, and the higher the pay adjustments the greater the decline in share. Still, the gender wage gap is down significantly in Washington state government and in the other jurisdictions where implementation has occurred.[119]

Proponents generally argue that Washington state fought comparable worth and, as a hostile environment, should not be considered a model for implementation. The domestic model they choose is Minnesota, which is the only state to require all its localities to develop and implement a comparable-worth plan for their employees. Until recently, the process at both the state and local levels has been overseen by Nina Rothchild, who from 1983 until 1991 served as the Minnesota state commissioner of employee relations. Rothchild, a former executive director of the Minnesota Commission on the Economic Status of Women, is a strong advocate of comparable worth, and much of her time as commissioner was spent trying to make its implementation a success.

As with Washington there are economic studies based on Minnesota data showing that there have been adverse employment results for women resulting from comparable worth at the state government level. Though no one who had a job lost it, the growth in employment of women relative to that of men is apparently less than would otherwise have been the case.[120] As with Washington, however, there have been substantial gains for women employees in terms of income.

As Nina Rothchild sees it, the bottom line is that comparable worth has "worked very well in Minnesota." Implementation has been smooth and the "doomsday predictions of opponents have not come to pass."[121] For example, women are still venturing into nontraditional occupations in increasing numbers. During the period that comparable worth was being implemented in Minnesota, the number of women in nontraditional state jobs was up 19 percent while the number of women in state employment overall rose only 6 percent. At the state level comparable worth led to no wage reductions, no layoffs, no strikes, no lawsuits, no big bureaucracy, no new problems attracting and retaining labor, and no fiscal crisis. Costs have been moderate, just 3.7 percent of payroll. Rothchild reports that an independent poll found that over 80 percent of state employees supported the pay equity system.

At the local level in Minnesota, advocates call for tighter monitoring and enforcement. But, still, results on the whole are seen as quite favorable. Most local governments appear to be making "a good faith effort to comply with both the letter and the spirit of the law."[122] Despite the use of sixteen different consulting systems, "all of the evaluation systems showed similar results."[123] Costs at the local level have been even lower than those for evaluating state employees, and the most poorly paid women seem to be getting the increases. There has also been no significant disemployment.[124]

The assessment of the Minnesota experience by two University of Minnesota professors, Barbara Nelson and Sara Evans, is more qualified than Rothchild's. Implementation fell short of achieving all that proponents had hoped for. There were conflicts and uneven results at the local level. Still, on balance, Evans and Nelson also see Minnesota as an example of "successful" implementation.[125] At both the state and local levels the economic gains for low-income women were substantial. There were no "economic dislocations in the form either of significant disemployment effects or of exorbitant and inflationary growth in the total wage bill."[126] The Minnesota experience shows that "comparable worth can be instituted with minimal disruption in large government (or corporate) bureaucracies which have professionalized their personnel functions and pay practices."[127]

Based on the reports of others, even comparable-worth critic Jennifer Roback has acknowledged that "a case can be made" that the early implementation of comparable worth in the public sector has "not created such dire problems."[128] Additionally, Ehrenberg and Smith conducted a simulation of the effect of comparable worth on female employment in state and local governments and found that the negative effect would be "surprisingly small," perhaps 2–3 percent for a wage increase of 20 percent.[129]

Roback and other critics expect far more adverse effects in the private sector, where businesses cannot simply increase taxes to pay for any pay increases. A simulation by Victor Fuchs and his Stanford University colleagues found "considerable unemployment of women" and, more generally, significant adverse effects on efficiency and real output.[130] On the other hand, two other simulations have reported very small expected amounts of private-sector unemployment if comparable worth were implemented. An author reporting on the results of one of these simulations states that the adverse effect on female employment would be so insignificant that "one need pay little attention to the efficiency costs of comparable worth actions."[131]

Though the simulations of U.S. private-sector effects have been mixed, the proponents can take more cheer from the reports of results abroad. After all, countries in the EC have had comparable-worth requirements for a decade and a half. These laws and regulations apply to private- as well as public-sector employees, including European subsidiaries of U.S. companies. After surveying results to date of Europe's "state of the art" comparable-worth jurisprudence, one Oxford professor concludes, "The sky has not fallen." He suggests that "the onus now lies with those who would argue that [the European subsidiaries'] parent companies should not be held to comply with an equivalent standard."[132] Moreover, most reports on comparable worth from Australia also report dramatic gains for women's wages (in the range of 20 percent) with a very small adverse effect on women's employment.[133]

The arguments and studies of critics reported herein have by no means been all theoretical. Their critical review of the comparable-worth studies examining U.S. state experience, for example, are especially telling. Still, on the whole, the critics are the most persuasive when they argue at the theoretical level, but the severely adverse results they expect do not appear in most reports from the field or in many retrospective quantitative studies. As NCPE said when attacking a Reagan administration document critical of comparable worth, "The report rehashes a lot of old arguments against the concept that have been proven wrong repeatedly in places where pay equity is actually being implemented."[134]

The remainder of this book looks at three cases that are at the heart of the proponents' argument on the basis of experience: Minnesota, the European Economic Community (especially the United Kingdom), and Australia.

# 3

## Implementing comparable worth in Minnesota

In their research on comparable worth, Sara Evans and Barbara Nelson find that states which pass such laws typically have public-sector collective bargaining, Democratic control of state politics, and energetic commissions on the status of women.[1] Minnesota had all these as well as a strong progressive tradition; a politically astute branch of the American Federation of State, County, and Municipal Employees (AFSCME); 154 women's organizations; and feminist (not just women's) caucuses in both major parties. Moreover, as important for the passage of comparable-worth legislation as any one of these was Minnesota's position as one of the first states to act, so that events transpired at a time when few knew anything about the issue and opposition forces had not mobilized.

In the late 1970s, Minnesota evaluated the state's personnel system. As a part of the evaluation Hay Associates did a study of salary and benefit policies, which included job evaluation point totals for 762 multi-incumbent job classes. Under prodding from Nina Rothchild, the executive director of the Commission on the Economic Status of Women, Hay did a brief analysis comparing male-dominated and female-dominated job classes. Hay reported a "slight tendency" to pay male-dominated classes at a higher rate than female-dominated classes, but considered the finding of no significance.[2]

Searching for ways to improve the economic status of women, Rothchild and fellow staffer Bonnie Watkins decided to look again at the relationship of points and pay for male- and female-dominated jobs. Watkins says they began pessimistically, expecting the Hay system to have produced a study justifying the status quo favoring male-dominated positions. They thought that they would then have to say "throw it out," a position that they knew the state would resist, having just spent much money on the reevaluation of the personnel system.[3] Rothchild and Watkins were surprised and delighted to find that the Hay study could be very useful to them since it showed that female-dominated job classes were paid less than similarly rated male-dominated classes. For example, delivery van drivers were paid 24 percent more than similarly rated clerk typists 2, and pharmacists were paid 20 percent more than similarly rated registered nurses 3.

Once it was clear that a consistent application of the Hay system would lead to a significant increase in the economic status of women, Rothchild had Watkins plot all the classes on a scattergram (such as Figure 2) showing the male classes in red and the female in green so that the disparities would be highlighted. The council had earlier appointed a Pay Equity Task Force that included six influential, friendly legislators from both parties. That task force's report to the legislature led very quickly to the State Employees Pay Equity Act. The applicable bills sailed through committees in both houses. For example, the Senate committee unanimously recommended passage after fifteen minutes of discussion with two individuals speaking in favor and none in opposition.[4] There was no opposition to the measure on the floor of the Senate, and it passed the House by 100 to 13 in March of 1982.[5] One knowledgeable lobbyist, a strong pay equity advocate, told me that many legislators did not know what they were voting for, with a number thinking the pay equity measure concerned equal pay for equal – not comparable – work. The press gave the matter almost no attention, with the bill's passage only briefly noted in the back pages of even the largest newspapers.

The law stated that it was the policy of the state to establish equitable compensation relationships between female-dominated, male-dominated, and balanced classes of employees in the executive branch. While not repealing an earlier law requiring reasonable pay relationships between similar jobs in and out of state employment, the law did say that the primary consideration in establishing pay would be "comparability of the value of the work" understood as "the composite of the skill, effort, responsibility and working conditions normally required in the performance of the work." Since Minnesota was in a severe recession in 1982, quick passage of the pay equity act would probably not have been possible had proponents not assured legislators that funding could wait till future years. As Evans and Nelson have noted, "Legislators welcomed an opportunity to go on record for 'equity' without having to appropriate money at the same time."[6] Though costs were nowhere mentioned, the act did require the Department of Employee Relations (DOER) commissioner to submit every other year a list of the female-dominated and the male-dominated classes for which a compensation inequity exists "based on comparability of the value of the work."[7] The commissioner submitted her list of inequities early in 1983, and the first money began flowing to occupants of underpaid female-dominated classes later that year.[8]

## IMPLEMENTATION OF THE STATE LAW

DOER counts the cost of pay equity as about 3.7 percent of state payroll costs per year. The money for the pay equity raises (about $26 million annually) was phased in over a period of four years. Money for general pay increases was appropriated separately from pay equity increases, and unions were permitted to bargain only about the timing of the equity increases for their members, not which classes would receive them and how much they would receive.

After implementation, the pay gap in Minnesota state employment declined from 27 percent (a female salary of 73 percent of the average male salary) to 19 percent (a female salary of 81 percent of the average male salary). (Nationally, during this same period, 1983–7, the pay gap was closing from 34 percent to 31 percent.) About one-third of the state labor force received a pay equity increase (60 percent of all females and 9 percent of all males). The big gainers were female nonprofessionals; 95 percent of clerical workers and 72 percent of health-care nonprofessionals received increases. These two classes of workers accounted for 75 percent of all individuals receiving increases.[9] To give one example, the lowest paid position in the state is clerk 1. For the year 1983–4 the pay for this entry-level clerk was $11,922. In 1986–7 the pay was $15,931 with $1,753 of the $4,009 gain coming from regularly negotiated raises and $2,256 coming from pay equity raises.[10]

In late 1982 Nina Rothchild moved from the Commission on the Economic Status of Women to become commissioner of DOER. In that position, which she held until 1991, she oversaw the implementation of comparable worth for state employees. Rothchild emphasizes the smoothness of the implementation process she oversaw and cites as evidence an Evans and Nelson survey of state employees. They report that 81 percent of employees support the concept of equal pay for jobs of equal value and that only a minority (36 percent) of employees believe that "pay equity causes many problems in the workplace."[11] Rothchild takes the 81 percent support for the comparable-worth "concept" as support for the particular Minnesota "program."[12] But even the expressed support for the *concept* may be artificially high. The question asked by Evans and Nelson was "If studies showed the work of delivery van drivers and clerk typists required the same level of skill, training, responsibility, and so forth, should an employer pay these types of positions the same?" As will be shown in Chapter 4, there is reason to doubt that multiple studies of van drivers and typists would agree about the equal value of these occupations or any other. If the question had said "a study" or "most studies," support for the concept might well have been somewhat lower.

There are more fundamental reasons why the Evans and Nelson poll results do not necessarily suggest that pay equity will be a popular, easily implemented policy. First, even after years of implementation, many Minnesota state employees know almost nothing about the policy. Indeed, as Evans and Nelson note, 45 percent of employees who received comparable-worth raises were unaware of that fact.[13] Neither DOER nor the unions notified employees of their pay equity raises. Moreover, in the documentation that accompanied employee checks it was impossible to distinguish pay equity from general raises. This policy of silence, suggested by AFSCME, was meant to head off potential concern among the union's male-dominated classes about the effect of the pay equity raises on what might otherwise have been a larger general salary increase.[14] Second, there is little reason for most Minnesota state employees to feel disgruntled. As Evans and Nelson note, they are "among the best-paid public workers in the country."[15] Moreover, during the years when comparable-worth wages were being implemented, female workers made dramatic real-wage gains and male workers made modest ones.[16] As we shall see, however, despite these gains, some employees felt very unfairly treated by DOER's policies for implementing comparable worth.

### *Ignoring "underpaid" balanced and male-dominated classes*

The Minnesota Association of Professional Employees (MAPE) represents about five thousand state professional employees, most of whom fall into male-dominated or balanced job classes. On the scattergram some of these classes fell significantly below the pay-per-point Minnesota trend line for men, and the employees in these classes felt that they were entitled to pay equity raises just as the men and women in the predominantly female job classes were. In support of this view, MAPE pointed to the sex-neutral language of the act – "It is the policy of this state to attempt to establish equitable compensation relationships between female-dominated, male-dominated, and balanced classes of employees in the executive branch."

Nina Rothchild and her staff strongly resisted this view, not only at the state level, but when implementing the local government pay equity law as well. Rothchild believes the intent of both laws was clear. In her view they sought to end sex-based wage discrimination. Neither law established a requirement that pay for everyone be based on job evaluation points. She sees nothing wrong with male (or female) job classes being scattered above and below the line. Whatever the reasons why some male classes fell substantially below the Minnesota state line, the reasons were not sex discrimination, and thus the pay equity law should not be used to remedy the situation.[17]

Many of the MAPE employees in question work in the Department of Natural Resources (DNR) in jobs such as forester, park naturalist, fisheries manager, and wildlife manager. These jobs do not attract large numbers of female applicants, possibly because, as one DNR employee put it, women "don't want to be out in the boonies" where "no one else is around" and where the facilities are often "primitive." Concern for safety is another factor mentioned. Many young men, however, find these jobs very attractive. DNR staff describe these young men as "top quality ... dedicated environmentalists" with strong commitments to their job. Usually well educated, a number have Ph.D.'s, and many more have M.A.'s.

When these people and others below the Hay line in the male and balanced classes learned that Nina Rothchild planned to do nothing for them, MAPE union leaders say they "went off the wall." MAPE had understood all along that the female-dominated classes would be adjusted first, but in negotiations, DOER had suggested that the turn of the other classes would come later. MAPE had no objection to this plan, figuring that on the whole it was "good to get the women up first to build up the base." But as one union leader put it, when "our feminist commissioner who did a hell of a job for the women" decided to do no more, MAPE was outraged. They knew that many of the job classes in DNR had lower entry pay levels than any other state professionals, including the female-dominated librarians who did receive pay equity increases.

There are many similarities between the female-dominated librarians and the male-dominated foresters and naturalists. Both groups are dedicated and highly educated. Both believe strongly that society undervalues the importance of what they do. And both have trouble getting jobs. Just as one sees would-be librarians getting another degree or taking subprofessional library jobs in hopes of having an easier entrée when a professional librarian job opens up, so one sees would-be naturalists getting the M.A. and then working as a laborer in parks, waiting for a full-fledged naturalist job to become available.

If one asks why the naturalists are paid so poorly, the answer that always comes back in one form or another is supply and demand: "Our money is tied to the game and fish fund. Fish stocking and wildlife management and personnel costs all come out of the same pot. The agency is always trying to get money for program substance by keeping personnel costs down." In negotiations, management will say: " 'Why should we pay more? There are many people lined up to take your jobs.' It's true. Plenty of people apply. That's why they can get people with an M.A." For "wildlife management, there are just government jobs." There is no private sector to compete. These responses from people at MAPE or DNR were echoed by a pay technician at DOER: "Perhaps these jobs are paid less because there is a good supply of these people. We get a good response whenever we announce openings."

Regardless of the reasons why these and other male-dominated positions were poorly paid historically, MAPE wanted the men and women in these job classes and in the balanced classes to be treated the same as the female-dominated classes represented most often by AFSCME. Whatever the intent of initiators of pay equity legislation, what the legislature passed appeared to be sex neutral. It sought "equitable compensation relationships" between all three types of classes and specifically required the DOER commissioner to submit a list of male-dominated classes, as well as female-dominated ones, "for which a compensation inequity exists based on comparability of the value of the work."

In the early stages of the dispute MAPE gave very serious consideration to filing a gender-based discrimination lawsuit. It thought it could win but also thought the process would be long and expensive, with appeals certain no matter who won at the first stage. Moreover, though its objection was only to the implementation, not the concept, of pay equity, it feared that the suit would be billed as against pay equity, and the right-to-work committees and other embarrassing allies might join its suit.

Most important of all was the knowledge that, regardless of who would win such a suit, Nina Rothchild would consider it a declaration of war. "This was her thing," and a suit early in her tenure would sour the relationship so badly that MAPE could lose the war in future pay negotiations even if it won the legal battle.

For the next few years the conflict was fought in small-scale skirmishes. MAPE was able to make some "nickel-and-dime" progress through reclassification studies and through abolition of the lowest-paid entry class for most of its members. Still, in 1989 MAPE found fifteen of its occupations not only were still below the line, but were below the informal corridor of 7 percent that the state had established on either side of the line. In May of that year MAPE requested "a general wage inequity [increase] for all positions that are currently compensated below the 'Ideal Compensation Code' as it relates to assigned Hay classification points." MAPE included a document showing that 65 percent of MAPE-represented positions were funded below their ideal compensation code. "This far exceeds other bargaining units and appears to be inconsistent with the intent of 'pay equity' legislation." MAPE said it "expect[ed] the employer to bargain in good faith and provide equity to those who are undercompensated."[18]

Before this "General Wage Inequity" complaint was formally filed, MAPE had checked with an attorney and was giving very serious consideration to a lawsuit if no breakthrough were obtained in the 1989 negotiations. MAPE knew that Commissioner Rothchild did not think the pay equity law applied to balanced and male-dominated classes, but it also knew that there were lawyers in DOER who felt otherwise.

As Nina Rothchild told me, "We gave in to them." The people involved in the negotiations at MAPE believe that it was only the threat of a successful comparable-worth lawsuit that led to their success. Over 1,500 employees gained from the "General Wage Inequity" settlement in late 1989. The ultimate cost to the state will be about $5 million a year.[19] Future costs could mount further since there are a few small classifications that are still not in the corridor, and, in any case, MAPE thinks all its members should be paid at least at the level of the line, not just the lower end of the corridor. They want to be paid for their full Hay-determined "job worth." Strong proponents of comparable worth at AFSCME are also unwilling to settle for less money per point than other job classes obtain. Thus, the trend toward ratcheting up of pay rates seems likely to continue.[20]

### *Salary compression and inversion of the hierarchy*

Linda Barton, commissioner of DOER since 1991, told me, "We're way over market on the lower end [of employee classifications] and way under at the upper end, and that's because of pay equity." As a "people's legislature" with strong union influence Minnesota's lawmakers had always made periodic efforts to "cap" managers' salaries, but Barton thought pay equity had clearly made things worse. Compressed managerial salaries "were causing morale problems and probably productivity problems too." Managers could not unionize, but they had formed an informal "nonunion" to try to do something about the pay compression problem.

Although relatively few occupations are poorly paid by the state as compared with the private sector, those in lower-paid occupations do particularly well so that the benefits of moving up to positions of greater skill and responsibility have sometimes been quite meager. One high-ranking supervisor of public-health nurses explained at length how hard it had been for her to get a member of the nursing staff to accept a promotion to a supervisory position because the job was more demanding and paid only $500 a year more. Comparable worth, which raised the pay of almost every clerical job and over 70 percent of the health-care nonprofessionals, accentuated historic pay compression problems. One MAPE official spoke of the cynicism he encountered from female professional supervisors wondering why they went to college for four years if their pay (their class was balanced) was to be $11 an hour while the clericals working next to them made $10. In the human rights enforcement area, most hiring for years had been of women, but at the supervisory levels there were holdover men making these classes balanced. Thus, women who were promoted gained little because pay equity money was not available to supervisors in balanced classes.

There were even a few cases where the failure to do anything about balanced classes brought a cut in salary with a promotion. For example, in the accounting area there were accounting technicians who did numerical/clerical work and accounting officers who often had a B.A. and did the more complex work of accountants. Comparable-worth raises for the technicians were not available to the officers, who therefore often ended up being paid less than some technicians. Thus, accounting technicians were resisting promotions to accounting officers.

The situation of one female technician who had accepted a "promotion" before all this became apparent was described as follows in the *Minneapolis Star & Tribune:*

> In April 1982, Carol Tembreull got her job in the St. Cloud State University business office reclassified. Her duties didn't change, but her pay increased a bit.
>
> A year later the state implemented its pay-equity raises, designed to end wage discrimination against female-dominated job classes. Tembreull figures she would have earned $1,800 more if she'd stayed put.
>
> Her old job title, senior account technician, was one of more than 150 female-dominated classifications that received comparable-worth pay increases in 1983. Her new job classification, accounting officer, is not female-dominated and received no special raises.
>
> So, even though an accounting officer is a step above senior account technician on the state's accounting career ladder, accounting officers earn less in most experience categories.[21]

In a few other cases a small class was not rated and a female-dominated one jumped past it, creating a similar hierarchical salary inversion. Over time the accounting officer and the other anomalies were resolved by "reclassification" studies that determined that the lower-paid supervisory positions had been underrated previously (see p. 53).

## *System maintenance problems*

Comparable-worth systems all have an arbitrary cutoff point for female-dominated classes. In Minnesota if a job class is a fraction of 1 percent above 70 percent female, it is treated as if below-the-line wages are held down artificially because of discrimination – presumably reflecting crowding, cultural undervaluation of women's work, and the other reasons discussed in Chapter 2. The class is thus entitled to pay equity raises. However, if the pay of a job class was over 10 percent below the line, but the job class was only about 69 percent female (e.g., social workers), it is assumed that the below-the-line pay was not a result of discrimination, and employees in this group are entitled to no pay equity raises.

The arbitrariness of these sorts of distinctions is magnified by the fact that the percentages of men and women in job classes are always changing. While in the midst of bargaining with DOER about which classes would get the initial pay equity raises, MAPE officials got frantic calls from employees whose "job class" had taken a sudden turn for the better: "Joe has left and we've hired Mary, so we should qualify too"; or "Joe has left, so we're down to only ten staff, seven of which are women, so we should qualify." Though less than two months had passed since jobs were put into one of the three classes, nothing could then be done to help these people.

The state takes a fresh look at the dominance of various job classes every two years, and the male line is adjusted accordingly. But balanced classes that have turned female dominated recently are not assured of pay equity money. They can try to negotiate for it, but in years like 1991 when there were no reassignments of job classes for any reason, they were out of luck. On the other hand, female-dominated classes that have since become balanced continue to get full pay equity raises. They are built into the base. Even before the 1989 MAPE settlement, 14 percent of those in balanced classes were getting pay equity money because their jobs were female-dominated in 1982.[22]

The 1989 MAPE settlement seems certain to lead to additional pay equity raises for female-dominated classes in the future. The male-class Hay line is adjusted every two years. Since the line represents an average of the salaries of all male-dominated classes, MAPE success in boosting the below-the-line male classes will in turn raise the line. Given the new higher line, the female classes will be entitled to a further pay equity adjustment. Indeed, some of the balanced and male-dominated classes below the new, higher male pay line will presumably again fall out of the below-the-line corridor, a situation that MAPE will seek to change. If they are successful in again boosting their male members' pay, there may be a need for a third round of pay equity raises as the male line again creeps upward. As one DOER pay technician told me, "The difficult part of pay equity is not getting it but maintaining it."

### *Surpluses and shortages*

Minnesota's version of comparable-worth doctrine holds that it is all right to pay male-dominated classes beyond what is indicated by job evaluation studies (JESs) if the increased salary is necessary to overcome documented shortages of labor.[23] It is not all right, however, to pay female-dominated classes less than the JES suggests simply because they are available for less in the market. As a generally high-paying employer, the state has not had much problem with shortages. For computer specialists, however, even though paying two steps above the line and at the top of the pay range, the state had great difficulty finding two people to take openings in a newly created data resources administrator category.

As for surpluses, in at least one case the state violated comparable-worth doctrine and paid a female-dominated class less than the Hay points indicated because it did not need to pay at the Hay level to attract labor and it wanted to save some money. Evans and Nelson relate without comment the following incident from the first round of negotiations over the distribution of pay equity money:

In most cases, implementing pay equity meant that a job classification moved to a higher step or range on the salary grid. In one instance, for Human Services Technicians, Senior (the people who work as patient aides in state facilities) the negotiators decided to extend the salary range, allowing long-term employees to make higher salaries, but not raising the entry salaries of these workers. The state felt that the entry-level pay for these positions were [*sic*] already compensated above the market, but did not oppose higher salaries for the long-term incumbents of this job.[24]

The human service technicians work in the "regional treatment centers," the Minnesota term for state hospitals. These technicians are considered the "backbone" of the centers. They represent about one-third of all treatment center employees, and they are the people who provide direct care for the mentally ill and retarded. As a pay specialist explained, most of the treatment centers are located "in rural [areas of] Minnesota. Our competitors there [nursing homes] were paying less than we were." The budgeting problem for state facilities was a concern. I do not know if there were other cases where budget and market considerations were used as a justification for holding back comparable-worth raises at the state level, but as will be shown, local government's reliance on these considerations is not approved by DOER.

## *Making pay equity look good*

As commissioner at the Department of Employee Relations, Nina Rothchild was more interested in comparable worth than in anything else.[25] In articles for personnel journals and in trips around the country she tried to energize the committed and persuade the skeptical by relating the Minnesota success story. She typically said little or nothing about the matters just discussed.

As already mentioned, Rothchild sees the more than 80 percent support among state employees for the pay equity *concept* as support for the Minnesota pay equity *program*. She also believes that the fact that women continue to flock to nontraditional jobs in Minnesota state employment (a 19 percent increase) shows that comparable worth has not and will not discourage women from entering traditionally male fields.[26] But the previous example of accounting technicians' resistance to promotion out of female-dominated job classes because of improved pay in those classes supports the concern of critics that comparable-worth pay will provide an incentive for continued job segregation. As for aggregate trends, the occupational choices that comparable-worth critics worry about would not be expected to show up in the brief four-year period about which Rothchild has reported, especially when salary changes have occurred only in a tiny segment of the total public-private labor market. Critics predict that if the relative wages of male-dominated occupations throughout the economy decline, the shift of women toward the male-dominated occupations will be slowed. But wages of men and women in Minnesota state employment are generally high and have risen faster than elsewhere in the economy during the era Rothchild describes. Critics would expect that these relatively higher wages in state employment would attract more women and men applicants, and Minnesota's affirmative action program helps ensure that a good number of the women applicants are hired.

The news on pay equity looks better if the base-line situation prior to pay equity looks worse. The Hay pay-for-points line did show that women's occupations were below the line before Rothchild got to DOER, but it did not show them as far below as the before and after charts that Rothchild takes around the country show. Soon after Rothchild got to DOER she began to try to rid the Hay system of the bias that she thought it carried over from the market system. (At a later stage the Hay consultants themselves were brought back.) All four Hay factors were looked at with sex bias in mind. Female occupations gained points in the clerical area because of factors like light-muscle fatigue and noise, and in the know-how area because of the ability and knowledge needed to deal with patients and clients. Rothchild kept a close eye on the whole process.[27] She also ensured that the scattergrams comparing male and female pay before and after comparable worth included as the "before" situation for female-dominated jobs the revised 1984 points for the job, not the original 1979 points.

Though there can be no objection to ridding any system of bias, as argued in Chapters 4 and 6, bias in job evaluation systems seem to be in the eye of the beholder. In any case, Rothchild told at least one non-Minnesota audience that the Hay system the state uses was set up before her arrival when comparable worth was on no one's mind.[28] She did not tell them, however, that the pay gap that she considers discriminatory (and that is pictured on her "before" scattergram) is larger than Hay originally found and that it is larger because of Rothchild's efforts to weed out the sex bias in the 1979 Hay results.[29]

At a women's-caucus-sponsored panel on comparable worth at the 1986 convention of the American Political Science Association, a speaker gave the practitioners in the audience advice based on her study of California comparable-worth initiatives: "It helps if you can keep costs low so the press can say it only costs 1 or 2 percent." Minnesota has never been able to keep costs that low, but in her speeches and writing Rothchild notes that the costs, 3.7 percent of payroll, were "less than the original estimate of 4 percent."[30] As we have seen, however, decisions not to give pay equity raises to the entry-level human service technicians were made in part because of budgetary concerns. A former DOER official has told me that the Rothchild decision to ignore "underpaid" male-dominated and balanced classes was also made not solely on her understanding of pay equity principle, but also because including them would have raised the costs so much that it could have killed the whole program. However, as already noted, in fact, the under-the-line, male-dominated and balanced classes *are* little by little getting their pay equity raises through the mechanism of reclassification studies or job audits. The accounting officers got two additional steps (about 7 percent beyond raises for other employees) so that the embarrassment that placed their pay beneath the accounting technicians could be remedied. Many other upgrades have occurred. Nina Rothchild counts none of these charges as a part of the cost of pay equity. She says, "We have always given equity increases based on reevaluations" of classifications. In her view this is "not a cost of pay equity" because it is not done to remedy sex-based discrimination.[31]

The people at MAPE are convinced that most of these reclassifications are a fallout of comparable worth. They think they would not have occurred had not hierarchical anomalies and fears about successful lawsuits threatened to sully the record of the Minnesota comparable-worth experience in a more fundamental way than would some added but easily hidden comparable-worth costs. Whatever these costs are called, they have been significant. As previously noted, they will add about $5 million per year to the $26 million or so on the official record. Moreover, whatever the unacknowledged costs of comparable-worth pay raises, a full accounting of costs would have to add the staff time devoted to implementing the system. This cost has also not been included in the 3.7 percent figure used by DOER.

Finally, because comparable worth increases the cost of predominantly female jobs, the state has hired fewer women than it otherwise would have. An overall increase in Minnesota state government employment due to other causes has masked the adverse employment effects of comparable worth for women. While there is debate over the extent of disemployment, researchers agree that it has occurred to some degree. Elaine Sorensen calculates that women's state employment declined 1.35 percent from what it otherwise would have been.[32] Mark Killingsworth calculates the job losses for women as perhaps three times as high.[33]

## THE LAW APPLYING TO LOCAL PUBLIC EMPLOYEES

Though there were more discussions, debates, and compromises before passage of the law applying comparable worth to local government than there had been before passage of the state employee law, the unorganized opposition was no match for the formidable coalition of proponents:[34] AFSCME and women's groups, an enthusiastic Governor Rudy Perpich, powerful legislative supporters, and Nina Rothchild, now speaking as the head of DOER. The Minnesota League of Cities and the Minnesota School Board Association tried unsuccessfully to substitute a voluntary bill for the state mandate that was passed. AFSCME reminded the Chamber of Commerce that the bill at issue applied only to public-sector employees and that if the chamber still planned to oppose it, it could be amended to apply to the private sector as well.[35] With higher-priority measures at issue during the 1984 legislative session, the chamber remained neutral. In 1984 the bill passed unanimously in the Senate and by 104 to 20 in the House.[36]

One Democratic legislator who voted for the legislation and is counted as a reliable supporter by proponents told me of his skepticism and "resistance in the back of [his] mind." But he said that he "didn't want to take on the politics" of a vote against the measure. "I'm in enough trouble with other people. Why fight it?" If the law had applied to the private sector, "then you'd be getting serious," and he'd have had to take a much harder look at it.[37]

The proponents of the law cared more deeply and were more powerful electorally. For others the bill had low visibility and attracted little attention in the media or in most legislators' minds. One local government lobbyist said, "I know for a fact a lot of people [legislators] didn't know what they were doing."[38] Nina Rothchild, who believes that pay equity and comparable worth are the same, was delighted that the bill's sponsors had adopted the less controversial pay equity moniker. One conservative female legislator had told Rothchild right before passage that she was glad to see that the bill was not a comparable-worth bill, which she could never support, but instead a pay equity one that she planned to vote for.

Two other factors were important to passage on the hurried last day of the legislative session. First, it was a presidential election year, and the Republicans' problems with a gender gap were much in the news. An amused AFSCME lobbyist told me how he went to the Democrats and explained how this bill could embarrass the Republicans and widen the gender gap and then went to plead with Republicans, "Don't let the Democrats turn this into a partisan issue." Second, and by all accounts of great importance,[39] the bill was considered after Judge Tanner ruled against the state of Washington in that state's comparable-worth case and before the Court of Appeals overturned the Tanner decision. The Tanner decision had awarded ten years of back pay to state employees and was expected to cost Washington over $400 million. Proponents could argue that Minnesota would save money in the long run if it took the planned route of legislation rather than the divisive one of litigation.

The law that passed required all political subdivisions (principally, cities, counties, and school districts) to set a pay equity policy and conduct a JES. Each was then to adopt a plan to remedy any pay inequities among job classes and to forward this plan to the DOER commissioner. Much of the language was like that of the law applying to state employees. But to pacify local government opponents and ensure passage, the state's law establishing comparable-worth value as "*the* primary consideration" in establishing equitable compensation became "*a* primary consideration" (emphasis added). As suggested later, this change together with a provision requiring compensation to bear a "reasonable relationship to similar positions outside of that particular political subdivision's employment"[40] has led many jurisdictions to link their policies to outside market relationships as well as internal comparable-worth ones.

## IMPLEMENTATION OF THE LOCAL GOVERNMENT LAW: THE PROPONENTS' PERSPECTIVE

The official view of Nina Rothchild and DOER is that the local government pay equity law is "working well." So says the "fact sheet" put out by the department and so said Bonnie Watkins when briefing congressional staffers at a May 1987 Washington, D.C., meeting.[41] Watkins and Rothchild acknowledge that "many" local government officials were at first resistant, but they argue that once the officials "settled down" to do the study, they "found that it wasn't as hard to do as they thought, and it did make sense."[42] At a fall 1989 session with Minnesota legislators, Watkins spoke with pride of the many local units who were a part of the major change in the way "we think about pay." There had been an end to picking "numbers out of thin air." People were now asking if we were paying less "just because the job is done by a woman." Many local units were clearly doing it right, and many employees who had been underpaid for a long time knew now that they were "being treated fairly."[43]

From the proponents' point of view the big gain from the local legislation has been the increased wages for women. Although almost one-half of local governmental units did not find inequities, most of these were very small governments or organizations with a predominantly female work force and few male jobs for comparison. Most government-employed women work for units that found inequities, and 47 percent of the female classes in these governments were or are to be included in the wage adjustments. The occupational groups with the largest number of employees eligible for pay increases were clerical workers, school aides, and food service workers; the average amount of pay equity increase is estimated at $246 per eligible employee per month.[44]

Despite these gains, in their less public moments comparable-worth proponents give a more pessimistic view of local government results to date. In an interview, Bonnie Watkins noted that most local officials did not like the law to start with, and she said that the results to date were "problematic." In 1989 DOER looked at a sample of 100 (of the 1,522) reports submitted by localities and found 29 out of compliance and another 12 possibly out of compliance.[45] Moreover, if proponents did not think there were significant problems in local results to date, they would not have invested so much effort in the 1989–90 legislative battles over amendments they were proposing to the local law.

Nina Rothchild had anticipated that most localities would use the state's "job match" system for job evaluation purposes. The job match asked localities to find state equivalents for their local jobs and then apply the state's Hay points to them. Commissioner Rothchild and the departmental "pay equity team" headed by Bonnie Watkins toured the state and urged localities to avoid disruption by using the simple and cheap job match system. In Rothchild's view, the job match guidebooks created by her pay equity team gave almost a "paint by the numbers" simplicity to pay equity implementation.[46] Rothchild was surprised and disappointed that, for the most part, only the smaller units of government used the job match system. Almost all the larger units chose to maintain local control by using consultants to establish their own job evaluation systems.

Rothchild considers the consultants some of the great spoilers in the comparable-worth process.[47] As she sees it, in pursuit of bigger contracts, they convinced local officials that pay equity was as complicated as the officials feared. The consultants reclassified everything, established a great technical edifice, and lost sight of the whole point of the exercise: putting an end to sex-based wage discrimination. Indeed, they suggested various cost-saving devices (discussed later) that perpetuate and institutionalize sex-based wage disparities.

In proponents' minds another important spoiler was Hennepin County (greater Minneapolis). Hennepin has 23 percent of the state's population, and its government employs 8,700 people. Both the professional managers and the county commissioners in Hennepin opposed comparable worth. Indeed, "the impetus for the local law had come first from leaders in AFSCME frustrated by the county's adamant refusal to negotiate a pay equity agreement."[48]

In implementing the law that passed, Hennepin adopted some policies to be discussed that had the effect of minimizing the costs of comparable worth. This result alone would have recommended the policies to many other local officials, but the Hennepin example loomed still larger because of the size of the county and because of its reputation for having a professional, well-run personnel department. Policies like those adopted by Hennepin were subsequently adopted by other counties and medium-sized cities.

One of the ways these localities resisted state implementation guidance was by abandoning the male line as the standard for nondiscriminatory pay and substituting instead a line that reflected the average pay for points of all employees or of balanced-class employees. Since "women's" jobs earn less per point than "men's" in most jurisdictions, the all-employee line is lower than the men's. So too is the balanced-class line. Localities do not have to raise the pay of predominantly female jobs as far to reach either of these two lines as they would have to raise wages using a male line. Moreover, using either of these lower lines makes some male-dominated jobs with very high pay for points seem to stick out on the high side. Management thus has an argument for wage freezes in predominantly male jobs as a means of meeting pay equity goals, not just raises for women.

All surveys have shown that the all-employee line has been far and away the most popular with localities. For example, 54 percent of counties and about 69 percent of school districts have used it.[49] Most comparable-worth proponents strongly oppose the use of the all-employee line. As usual, Nina Rothchild puts the case the most pungently: "I was a math major at Smith College. I know enough not to include the salaries of women's jobs, which have been held down by discrimination, in my standard for nondiscriminatory wages."[50] This position assumes what even crowding theorists and other economist *supporters* of comparable worth explicitly deny, that discrimination against women lowers their wages but has no effect on men's. In fact, by reducing the number of competitors (i.e., supply) in "male" occupations, discrimination would inflate the male salaries.

Regardless of the substantive arguments made against the all-employee line, comparable-worth proponents realize that it causes them substantial political problems. As long as pay equity means pay raises for governmental women and very small, perhaps unnoticed, and certainly unidentified tax increases or program cuts for others, pay equity can be politically popular. But if the all-employee line puts the "overpaid males" issue on the bargaining table, it becomes clearer that there are losers as well as gainers from comparable worth, and the losers may cause trouble for pay equity.

Many jurisdictions, especially large ones, combine an all-employee line with corridors, usually around 10 percent, on either side of the line.[51] Jurisdictions argue that job evaluation is not precise enough to require that all jobs be exactly on the line and that a 10 percent variation in either direction should be considered acceptable. While not objecting to corridors per se, comparable-worth proponents note that jurisdictions having them usually show most of the predominantly female jobs clustered in the corridor beneath the line and most of the predominantly male jobs clustered in the corridor above it. In effect then, proponents charge, the corridors simply reduce the number of female job classes eligible for pay increases and institutionalize "an 'acceptable' percentage for continued disparity between male and female jobs."[52]

From the perspective of proponents, matters were made even worse by the decision of many large jurisdictions to forbid any wage to go more than a fixed percentage away from the market rate regardless of JES results. For example, Hennepin County refuses to pay any job more than 10 percent above or below the market rate. As a result, some "female" jobs might not even reach a lower-end corridor if the salary paid is already 10 percent above the going rate.

Jurisdictions that apply the market constraint are relying on the portion of the law that allows for consideration of factors other than comparable-work value such as "reasonable relationship to [wages of] similar positions outside of that political subdivision's employment." DOER argues that this language is meant only to allow exceptions for wages above comparable-worth value where such higher wages are necessary to overcome recruitment difficulties.[53] The language is not meant, DOER argues, to allow the historically discriminatory market wages to set limits on comparable-work-value gains of predominantly female jobs.

The question of whether comparable worth also applies to under-the-line, male-dominated jobs arose at the local level just as it did with the state law. Though about 29 percent of localities ignored under-the-line, male-dominated classes, 71 percent gave raises to all classes that were inequitably paid.[54] The Department of Employee Relations argued that the intent of the 1984 law was to give priority to establishing pay equity for female-dominated classes "where historical discrimination against women" had occurred. DOER maintained that state-level implementation had been limited to female-dominated classes and noted that all comparable-worth court cases had been brought on behalf of female-dominated classes.[55]

Comparable-worth proponents and some legislators are particularly incensed that some jurisdictions use the pay equity law to justify pay increases of 40 or 50 percent to well-paid executives most of whom are male.[56] In their judgment such raises have nothing to do with remedying sex-based wage discrimination, which is what the local government pay equity act is intended to do.

Aside from the broad conceptual quarrels, comparable-worth proponents also object to the practice in many localities of avoiding pay equity increases for women by various evasive techniques. Two of the most discussed are the two-tiered wage schedule and contracting out. The former involves cutting the wage for above-the-line "male" jobs (e.g., school janitors) for new hires only. Most men continue to get the previous high wage, but the "official" wage used to establish the line is the one paid newly hired employees. Contracting out of relatively high-paid predominantly male jobs (e.g., janitors) or relatively low-paid predominantly female jobs (e.g., cooks) also enables a pay equity organizational problem to be quickly solved because the organization no longer employs the overpaid men or underpaid women.[57] Various evasive devices used by localities are discussed further in Chapter 4.

## IMPLEMENTATION OF THE LOCAL GOVERNMENT LAW: THE LOCAL PERSPECTIVE

When the law applying to local governments passed the state legislature, St. Paul, Minneapolis, and a few other localities had already begun to study and implement comparable worth on their own initiative. In these localities and in some others with committed elected female politicians or school board members the law's passage caused few waves. However, in much of the state the law came as a surprise and a shock. Most of the newspaper commentary and attention to the issue came only after passage. Suddenly, local officials were faced with a mandate to pay their employees according to practices very different from those they had used in the past. These past practices varied widely. In small rural counties and cities there was often no central personnel system at all. Department heads individually negotiated for raises for their employees with the local powers. Even in the handful of localities that had previously embarked on job evaluation systems, the pay among men as well as between men and women was not correlated closely with job evaluation point totals.[58]

In most places there was, and still is, belief that wages should be market sensitive.[59] Sometimes the market rate is inflated because of union power, but whatever the source of the prevailing wage, most local officials think it makes no sense to pay more. A consultant active in the state told me of instances, before comparable worth, where he and other consultants had been fired because their JES results were too far from the market to be credible with localities. Other local officials described their initial reaction to the law in words such as "We pay a market rate; why should we pay for someone's social theory?" or "They're [home health aides] readily available when we look to hire; why pay more?" These local officials were not just stingy penny pinchers. They looked to an alternative ideal to that emphasized by comparable-worth supporters, namely, "It is the business of government to provide good services at low cost." Comparable worth seemed a direct affront to this principle. As the Lake

County auditor said at the time that he reluctantly implemented his comparable-worth raises, "What do we get for it [this money]. Nothing. We have the same people doing the same things."[60]

Despite their feelings local officials had no choice but to bring their pay systems into compliance with the new state mandate. Evans and Nelson nicely summarize some reasons why so many local officials decided not to adopt the job match method of compliance touted by DOER:

> Local jurisdictions of any substantial size argued that their labor forces had unique characteristics not captured by state-level job classes. Police and fire-fighters in cities, like teachers and school secretaries in school districts, were employees central to the jurisdiction's mission. But analogous employees of the state had somewhat different duties and responsibilities as well as significantly different relationships to the central mission of the governmental body in question. In addition, jurisdictions whose employees were organized into a variety of unions faced pressures from male-dominated unions. These localities wanted a system that would be credible with all employees and doubted that a job match would serve the purpose.[61]

Like Evans and Nelson, I too found local administrators, some quite sympathetic to comparable worth, who were critical of job match. One librarian said, "I can't believe it would be easy to do or be very accurate – someone running a single person library in northwest Minnesota being matched with a reference librarian for a state office." Though Nina Rothchild blamed the consultants for making things too complicated and technical, one personnel administrator from the city of Minneapolis said the city should have paid *more* attention to reclassification issues before proceeding: "We had a twenty-year-old system. We're finding some increases already given were inappropriate, and that's money down the drain."

Many localities' systems were not twenty years old, but nonexistent. A number of these localities thought that they needed help setting up job classes before they could even think about job match or some alternative. And once classification systems were set up, consultants, understandably, thought they should finish the job rather than leave things to the local officials and the job match manuals.

At every stage of the implementation process local officials' fears about litigation were pervasive. Their lawyers expected lawsuits, and Nina Rothchild and Bonnie Watkins warned the recalcitrant that in time, they would surely come.[62] This is ironic because both were assuring their national personnel audience, concerned about the effects of comparable worth if they should adopt it, that the Minnesota program had led to no lawsuits. This statement, though ambiguous in context,[63] was presumably meant to apply only to the Minnesota program for state *employees* not to the state in general, for there have been a number of lawsuits against counties and other jurisdictions. At least six were underway in early 1990.[64] The use of a *threat* of suits is more pervasive still. In any case, though DOER was saying job match would protect against suits, consultants were saying that only a tailor-made, state-of-the-art classification and job evaluation system could be defended when challenges came. To be safe, the locals often went with their consultants.

Those localities that followed DOER advice and used a male line often did so not because they agreed with DOER about comparable-worth theory, but because their lawyers told elected officials that this was the safest course to avoid lawsuits. Since the male line meant bigger raises for women in predominantly female job classes and fewer, if any, pay cuts in male-dominated classes, employees were less likely to sue. Some localities tried out alternative lines and went with the male line for legal protection reasons if the costs were not substantially higher.

For most employers the costs were substantially higher, however. These cost differences were important to the majority of localities that adopted an all-employee line; but localities saw other advantages to the all-employee and balanced-class lines. Hennepin County noted that, in Hennepin, the balanced classes were the most uniformly represented at all compensation levels. Moreover, being neither male nor female, they were "the least likely to have sex bias reflected in their compensation."[65]

Perhaps the biggest advantage of the all-employee line was that it provided somewhat greater stability in pay equity implementation plans. As we shall see in Chapter 4, the process of ranking jobs brought acrimony to most workplaces. Once the process had run its course, localities wanted to be able to implement agreed-upon comparable-worth raises over a determined time period and put the matter behind them. But with the use of a male line, the line, and thus plans, could change every time a job class became predominantly male or ceased to be predominantly male. This happened periodically since, in counties, the majority of job classifications have only one occupant. If a high-priced (in terms of pay per points) man retired and a woman took his place, the male line would fall, and employees below the line could suddenly find that the pay equity raises they had expected were shrinking. The same phenomenon would occur if a low-paid woman quit and a man took her place. The opposite phenomenon would occur if a low-paid man quit and a woman took his place or a high-paid woman quit and a man took her place. In these cases, the male line would go up, and the costs of pay equity to localities would go up accordingly.

These are not just hypothetical developments, but ones that loom larger and larger for localities that are reaching the point where they think it is time to recalculate the male line. When I spoke to one personnel expert from a county using a male line, he was mulling over what to do about a high-paid systems programmer job class. It had previously been an innocuous "balanced" class with three occupants; it had become an expensive line-raising monster with just one male incumbent. This random change had nothing to do with changes in sex discrimination, but given DOER doctrine, it would have a significant effect on the costs of implementing comparable worth.

Even the all-employee line requires frequent tinkering because, as female classes get increases, the all-employee line goes up, requiring still more increases. Thus, none of the lines really achieves the local unit's desire to get the matter behind them once and for all.[66] But the localities argue with perfect justification that the pay equity law does not mandate the use of a male line.[67] And they genuinely believe that existing inequities often stem from overpaid males, not underpaid females. Some using the all-employee line are trying to close the pay-per-point disparities by, for example, freezing the pay of school district janitors or hiring new ones at a new lower rate.[68] These localities think that such measures to end disparities should be applauded, not condemned. Corridors also seem justified to localities perceiving imprecision in job evaluation; indeed, such corridors seem indispensable in a union environment where everything must be negotiated. Local officials that have taken the heat and imposed freezes on *above*-the-corridor "male" occupations while funding raises to bring low-paid women up to the lower edge of the corridor are impatient with those who insist that they should be able to do without corridors altogether or at least ensure an even distribution of male and female occupations within the corridor.

Localities wonder how they can find the money to pay inflated wages in male-dominated trades relying on laws effectively requiring payment of union-level wages and then pay similarly "rated," female-dominated jobs the same inflated wages. They also wonder how they can keep police, fire, and other "essential" personnel from saying "you can take that law and shove it" as they exercise their legal right to let an arbitrator make a binding decision on an appropriate raise. As originally passed, the local government pay equity law required arbitrators to "follow" the equitable compensation standards established by the law. Pressure from police and fire unions got the term "follow" changed to "consider" in 1986.

When making their awards, some arbitrators (especially female ones) weight heavily the conclusions of the jurisdiction's JES, but others continue to give more weight to inflation and police and fire fighters' wages elsewhere just as they have always done.[69] For example, the city of Moorhead had a study that put fire fighters within a few points of police officers, but police had historically been paid significantly more. Fire fighters' pay was above the Moorhead line, but police were even further above it. However, the arbitrator for the fire fighters' case essentially agreed with the city's position that the fire fighters should get no more than they had, while a different arbitrator for the police case granted the police a higher base increase than any other job class in the city. When arbitrators let the police officers or fire fighters break out of the internally determined comparable-worth standards, those in other job classes quickly demand that they be brought up too.

The localities consider this de facto exemption of certain employees the principal implementation problem because government units are required by DOER to include police and fire fighters in the determination of the pay equity line though they have no control over their salaries. The problem goes beyond just police and fire fighters since the Minnesota merit system mandates minimum wages for some social services occupations, and the Corrections Department specifies wages for local probation and parole officers (often above comparable-worth levels) and withholds local aid for violations. Moreover, comparable worth encourages other occupations (e.g., jailers and public safety dispatchers) to try to be deemed "essential" so they can break out of the comparable-worth constraints and thus set everyone else on a new chase after them.

The localities have been trying to get reinstated the original language requiring arbitrators to follow comparable-worth standards. They have no prospect of success or of much help from comparable-worth supporters. These supporters realize that exemption of essential employees is a major problem, but value union support for pay equity and are reluctant to do anything that would strengthen further the opposition of police and fire unions to the total concept. In 1989 an obviously frustrated Nobles County administrator wrote Senator Linda Berglin, a strong comparable-worth supporter, explaining how arbitration and the other exceptions for particular occupations made it impossible for localities to establish an equitable pay system. Berglin's short response noted the controversial nature of the pay equity amendments already under consideration at the request of others (especially DOER) and said arbitration could be addressed in the future.[70]

In her travels, Nina Rothchild seeks to combat the "myth" that comparable worth "will destroy the integrity of the collective bargaining process."[71] Since Minnesota's laws do not establish a rigid pay-for-points system, she argues that collective bargaining remains "the most important influence on pay-setting."[72] However, she seeks a system where on *average* female-dominated jobs will get paid as much per point as male-dominated jobs. And male-dominated jobs are more likely to have the strong unions. As Evans and Nelson note, in the medium-sized cities, police, fire fighters, and engineers/maintenance workers are the occupations that bargain collectively and have the most "clout."[73] One sign of union clout is the ability to get more for your membership than can the unorganized with comparable skills.[74] If the male-dominated unions can no longer negotiate to raise their members' salaries above those of the less well organized, then collective bargaining cannot be "the most important influence" on pay. Indeed "male" unions often resent pay equity because they think it seeks a costless way for women to gain what male unions could get only through organizational costs, strikes, and tough negotiating.

Though localities are still required to negotiate in good faith with unionized employees, they were also required to implement their pay equity plans prior to 1992. As Peter Bergstrom, until recently general counsel for the Association of Minnesota Counties, has argued, a county cannot negotiate in good faith something that it has no choice but to implement.[75]

Pay equity advocates also seek to interfere with traditional collective bargaining results when they object to the way that localities have interpreted the law's requirement that localities "shall assure" that compensation for positions bear "reasonable relationship" to similar positions elsewhere. This provision has historically helped male-dominated classes with strong unions just as it has hurt female-dominated classes whose job evaluation points suggest a wage much higher than has historically been paid. DOER's view that this provision is meant to apply only to exceptional cases where there are demonstrated recruitment difficulties[76] seems strained since nothing of the sort is suggested in the language.

DOER also maintains that the law's provision making comparable work value "a primary" consideration in compensation is almost identical to that of the state law that makes comparable work value "the primary" consideration.[77] However, this change in the law was not inadvertent, but part of the floor negotiations that were essential to get the bill passed. The localities think they got something from the compromise language. The substitution of "a" for "the" suggests that there may be other primary considerations. And a mandate to "ensure" reasonable relationships to salaries elsewhere would seem to be one of them.

Though proponents' interpretation of the "reasonable relationship" provision seems strained, they are right to see that the localities are striking at the heart of comparable-worth doctrine when they allow market rates to limit the power of job evaluation results to change market rates. The proponents' opposition to this practice is thus quite understandable. More curious is their opposition to localities that do a standard JES and then implement its results for all employees – i.e., those in balanced as well as in both predominantly male and female classes.

Nina Rothchild and DOER have always said that localities are free to establish a program that reflects "their own unique value systems."[78] Most local jurisdictions have decided that their value system will not permit them to conduct a JES and then raise the pay of female-dominated classes found to be underpaid, but not the pay of male-dominated and balanced classes found to be underpaid. They strongly believe that such a policy would be discriminatory and bad personnel practice. Questions of basic fairness aside, such a policy also causes serious implementation problems since, as time passes, the classes that are female dominated and thus eligible for increases will change just as they have at the state level. Moreover, local officials who wish to adopt a sex-neutral policy have a strong argument that the 1984 law as passed encourages such a policy. In a letter to a state senator in 1989, a St. Paul personnel specialist noted that though the original proponents of the local government pay equity act may have wanted it to apply only to females, the Act that was passed in 1984 applies to both males and females. The Act specifically states that "every political subdivision of this state shall establish equitable compensation relationships between female-dominated, male-dominated, and balanced classes of employees." ... The Act literally says that all employees must be paid equitably in comparison to each other. ... In other words, the Act requires that we use a gender-neutral job evaluation system to study all of our jobs. We must then assure that all employees are paid equitably based on this system, not just females and not just lower level employees, but all employees regardless of gender and level within the organization.[79]

This letter was occasioned by the brouhaha that erupted in 1988 and 1989 when it was learned that pay equity was being used as a justification for increasing the wages of some high-level male administrators. The Commission on the Economic Status of Women, Rothchild, and friendly legislators were outraged, and an unsuccessful attempt was made to pass a law that would have forbidden any locality to give a salary increase of more than 4 percent to managers, officials, and administrators.[80] The publicity did lead to a rescinding of comparable-worth raises scheduled for executives at the Metropolitan Airports Commission.[81]

So far as I can determine, there were no unusual job evaluation shenanigans that led to the results that most outrage proponents, such as at the airports commission or in Hennepin County. At the Metropolitan Airports Commission the original, much-criticized proposal for male executive raises grew out of a study using a Control Data JES adopted by many cities in Minnesota. Under the airports commission's plan, more female-dominated jobs were due for raises than were male-dominated or balanced class positions. In Hennepin County 83 percent of employees receiving increases were females. Moreover, consultants I spoke with were not surprised to learn that studies might find male public-sector executives underpaid since the "pay compression problem" was widely discussed. As one consultant said:

The private-sector pay line is below the public sector's except at the top. Traditionally "essential" employees [like police] got theirs first, then the organized workers, then the nonorganized. Increases for the managers were always politically sensitive.

Indeed, some localities using standard job evaluation techniques found more underpaid male-dominated positions than female-dominated ones. In Cass County such a finding occurred because women held more Social Services Department positions that were tied to higher, state merit system pay scales. Aitkin County used the state's own job match system and found more men below the pay equity line than women. My personnel department source there thought that the women had previously been ahead because clerical workers and other female-dominated jobs had more votes in the relevant bargaining unit.

What we are left with is this: In their debate with opponents, comparable-worth proponents use the language of science and technique. In Nina Rothchild's words, pay equity is "a very simple concept: People doing jobs of comparable worth should receive comparable pay."[82] Proponents say that comparable worth can be determined through the use of objective, quantitative job evaluation that can establish the relative "value of the job."[83] Or as Helen Remick puts it, comparable worth means "the application of a single, bias-free point factor job evaluation system."[84]

So the localities were told they must abandon their historic, unjust pay practices and adopt comparable worth. They donned the white coats of science, conducted the state-mandated job evaluation studies and implemented the results. But when the study results benefited the male-dominated classes, they heard from Nina Rothchild that they were taking the system "one step further than the law intended" by paying "everybody according to what their evaluation showed they should be getting paid."[85] And they were told that they were "twisting" the system and substituting a "technocratic" definition of fairness,[86] "pay for points," for the real purpose of the law, remedying "sex-based wage disparities."[87]

But what does Remick mean when she says she wants pay based on the application of a "point factor job evaluation system" if *not* pay for points? To be sure, Rothchild has told national audiences that she does not favor the inflexibility of a pay-for-points system.[88] However, she has also told national audiences that job evaluation enables one "to determine *to what extent* persons in female-dominated jobs are unfairly underpaid" (emphasis added),[89] and that job evaluation determines the "value of the job."

The only job-specific evidence comparable-worth proponents have to show discrimination is a low pay-for-points ratio in "women's" occupations. That ratio is meant to prove the discrimination in the localities' pay scales and point the way to a specific remedy. But though this technique can spot pay inequities in "women's" jobs, it is apparently powerless to do so for "men's." Low pay-for-points ratios in predominantly male jobs, such as forester, must be caused by "something else" and are no sign of policy relevant "sex-based wage disparities." Or as one consultant told me, "When Nina complains about technique taking over, she is really saying, 'It is a political issue; raise the wages of women.' " Bonnie Watkins seemed to agree completely when she said of New Mexico, which simply raised the wages for low-paid women without conducting a study, "Nina and I said, 'Great.' "

In practice almost all states that have a comparable-worth system have a sex-neutral pay-for-points system. It has proven difficult to maintain that a single JES spots underpaid women with ease but is powerless with respect to underpaid men. If the law assumes that the JES scores represent the value of the job, the pressures will be to pay accordingly.[90] As previously noted, even Rothchild was eventually forced to raise the pay of below-the-line male-dominated state job classifications though she has attributed the costs to something other than pay equity.

At the local level, Rothchild also insisted that only gains for female-dominated classes be counted as costs of pay equity. Though 71 percent of localities have acted on the belief that pay equity should apply to all classes,[91] the forms for reporting costs to the state allow localities to say nothing about costs attributed to raises for male-dominated and balanced classes. Thus, when Rothchild tells her legislature that localities "report" costs that average 2.6 percent of payroll, she does not give them a figure that reflects what localities see as the costs.[92] These localities do not "report" the costs for raises for male and balanced classes because the forms provided by the DOER do not allow it.[93] There is also no space provided to report costs for consultants or for the internal process or morale costs of establishing a system.

Though the reported "costs of pay equity" are not those that the localities think they encounter, they are also not really the costs that DOER thinks they would be if pay equity were done right. If all localities had to use a male line and had to have female-dominated classes scattered around the line in the same way that male classes are, costs for some localities would increase dramatically. The Minneapolis school district figures that their costs would go up from $900,000 to $9 million.[94] Hennepin County says their annual costs would go from $16 to $31 million.[95] Financially, the city of Burnsville has been disrupted less than most to date, incurring annual costs of $110,000 on a $9-million payroll. However, a male line and an even scatter of male and female classes around it would take costs from $110,000 to $310,000. This $200,000 increase represents the total normal tax revenue increase in Burnsville over a four-year period.[96] The costs of comparable worth that are reported on DOER forms are thus not accurate from either DOER's or the localities' perspective, but being smaller than either would figure, they may be reassuring to those who hear them.

While not allowing the localities to report to the state their full costs of comparable worth and while ignoring their problems with litigation, collective bargaining, arbitration, and shifting pay lines, Nina Rothchild tours the country saying the costs are low, the problems few. She also reports that "many local employers have a sense of satisfaction in developing a more rational, defensible, and bias-free pay system for all employees."[97] Though I encountered some local officials, especially in personnel departments, who took pride in their new systems, I also encountered a large number who were very frustrated by the pay equity process.

Evans and Nelson report that "stories of intense conflict... pepper accounts" of local pay equity implementation with respondents still in the middle of the process using "apocalyptic language: 'agony and pain,' 'the biggest upheaval any employer will see.' " However, Evans and Nelson downplay the significance of these reports, arguing that change always means conflict and that the struggles were primarily within government (not in the broader political arena) and lasted for a fairly short time.[98]

The anger and turmoil were especially intense and public in the first years after passage. In 1985 the annual meeting of the Association of Minnesota Counties recessed quickly, and the whole section of the platform on general government policy was tabled after the delegates passed by a 179 to 95 vote a resolution rejecting comparable worth. By the next day the leadership had regained control with the help of the association's lobbyists, who warned against "slap[ping] the legislature in the face" through an action thoroughly repudiating a law so recently passed.[99] The platform plank as finally passed urged a legislative review, extension of deadlines, financial aid to cover the costs of pay equity studies, and the like.

My respondents tell me that eight years after passage, pay equity remains the number one personnel concern of local officials. Staff at the Association of Minnesota Counties report that their members constantly "bitch" about how the law makes it nearly impossible for them "to respond to the market." Phrases such as "the stupidest law ever passed by this state" are still around. *Public* attacks on the concept are more guarded now because it is the law, and attacks on it may be used as evidence in lawsuits claiming indifferent and inadequate implementation. Thus, one county's labor relations expert told me: "When I first heard of it, I said, 'you have got to be kidding.' Now we're in court advocating our version of it.... Though it's not the system I might devise, our job is to make it work as well as we can." Similarly, news accounts often quote city managers or county commissioners making statements like "I don't agree with the darn thing, but we're going to get it done"[100] or "It just doesn't make sense... but our job is to implement the law."[101]

## THE 1989–90 FIGHT OVER CHANGES IN THE LOCAL LAW

As they surveyed the pay equity situation in Minnesota in the late 1980s, comparable-worth proponents saw three principal problems. First, many localities were refusing to acknowledge that the law was solely concerned with raising discriminatorily low wages in occupations dominated by women. As a result, whether because of manipulation of their systems or because of adherence to a "technocratic" sex-neutral pay-for-points philosophy, localities were giving too many pay equity raises to male-dominated occupations. Second, through the use of corridors and other devices, many localities were paying female-dominated occupations less than male-dominated occupations rated equally according to their own job evaluation systems. Third, existing law gave DOER some authority to penalize localities that refused to implement *their* plans but no authority to examine the plans themselves to see if they, in fact, would bring about a fair pay system.

Throughout 1989–90 Nina Rothchild led a coalition of women's groups and friendly legislators in efforts to correct all three of the problems that proponents saw. They were opposed by an unusual coalition of employers, represented by the Minnesota League of Cities and the Association of Minnesota Counties, and employees, represented by a number of strong predominantly male unions, including those representing the teamsters, operating engineers, and law enforcement officers. Though they had to make compromises, the proponents of comparable worth achieved progress in the legislature on all three of their concerns.

The 1990 law changed the original law so that the definition of "equitable compensation relationship" was no longer sex-neutral. Instead of general language emphasizing payment based on comparable-worth value, the new law read, " 'Equitable compensation relationship' means that the compensation for female-dominated classes is not consistently below the compensation for male-dominated classes of comparable work value."[102] Proponents had originally proposed language requiring that the average compensation for male- and female-dominated classes be equal. The "not consistently below" language was a compromise.[103] In addition to this change in the definition, the "establishment" section of the law that had emphasized equitable compensation relationships among all classes was followed by language saying "in order to eliminate sex-based wage disparities in public employment in this state."[104]

Finally, the DOER commissioner's enforcement power was increased substantially. Localities are required to submit much more detailed information about such matters as lump sum payments, the minimum and maximum salaries for each job class, and "any other information requested by the commissioner." The commissioner can impose fines on governmental subdivisions that he or she finds have not established equitable compensation relationships. In an effort to assuage the opposition of localities, the commissioner is required to "consider" recruitment, retention, and arbitration problems before finding a jurisdiction out of compliance. Moreover, appeals to both the commissioner and an administrative law judge are provided for; and in addition, no penalty will be enforced before "the end of the first regular legislative session after a report listing the subdivision as not in compliance has been submitted to the legislature [1993 at the earliest]."[105]

The legislature clearly had not expected the opposition it encountered to the amendments proposed by DOER. At the end of the first day of the 1990 hearings before the House Committee on Governmental Operations, a host of witnesses remained unheard. An obviously frustrated and annoyed committee chairman, Representative Leo Reding, made it clear that he was not happy that the proponents of the legislation had left so much conflict for the committee to resolve:

> I had assumed when we scheduled the bill that it had been heard in the Senate for six hours and that there had been some agreement out here in the crowd. There is no agreement out here. We will schedule for next Wednesday. We will have the whole two hours. At the end of the time we're going to vote. The author of the bill pretty much set the stage for what is happening in the crowd.[106]

Despite the efforts of the chairman to move things along, the hearings actually concluded after not one, but three additional sessions. In his lengthy testimony the teamsters' representative was particularly outraged by frozen wages incurred to date and the prospect of more if the amendments should pass.[107] Aside from the testimony of interest group representatives, there was a heavy equipment operator who asked to testify about the effect of wage freezes on his family and about the inequity he saw when his salary was well below the private sector's level while his city's secretaries' wages were way above market levels.[108]

Though the antagonists differed on important issues of substance, the hearings made it clear that the differences were accentuated by the strong feelings opponents had about DOER commissioner Nina Rothchild. Proponents, in and out of Minnesota, consider Rothchild one of the great heroines of the comparable-worth movement. Bright, witty, confident, and combative, Rothchild is particularly admired for her famous slide show in which she "lets the air out of opponents"[109] with her discussion of excuses to avoid implementation "ranging from the 'ostrich' (if we don't do anything it will go away) to 'Chicken Little' (implement pay equity and the sky will fall)."[110] Many local officials, however, see this speech as indicative of Rothchild's general unwillingness to take seriously important implementation problems.

In the House hearings Representative Wayne Simoneau, the House sponsor of the proposed amendments, pressed Bill Bassett, the Mankato city manager who was testifying on behalf of the Coalition of Greater Minnesota Cities, as to why the language saying the commissioner "shall consider" recruitment and retention difficulties was not sufficient. Simoneau asked; "Is it that all this language is here and you don't trust the Commissioner to do what is right? Is that what you are saying?" Bassett replied, "That is correct," and (on the tape of the hearing) the whole room seemed to burst into laughter and applause.[111]

The following day Representative Linda Runbeck was narrowly defeated in her attempt in committee to require the commissioner to establish an advisory task force made up of representatives of local governments and employees of these governments. Runbeck made it clear that the task force was her attempt to get the commissioner to enter into a dialogue with the localities and cooperate more with them.[112] Though this measure failed, the final bill's provision that required a full regular legislative session to pass before any fines on localities could be enforced was clearly a result of the tension between the localities and Rothchild. As former Senator Donald Moe, then chairman of the Senate Government Operations Committee, told me, the localities were saying, "Don't throw us to the mercy of Nina Rothchild."[113] This provision in the law allowed a further appeal to the legislature to extend deadlines or perhaps provide funding.

Despite the compromises in the final legislation, proponents made legislative gains in the 1990 battles. The localities strongly opposed the definitional language which suggested that inequitable compensation relationships could exist only if female-dominated classes were consistently paid less than male-dominated classes of comparable-work value. Testifying before the House for the Minnesota League of Cities, Joel Jamnik said:

> There has been concern about local government implementation, especially adjustments of male-dominated classes. Quite frankly one of the reasons that has been done is simple fairness – that if you're using a job evaluation system and saying that you're going to use that system for compensation either for negotiation or setting salaries, it only makes sense that that system be applied across the board. Also there is concern that if you *don't* do that you'll be exposed to Title 7 civil rights reverse discrimination action.[114]

There were representatives who strongly agreed with Jamnik and proposed a return to sex-neutral language about pay inequities. They were defeated in a voice vote in the House committee.

I argue at length in Chapter 4 what is briefly suggested here: A job evaluation system that finds predominantly male jobs underpaid has not necessarily been manipulated. Legislators, however, know little about job evaluation methodology or processes. Proponents were telling them about cities like the one that reduced the "on paper" requirements and points for female jobs while leaving actual duties and pay unchanged. Such shenanigans enabled them to give a comparable-worth pay raise to the police chief.[115]

The legislators were clearly affected by such stories of abuse. I argue in Chapter 4 that a fair, rather than a manipulated process led to a substantial comparable-worth pay increase for St. Paul police. But when I interviewed Senator Donald Moe, 1990 chairman of the Senate Government Operations Committee, he said he thought the pay increase for the St. Paul police was "just outrageous." Similarly, the chairman of the House committee, Representative Leo Reding, told me: "The scenario is always the same. If people are smart enough, they can make the process help them. Administrators got their pay up using pay equity." When Linda Barton, then city manager of Burnsville, emphasized the cost of comparable worth in her testimony before Senator Moe's committee, Senator John Marty asked:

If you spent $110,000 and all of it went to the female-dominated classes, might not you be in closer compliance? I mean it seems to me that the $15,000 you are spending on the male classes puts you $15,000 further behind.[116]

Minnesota legislators are proud of their state's leadership on pay equity. At the start of one hearing Representative Reding passed around a current *New York Times* article that mentioned Minnesota when discussing comparable-worth developments,[117] and he took pride in calling the Commission on the Economic Status of Women, a "national and international leader."[118] In the early 1980s Minnesota legislators were persuaded that predominantly female jobs were not being paid their comparable-worth value. They passed legislation to do something about it and were understandably surprised and suspicious when the supposedly objective job evaluation systems produced large numbers of underpaid male-dominated jobs.

In addition to their efforts to keep sex-neutral language in all parts of the law, the local jurisdictions tried hard to get the language making comparable-work value "a primary consideration" changed so that "primary considerations" became both internal comparable-worth comparisons and "external comparisons with similar job classifications." They achieved considerable legislative support for this change, which actually passed the House Government Operations Committee by a 14 to 8 vote.[119] The change was strongly opposed by comparable-worth proponents, who said it would "kick the legs out of pay equity."[120] The language did not survive the House tax committee, where the bill was sent before going to the House floor. Two female legislators on the tax committee, Ann Rest and Sidney Pauly, proposed omitting the "external comparisons" language, and it was taken out without a formal vote being taken.

Though the localities did not get strengthened language allowing external comparisons, the existing law already *required,* in another section, that localities "assure that . . . compensation for positions bear reasonable relationship to similar positions outside of that particular political subdivision's employment."[121] No attempt was made to repeal this provision. Comparable-worth proponents also decided that they could not get the legislative support necessary to make comparable-work value *the* primary consideration (as in the law applying to state employees) rather than just *a* primary consideration. Thus, local jurisdictions that choose to give the market a role in their pay systems still have support in the law.

## PENDING REGULATIONS TO IMPLEMENT THE 1990 LAW

The amendments to the pay equity statute applying to local governments were signed into law in the spring of 1990. As of the summer of 1992 the administrative rules relating to compliance were not yet finalized. In 1990 DOER had moved quickly, publishing a revised handbook that spoke of assessing locality plans by "viewing the scattergram as a whole" to see if "there is a good mix of male and female classes at the various pay levels."[122] This approach to compliance came to be called the "eyeball method."[123] The whole effort fizzled when the attorney general's staff informed DOER that the department needed specific rule-making authority before it could issue pay equity rules. The department independently came to realize that before assessing penalties for noncompliance, it should have a less time-consuming and more legally defensible approach than an "eyeball method."

In November of 1990 a Republican governor was elected, and in January of 1991, Linda Barton, formerly the city manager of Burnsville, replaced Nina Rothchild as commissioner of DOER. She was soon armed with pay equity rule-making authority granted in the 1991 legislative session.

Barton inherited Faith Zwemke, a classified employee who was the pay equity coordinator under Rothchild. She also inherited a methodological advisor drafted by Rothchild, Charlotte Striebel. Striebel, a professor of mathematics at the University of Minnesota, was working on a statistical method for determining local government compliance.

Barton appointed a pay equity rule-making advisory committee representing various interests including, among others, AFSCME, the Teamsters Union, the Minnesota National Organization for Women, the Minnesota Library Association, the Association of Minnesota Counties, and the Minnesota Pay Equity Coalition, represented by Nina Rothchild. Eight meetings were held between May 3 and July 17. The number of people at each meeting "ranged from 26 to 33, and a total of more than 850 person-hours" were spent in the meetings.[124]

Despite the lengthy discussions on the proposed rules, there was no consensus on a host of issues. Localities, for example, objected to the DOER requirement that they use a male line. Male-dominated unions wanted the rules to pay more attention to collective bargaining history. And AFSCME objected to the proposed "four-fifths rule," which allowed localities to have more underpaid female classes than male classes as long as the underpaid male classes were at least four-fifths as great as the underpaid female classes (e.g., a locality could just comply if 40 percent of the female classes and 32 percent of the male classes were under the male regression line).[125]

The proposed rules and these and other controversies were passed along to an administrative law judge. The judge found the rules reasonable but agreed with the localities that the proposed rules would have a fiscal impact greater than $100,000. According to Minnesota law, the department should have included with the proposed rules formal notification of such significant fiscal impact. The failure to include "an adequate Fiscal Note in the Notice of Hearing" was a defect in the rule that would require DOER to republish the rule and provide an opportunity for another hearing.[126] The process will not be completed until the end of 1992.

Linda Barton was formerly a city manager charged with implementing at the local level the state-mandated comparable-worth law. When I interviewed her five months into her new job as DOER commissioner, her personal views about pay equity remained like those of most local officials. Though she thought the 1990 law focused only on raising the pay of underpaid female-dominated classes, she personally believed that underpaid male-dominated and balanced classes should have been made equally entitled to pay equity raises.[127] Her principal interest in pay systems was in encouraging more pay for performance. When asked, she quickly agreed with the frequently stated local philosophy that government's job was to provide good service for low cost. After I mentioned that some local officials complained that pay equity bought nothing since it left the same people doing the same things, she corrected me – it bought "less than no return." Barton said that, in Burnsville, "morale went further and further down the more we got into it." The city's police dispatchers "got large increases, but believed they should have gotten more." No one was happy. People would say, " 'I work as hard as that person.' " There were "lots of bad feelings."[128]

Despite her personal views, Barton has sided with comparable-worth proponents rather than the localities on most of the disputes that have come before her. She believes the law gives her no leeway on some of the issues. Moreover, several local officials noted that she has had little room to maneuver since her pay equity staff was inherited from Nina

Rothchild, many rule-making decisions had been tentatively made before she took office, and a host of interest groups and legislators friendly to comparable worth would protest at any signs of retreat.

Some local officials think Nina Rothchild would have insisted on complete parity between underpaid male- and female-dominated classes and would not have supported the four-fifths rule.[129] But this issue aside, they are hard pressed to think of other substantial decisions that would have been different under a Rothchild-led DOER. Still, the local officials have high praise for Barton. They say she listens to them and returns their phone calls. Comparable-worth proponents such as Aviva Breen agree that she is a good listener, and all sides think the hearings before Barton's broadly representative advisory committee were well run and helpful.

Despite the good feelings toward Commissioner Barton and all the hours that have been devoted to the rule-making process, the controversy in Minnesota over comparable worth is by no means over. To be sure some localities are seeking to come into quick compliance with DOER-proposed rules. Hennepin County, for example, wants to get the issue behind it. Hennepin has found some female-dominated classes that have few employees and are near the male line, and by moving them to the line, it thinks it can come into compliance with state doctrine. (Under the proposed state rules the cheapest way to come into compliance is to raise the pay of those in small classes who are closest to the line while ignoring those furthest from the line who are, presumably, the most unfairly paid.) Hennepin still considers its preexisting pay equity program based on a balanced line to be its real program. It will provide other pay equity money to some female-dominated classes furthest below this balanced line.

Other localities and unions, however, are considering lawsuits testing the ambiguities in the law about external comparisons. The question of underpaid males may also lead to "reverse discrimination" suits. Despite the changes in the definitional clause, there is nothing in the law that would prevent the continuation of sex-neutral policies, and certain sections of the law would seem to require them.[130]

Another issue very troubling to localities is the relationship between the Striebel-developed computer model and the pay equity statute. Local governments received the software in June of 1992, and within weeks they found that "lots of oddities were coming up."[131]

A blunt June letter to Faith Zwemke from Jeanette Sobania, the personnel coordinator of the city of Plymouth, alluded to one case in the city of Fridley. Fridley thought it would currently be in compliance with the proposed rules, but it expected one of its four male police sergeants to retire soon. The next eligible person for promotion was a woman. If this promotion took place, the highly paid, above-the-line, sergeant position would move from a male-dominated to a balanced class.[132] This would make for a lower male pay line, which in turn would mean some male-dominated classes, currently just below the line, would move above it. Fridley would consequently fall out of compliance since the number of male classes below the line would become less than four-fifths of the number of female classes.

Sobania could not believe that the pay equity statute intended to penalize a city that wished to promote a woman to a highly paid male-dominated position. The letter also noted that Fridley might come back into compliance if it raised the pay of some male-dominated group, thus raising the male line again so that the aforementioned male-dominated classes, which had moved above the line, then moved back below it. In a blunt conclusion, Sobania, speaking for the coalition of metro-area suburbs, warned of a "time consuming and expensive judicial process" if DOER refused to consider modifications to its rules and computer program.[133]

When I spoke to her briefly in June of 1992, Linda Barton said she expected a group of localities to approach the legislature urging changes in the law in January of 1993. If legislative changes were not made, she expected a lawsuit to be filed challenging the department's rules.

# 4

## Job evaluation in Minnesota localities

Despite all the serious implementation problems enumerated in Chapter 3, the most fundamental weakness of comparable worth in Minnesota lies not in shifting lines and the like, but in arbitrary job evaluation systems unanchored to labor market signals. The very presentation of female and male lines with points on one axis and pay on the other suggests more solidity to the outcomes of job evaluation than ever exists in fact. To see how tenuous the figures are, one must probe beneath the seemingly objective "total points" for a job on a graph and focus on the political process and subjective criteria that produce the total.

The Department of Employee Relations (DOER) guide for local government implementation takes the standard position that job evaluation "measures job duties against objective criteria such as skill, effort, responsibility, and working conditions." But if the criteria are objective, phrases like "such as" will not do. We need to know what the criteria are and how they should be weighed and measured. Instead of providing such standards, the DOER guidebook provides a list of sixty-six "possible" criteria and assures its readers that the list is not "exhaustive." Some of the suggested factors clearly overlap, for example, "work environment" and "working conditions." To make the whole conceptual mess complete, the guidebook tells local officials that, though the criteria are objective, they can decide for themselves "what they value most" and "pay accordingly."[1]

### CONSULTANTS

A number of consultants helped localities with the job evaluation process, but Arthur Young, getting most of the school board and county business, and Control Data, serving 134 jurisdictions including most of the suburban cities, were the big winners.[2] The objectivity of job evaluation is immediately called into question if one notes the great differences in the usual methodologies of the two leaders. Control Data relied on very lengthy questionnaires that were meant to tell how much time jobholders spent on up to a thousand different tasks. Tasks were then valued based on their complexity, importance, unfavorability, and a fourth "overall" measure that was meant to combine the other three elements. Arthur Young's popular decision band method assumes that the value of a job is related to its decision-making requirements. Higher-banded decision-making jobs deal with more uncertainty and are seen as requiring more skill and effort.

As the comparable-worth movement generated new business for consultants, so it generated new marketing strategies. One advertisement in the *Public Administration Times* read:

> COMPARABLE WORTH?
>
> Finally! A comprehensive six factor (21 subfactor) system to compare jobs point by point to prove sex discrimination (or disprove).[3]

In Minnesota the challenge was to differentiate oneself from competitors while still appearing solid and sensible. Control Data emphasized up-to-date technology. Its system was "highly structured" and "computer based." Arthur Young played on its flexibility. Their chief public-sector consultant told me what he told counties: " 'It's your choice. We're flexible. If you don't like this system, here's another one.' " This consultant told his clients that if they wanted computerized job evaluation, he had a system "to match Control Data" and if they wanted a point factor system like Hay, he had one. For those who wanted "something different," he offered "the decision-band method." One county had had a point factor system and said that they could not stand it. Having a different system helped get the business for Arthur Young.

Though comparable-worth proponents often see the consultants as spoilers, forgetful of the purpose of the pay equity law and out to complicate things, they sometimes use the consultants' supposed expertise when it serves their purpose. During the 1989 Minnesota legislative hearings several representatives asked about the rigor of job evaluation, and one reported that he had heard of a lot of unhappiness with one system. Representatives were told of the long-time use of these systems in the private sector and of the development of expertise and "universal standards" through time as more and more organizations used the systems both here and abroad.[4] Nina Rothchild and DOER have maintained that "all the evaluation systems showed similar results."[5]

Sometimes the studies did yield similar results, but this correlation can be attributed more to decisions by similar jurisdictions to use the same evaluation system than to agreement among the results obtained from different systems. For example, the suburban cities decided to enter into one big joint study with Control Data because they feared that otherwise "if thirty or forty cities do their own [pay equity] plans, the unions would come back and hold up the highest one as the standard."[6] But as will be argued, there was substantial variation in many outcomes, and this variation was in part caused by the use of different systems. Certainly the occupational interest groups thought the systems differed, and they paid attention to which ones favored their members. The police liked the DCA Stanton system with its greater emphasis on accountability. An imaginative state-level overseer of library services told local librarians; "Don't worry about the system. With any of them you'll do better." But she also said that "Hay and Control Data do better by us than Young" because of the latter's deemphasis of knowledge and emphasis on decision making. She had systematically looked at results obtained through three of the most popular systems in hopes that there would be a male occupation that was always ranked quite near librarians. There was not, and thus her effort to come up with a rule of thumb for her membership – "We deserve what the [male occupation] get" – bore no fruit.

## BIAS IN JOB EVALUATION

As noted in Chapter 2, at the same time that proponents of comparable worth are calling job evaluation objective, they are charging that consultants and their evaluation systems are biased against jobs held predominantly by females. What little evidence there is on bias in evaluation does not offer much support for the proponents' charge. For example, one study provided compensation practitioners with detailed job descriptions and asked them to evaluate the jobs and set their rates of pay. When the sex composition of the incumbents in the positions was varied, no effect was found on the relative job ranking and pay.[7] Nevertheless, comparable-worth proponents have put pressure on job evaluators to reshape their systems in ways that will lead to higher ratings for predominantly female jobs.[8] The pressure has been successful. As Ronnie

Steinberg notes, "Completed comparable worth studies . . . introduced some changes in methodology for the purpose of gender equity."[9]

Particular attention has been given to working conditions where the consultant's rule of thumb often had been that indoor work was more pleasant than outdoor work. After taking over at DOER, one of the first actions that Nina Rothchild took was to have working conditions reassessed with the result that clerical workers received points because of conditions such as light-muscle fatigue and noise. In the guide put together to assist localities with implementation, DOER explicitly asked local governments to guard against the assumption that the only bad working conditions were those "typical of male jobs, such as outdoor work or heavy lifting."[10]

At the local level women city council members, AFSCME, and others sometimes pressed hard for an end to bias in job evaluation systems.[11] Consultants looking for contracts would naturally be sympathetic to such demands, but I found some genuinely sympathetic as well. As one told me, "I think it is good for job evaluation that we were pressured to take another look at how we assess women's work. Carrying bed pans [nurses] is as disgusting as cleaning toilets [janitors]." At the local level, nurses, cooks, and home health aides gained points for their "dirty" work as did social workers for the danger involved when dealing with child protection cases.

Despite the improvement in making job evaluation systems sensitive to the demands of traditionally female jobs, women frequently thought there was much more work to be done. One consultant remembered vividly a two-hour session with fifty representatives of a clerical union in which he was called "a raging, discriminating fool" for ignoring things such as the pain from "paper cuts." I myself spoke to many women angry at the bias they perceived in the evaluation systems and the rating processes that used such systems. One nurse revealed:

> The whole perception of what nurses do is off. They risk AIDS and other communicable diseases, having guns pulled on them. But it wasn't considered a hazardous occupation compared to a truck driver or a sheriff.

Similarly, a head librarian, librarian "A," said that she could not convince others in the process that her people faced unfavorable working conditions. She thought it "tiring to deal with the public" and be "constantly interrupted." But her colleagues would say, " 'Sure, I understand, they use a scannerpen and check things out.' "

But if the women were angered at the bias they saw remaining, the men were angered at the bias they saw created by the feminization of the evaluation systems that has already taken place. Like the women, they too focus in particular on the treatment of working conditions. Police officers and fire fighters were especially upset at the fact that secretaries facing "the stress of working between four walls" or of "meeting deadlines" were getting working condition points close to or equal to theirs when the secretaries encountered no rotating shifts or risk of physical harm. One police officer, St. Paul's Dan Vannelli, put it this way:

> Stress and hazard were lumped together. The maximum you could get for stress was 5 and the maximum for hazard was 5, but the maximum for both combined was also 5. So fire fighters would get a 5 and secretaries with deadlines to meet would get a 5 for stress.

What upset the men the most, however, was not their relative ranking within the working conditions category, but rather the paltry weight given to working conditions. All the consulting systems weigh working conditions relatively low. One study found that the working conditions category accounted for only 1.4 percent of the total score in the average Hay study.[12] The Willis study done for the state of Washington "assumed a maximum award of 280 points for knowledge and skills, 140 points for mental demands, and 160 points for accountability, yet awarded only 20 points for working conditions (which included the risk of injury or death)."[13]

During a period of tension over comparable worth in St. Paul, the local press contained complaints by fire fighters about an evaluation system that they said gave more points for skills such as "finger dexterity" or "the ability to drive a car" than for the "conditions fire fighters faced – such as exposure to toxic materials, lifting heavy objects and climbing high ladders."[14] One St. Paul fire fighters' union leader told me that the system was "preset" so that it's "the women who get the raises." On another front, even those not working in public works commented to me that they were surprised and troubled that public works jobs were not ranked a little higher. A policeman who was a member of a job evaluation committee noted that "in the year we looked at, two street workers were hit and hospitalized." A personnel specialist commented:

In Minnesota the snowplow unit has a very difficult, demanding, unpleasant, and important job. [Also] it's not much fun pouring hot asphalt in the blazing heat in the summertime.[15]

This personnel specialist went on to say of the public works crews, "But we don't have any trouble filling these jobs." As this comment suggests, it is the historic tying of job evaluation to market outcomes that explains the low weighting given to working conditions. A Hay consultant further explained that those with bad working conditions "have more restricted choices." Moreover, there is "a natural cap on how high the working conditions" points can go if you are going to preserve the job hierarchy. If you have laborers, crew leaders, and crew supervisors, the laborer will have the worst conditions; the supervisor may be "in an air-conditioned office most of the time." The points for working conditions must be "low enough" so that the supervisor comes out poorly on that factor but is still ranked highest.

Bad working conditions count for relatively little in job evaluations because the market finds a ready supply of people willing to put up with them for a small wage premium. Comparable-worth proponents attack this sort of surplus-of-labor argument when it is used to justify low wages for predominantly female jobs. They are silent when it causes a low weighting for working conditions, perhaps because raising the weight given this factor would benefit males more than females.[16]

Faith Zwemke was the mayor of Princeton, Minnesota, before she became pay equity coordinator for DOER. As mayor she brought comparable worth to Princeton even before the state law mandating it had been passed. Together with another council member, Zwemke designed her own evaluation system, which included five factors: knowledge and experience, accountability, responsibility for planning, variety of work, and responsibility for work of others. The police officers in Princeton complained because no credit at all was given for working conditions. Zwemke considered but decided against compensating police officers "for the danger factor on the job." She quoted approvingly the advice she got from someone at the state personnel department: "There is stress across the board. Every job has a certain amount of stress, and everyone is going to say they have a certain amount of it."

The police officers were bitter at their $.20 an hour raises when three female jobs were all going up over $1.20 per hour. Zwemke offered her opinion that it was "a mistake for employees to compare themselves between departments."[17] But such comparisons among departments would seem to be the essence of comparable worth itself.

In Minnesota, as elsewhere, bias in job evaluation seems to be in the eye of the beholder. There is no agreement on factors to be included, how they should be weighed, or even how factors (such as working conditions) should be measured once decided upon. Since "it takes all kinds," people will never be able to agree on the appropriate amount to compensate someone for facing risks. Some people *like* risk. One young Tampa reporter on local news, desperate for a job as a foreign correspondent, spent his vacation in the lawless coca-growing region of Peru. He was murdered there. What for others was a risk too great to bear was for him an adventure.[18] For others attracted to the helping professions like nursing, the occasional bedpan or vomit may be a minor unpleasantness, not a disgusting part of a job. We cannot be sure how atypical these people are or how many others there are like them, but we can be sure that one job attracts the atypically risk loving and the other the atypically empathetic. Thus, the unpleasantness of working conditions as determined by committee consensus will bear no relationship to how unpleasant the conditions seem to the atypical job occupants themselves. And, as indicated throughout this book, no agreement is likely in any case. At this stage, Minnesotans cannot agree even about which sex is being unfairly treated by job evaluation. Comparable-worth proponents think they know for sure, but so do their opposites in the male-dominated unions. And what they each "know" the other would deny most emphatically.

## BAD FEELINGS IN THE WORKPLACE

Evans and Nelson note that advocates think comparable worth will reduce friction in the workplace, while opponents think that it will increase it.[19] As argued in Chapter 3, Nina Rothchild maintains that a poll showing hypothetical state employee support for the concept of pay equity demonstrates support for the Minnesota comparable-worth program. She also believes that this Evans and Nelson poll disproves the view that pay equity "cause[s] disruption and low morale in the work force."[20] Rothchild ignores Evans and Nelson's findings on local implementation, which include reports of "hours and hours" of time spent on an intensely conflict-filled process leading to results greeted by a "general outcry" from "confused and sometimes angry" employees.[21]

If anything, Evans and Nelson's findings understate the picture I was given in my interviews. Whether I spoke to proponents or opponents, there was nearly universal agreement that the *process* was disruptive. It produced "ill will," "bitterness," and in some cases "bad feelings which carried over afterwards to other business."[22] DOER told the localities that substantial employee involvement in the rating process would help build support for the system.[23] But neither Evans and Nelson nor I found this to be the case.[24] Indeed, though Arthur Young let localities decide how much employee participation they wanted, the "crying and shouting" that occurred gradually led them to recommend less employee involvement than they had experienced in the first jurisdictions studied.

Even the managerially sophisticated localities were plagued by a large number of appeals on ratings. In Hennepin County there were 3,500 individual appeals (out of 8,700 employees) in addition to departmental appeals. Some jurisdictions did as many as four different studies, but multiple studies did not often ease employee discontent. Some employees always preferred the first study to the last, and when consultants made changes in employee committee decisions, the committee representatives felt "used and abused" at the changes "made in the dark."

It would seem that almost any job evaluation system risks damaging employee morale. One personnel chief reflecting on the ill will caused by the "comparing you and me business" seemed to long wistfully for the days when "the market decided." Another former local official who had been through the process asked me to imagine this situation:

> You go to a clerk who has been there for thirty years and thinks she is doing important work and say, "Tell me what you do." [Then you come back later and say,] "I'll tell you what it's worth." *Nothing* is more degrading than when your position comes out lower than you thought it was worth. That's *hard* stuff. "This is what your job is *worth*."

My respondents seemed particularly upset about the effect on lower-paid workers. One librarian said she thought her evaluation committee had given a few more points than were justified to clerical workers because "they wanted so much to get recognition. They didn't want low numbers. Their pride was involved." But hurt feelings and anger were found among many of the better paid as well – especially men – who saw their relative pay go down even if their real income did not. One personnel chief who said he supported the concept of comparable worth nevertheless thought the process

> one of the most divisive things imaginable. . . . it was the most dreadful experience in all my life. I'll never forget it. I lost some of my closest friends. They just couldn't handle it [when others were] ranked higher on "responsibility."

These experiences certainly suggest caution to any state government considering making job evaluation mandatory for local governments. Caution is also suggested by consultants who find the legally required job evaluation systems much more difficult than the voluntary ones. As one consultant told me, the employers "do not want to do it," and the employees do not understand this esoteric system that determines their pay. You face anyway in the public sector employees with great job security so "they can be contentious and not be canned." Since there is no pay for performance the "only way that an intelligent employee with initiative can affect [his pay] is by haggling over classifications." On top of this with comparable worth you have

> the heightened anxiety of males who now focus all their energy on the consultant. "You don't know what you are talking about putting me in grade 62. I belong in 67. But 69 would be okay too."
>
> From the consultants' point of view, even though our salary is based on contracts, these projects became a grind. We sickened of them.

As I got up and thanked another personnel expert for the interview, he said: "My pleasure. I am glad to talk about this in a setting where I am not getting yelled at."

## COMMITTEE POLITICKING

In their book, Evans and Nelson say of the local government implementation process, "Everyone had discovered that the people who controlled job evaluation won the comparable-worth sweepstakes."[25] This statement does not suggest that objectivity, science, and technique were carrying the day, and in fact they were not. With no standards to resolve disputes about bias and other problems, the interests fought it out, with the advising consultants trying the best they could to make the politicians and managers who hired them happy by keeping the costs tolerably low and the conflicts out of the papers.

About three-quarters of the local jurisdictions used committees to evaluate jobs. Some committees were made up of only employees and some of only management, but most often representatives from both were included.[26] Committee members thought that they had real authority and were much more influential in determining final outcomes than the consultant was. Among the big gainers in the evaluation process were those jobs that had articulate, forceful representatives on the committees or that had occupants who were creative in filling out the questionnaires.

The majority of job evaluation systems relied heavily on questionnaires – usually filled out by employees, but occasionally by their supervisors. The questionnaires were very elaborate, with those by Control Data containing up to a thousand questions. Still, there were complaints that Control Data's "fill in the circle" method did not capture the essence of a job. One librarian commented that, in small libraries, work is part administrative, part professional-technical, and part clerical, so in principle these librarians should have been filling out three different Control Data questionnaires. A disgruntled employee noted in the press that nearly identical jobs could look very different depending on how the forms were filled out.[27] Similarly, a respondent told me that "a lot had to do with the savvy of the people who answered the surveys – being able to read between the lines."

I spoke to nurses and librarians who had worked closely with others in their profession to be sure that no function or role had been overlooked. Likewise, a Minneapolis police federation representative spoke of trying to get more city attention paid to his "idealistic" composite responses to the job surveys:

> We got three hundred and fifty questionnaires filled out and gleaned the good stuff – no inventing but taking innovative suggestions about what to include. Then I tried to get this submitted as representative of the jobs for each rank.

In systems where questionnaires allowed employees to describe their responsibilities in their own words, committee members told of receiving "M.A. theses" for some jobs and lengthy job descriptions for others such as "light equipment operators." Employees who were less alert to the importance of the questionnaires, however, got burned. Aviva Breen of the Commission on the Economic Status of Women says she received phone calls from employees who complained that they had not known how their answers would be used. One strong supporter of comparable worth, a nurse who had served on an evaluation committee, told of her anger at the responses of one male employee in the parks department: Under duties "he said, 'I mow grass.' " Then under "education required" he put, " 'Get real, I said, I mow grass.' "

I said to hell with him. If he won't take this seriously, give him the lowest points on everything. Others [on the committee] reacted differently, and it balanced out.

Whatever the degree of balancing, it is clear that this poor fellow's pay was determined disproportionately by his unwillingness to take comparable-worth questionnaires seriously, as opposed to what he actually did on the job every day.

One former employee of the city of Coon Rapids wrote of his disgust at the doctoring of questionnaires that he saw going on around him:

When I was instructed to complete the comparable worth questionnaire, I was unaware as to its intent. Prior to the completion of the ranking of job scores, I spent approximately 1½ hours with public works director Russ Ward reviewing my survey. I had answered the survey to the best of my ability, but my raw score did not reflect my salary level as compared to others.

So the process became one of justifying salary levels by changing answers in the survey. Because my salary level was higher than most, my test score needed to be increased....

I know that there was a period of review in which employees could formally request that answers be changed. I'm unaware of any, other than management staff, receiving counselling by their supervisors to do so....

I believe that the pay structure at the city is such that the more the mid-level managers are paid, the more the department heads are paid. In other words by paying me more than I was actually worth, the public works director gets paid more than he is actually worth. By paying him more than he is worth, the city manager gets paid more than he is worth, and so on, up or down the line....

I was uncomfortable with the process when I participated, even though I benefitted greatly. I am, for seemingly obvious reasons, extremely discouraged by the manner in which the city of Coon Rapids is managed and governed.[28]

Nina Rothchild and Bonnie Watkins told me that they did not think that those occupations with representatives on the evaluating committee fared much better than others. But everyone else I asked thought committee membership was a big help. A supervisor of public health departments throughout the state told me that nurses in some departments fared well and in others poorly, and the differences seemed to depend on which job evaluation system was used and whether a nurse was on the evaluation committee. Interest group representatives of school personnel, librarians, and police also thought committee membership helped, with some saying "most definitely" or "absolutely." Two respondents emphasized that "the paper" was not enough, and that you had to be able to really explain what your occupation did when questions arose even if you were not able to vote for a rating for your specific job.[29]

One nurse emphasized time and persistence in going to meetings when describing the qualities needed to succeed when the Control Data intercity system was being set up:

> I spent thirteen or fourteen months with Control Data. I got to know them well. I went to at least twenty meetings, another staffer to at least thirty-five. Those who took it less seriously and didn't attend all the sessions lost out.

One head librarian, librarian A, echoed this sentiment, remembering the "aeons" she spent at Control Data and emphasizing the importance of regular attendance at meetings since Control Data did not know all the tasks themselves.

Once in committee, it was important to be prepared. The librarians especially seemed to have spent a lot of time looking for parallel tasks in other departments. At the appropriate time they would say, "You gave that task '*x*' points in '*y*' department. I do that task too." Success in committee also depended on being "articulate" and a "good sales person." One nurse remembered being impressed by the representative from the fire department: "He was emotional but good. His description of breathing smoke, falling off ladders, trucks traveling at great speed. It was real emotional stuff." Success also depended on being willing to "fight it out for what you are doing" or "sticking up for your group." One nurse made it clear that, for her, the "group" was all women: "I felt a deep sense of responsibility for helping women. I really did. I fought for the clericals. I was consistent throughout."[30]

The "lobbying" seemed to be done almost entirely in committees, not in the hallways, and some respondents said you could overdo it. You could fight only to a point or you lost credibility. But being "aggressive" and "willing to do battle" was important to success in comparable worth regardless of its importance on the job.

Committee members remember their sessions as exhausting, but also very educational – they learned a lot about what people did in other departments, and the committees did their best to reach fair conclusions. Still, the members often sensed that they did not really know as much as they should know when making their decisions. One nurse ruefully remembered being convinced by another committee member that it took an inordinate amount of time to learn how to operate a heavy road grader only to find later that it was not nearly as difficult as she had been led to believe.

Some women felt that the men did not read the written material and then were very vocal and aggressive in meetings. One nurse did not like the feeling that she always had to justify her needs, and she felt criticized when others objected after she made her points. One consultant who had seen the committee process at work over several years reported:

> Because of the political nature of the process, you feel you must have employees from all levels of the organization on the committee. From the county attorney's office the guy is an oral expert. With him is maybe a matron from the sheriff's office and a clerk. [The sessions are] heavily influenced by articulate members. The lower-level job members on the committees can't envision what the supervisors do. [You] can get some crazy results.

## STILL MORE MANAGEMENT PROBLEMS

The previous chapter discussed the travails of local government officials plagued with shifting lines, arbitration awards that conflicted with their comparable-worth plans, and lawsuits that challenged those plans. These officials also had to deal with the complaints of those who lost out in the committee politicking and with the general morale problems discussed in this chapter. The results of job evaluation studies provided still more problems for a number of administrators throughout the state.

Sometimes the problems were a simple result of high costs for raises that political authorities thought unjustified. In 1987 the St. Paul school district faced a projected budget deficit of more than $5 million. It also had in hand a market survey showing that the district paid women relatively well. For example, the district's clerks were paid 16 percent more than clerks working for business. Nevertheless, the board was presented with a second comparable-worth study claiming that the earlier study showing fifteen female-dominated classes underpaid to the tune of $1 million was in error and that, in fact, there were twenty-eight female-dominated classes underpaid, and the total cost of remedying the inequities would be over $2 million.[31] Another school board refused to grant the large raise for "paraprofessionals" recommended by a committee and insisted that the category be broken down into more descriptive job titles such as "hall monitor" or "behavioral management aide." In the city of Rochester, a plan calling for some raises as high as 45 percent was approved by the city council only because it felt "forced into the action" by the state law. One alderman noted that "if there were vacancies in many of the city positions, there would be long lines of people applying because the pay is substantially higher than for similar work in private industry."[32] Morrison County went through three studies and much acrimony. It ended up with a plan that outraged county commissioners by raising one employee's pay by $800 a month. At the same time, the plan left some other employees at the top and bottom "way below market."[33]

Morrison County had settled for less well known consultants, but even those who chose Control Data and Arthur Young encountered some major problems with their results. When the Metropolitan Area Management Association (MAMA) chose Control Data from a final list that also included Hay Associates, the selection committee could not have been more enthusiastic. News accounts noted that the Control Data proposal, at a cost of $345,000, was the most expensive submitted, but "the unanimous feeling of the MAMA Committee was that it was the one proposal that would provide the best and most legitimate results and would be the most easily maintained system over a period of years."[34] Even in 1989 rival consultants were saying that Control Data had "good people" and that their time-on-task, computer-based scoring system had been "thoroughly tested." But few were happy with the way things turned out.

Control Data, working with representatives from many cities, had divided jobs into five thousand tasks in seven different job groupings and was at work on the tedious business of ranking jobs when it became clear to corporate headquarters that the whole process was taking much too long and that the company was going to lose a lot of money. There was suddenly great pressure to finish quickly. Just about the time that some jurisdictions expected results, Control Data sold off its system and got out of the business. Even before then the company had been fired by some jurisdictions. One of the main reasons was the tendency of its elaborate system to produce bizarre results. Police lieutenants were rated higher than police chiefs, and utility directors came out ahead of city managers. Librarian "B" laughed and said:

> I was [ranked] third. I know very well that I was ranked too high. [The results were] not useful. [I was] ahead of the chief of police. If you look at budget or number of personnel under us, it makes no sense for me to be [ranked] ahead of the police chief.
>
> The utility director [got] more points than the city administrator. [The administrator] gets coffee, gets meeting rooms ready. It makes him successful. He really cares about the people who visit. [But] his [tasks] seemed odd.
>
> [The system was] not useful as it stood. They [finally] got another consultant.

Control Data's system also gave higher ratings to managers with an authoritarian style than to those who were good delegators.[35] Arthur Young's decision band system did the same with even greater impact, since a premium was put on making decisions. One large county encountered severe strains during the process because department heads figured out that if they were to make some decisions made now by subordinates, they could improve their own ranking. What the Young system counted as a decision was also controversial. One sign language interpreter told a legislative committee that she had to make four decisions at the same time in her work, but under the Young system, these decisions did not count at all.[36]

Other common problems with job evaluation results flowed straight from comparable-worth doctrine rather than from the methodology of particular consultants. For example, comparable worth insists that the focus be on the value of the job, not the value of the employee. As the DOER guide for localities put it, "Job evaluation evaluates jobs, not people or job performance."[37] This approach may work in the private sector if performance can be rewarded separately. But in the public sector, everyone knows everyone else's pay, and it is harder to make a pay-for-performance system work. In a heavily unionized state like Minnesota, it is harder still. Some administrators and courts have thought this perennial problem was made worse by the rigidity of the comparable-worth system.[38] Previously, whether managers were paying for the person or the job might be left vague, especially for single incumbent positions. One virtue of unsystematic, seemingly chaotic public personnel systems is that they enable managers to pay for performance without anyone really knowing or getting upset about it. Comparable worth made this kind of payment more difficult. As one observer noted, the tendency was to look at a bright clerk who was doing much more than her job description said and say either she was overpaid or everyone else was underpaid. In one case a school district pilot study was completely abandoned when the school superintendent determined that his secretary, whose actual duties were far greater than secretarial, was classified at too low a level by the comparable-worth system.

More troubling still was the frequency with which an equal pay for comparable worth system made it necessary to abandon a system in which there was equal pay for equal work. For example, in Minneapolis, the city council, the parks and recreation board, the library board, the school district, and the community development agency each conducted its own labor negotiations. Thus, under the comparable-worth law, they were considered separate employers. Though legally separate, each used the same civil service system, and the pay rates were generally the same for the same job. After comparable worth, however, employees doing the same job but working for different city governmental groups received varying salaries. Since there were more high pay-per-point males in the city government than at the public library, secretaries at the latter seemed less discriminated against and obtained lower wages. Because a secretary can transfer from the library to the city and maintain her seniority, the library management is understandably concerned about retention problems when slots open up with the city government.

In St. Paul the school district and city shared a tradition of bargaining with employees for a single contract as well as a common civil service system. Before comparable worth, pay was identical in the two systems for common classifications. After comparable worth, school employees were paid less. Though the same consultant used the same job evaluation system with both employers, results differed because, again, at city hall there were more high pay-per-point males to compare with the female-dominated classes.[39]

It seems efficient and just for cities to pay the same wages to secretaries doing very similar work whether the secretaries work in city hall, in the parks and recreation department, or at the community development agency. Yet, in localities in Minnesota, arbitrary comparable-worth results have completely dismantled this widely shared foundation of equity. There is no remedy for pay inequities for fundamentally equal work under any employer-centered comparable-worth system, the only kind advocated by U.S. proponents. Though no one seems to think the Minneapolis city government discriminates more than the Minneapolis public library, the employer-centered law required studies that led to the conclusion that the city does. As for the library secretaries paid less than those doing the same work at city hall, Aviva Breen, the executive director of the Commission on the Economic Status of Women, told me that they were simply "out of luck." Breen was not unconcerned but said: "We looked at that," and there was "nothing we can do about it."

## LIBRARIANS AND NURSES

From the start, librarians and nurses have been among the female-dominated professions most often cited by proponents as being seriously underpaid.[40] Both have also taken leading roles in the movement for comparable worth. It was the librarians in San Jose, California, who took the lead in that city's strike and thus began a process that led to the first major political victory for comparable worth in the United States. Nurses were involved in some of the most significant early court cases challenging pay classification systems in Denver and elsewhere.[41] The national interest groups representing both professions have been involved from the start, and the American Library Association has prepared a number of "how to" publications for use in the states and localities.[42]

Given the prominence of these professions in the arguments made by proponents, I decided to take a special look at how they had fared in Minnesota. I spoke to statewide interest representatives of both professions and to a number of head librarians and county directors of public health nursing throughout the state. On the whole the benefits for librarians dwarfed those achieved by nurses. The following pages explain why and comment on the public policy implications of this outcome.

Not all librarians have gained from comparable worth. An occasional study has found librarians to be overpaid.[43] Other localities have tried to ignore their studies showing librarians to be underpaid. And as mentioned in the last section, libraries whose library boards have substantial powers are sometimes considered separate jurisdictions, and with few higher-paid males available for comparison, librarians who work there can gain much less than their peers elsewhere. Librarians face a similar problem in regional libraries shared by several localities under joint power agreements.

Still, on the whole, the head librarians I interviewed reported staff wage gains of 20 percent or more, and they occasionally made comments such as "we led the pack" in citywide gains. A 1989 memorandum to state Senator Moe from Aviva Breen of the Commission on the Economic Status of Women listed results for seven different cities' librarians and noted that, when plans are fully implemented, one will have gained a comparable-worth raise of over 60 percent, one of 33 percent, and three others of 20 percent.[44] State-level librarians also earned pay equity increases in the earlier process.

While the gains for most librarians have been substantial, on the whole they are not happy with results to date because many cities, though granting substantial raises, are still not bringing librarians up to the level of their cities' equivalently rated male-dominated professions. Thus, when Breen reported the comparable-worth librarian results to Senator Moe, it was not with satisfaction, but by way of complaint. None of the seven cities would achieve pay equity even after its plan was implemented. For example, the city that planned a $629 per month pay equity raise (over 60 percent) for librarians would still pay librarians 15 percent below a lower-rated predominantly male job.

Despite the unhappiness, the comparable-worth gains for many librarians have been very substantial. In part the gains were achieved because librarians are paid relatively poorly compared with many professions. Moreover, they tend to get good scores on criteria such as skill and knowledge required. In addition, some job evaluation systems give credit for levels of education required, and since many librarians have masters degrees, they tend to score high on this count as well.

Though librarians rate high according to the criteria job evaluation systems usually value, equally important to their success were the attitudes and skills that they brought to the evaluation process. Librarians were primed and ready to go when comparable worth passed. They knew how important the answers to the questionnaires would be, and they gave each other tips on how to improve their scores. They went to the committee meetings, and they went prepared. It was the librarians who systematically looked for parallel tasks in well-paying jobs in other departments. It was a librarian who took the time to contact the civil service commission to find out how much supervising biologists and chemists actually did and how much education current occupants in those classifications had. When Aviva Breen needed some hard examples of remaining inequities for Senator Moe, it was the librarians who had them at the ready. Similarly, I found the librarians to be the only occupational interest group to have systematic comparative evidence on how their profession was faring under the most frequently used job evaluation systems.

The librarians I spoke with seemed quite smart, but even more impressive was their talent in preparing a brief. Their usual job skills involved finding data and doing research. Though, in principle, this esoteric skill should not count for more in comparable worth than an equivalent skill of a nurse or chemist, that the librarians' skill was so much more helpful in comparable-worth politicking gave them a big advantage in the process. The librarians usually knew the systems inside and out.[45] One head librarian, librarian A, readily acknowledged that the police chief was responsible for far more money and personnel than she, but she also knew why she came out ranked as his peer: "[Legally] he doesn't hire and fire. The city council does. He doesn't do the labor negotiations; the city coordinator does." Librarian A had originally been rated ahead of her city coordinator (the local name for the city manager). When he came to her puzzled, she said, "How did you answer your questionnaire?"

> I sat down with him. He had not included certain elements of his job. We sent the revised questionnaire back to Control Data for reevaluation, and he got fifteen more points.
>
> The Control Data system was determining it. He had not put in all his tasks. . . .
>
> No question, we [in the library] were ready. We knew what was going on [and how the tasks were] weighted. Many people [elsewhere] got the questionnaire and said: "What is this? Is it like a test?"

Some factors that seemed to distinguish librarians who got good raises from those who did not were aggressiveness, self-confidence, and a sense of grievance. Successful librarians were not afraid to threaten to go to the local newspaper or to file suit. They "kept after them," "fought" for what they were doing, and appealed adverse decisions. They were true believers, convinced that they had been discriminatorily underpaid for years and that comparable worth was crucial to how "these [library] people think about themselves" and to "what they can do with their lives." To them huge raises were not manna from heaven but badly overdue, hard-earned salaries that in many cases still left an inequitable pay gap that should be closed further very soon.

Librarian A had mastered the Control Data process and had no doubt that she deserved a salary equal to the police chief's. When asked to consider why some librarians studied by the Control Data system had received large raises and others had not, she was not sure, and she commented in particular on a nearby city, similar to hers in many ways, where the librarian had not done well: "They threw out the study. They thought [the rankings] were ridiculous."

When I interviewed the head librarian from the nearby city, I found librarian B, the person quoted earlier (p. 93), who said it made "no sense" for her to be ranked above the police chief who had a much bigger budget and more personnel under him. Though some of her staff librarians had received modest comparable-worth increases, she had received nothing. She had no complaints, believing that she and her staff were now well paid. She had found the Control Data system interesting but confusing, and she thought the results it produced "very peculiar." Compared to librarian A, she believed less in job evaluation, understood it much less well, and lacked a strong sense of grievance about historic salaries for librarians.

In librarian B's city most librarians received modest comparable-worth raises; in librarian A's most received substantial ones. But in one important way the two cities were the same. In both cities there were almost never job openings for librarians, and when there were openings, there were always scores of well-qualified applicants *before* the comparable-worth salary increases for "underpaid" librarians. In librarian A's city the last opening had occurred about the time the comparable-worth process had gotten under way. They had "sixty some" applicants for that children's librarian opening. In librarian B's city the last opening had been in June of 1983. They had forty to sixty applicants for a reference opening even though at that time the position "didn't pay well." These numbers of applicants were about the average that I encountered in my interviews with head librarians. The range was from 6 in a small outlying city to 120 in a more attractively located one.

A policy that grants substantial raises not needed to attract people to a profession or to attract people in the profession to particular locations incurs a number of costs. The most obvious cost is the one city administrators focus on: This money buys nothing for the public – "You have the same people doing the same things." The benefits of taxpayer relief or expanded city services elsewhere are forgone.

In the case of librarians, the policy worsens the tendency of libraries to spend too much on personnel and not enough on books and materials. This is a common criticism of outsiders who look at library operations and note that more than 60 percent of the budget typically goes to personnel.[46] In Minnesota there were cases of comparable-worth raises shifting more money from book purchases to personnel expenses.[47]

In Minnesota, I encountered cases of would-be librarians with B.A.'s or even M.A.'s in library science taking clerical or library trainee jobs in hopes of getting their "foot in the door" when future professional openings occurred. I also heard of cases where head librarians had been successful in getting positions upgraded from subprofessional to professional in part because they felt badly that a "poor Jane" was paid so little for one with her qualifications. Another step in the cycle is to make an M.A. a "requirement" for jobs where one is certain to have many applicants with that degree. And finally, come comparable worth, one can point out that librarians are paid so much less than other jobs where "the M.A. is required."

From the point of view of economists concerned about economic efficiency, librarians have historically been paid too much, not too little. For economists, the sign of this excessive wage would be the large number of qualified applicants available when jobs become vacant.[48] Comparable worth just exacerbates this historic problem. The higher pay makes still more talented women (and men) take a chance that something will open up. In the meantime, they become still more likely to take subprofessional library jobs for which they are overqualified or to go back to school to get an M.A. – all in hopes of increasing their chances of getting the now more attractive, because higher paying, job of librarian. There are efficiency costs from this process that are surely not fully reflected in unemployment figures.

In a well-functioning market economy a sudden surge in the price of something means that the public wants more of that thing. But city councils are not generally trying to hire more librarians, and if the elected representatives are accurately reflecting the public's wishes, the public does not want more librarians. Indeed, the public cannot fully use the talents of those it already has. So the sudden surge in the wage for librarians makes the economy work less well. It sends the wrong signals. At pre-comparable-worth wages, there were more people wanting to be librarians (and foresters) than there were jobs available. If instead of rising, their wage were to go down, there would be room in library budgets to hire more librarians, and some of those in the profession or contemplating entering it would go elsewhere – to professions for which the relative wage and job prospects were much higher.

If we are not going to compel people who would like to be librarians to do something else, we need some other way to induce them to change occupations. In a way, it seems just that would-be librarians who agree to shift fields to jobs of greater scarcity get something (added pay) for their sacrifice. Some readers will be surprised to learn that nurses are among those who gain when a shift from a comparable-worth to such a market-oriented wage policy occurs. So, at least, the Minnesota experience suggests.

Like the national nursing associations, those in Minnesota are on record as being supporters of comparable worth. But if one asks nurses at any level what it has done for the profession in Minnesota so far, the answers are less supportive. Some county directors of public health nursing will say that "it has helped" or even occasionally that "we did super." However, if one then asks these same respondents if the local public-unit nurses have done *better* than local private-sector nurses who have not had comparable worth, the answer is almost always no. And many other respondents complain readily about the effect that comparable worth has had on public-sector nurses and the organizations they work for. No matter how disappointed, there were no librarians – as there were many nurses – saying that comparable worth had made their situation worse.

The complaint of public-sector nurses is that salary increases have been less generous than those in the private sector. This view is held by a statewide lobbyist for nurses, by the director of public health nursing for the state, by several county directors of public health nursing, and by two regional supervisors of county public health departments. "We were more competitive before" is the way one local public health nursing director put sentiments expressed by many others. A lobbyist for the Minnesota Nurses Association said, given the current shortage, the counties would "do better with the market."[49]

Most of the nurses who voice these sentiments do so reluctantly. One closed her tale of woe by saying, "I hope I've been positive in my comments." These nurses generally like the *idea* of comparable worth, and some are pleased that it is helping women in other predominantly female professions. Others believe that the problems could be corrected if only the job evaluation systems would properly consider that nurses are exposed to communicable disease, supervise home health aides, and confront other difficulties. But for now, as far as salary is concerned, public-sector nurses say, "pay equity is holding us back."

The registered nurse vacancy rate in the nation's community hospitals increased from 4.4 percent in 1983 to 11.2 percent in 1987.[50] The need for nurses outside the hospitals has also increased. These shortages have been felt in Minnesota, and like other shortages, they have led to price/wage increases. I found articles describing hospitals that had unilaterally raised weekend and night shift premium pay for nurses significantly beyond that called for in union contracts[51] and public health nursing directors whose staff was being tempted by Florida- and Arizona-generated advertisements offering twelve months' pay for six months' work for those willing to relocate for the busy winter season.

Many public health directors complain that they cannot meet the competition for nurses because their locality's job evaluation system has determined that nurses are already overpaid. Vacancies exist many places and are increasing. One nursing director expressed her frustration by saying: "We started losing nurses to ____ thirty miles north." They were paying more than \$2.00 an hour more. "Two nurses left for the money," and "we could find no one for three to four months.[52] We spent \$2,000 trying." This nurse was "reconciled" to the fact that nursing will "always be a women's profession," and she expected to lose nurses through "pregnancy" or because a husband got a better job elsewhere. But for the first time she was beginning to lose them for money.

Some localities have had to violate the spirit of their comparable-worth plans by giving nurses credit for experience elsewhere (unlike, say, equally rated social workers) or by paying new nurses more than some currently employed nurses. Since the pay equity plans have usually compared maximum salaries, hiring new nurses at midrange has not been an easily seen violation as long as the maximum pay does not rise. Still, localities employing these tricks sometimes remain \$3 per hour or more behind private-sector wages for nurses. Thus, one hears directors of local public health nursing as well as personnel managers praising their locality's pay plans but also asking legislative committees for some flexibility. As one said, "Though I have a concern about putting in the job, market values, there must be a way of doing it." Why? Although her staff's salaries were higher than those of many surrounding counties, they were "much lower" than those paid "in the hospital or what you can drive to Sioux Falls and work for."[53]

My clear impression from the interviews was that Nina Rothchild, Bonnie Watkins, and Aviva Breen had no real sense of how serious were the problems that comparable worth was causing for many public health nursing directors in Minnesota; and Washington, D.C., proponents I interviewed could not imagine that nurses might be hurt by comparable worth. When I explained to these proponents that nursing supervisors had told me that they could not recruit and retain staff because of pay equity all reminded me of the exception allowed for precisely these reasons. When there are "documented" recruitment and retention problems, "temporarily" paying nurses (or others) more than similarly rated jobholders – even paying above a pay corridor – is perfectly all right. Indeed, in the case of nurses, since paying them more would not suggest a pattern of sex discrimination, such pay need not be only temporary.

Despite this all-clear sign from proponents, many local officials fear that granting such exceptions will cause them headaches. As discussed in Chapter 3 a number of officials are involved in lawsuits defending their pay plans against some employees' claims that the plans are discriminatory. The last thing officials want is to open themselves up to the charge that their plans are discriminatorily implemented as well.[54] Other localities not involved in suits nonetheless worry about what social workers or other jobholders will say if an exception is made for the nurses.

Nursing directors sometimes make comments such as "this county has spent a fortune trying to do the right thing." They sympathize with their bosses and readily acknowledge that nursing pay and recruitment woes are not an antiwomen plot but rather a policy of "trying to get everyone right at the line" or "making sure that no one is outside the corridor." Some of the county boards have been willing to spend thousands of dollars on advertisements for nurses and have been willing to see state and federal moneys lost because the short-handed local nursing staff had no time to file for reimbursement. But they resist market wages for nurses because they fear that it will not be possible to break the link between nurses' and others' salaries once an exception is made. It is one thing to pay higher, market wages to nurses when paying market wages is the established local policy. It is something else to pay higher wages to nurses for market reasons but then refuse to pay social workers and others as much even though there is an official county plan that declares them equally valuable.

Comparable-worth proponents have long used the behavior of nurses' salaries as their prime example showing that shortages do not lead to substantial wage increases in women's occupations, as the mainstream economists argue. Instead of raising wages to overcome shortages, employers are said to pay their own nurses bonuses to lure nurses from other places, or to make "international forays to the Philippines" to increase the supply.[55] At the NCPE tenth anniversary conference keynote speaker Eleanor Holmes Norton said that if markets responded to female shortages as they did to male shortages, nurses' wages would be "sky high."

In Minnesota, Aviva Breen told me that she had clipped a *New York Times* article headlined "Shortages Cause Nurses' Wages to Go Up." But she saw the article not as evidence supporting mainstream economists, but rather as evidence supporting comparable-worth proponents. "Nowhere else would this be worth a headline." As this comment suggests, the shortages of nurses in Minnesota accompanied by rapid salary increases has not caused proponents there to rethink anything. When these facts are pointed out to them, they say, "Why did it take so long?" and "Nurses' salaries are still nowhere near as high as they should be."

Over the past three decades there have sometimes been complaints about nursing shortages when none existed.[56] But through much of the period, nursing shortages did exist, and through most of the period, nurses' wages did rise more rapidly than those of most employees. For example, from 1960 to 1978, "the salary of registered nurses increased by 250 percent, while the pay of all men rose by 206 percent and the pay of all women rose by 193 percent."[57] From 1980 to 1986 the earnings of nurses went up by 55 percent, while those of all men went up 30 percent and those of all women 42 percent.[58] Recent trends in real (inflation-adjusted) earnings show that, from 1981 to 1990, registered nurses' salaries went up by 27.7 percent. During that period the average male salary declined by 2.8 percent and the average female salary increased by 8.07 percent.[59] Registered nurses in 1990 made 99.7 percent of the median wage for professionals ($608 versus $610 per week). Their pay exceeded the median for skilled blue-collar craft workers by 27 percent.[60]

Debate over whether these gains are "fast enough" or whether the level achieved is "high enough" would no doubt be unending and fruitless. But the evidence does suggest that shortages in this female-dominated occupation lead to increased wages.[61]

Those who believe that the market does not pay nurses enough assume that they will be paid better through some nonmarket mechanism that they have in mind. One of the most curious aspects of the debate over the proposal for a comparable-worth study of the federal pay system is the way that proponents use the crisis in nursing. That the federal government forces the National Institutes of Health and the Veterans Hospitals to pay nurses annual salaries thousands of dollars below the market, that severe vacancies have resulted, and that attempts to remedy the problem and get permission to offer special pay rates have been plagued by delay and red tape are all seen as evidence not that we should let markets set salaries, but rather that we have the wrong *kind* of administered wage system.[62] Minnesota shows what has happened in a state that should be able to produce the "right" kind – a state where the comparable-worth process has been guided by a tradition of law-abidingness and, at the critical stages, a thoroughly supportive director of employee relations. The result has been that one of the few professions in the public sector that frequently receives less than market wages is the female-dominated one of nursing. Nationally, rapidly rising wages for nurses have helped reverse the decline in enrollments at four-year nursing colleges.[63] The Minnesota experience suggests that a national comparable-worth policy would have made rapid changes in wages and thus in supply responses much less likely. Since changes in salary affect the career decisions of at least some men and women, still more people would have sought to become librarians, and the shortage of nurses would have been even more severe.

## POLICE

If librarians and nurses have represented the "worthy but underpaid" in the lore of comparable worth, police officers have been seen as a prime example of those unjustly paid more than the female-dominated professions. Comparable-worth proponents believe that the police and fire fighters have a privileged position in many localities. They have the most clout and have first claim on local budgets.

Most studies by local jurisdictions did find their police to be paid above the line, especially in localities that used the Control Data methodology. Howcver, many policc facing pay freezes took their cases to arbitrators, some of whom ignored comparable-worth standards. And among the larger cities, there were cases where the police were found to be underpaid and entitled to a comparable-worth raise.

The most prominent of these exceptions and the one that attracted more press attention to comparable worth than any other case involved the St. Paul police. They eventually received an 11 percent pay equity increase, but not before they marched en masse on city hall and took part in several bitter, public disputes with the mayor.[64] After the police won their raise, the fire fighters took over, demanding a comparable-worth raise of their own and a continuation of the policy of pay parity with police.[65]

Proponents of comparable worth have a ready explanation for why the St. Paul police did so well: politics. Nina Rothchild, who tells national audiences that police and fire fighters "always" end up above the line,[66] explains the St. Paul exception as follows:

> The cops put political pressure on, and the city reevaluated their jobs and gave them more points. The original study showed the cops well above the line....

> [It was] really just all caving in politically. The police and fire do all the political work [in St. Paul]. They deliver the campaign literature.[67]

Evans and Nelson tell a similar story. The police and fire fighters had reacted angrily to the results of the first study, so a second was done.[68] The St. Paul case is also seen as a negative example of employee-based evaluation since the consultant supposedly lost control of the process, and when employee groups began to negotiate, the whole process became suspect.[69]

St. Paul city hall sources told me that Sergeant Dan Vannelli was the police officer with the most detailed knowledge of comparable worth in the city. When I called him, I expected to encounter a tough cop who could tell me just how political muscle had been used to win comparable-worth wage gains for the police. In the most unexpected interview of all my travels, I encountered instead a soft-spoken, well-informed, comparable-worth strategist. In his approach to comparable worth, Vannelli reminded me a lot of the most savvy librarians I spoke to.

I first asked why police in St. Paul had fared so much better under comparable worth than police had elsewhere. Vannelli said, "One thing that was probably unique" was that the employees had real "involvement in the process.... We were able to challenge the stereotypes that were around."

Vannelli also noted that he had been "able to get the addition of [a new factor] consequences of error." He was able to show that suspensions were much more prevalent in the police department than elsewhere. They had them "every month." Maybe there were just more screwups in police work than elsewhere, but since the psychological and other screening was so much greater, he thought that unlikely. It must be the "more serious consequences of error that result in the suspensions."

Vannelli also provided his evaluation committee data showing that police have an adverse "work environment with rotating shifts and days off." Moreover, he had life expectancy tables showing that police live less long after they retire.

What had really "energized" Vannelli "to take this seriously" was what had happened to his deputy chief who had thought the police would do well. The deputy chief had asked the consultant, " 'How much weight should be given for a job where a person must decide whether to shoot [someone] or not?' " The consultant said that that was less important than the decisions of the personnel director, who must decide "whether to hire this guy who must decide whether to shoot someone or not."

Vannelli continued:

> I called all around the country on these [evaluation] surveys. I was really familiar with them then.... Police always think that you should emphasize the risk of getting shot or the decision to shoot. But the public knows about that, and they'll give us credit for it.... You need to rephrase what you're doing in bureaucracy terms.

Vannelli explained that if you ask a police officer what he did, he'll say:

> "I set a plant on a liquor store." [If instead you say,] "I *decided* to set a plant on a liquor store," [you can show that] there is really a lot of allocation of resources going on. If you can change [the activity] to a thought process, police will do better.... There is really constant decision making [in police work,] and you need great people skills. But police officers don't recognize this.

In the end, Vannelli returned to his first explanation for success – the employee committees had some real impact on the St. Paul system. "On the first day" the consultant "passed out a factor sheet with all the definitions for knowledge level written in and the job titles listed to go with them. We had them give us clean sheets instead." The sheets described the knowledge needed to reach a level, but the job titles were not written in.

Originally, the sheet had put police and secretaries at the same knowledge level. Vannelli had argued, however, that police have to have a two-year degree, and four years was usually expected in the metropolitan areas. In St. Paul you must go to a sixteen-week academy beyond that, and there is an ongoing requirement for fifteen hours of training a year. When the committee finished, it put secretaries one level higher on knowledge than they were in the original grid and police several levels higher.

The decision-making process Vannelli described was not at all that suggested by Rothchild, Evans, and Nelson. There was "a lot of discussion in committee." He thought "it was a fair process" and that he was "open-minded":

> I thought many [of the female occupations] were underpaid. Elementary school secretaries are really administrative assistants to the principal. They deserve much more than a clerk 2. They clearly deserve a jump [if you look at their] actual duties regardless of their paper duties.

I told Vannelli that there had been reports of political back scratching and negotiating in the committee. He said that he had seen none of this.

To check on Vannelli's story, I spoke to committee members likely to have noticed and been troubled by unfair politicking by police if it had occurred: a librarian and a nurse. The librarian denied having seen any horse trading, negotiating, or the like. She noted that the memorandum going out asking for departments to nominate committee members had said, "Give us your best, the ones you can't do without." But as far as negotiating was concerned, she "saw none of it. We were just petty employees. We had no real power."

When I brought the subject up again toward the end of the interview, she responded more forcefully:

> These people who say it was all political. What's their beef? What do they know that I don't know? I watched the numbers march by, and they were pretty much the same at the end of the process as at the beginning. [It's] probably just disgruntled city employees saying this.

This librarian had found the process "long and boring," but "fair." The nurse was in complete agreement. There was "lots of lobbying," people "sticking up for their group." But the "lobbying" all occurred inside the committee, and the group was "large and diverse enough to control it pretty well." On the whole, "it was a fair process. [The] group tried to do our best, and I think we did a good job." When I asked if there might have been negotiating going on outside the committee that she had been unaware of, she said she doubted it: "We were all anxious to get away from it" after the committee sessions were over.

Both women remembered Dan Vannelli. The nurse remembered him as "vocal, lobbying for his group, a good representative for his group. He had good arguments." The librarian concurred, "He was among the most effective advocates." She added that both the police and fire fighter representatives on the committee were "educated and verbally skilled." She had "learned a lot she didn't know" and "came away with real respect for police and fire. I was impressed that we were getting that quality of person."

Previous explanations of why the police fared so well in St. Paul seem off the mark. Both the police and fire fighters were slated to receive bigger raises from the original study than they ended up with. In the case of the police, a scheduled 17 percent raise became 11 percent. The alterations occurred because the city decided that the figures for police and fire fighters were too high and asked the consultant to look again on his own at these and other ratings with an eye to lowering costs. Vannelli believed this is where the politics may have entered. His union had never supported the mayor, while AFSCME had: "The higher-ups didn't like police and fire turning out so well. It was supposed to be AFSCME." As the nurse on the committee also saw it, it was here that the unfair extracommittee politicking occurred. The committee's work "was done over again" by the consultant. "I felt used and abused.... Things [were] changed in the dark."

After the consultant had reduced the ratings for police and fire fighters, there was then a third look at the ratings of the fire fighters, which did lead to an increase in their ratings.[70] The increase occurred at a time when the fire fighters were putting great pressure on the politicians to regain pay parity with the police. But the revised fire fighter ratings were still not higher than they had been in the original study. And the police were not involved in this episode at all. They marched on city hall to get what AFSCME had received without the need for a march – their comparable-worth raises and some back pay related to this raise.

What the St. Paul episode shows is that a cross section of employees of both sexes examining the police and fire fighter occupations using comparable-worth standards will not necessarily agree with comparable-worth proponents. If they hear effective advocates for these professions who have the time and skill to prepare as well as the librarians, such a cross section may instead conclude that police and fire fighters are underpaid relative to most professions, female included. In Minnesota's other large city, Minneapolis, the first completed study also determined that police deserved a large comparable-worth raise. There were no differences between males and females on the committees that reached this conclusion.[71]

To be sure, the St. Paul results ranked the police higher than the consultant's system had ranked police in other states. Dan Vannelli thought the police ranking improved because they were able to add factors to the system and because Minnesota police were better trained and educated than the typical East Coast police force where the system had been used in the past. But in any case, surely comparable-worth proponents cannot object to letting ordinary employees consider again the factors used and the weighting given to factors in consultants' systems. They regularly urge employees to look again at the systems with an eye to eliminating bias. They applaud people who set out to do what Vannelli set out to do – "challenge stereotypes." And with further reference to the case at hand, Vannelli's success in having a consequence-of-error factor included would have to be unobjectionable to DOER since "Effect/impact of error" is one of the sixty-six job evaluation factors listed in the planning guide for localities put together by the department.

Comparable worth cost St. Paul much more than it did most localities – about 10 percent of payroll.[72] The original committee results would have cost more still. One can understand why the city looked with suspicion at expensive ratings that did not seem consistent with past results. But one can also imagine the complaints from comparable-worth advocates that would have greeted any attempt to lower committee-determined results for secretaries or librarians because they were thought too costly or not in conformance with the usual consultant's results.

The St. Paul raises for police may reflect widely shared societal values. Most people see the work police do as terribly important and very risky, whereas many of the police themselves see it as important and exciting.[73] The excitement attracts them in ways that no "desk job" could. Or at least something does because there is no dearth of applicants when police jobs open up. By the standards of economic efficiency, if not comparable-worth job evaluation, police are probably overpaid.[74] Vannelli told me that there were "plenty" of qualified applicants for police work before as well as after the comparable-worth raise. There are in most places across the country.[75] The process librarians and their employers engage in seems at work here as well. To get an edge, would-be police officers get more education, and police departments, seeing a plethora of educated applicants, heighten the minimum education required – which helps raise comparable-worth scores. As with librarians, we need to consider lower, not higher, wages for police so fewer people waste their time preparing for jobs that do not exist.

## STILL MORE SURPLUSES AND SHORTAGES

By the standards of economic efficiency, librarians and police were not the only overpaid workers to be affected by comparable worth. Like most police officers outside of St. Paul, the effect on the wages of other male-dominated occupations was usually negative but in the desired direction from the point of view of reducing the surplus of qualified applicants and improving economic efficiency. For example, custodians and public works personnel were well above the line in many jurisdictions. They sometimes faced wage freezes or, in the case of custodians, contracting out or two-tiered wage structures. The effect on most of the female-dominated occupations that were overpaid by efficiency standards was far different. Librarians, cooks, teacher aides, child care workers, home health aides, and clerical workers received substantial raises in most jurisdictions of any size. Applicants for all of these jobs were plentiful before comparable-worth raises were implemented. Where there were private-sector equivalents, as with cooks, child care workers, home health aides, and secretaries, those in the public sector were usually better paid before comparable worth. Nevertheless, the average pay equity increase, the bulk of which went to these groups, was substantial – an estimated $246 per month per eligible employee.[76]

Secretaries and other clerical workers are like nurses in that they have been in relatively short supply over the past decade and have consequently enjoyed above-average wage increases in the private sector.[77] But unlike nurses, secretaries were big gainers from comparable worth in Minnesota. More clerical workers received comparable-worth wage increases than did occupants of any other job category, and their total wage gains far outpaced those of clerical workers in the private sector. As one county personnel officer told me, "Every secretary in the city wants our job. When we advertise, we get seventy-five to a hundred applicants, applications from Iowa, from Southern Wisconsin, from all over." However, according to its pay equity study, this county still discriminatorily underpays its secretaries. Indeed, the secretaries have not yet reached the bottom of the corridor surrounding the county's line. In another county, I heard tales of clericals, now paid one-third more than those in the private sector, who were nonetheless quite irritated that they were still paid less than equivalently rated men in public works.

The costs of these comparable-worth raises where surpluses already exist include those discussed in the section on librarians: a loss of otherwise obtainable city services (e.g., books) and a missignaling of labor needs in labor markets through the artificially high wage. For example, some supervisors of public health programs were concerned about salary compression as it affected the differential between nurses and home health aides. They felt that the shrinking differential did not give sufficient recognition to or incentive to train for the job with greater responsibility and requiring much more education. One head of personnel in a large suburban school system explained in detail how comparable worth had affected his management decisions and led to less efficient schools.

"In the sixties and seventies teacher aides were cheap support." They would do "Xeroxing" for teachers, provide "leg work" and "technical support."

> It used to be that you could get two and a half aides for the cost of one teacher. Now if you include fringes, it's more like one and a half. . . . I'd have more aides if I could pay what private sector hospitals and other places pay [them]. . . . I have fewer aides per teacher than I had four years ago. The bottom line is that the teachers have less time for the kids because they're doing more manual stuff.

A more indirect effect on resource allocation was also of concern to school administrators. Local business executives would tell the administrators, "You're already above market, and now you want to use my taxes for a big raise so you can steal my secretaries."[78] There was concern that this effect on local businesses was reducing support for the school budget. Even worse, perhaps, was the city that deliberately tried to hold back knowledge about the high salaries it paid secretaries to avoid stirring up such opposition. It paid much more than market wages, but since its pay rates were not advertised, it could not be sure it was attracting above-average secretaries.

Aside from these costs to the general public welfare, there were more direct costs to some of the employees who were meant to be the beneficiaries of the comparable-worth raises. Some cooks, child-care workers, and home health aides lost their jobs. For cooks, the job loss came via contracting out of their function to private enterprise. I was told that one school district saved over 20 percent of its pre-comparable-worth food budget by such a mechanism. The prospect of yet higher costs in the wake of comparable worth precipitated the move.[79] Contracting out aside, since school district policy and state law require that education moneys not be used to support food expenses, the cooks faced a further threat to their jobs from consumer sovereignty. As cooks' wages, cafeteria costs, and prices rise, more parents pack lunches, and the revenues needed to help pay cooks' salaries may shrink.

Middle-aged adults with children who need day care or parents who need home health care also have non-public-sector options. A survey of child-care options at public schools and universities and under early childhood family education programs found that the typical pay inequity was over $10,000 a year per employee. Sometimes the local jurisdictions increased subsidies to help pay for the added expense, but most programs had to finance the salary increases themselves. Eighty-one percent of these raised parental fees. (Unfortunately, the survey asked for no information about the effect of higher fees on parental patronage.) Fifty percent of the facilities forced to pay for their own raises either took more children without adding staff or actually cut staff.[80]

A further sign that jobs may have been lost as a result of comparable worth were articles in the Minnesota press with headlines such as "Pay Equity May Cost Health Aides Jobs."[81] In them, the aides said that the scheduled raises of 25 percent or more were not worth it if they meant unemployment. One lobbyist for nurses confirmed that there had been cases of home health aides asking that they *not* get their full comparable-worth raise because of their fear of unemployment. Earlier in her career she had even sat on a job evaluation committee where the issue came up. A projected 40 percent raise for home health aides would force the county that was already subsidizing home health care to make "hard decisions." They might take the available options of contracting out or just getting out of the home health business altogether. Facing an "ethical dilemma" – "do I fight for what I think is right and risk these people's jobs?" – she decided to make the case for the increases and "cross the next bridge later."

These cases are especially interesting because they call into question the comparable-worth proponent's vision of the discriminating employer as the prime mover in most pricing decisions. Instead, if there is a villain at all, it is the ordinary consumer. City councils can get away with paying librarians inflated salaries because taxes pay for the salaries, but because child- and home health-care providers charge fees, private-sector alternatives can compete, and we can observe consumers' preferences. Consumers frequently are unwilling to pay what comparable-worth proponents think these occupations should earn.[82] Employers, the hapless go-betweens, can do nothing to compel care providers to work for less than they are willing to work for, and they cannot force consumers to pay more than they think a service is worth. Indeed, in private-sector child care the providers often have no employees and set their own fees for their own labor.

As at the state level, pay for local government employees in Minnesota is above that in the private sector for most jobs in most jurisdictions. Thus, labor shortages have been less frequent than surpluses. There are exceptions however. As noted, nurses get below-market pay in many jurisdictions. Those in the computer field are also paid below market average in most jurisdictions. Though underpaid by market standards, these occupations were often overpaid by comparable-worth criteria. Thus, for example, though the potential maximum salary increased for 85 percent of the employees of Olmstead County, a newspaper article noted that "most of those whose salaries are scheduled to be frozen are in the skilled and technical fields."[83] Caught between the rock of actual markets telling them their wages for technical personnel were too low and the hard place of a legally required comparable-worth plan telling them they were too high, local personnel officers "more and more" frequently went to their consultant and said: "I can't get these people at the pay equity rate, but I don't want to screw up my line by paying more. How can I get them off the line entirely and out of the system?"

As noted in the discussion of nurses, comparable-worth proponents plead innocent to the charge that they have caused this mess. They say that exceptions are allowed for recruitment and retention reasons. As also noted, local officials nonetheless fear lawsuits and employee morale problems if they seem to be making exceptions to their pay equity plan. One county personnel specialist told me, "If we pay *them* more, everyone else in the band must come up. It will come up in negotiations." A consultant I spoke to reported: "Most of those I advise have been conservative in using the shortages exception. Given public employees' litigiousness it's a high-risk strategy. You're usually better off making do with an incompetent programmer." Another consultant acknowledged that there are data one could look at that would indicate labor shortages, but also worried about how the process would play out.

> You could look at the number of applicants, turnover rates, market surveys. Still, you could waste a lot of time trying to prove that the two with questionable work histories who applied for the management job listed at $37,000 were not in fact qualified.

Though proponents respond to complaints by quickly pointing to the allowable recruitment and retention exception, they are in fact suspicious of the "shortages" excuse and worried about how the exceptions will be used. Thus, a legislative supporter of comparable worth reminds her listeners that these exceptions are temporary and that the salary should come back down after "there no longer are shortages."[84] But shortages that have been gone for years after wages went up may still reappear when wages come back down. How often will localities be asked to show that they cannot hire and retain personnel in technical fields at the wages called for in comparable-worth plans? When describing the Minnesota pay equity laws, Bonnie Watkins says that supply and demand considerations are permitted "as long as the impact is nondiscriminatory."[85] However, if the shortages are mainly in the technical fields, the impact will seem discriminatory since a high proportion of the jobs floating high above the line will be male dominated. Systems programmers, systems applications development specialists, and the others near the top in the computer field are overwhelmingly male.

Newspapers rarely give attention to internal management processes and problems in local government, but in late 1986 a Rochester newspaper commented on the problems comparable worth was causing for managers of information systems in Olmstead County. The pay equity plan had determined that computer systems programmers were overpaid, and their pay was to be frozen. The county's information systems director and its only experienced systems programmer were quoted as saying that adoption of the new pay ranges "would make it nearly impossible to keep and hire qualified people for the position. They said the county spent months attempting to find someone for a second systems programmer position earlier this year and finally settled for a trainee whom Tullidge [the experienced systems programmer] will tutor."[86]

In 1989 I called the information systems director quoted in this story and a personnel specialist in Olmstead, and both confirmed the accuracy of the newspaper's account. The information systems director said the problem existed in the public sector throughout the state. He discussed the problem at length and explained how Olmstead was dealing with it. "The comparable-worth purists say each organization is to be treated as its own little world, but in the real world you have to compete." He was able to get a market survey done on the systems programmer positions, and it showed that Olmstead was "eighteen percent below the midpoint" of what was paid elsewhere.

> We decided arbitrarily to allow market results plus or minus ten percent from the line, but the other eight percent [we're paying these people] on a contingency basis. This is totally separate from [what affects] the line [i.e., the "official" salary ignores this eight percent payment].

The information systems director said that most of his technical people – for instance, "management information systems" specialists and "senior program analysts" – were overpaid according to Olmstead's Arthur Young designed "decision band" job evaluation system. The director said "decision band is hard for most people to grasp. The people here finally gave up. [We just said,] 'Let it go.' "

He had no openings at the time, but if he had had, he would "have problems getting good systems programmers, no doubt":

> I'm going to propose a new category of senior systems programmer. Even that won't put pay in the private sector [range, but it will be in] the ballpark. Personnel will [decision] band it informally when we get this new position.

I asked this man how he managed to keep his people and deal with his management problems. He said they used consultants frequently to install new software and train people. I asked if the consultants got paid more than anyone on his staff and he replied, "You bet. They are not cheap." To keep his personnel he would give them unusual nonmonetary benefits:

> I'm probably less demanding timewise compared to IBM. I allow more independence and flexibility on hours. I give them the time in lieu of more pay. I let them go to their kid's first day of kindergarten.... That means something to them.

I asked if this flexibility was unusual for Olmstead County employees, and he said that it was.

In all the phone calls I made throughout Minnesota, I only twice encountered recorded messages. The first was when I called a hospital number for the senior nurse anesthetist – a specialist so scarce and so well paid that one personnel manager told me, "I wish I was one." The other message was at the office of this Olmstead County director of information systems. It said, "Systems information is presently unable to answer your call. Please leave a message and we'll get back to you when we can." I asked the director if there was any connection between recorded messages and very busy offices. He said:

> There could be. Answering machines are one way out. Much of our staff is in the field. The secretary may be [away from her desk] helping with technical duties. We're running pretty lean here. Our answer is technology and the answering machine.
>
> For secretaries, comparable worth has helped. We can get really good people, good enough to help with the technical stuff. That's a real positive from pay equity. We get lots of applicants. We get them to do more – [they] can do the technical stuff, spread sheets, [answering questions about] software.

When the information systems' secretaries got calls with questions from "the courts or social services," they answered them themselves rather than referring them to technical staff who would answer these questions in other offices. "Our technical people are out in the field," so the secretaries called to help on technical stuff "can't keep up" with their other duties. So the information systems office used the recorder "so [they did not] miss calls."

## EVADING THE LAW

Chapter 2 noted that comparable-worth opponents predict that benefits from any mandated system will be much less than proponents anticipate since employers will find that there are many legal ways to evade the law. In the management of information systems in Olmstead County, there are several examples of evasive action. A statewide pay equity regulatory department might be able to spot and disapprove of the 8 percent premium paid to systems programmers if it thought documentation of shortages was insufficient, but will it have any grounds to complain if Olmstead adds, say, a duty or two and creates a more highly rated "senior" systems programmer? If Olmstead says it needs such a new position, can the state say it does not? Will it have any grounds to complain if Olmstead pays still more to hire a consultant to do the work? Will it be able to spot and countermand the additional nonmonetary compensation (i.e., time off) given to its much-in-demand computer specialists or the gradual increase in duties given to its highly paid, highly skilled secretaries? The Olmstead comparable-worth reports will suggest all is well, but the occupation rated as equivalent to the computer specialist will not really be paid the same because the computer specialist's job will have been made less demanding, and the added time off will not be available to the equally rated occupation in another department. And the pleasure that proponents would feel in the state office at seeing the high salary finally commanded by secretaries would disappear if they knew that the secretaries' jobs now include computer-related duties for which they are not additionally compensated.[87]

From the start, Nina Rothchild and her staff made efforts to head off likely evasive techniques. For example, DOER required that even very small one- and two-person job classifications be included in pay equity plans because they feared that otherwise localities would break their employment categories into a large number of small classes that need not be included. In her December 1989 analysis of pay equity plans ("Analysis 100") Faith Zwemke of DOER noted that even jurisdictions that had the requisite scatter of female jobs above as well as below the line might still be out of compliance if they had excluded some jobs (as many jurisdictions did for their high pay-per-point blue-collar jobs) or blended male- and female-dominated classes into a balanced class so as to make inequities disappear.[88]

However, there are many evasive techniques not mentioned in Zwemke's Analysis 100, and most have been used successfully by local governments. For example, one locality takes advantage of the accepted exclusion of part-time employees by forbidding home health aides to work more than twelve hours a week. Thus, their pay need not be changed. Another evasive technique used by localities that adjust only the pay of the underpaid female-dominated jobs is to hire a male cook so as to turn an underpaid female-dominated class into a balanced one.

Some of the evasive techniques used by localities will be eliminated under the proposed DOER regulations. But it would be very hard to come up with reasonable regulations controlling the creation of new jobs or the merging of old ones. Some localities clearly are blending male- and female-dominated classes into balanced classes to avoid pay equity salary increases,[89] and despite her Analysis 100 warning Zwemke told me in 1992 that localities did not report on newly consolidated or split classes, so there was no way to correct the situation. And surely comparable-worth proponents could not complain about making job classes more sexually balanced even if it might have the effect of keeping female cooks underpaid. There have been a number of complaints about job descriptions and titles being changed so as to pay highly rated but easily filled "women's" jobs less, even though actual duties had not changed at all.[90] Though the most extreme manipulation of job titles and job descriptions might be regulated, it would be easy to change the duties a little and *then* pay less (or more, as for the "senior" systems programmer in Olmstead). When I questioned them, neither Aviva Breen nor Bonnie Watkins thought this sort of manipulation could be effectively regulated.

More thought has been given to the contracting-out evasion than to any other, but neither of the two most-discussed remedies is very satisfactory. One proposed remedy would require contractors to have a comparable-worth plan. But if a school district contracts out its low-paid cooks or a county its home health aides, the cooks or aides in the new, more specialized organization will not have many high pay-per-point males to compare themselves with, and their pay will not be boosted much if at all. Apparently realizing the weakness in this remedy, some comparable-worth proponents are now proposing that contractors be required to pay their food service employees at the levels they would be paid if they worked directly for the school district.[91] However, this attempted solution would mean that a contractor's cooks often would be paid unequally for doing equal work depending on which school/pay plan the cook was assigned to. Moreover, some of the contractor's employees would service more than one school, and thus the contractor would be unsure which of the schools' pay plans should be controlling.

Even regulating out of existence all the evasive maneuvers used to avoid changes called for by job evaluation results might accomplish little because it is so easy to manipulate the job evaluation results themselves. Since there are no standards for how to conduct comparable-worth job evaluation, there is no standard by which to criticize any scheme localities may use. A number of localities have done multiple studies. Some county boards changed their consultant's studies in executive session. Some never used job match or a consultant. As Faith Zwemke had done in Princeton, they simply came up with a plan on their own. An Arthur Young consultant told me that he had been fired by a locality because his plan was too expensive, and the newly hired consultant was given clear instructions to make the plan less expensive.

Spotting manipulated job evaluation scores would be very difficult since, as in the St. Paul police case, unusual-looking results are not necessarily manipulated. DOER's implementation guide states that localities may use any of their sixty-six "sample" job evaluation factors or add to the nonexhaustive list. It also says that the law allows governments "to make their own determinations about what they value most."[92] As already indicated, there is not even agreement on how to measure factors such as working conditions once they are decided on, much less agreement on the factors themselves or how they are to be weighed.

Nina Rothchild told me that it is "so easy to play games" with the job evaluations that she was surprised that, for the most part, the evaluations were so honest. She thought that the public visibility of the process mitigated the temptation toward manipulation. It is impossible to tell how much manipulation occurred. Most of the gross kind – such as that noted in the lengthy letter from the former employee who had benefited from doctored JES results so that his supervisors could benefit still more – will never see the light of day. I suspect that most of the evasive techniques were of the more subtle kind such as those used in Olmstead County.

Certainly, most elected officials will not want to be seen as sabotaging a process meant to bring pay equity to female workers. And there were many cases of localities bending over backward to be fair to women workers and to avoid undermining the process. For example, librarians were often allowed to be compared to all city employees even though technically the city and library board could have insisted that librarians be compared only with other employees hired by the library board. The University of Minnesota hospital lacked enough male-dominated jobs to form a decent pool for some comparisons, but the university agreed to form a male market pay line for the jobs dominated by men at other hospitals but by women at the university.[93] In my interviews, I was told of one school district that decided against contracting out for janitorial services even though it could thereby have changed its pay equity bill from $750,000 to zero and of another school district that would never consider contracting out for the cooks because "the cooks are like family. They have a good relationship with the students and staff."

Some readers will be pleased by such instances of concern for employees and willingness to support the spirit as well as the letter of the comparable-worth law. Others will think it too easy to be generous with taxpayers' money and wonder if the funds involved could not have been better spent elsewhere. But I think it beyond dispute that these examples are far less likely to occur in the private sector than in the public. Evasions of the law will be far more frequent in industry because media exposure and political costs from it will be much less likely. Moreover, the owners and managers who make such decisions will be those who lose the $750,000 savings when they do not contract out. Businesses that do not contract out expensive labor or work to ensure that their job evaluation results reflect market forces will have higher costs and will lose business to those that do. A representative of the Minnesota School Boards Association told me that school districts could sometimes save $6–8 an hour if they contracted out for bus drivers, custodians, and food service personnel, even without considering comparable-worth savings. Given the different personal financial incentives involved, the private sector will use contracting out as a technique to avoid comparable-worth strictures much more readily than public-sector employers have. Thus, in the absence of a far more detailed and intrusive regulatory regime than has yet been contemplated, comparable worth in the private sector is likely to accomplish much less than proponents hope.

## CONCLUSION

Minnesota has a worldwide reputation for implementing the most successful comparable-worth program of any state in the United States. On the day that I interviewed Bonnie Watkins, she was also scheduled to brief a delegation from Africa on the Minnesota experience. Nina Rothchild calls herself a political type, and I believe she deserves most of the credit for the good reputation of Minnesota's comparable-worth program in political circles. She presents her story very effectively in national forums. When traveling to Minnesota, we researchers are always grateful for her willingness to spend hours answering questions. Nevertheless, though Rothchild deserves most of the credit for the story of Minnesota's success, the story is not persuasive.

When I first spoke to Bonnie Watkins about my impending trip to Minnesota, she strongly suggested that I speak to Faith Zwemke of Princeton, Minnesota, about local implementation. Others who spoke to Rothchild and Watkins must have gotten similar advice, for a number of news articles quoted Zwemke or were datelined Princeton, Minnesota. For example, a 1985 *Wall Street Journal* article filed from Princeton, Minnesota, discussed at length Princeton's experiences and Zwemke's belief that Princeton's comparable-worth plan was "just pure justice."[94] Princeton is also one of twenty-four localities studied in depth for the Evans and Nelson book *Wage Justice*. What is odd about the emphasis on Princeton is that its population is only 3,193, and it had completed its comparable-worth plan before the local government pay equity law was even passed. Although Zwemke, who later became DOER pay equity coordinator under Rothchild, could be counted on to tell a story of successful implementation, the Princeton police would have told a different story (see p. 85).[95]

Rothchild underestimates the budgetary costs of comparable worth at the state level and requires that localities report their costs on forms that do not allow the localities to list their comparable-worth raises for balanced and male-dominated classes (see Chapter 3, pp. 53–4, 69–70). But the most important costs are not budgetary. When Rothchild reports the facts about "the state's program," she says there have been no reduced or frozen wages, no laid off employees, no lawsuits, no disruption or low employee morale, and no change in the state's ability to attract or retain qualified workers. This summary of results immediately follows a discussion on implementation of the local government law, and many readers will take this description of "state" results as applying to the state's program for local government employees as well as the one for state employees.[96] Certainly there is no hint of what is in fact the case: that every one of these costs of comparable worth has occurred at the local level in Minnesota.

Beyond these costs, comparable worth has produced a problem with pay compression and occasionally even an inversion of the pay hierarchy. There have been problems trying to maintain the system because some supposedly discriminated-against female-dominated jobs disappear as a decreased proportion of females puts them below the 70 percent female-dominance, cut-off line. Likewise, some jobs previously not considered to be subject to discrimination appear as the proportion of females increases to put them over the 70 percent mark. Employees of both sexes feel a new sense of grievance as they contemplate aspects of their jobs that may have been ignored or undervalued in the past. Under the new comparable-worth regime, their pay is dependent on which consultant's system their locality happened upon, on how they fill out questionnaires, and on how rhetorically effective their representatives are in the job evaluation committees. The vagaries of the process are such that even the more widely accepted norm of equal pay for equal work must sometimes be abandoned.

Perhaps worst of all, the important work of government gets done less well. Localities that know there are large numbers of talented librarians willing to work at existing wage rates are nonetheless compelled to give their current staff large raises, after which they face charges that their librarians are *still* discriminatorily underpaid. At the same time, facing nursing shortages and gladly willing to pay nurses more to alleviate the shortages, some localities risk lawsuits from employees that their equity plans deem equally valuable if they spend more on nurses than they do on these equally rated employees.

The only benefit said to outweigh all these costs is that women are finally paid fairly based on the objective value of their work, not on long-standing cultural stereotypes. But in Minnesota, do the results of comparable-worth represent the value of the jobs? Does this mix of sham science and employee participation persuasively show that librarians deserve much more than markets would provide, but nurses and computer scientists considerably less? Or does it show that St. Paul police are worth more than their previous wage provided, but most cities' police are worth much less?

Most employers and most economists would probably say that the worth of an employee to an employer depends not just on his or her skills and responsibilities, but also on how many other employees that employer has. The first counter person at McDonald's is worth more than the fourth, and the fourth is worth more at rush hour than at 10:00 p.m. and worth still more at busy branches than at less busy ones. There simply is no intrinsic or all-purpose value. What these employees will be paid in the market is not determined by whether the job is associated with womanhood or nurturing and helping. Both nurses and secretaries fit the nurturing and helping category well, but despite these historic associations, both have managed to command above-average salary increases in the private sector for years (see pp. 104, 111 and Chapter 4, note 77). These trends began before passage of the first comparable-worth law.

The Minnesota experience gives ample evidence of how supply and demand powerfully affect wage rates. Foresters and librarians, for example, are paid less than most similarly educated professionals because the supply of foresters and librarians is larger relative to the demand for their services than is the supply of other similarly educated workers relative to demand. Likewise, nurses' salaries have risen sharply in recent years because the supply of nurses relative to demand is small. Yet when Aviva Breen saw evidence highlighting trends in nurses' salaries, she thought the very highlighting of the facts showed that they were unusual, and when I spoke to Bonnie Watkins, she remarked on the "fantasy" of the supply and demand explanation for wage rates.

Despite the neutral-sounding goal of pay based on the value of the work, what advocates really want is more money for women workers. Much emphasis is given to the gains for clerical and health-care workers at the state level and for school aides, clericals, and food service workers at the local level. Evans and Nelson add some figures showing that an entry-level clerk supporting a family of four and working for the state would have an income 42 percent above the poverty line after pay equity, whereas it was only 17 percent above before pay equity. In these listings of wage gains, proponents of comparable worth never so much as hint that men and women elsewhere may lose something because of the wage gains for these women. Indeed, Rothchild, Watkins, Evans and Nelson, and others suggest that if comparable-worth means lower or frozen wages elsewhere, it is because it is being used divisively.[97] But even if there is no explicit pay freeze or pay reduction in the public sector resulting from comparable worth, there are losers elsewhere, even if they are only taxpayers or library patrons with fewer new books.

Advocates of comparable worth find valuable the higher wages for women in predominantly female occupations paying below-average salaries. But to justify these increases by referring to the poverty level and family needs seems to resurrect the philosophy that was used to justify reserving the good-paying jobs for fathers who had family responsibilities.[98] The comparable-worth philosophy says that pay should be based on the value of the work performed regardless of family needs.

When Evans and Nelson tell their readers that comparable worth enabled entry-level clerks 1 (already paid enough to put a family of four 17 percent above the poverty line) to be paid enough to put their families 42 percent above it, they also acknowledge that "not every Clerk 1 supported a family of four." Still, for them the change in salary indicates "the change in the capacity of people working as clerk 1s to support or help to support families."[99]

In fact, entry-level clerks 1 in Minnesota are very rarely the sole support for a family of four. According to the state personnel office, they are typically fresh out of high school. When they do have families to support, they often have spouses to help support them. Those with no spouses and with families to support have often been promoted beyond the entry-level clerk 1 classification.

Experts on antipoverty programs usually argue that good programs are well targeted at the poverty population and minimize adverse effects on economic efficiency. As an antipoverty program, comparable worth fails badly on both criteria. Even the clerks 1 with families of four and no spouses had incomes above poverty level before comparable worth. Priority should probably be given to those who cannot get jobs at all – who need job training or basic education – or even to the *private*-sector clerk 1 equivalents supporting families of four. Many of their incomes are under the poverty level, and they are paying taxes to boost the wages of public-sector clerks 1 not in poverty. And what of all the comparable-worth money going to professionals like librarians or to women with working spouses? In fact, unlike money spent to expand the earned-income tax credit, almost none of the money spent on comparable worth in Minnesota fights poverty.

As well as being poorly targeted toward the poor, comparable worth badly fails the efficiency test for antipoverty programs. If fully implemented, it would tend to isolate wages, about 73 percent of national income, from the forces of supply and demand. Mainstream economists, liberal and conservative, agree that fighting poverty by subverting market price signals is very inefficient.[100] They also agree that overpaying workers – paying them more than the market equilibrium wage for the job – reduces societal well-being (see Chapter 2, pp. 30–2). Thus what is bad in comparable-worth circles seems good to ordinary economists. Take the two-tiered wage. Suppose that all existing teacher aides kept their comparable-worth-inflated wages, but that new aides were hired at 20 percent less. The taxpayers, teachers, and parents would be delighted that they could now free teachers' time by hiring more aides. The newly hired aides would be pleased by the new job opportunities; otherwise they would not take them.

As for contracting out, the Organization for Economic Cooperation and Development, a body the *Washington Post* has called "a Council of Economic Advisors for the industrial democracies,"[101] says that "greater competition in, or recourse to, contracting out of public services may provide an essential check on public sector pay demands." It further speaks of the obligation governments have to keep pay at levels comparable to those in the private sector.[102]

All women have a stake in a well-functioning economy that allows wages to help channel labor to the areas where consumer demand for products and services is greatest. Wives who do not work or who work part time and rely mainly on their spouse's income and the increasing numbers of women in predominantly male or balanced occupations are likely losers from comparable worth. But even some women who might be presumed to have direct gains to balance off the losses from inefficiency may not have them. Remember, in Minnesota nurses were losers.

Moreover, past comparable-worth results may not accurately reflect future ones. The librarians and many other "female" professions hit the ground running. They knew the system and how to make it work for them. Even Nina Rothchild could not keep MAPE from getting pay equity benefits later on. On an economywide playing field, unlike a public-sector one, there will be real wage losers for every gainer in the relative wage skirmishes, indeed more losers once one considers inefficiencies. With such heightened stakes, male-dominated professions are likely to be aggressive participants in the skirmishes and to achieve accordingly.[103] This has indeed already occurred in Australia as will be discussed in Chapter 7. The Minnesota experience, in short, serves on close examination less as a shining example than as a beacon of caution.

# 5

## Equal pay for work of equal value in the European Community

What people in the United States call "equal pay for comparable worth," those in the European Community (EC) and Australia call "equal pay for work of equal value." By its equal-value name, comparable worth has been a legal requirement in the EC for over a decade and a half. Christopher McCrudden, a fellow and tutor in law at Lincoln College, Oxford University, has correctly noted that many U.S. participants in the debate about comparable worth are completely unaware of this fact. McCrudden believes that European experience can provide evidence to rebut complaints leveled against the concept – such as the charges that it ignores the economic realities of supply and demand and requires courts and agencies to undertake the impossible task of ascertaining the worth of dissimilar jobs. However, like most people who write on the subject in Europe, McCrudden is interested primarily in a legal analysis of comparable worth. In an article written for a U.S. audience he discusses statutory and case law but explicitly omits analysis of "the *practice* of comparable worth in Europe, except to look briefly at the extent of litigation."[1] Though he thus says nothing about European methods of comparing various jobs or about the economic effects of their efforts, he nonetheless makes it clear that he thinks Americans have spent too much time debating the merits of comparable worth and worrying about possible ill effects. After more than a decade of experience in Europe, he states, "The sky has not fallen."[2] In McCrudden's view, it is time for Americans to consider institutional modifications that would facilitate the effective implementation of the concept.

But without some assessment of comparable worth in practice, it would be a mistake to rush to follow the European example. And it would also be a mistake to assume that, because EC law requires comparable worth, the member states (Belgium, Denmark, France, Germany, Greece, Ireland, Italy, Luxembourg, the Netherlands, Portugal, Spain, the United Kingdom) actually have it. If problems exist in the countries and if Community law requires that employees with grievances have a judicial remedy, one would expect to find evidence of substantial equal-value litigation as "one indication of the degree of change occurring."[3] Yet in at least four of the member states (Portugal, Luxembourg, Germany, Greece), there have apparently been "no cases at all on equal value,"[4] and in all the rest except Ireland and the United Kingdom,[5] there have been very few. Moreover, one member of the EC's network of experts on the implementation of the equality directives told me that, when the experts gather, only the English, the Irish, and more recently the Danes have anything to report about equal-value developments in their countries.

The Italians were one of the few states in the EC who were left untouched when the EC's executive organ, the Commission, decided in 1979 to get tough with members thought to be infringing the equal-pay directive. The Italian law does look strong, including provisions for fines and for financial assistance for litigants with low incomes.[6] There is even a law allowing equal-value claims to be taken across industries.[7] But in fact, as in several other EC countries, enforcement of the law is pretty much left to the labor inspectorates, an arm of government. Most observers agree that the inspectorates' main interest is health and safety and that they have little interest in or knowledge about sex discrimination. In any case, since Italian case law says that equal value in a job is "normally evaluated by collective agreements or company practices," it is easy to see why few women bring cases challenging such agreements and practices.[8] In my U.K. interviews, I frequently encountered respondents in business and government who complained that Italy was merely one of the more egregious examples of countries whose legal and/or administrative systems made it incapable of carrying out Community mandates such as equal value.[9] According to my respondents, British business, on the other hand, was actually constrained by such laws.

If the EC example on comparable worth is to provide any guidance at all to the United States, one must look to the United Kingdom to find it. That country has provided most of the equal-value litigation generated in the Community as a whole. Moreover, because businesses there have feared lawsuits, they have also had to negotiate seriously with unions demanding equal-value raises for female-dominated occupations. In addition, Britain has a relatively powerful Equal Opportunity Commission (EOC), one that not only can investigate firms, but "can support a woman all the way through her case, from financial help, to legal advice, representation, and publicity for her cause."[10] And finally, British courts have taken Community law quite seriously, frequently asking the European Court of Justice for preliminary rulings on points of EC discrimination law.[11]

Because equal value is a real, rather than just a paper, phenomenon in the United Kingdom, experience there is of special interest to Americans. Because the United Kingdom shares with us an adversarial, common-law-based legal system and a firm-centered approach to comparable worth, its experience is doubly relevant. But Britain would not have comparable worth if it were not for EC law. And the story of how the Community came to have its equal-value law is itself an example of a political process spun out of control – one in which determined supporters of equal value have parlayed a dominant bureaucratic position and a sympathetic, activist court into law vastly different from that envisioned by the elected representatives who originally approved it. Having taken on a life of its own, equal value in the EC should give pause to those customers of comparable worth who think they know what they are buying. The remainder of this chapter will examine the politics that brought equal value into Europe, while Chapter 6 will discuss implementation in Great Britain.

## THE TREATY OF ROME AND EARLY EC EQUAL-PAY INITIATIVES

The peace treaty of 1919 that ended World War I also established the International Labour Organization (ILO). In 1951, the ILO adopted Convention 100, which required signatory nations to ensure that men and women receive equal pay for work of equal value. However, member countries were bound to do so only insofar as was consistent with their then current methods for determining rates of remuneration, and it was clear from the debate that a number of delegates to the ILO assembly voted for this phrasing "as an acceptable method of expressing what we today understand by 'equal pay for equal work.' "[12]

There is no enforcement mechanism for ensuring compliance with ILO conventions. There is, however, a means of enforcing violations of provisions of the Treaty of Rome, which established the EC in 1957.[13] Thus, the wording of the treaty's provisions was quite carefully considered by the representatives of the six nations that made up the original Community. Though the treaty said the EC Commission should promote "close collaboration" in the social field, this goal was to be reached through the issuing of opinions, studies, consultations, and the like.[14] The binding portions of the treaty were all narrowly economic with one exception – the provisions regarding equal pay. Even here there is agreement among commentators that the motive for including an equal-pay article was strictly economic. The provision was meant to ensure that all countries competed on an equal level. The French, who were about to introduce equal-pay legislation nationally, did not want to be priced out of markets by other countries who could pay their women less and thus lower production costs.[15] The equal-pay article was granted as a concession to the French to ensure that "free competition was not distorted by the employment of women at lower rates than men for the same work."[16]

As this quotation from a 1979 EC Commission report suggests, there was no hint of "equal value" in the equal-pay language of the treaty. The member states explicitly rejected this more expansive language contained in ILO Convention 100.[17] Instead, Article 119 simply required that men and women receive "equal pay for equal work." It further defined equal pay as equal piece rates and time rates for the "same" job.[18]

At the end of 1961, as the second stage of the transitional period of the Common Market was fast approaching, it was clear to the Commission and to others that a number of states were not paying women as much as men for equal work. The member states then further agreed to gradually eliminate sex-based wage differentials on a schedule such that all discrimination would be abolished by the end of 1964.[19] There was disagreement, however, as to whether the equal-pay principle should be applied to more than the exact same job performed by members of both sexes.[20] The Commission thought the principle should have broader impact, and throughout the 1960s it occasionally drew the attention of members to inadequate implementation. Still, in 1968, even the Commission agreed that, in all member states, female rates were going up faster than male rates, and separate wage scales for women for the same job had nearly vanished from collective agreements.[21]

## THE POLITICS OF PASSAGE OF THE EQUAL-PAY DIRECTIVE

The most powerful of the EC organs is the Council of Ministers. The Council consists of representatives of each of the member states, but its membership changes with the subject matter, for example, agriculture ministers for agriculture, industry ministers for industrial subjects, and usually, labor ministers for social affairs. In late 1973, the Social Affairs Council of Ministers gave preliminary approval to a Community social action program. Together with many other initiatives, the Council took note of the Commission's having already submitted to it a proposal for an equal-pay directive. (Directives are binding on the member states as far as the results to be achieved are concerned, but the methods of achieving the results are left to the discretion of each nation.) Among the provisions of the draft directive were requirements that member states supervise collective agreements and provide sanctions against those that discriminate, that they provide employees with access to a court on equal-pay complaints, and that they protect complaining employees from dismissals and other sanctions. Though in most respects this draft directive was stronger than the one passed a year later, in one crucial way it was weaker. There was no mention of equal value or comparable worth. Throughout 1973 and the first half of 1974 the Commission maintained that the principle and definitions of equal pay were clearly stated in Article 119 of the Treaty of Rome.[22] The draft directive described the principle as "equal pay for equal work."

Before the Council of Ministers could take action on legislation, it had to get the advice of the European Parliament and the Economic and Social Committee of the EC. The European Parliament has limited powers and attracts little public interest.[23] Its resolutions on proposed Council legislation are usually based on reports from committees, which in turn attract members with strong interest in the matters under their jurisdiction. Committees considering women's issues attract a large number of feminist members. Similarly, the Community's Economic and Social Committee, which represents employers, workers, and other interest groups (e.g., those representing farmers, professionals, and consumers) adopts procedures that favor groups in their areas of special interest. Thus, the resolutions of the social section usually have an interventionist tilt, and they are rarely reversed in plenary sessions.[24]

Given the composition of the important social affairs figures in the

Parliament and the Economic and Social Committee, these bodies usually end up as strong supporters of measures meant to help women. Though the Parliament and the Economic and Social Committee have limited powers, the equal opportunity unit of the Commission can use these bodies' advisory opinions as justifications for its own wish to propose strong actions to higher-ranking officials in the Commission and to the Council of Ministers. In 1974 both the Parliament and the Economic and Social Committee supported the proposed equal-pay directive and demanded the strengthening of many of its provisions. Yet interestingly, neither asked for an equal-value component.[25]

In June of 1974, however, staff members of the Commission met with sympathetic staff members of the Belgian and Dutch permanent representatives (i.e., ambassadors) to the EC. These staff members served as part of a group of member state representatives called the Working Party on Social Questions. The Working Party did most of the preparatory work for the equal-pay directive eventually approved by the Council of Ministers in December of 1974 and formally promulgated in early 1975. At a June meeting of the Working Party, Belgium and the Netherlands first floated the idea of an equal-value definition for equal pay, and the Commission endorsed the idea.[26] By the August meeting of the Working Party, the Commission representatives were strongly pushing for this language.

The Commission had no previous problem with the Article 119 principle of equal pay for equal work and the accompanying definition of equal pay as equal piece and time rates for the "same" job. But now these seemingly clear principles and definitions were viewed by the Commission as unclear and imprecise. "Difficult problems of interpretation" had developed because some states had been interpreting the principle of equal pay in too "restrictive" a fashion.[27] By this, the Commission seemed to mean that the states had been interpreting the words to mean what they said – that equal pay applied where men and women were doing the same job. In defense of its desire to have the equal-pay principle of Article 119 interpreted as requiring equal value, the Commission cited a 1961 resolution of the member states that urged an end to the use of job evaluation criteria unrelated to "the objective conditions" of work[28] and the ILO language, which as of the following December, would have been ratified by all the member states.

By November the Commission had been joined by six delegations – Belgium, France, Italy, Ireland, Luxembourg, and the Netherlands – in support of a directive that would define the principle of equal pay as "the removal of any discrimination on the grounds of sex for identical work or work of equal value with regard to all aspects and conditions of remuneration."[29] However, directives could not be issued without unanimity, and the German, Danish, and U.K. delegations opposed any reference to equal value. The German delegation argued:

> As far as was known at present, it would not be possible to impose standard criteria for *assessing work of equal value,* since scientific research into this subject had not yet yielded conclusive results. It would be inappropriate, therefore, to invoke in Article 1 a principle the technical application of which seemed impossible at this stage.[30]

The U.K. delegation argued that the brief mention of equal value in the proposed directive "left complete uncertainty as to its interpretation. This was a subjective concept, where the standards to be incorporated into the various national legal systems required that objective concepts be introduced."[31]

While preferring no reference to equal value, the United Kingdom did propose compromise language that would have stated that equal pay would apply to identical work and to "broadly similar work to which equal value has been attributed on the basis of a system of assessment using the same criteria for both men and women."[32] This language was roughly parallel to that already incorporated into Britain's own domestic equal-pay law.

Aside from this definitional quarrel, the delegations had other remaining language differences that would have to be resolved at the Council of Ministers meeting in December. Most of these were fairly minor, but one would prove important in the final negotiations because its resolution probably affected the final decisions made on the definitional quarrel just described.

While supporting the United Kingdom on the definitional question, Germany and Denmark were even more concerned about a proposed article that would obligate member states to supervise at the plant level the application of the principle of equal pay and to provide sanctions against any infringements. In Germany the unions or workers' councils had the responsibility for seeing that the labor laws were applied, and they would not accept any interference by the public authorities. The Danes had similar problems for similar reasons. Both countries thought it sufficient for employees with equal-pay grievances to have access to a judicial process without also requiring state supervision of the workplace.

On December 17, 1974, the Council of Ministers (Social Affairs) met, with French Minister for Labor Michel Durafour presiding. The agenda was quite full. Up for consideration were a regulation establishing a European Centre for the Development of Vocational Training and a directive on collective dismissals in addition to the equal-pay directive. There were further proposals to create a European Foundation for the Improvement of Living and Working Conditions and to develop an interim program of food aid to Ethiopia and Somalia.[33] The permanent representatives had been unable to reach agreement on many of these items, so they required deliberation by the Council of Ministers.

The equal-pay directive took up all of the morning session, and the debate over how to define equal pay took more time than any other item. John Fraser, parliamentary undersecretary of state for the Department of Employment of the ruling Labour government, headed the British delegation. Fraser remembers the U.K. strategy well, and he suspects that it was the same for the other delegations: "We'll agree [to a new directive] provided we don't have to do anything."

In the British case this strategy was "not simply cynical."[34] The government had recently passed an equal-pay law, and neither the unions nor the government wanted to change it. Barbara Castle, who saw the bill through to passage, had argued on the floor of Parliament against equal value before the bill was passed. She thought it too "abstract" and "indefinite." Since men had never had equal pay for equal value among their own jobs, there would have to be an evaluation of all men's and all women's work in the whole population. Castle said that even the ILO convention gave only a faint-hearted nod toward job evaluation and envisioned nothing remotely like an economywide evaluation of jobs.[35] "Besides, the (ILO) convention leaves open whether the principle of equal pay shall be applied by legislation or through collective bargaining."[36]

Castle was an anti–Common Market Labourite. The Labour government did not want her recently passed legislation to be found wanting by the EC. Other anti-EC types like Tony Benn would, in Fraser's words, "kick up a fuss." Harold Wilson, the prime minister, and his foreign minister were from a faction of the party that wanted very much to stay in the EC.

But just as it would not do to have the EC find the recently passed U.K. legislation inadequate, so it would not do to have to veto the directive. A veto would suggest that EC and U.K. aims were in tension and also give ammunition to the anti-EC wing of the party. Far from wanting to be seen as obstructionist, Britain wanted to be seen as "leaders on this," as "making others do what we already had." Still the linguistic questions were important to Fraser because he knew that, unlike the Italians, the United Kingdom had a functioning legal and administrative system, and it would "want to see enforced" whatever passed. Caring deeply about Britain's wording preferences, but for political reasons being in no position to veto the directive, Fraser had a tough hand to play.[37]

He did his best, but lost in the end. Fraser went out of the way to withdraw all British objections and yield to a Council consensus on all matters except the equal-value issue. On equal value, he argued that its inclusion would create a subjective test that would produce labor difficulties and be difficult for courts to apply. Moreover, equal value would not help harmonize labor relations between the member states. Since the valuing process was subjective, one country could find clerks equal to typists, while another could find they were not. Still, he quickly proposed compromise language: "The principle of equal pay means for equal work and in particular for work which has been established to be of equal value." The "has been established" phrase was meant to limit application to employees of employers who had already voluntarily established a job evaluation system. The language would be compatible with Britain's own law. Germany supported the United Kingdom, and for a moment it looked as if the British language might gain a consensus. However, after the Commission strongly opposed the U.K. language, the French president of the Council proposed the following language: "The principle of equal pay implies for the same work or for work to which an equal value would be attributed, the elimination of all discrimination." The United Kingdom asked for time to consider the matter, and other articles were debated.

By the time the definitional article reappeared, several delegations had discussed the need to compromise, and the president had suggested that those who had their way on one item should give way on others. The president then proposed a grand compromise covering three articles in dispute. He bowed to the British preference for the past tense by substituting "has been attributed" for "would be attributed." Belgium and Italy said they could agree, and Germany could agree on all but the state supervision question, where it asked for language granting more flexibility in implementation in accordance with differing national systems.

At this point the Commission representative intervened again, agreeing to almost all of the president's proposal but asking for one "slight change": that "has been attributed" be changed to "is attributed." The

Netherlands and Luxembourg supported the president. Fraser then said he could accept the president's proposal. France said it could accept the whole package of compromises if "has been" became "is."

The French president then expressed a preference for "is attributed" and acted as if there was now agreement, but the United Kingdom said it could not agree to this modification. The president said it was a mere literary point with no substantive effect. Fraser disagreed. The president then switched and asked for agreement on "has been." He asked the Irish representative if he still suggested returning to "has been." But before the Irish representative could speak, the Commission vice-president, Patrick John Hillery – also an Irishman – jumped in and said that the "has been" phrase would put the women of the community "in a worse position than they now are" since they would have to wait for a job evaluation before advancing.

An exasperated president swore that they were wasting time "over a battle of verbs." He proposed returning to "has been attributed," which had "seemed, moreover, at the beginning, before [Commissioner] Hillery's speech, to have gathered a certain level of agreement." But now the Belgians objected and suggested including *both* phrases, that is, "for work to which an equal value has been or is attributed." Fraser again objected. The president said they could not debate this issue indefinitely and moved on to other articles, including the "supervision" article the Germans were most concerned about. The president made a direct appeal to the Germans, saying they should compromise, but they refused, arguing that the proposal on the table would require them to modify their whole legal system since they did not have the possibility of intervention at the level of work laws. Denmark supported Germany. Belgium then suggested language that Germany could agree to.

At this point, the president returned to the British and pressed for agreement on the present tense. Fraser pretended that the president was seeking agreement on "has been," and the French president, equal to this game, in turn pretended that Fraser was now willing to accept using both tenses, that is, "has been" or "is." Fraser said he would give the matter some thought, and he suggested returning to the matter after lunch.[38]

During lunch a member of the U.K. delegation called London and obtained permission to concede on the definitional quarrel. However, Fraser then arranged "a linguistic out" so that "both sides could go out victorious." In an unusual way of splitting the difference, the press release in English would use "has been attributed," while the release in French would say "is attributed"! But Fraser understood that since French was then the working language of the EC, the French text would control when the technicians had finished perfecting the texts for formal adoption in early 1975. Indeed, on December 20, 1974, in a brief report to Parliament, Fraser used the "is attributed" phrase.

Fraser, however, remembers being pleased about the outcome. His delegation had made some compromises, but they had an equal-pay directive, and it was "better to have the will to make progress." Fraser also thought it unlikely that the U.K. legislation would be challenged in Europe. As he had had his delegation member tell London during the lunchtime phone call, the United Kingdom had obtained agreement to insert in the minutes of the meeting during which the directive would be adopted an entry that would control the Commission's interpretation of the directive. The minutes' entry would say:

> In connection with the expression "work to which equal value is attributed," *the Council* notes the following statement by the United Kingdom delegation:
>
> The circumstances in which work is considered in the U.K. to have equal value attributed to it are where the work is broadly similar, or where pay is based on the results of job evaluation.[39]

One member of the 1974 U.K. delegation believes that the delegation would have known even then that the minutes' entry was the "weak reed" that it turned out to be. But a more senior member of the delegation, John Rimington – the U.K. permanent representative to the Social Affairs Council – and another member who seemed to have excellent recall of events that were later confirmed by the written record sharply disagreed and supported Fraser. At the time the U.K. delegates thought, and were assured by a Council lawyer, that statements for the minutes had considerable interpretive significance. At the very least it was thought that the statement for the minutes would bind the Commission and prevent it from bringing an infringement suit. Even in 1988 an experienced Commission operative told me that when the Council "takes note of" such a statement, it is almost like "an order to the Commission" to interpret a certain way.

All members of the U.K. delegation thought that their influence was weakened because they had only been members of the EC since January of 1973. The permanent staffs did not have the personal relationships with other delegations' staffs that those delegations had among themselves. Thus, Fraser had to play a weaker hand than he could have played a few years later. Rimington also remembers that everyone was having a hard time taking EC politics seriously, especially the politicians: "The different languages, the bowing, the clicking of heels, the very strange meetings. It was not like our politics at all. . . . 'Europe' was a pure abstraction. [It had] nothing to do with Britain."

## INFRINGEMENT CASES BROUGHT BY THE EUROPEAN COMMISSION

In 1979 the EC brought infringement proceedings against seven member states for violation of the equal-pay directive. Some of the Commission's objections were fairly easily remedied through negotiation and subsequent national legislation. For example, Belgium had granted a household allowance to married male civil servants, but gave one to married female civil servants only if they had children in their care. Germany's successful maneuvering at the 1975 Council of Minister's meeting proved for naught as it was charged with inadequate supervision of firms as well as with failure to adopt specific equal-pay legislation.[40] Still, after negotiations Germany made legislative changes that both satisfied the Commission and apparently made no domestic waves since subsequently little on equal value seemed to happen there. Britain, Denmark, and Luxembourg all resisted the Commission's charges, but lost their cases before the European Court of Justice.

In one sense it is surprising that the United Kingdom should be among those whose equal-pay law was found seriously wanting by the Commission. Even at the time of the infringement proceedings the United Kingdom had had more equal-pay cases than others in the EC, and everyone I spoke with at the Commission thought that there were serious problems in every country and that legal cases brought and won were signs of beneficial change.[41] Moreover, in the very year that infringement proceedings were begun, the Commission issued a report singling out Britain for its progress in implementing equal pay![42]

In the U.K. government there is a feeling that the EC picks on the United Kingdom with their frequent infringement proceedings against it on equal pay and other matters. To my surprise, when questioned about this charge, people at the Commission often agreed with it. One explanation was that the Commission staff from Britain were less "partisan" than many from the Continent and more willing to bring cases against their own country. There are many U.K. lawyers at the Commission, and one acknowledged that he was probably *more* likely to bring a case against his country. He mentioned a potential action against one of the less developed member states that he was then considering. Problems were everywhere. He did not speak the language, and there were communication problems with his contact lawyer who did. He suspected that this lawyer's reserve was connected to embarrassment about fraud. He did not really understand the country's legal system. In contrast, England was familiar. There were an active EOC, unions, and fellow anti-Thatcherite U.K. legal experts to feed him relevant information. In a situation where there were always lots of files of potential cases floating around, the chances of success were greater if one chose the U.K. file. Make them the pioneers, and build up some solid case law that advances Community social policy.

Before the European Court of Justice, Britain relied heavily on its statement for the minutes at the time the equal-pay directive was passed. The government argued that the United Kingdom might not have accepted the directive if there had been objections to its statement at the time, and since the Commission and others did not object then, they no longer could do so. The Commission replied that the Council had not supported or discussed the U.K. statement for the minutes, and as a matter of law, unilateral statements "by a Member State cannot influence the interpretation of a part of Community legislation."[43] The European Court of Justice's opinion did not record that the Council had "take[n] note" of the British minutes entry, and it sided with the Commission. More generally, it held that the United Kingdom had no mechanism for a worker to claim that her work was of equal value to another worker's in cases where her firm had no job evaluation system. Thus, the United Kingdom had failed to fulfill its obligations under the Treaty of Rome.

I asked four knowledgeable lawyers if they thought the court's decision would have been different if Fraser had prevailed and the directive had said "has been" rather than "is attributed." The two from the Commission thought not, but the woman who argued the U.K. case before the court thought it "could have helped." Christopher McCrudden, a strong proponent of equal value and one of the leading experts on EC equality law, thought the wording change would have led to a different outcome. McCrudden did not see how the European Court of Justice could have found in favor of the Commission since "has been attributed" would essentially have reproduced the U.K. law.

THE EUROPEAN COURT OF JUSTICE AND EQUAL PAY

Most lawyers who closely follow equal-value developments in the United Kingdom and at the Commission support an expansive understanding of European law on the subject, and most have high praise for the role of the European Court of Justice in advancing the equal-pay agenda. Though the court's decision on the British infringement case seems justified if the minutes' entry is assumed to have no legal force, a number of their other decisions seem to ignore or go far beyond the intentions of the politicians who enacted the legislation. The U.K. equal opportunity legal establishment cheers on these extensions of Community law.[44]

Article 119 of the Treaty of Rome calls on "each Member State" to ensure and maintain "the principle" of "equal pay for equal work." Though the article goes on to define equal pay, most lawyers and the Commission had assumed that the member states addressed by the article would have to pass implementing legislation before any employee could bring action against her employer.[45] But in a 1976 case, *Defrenne v. Sabena,* the court held that Article 119 was directly effective and that it gave a woman a right to ask national courts to enforce Article 119 directly even in the absence of national implementing legislation.[46]

Later, in a 1981 case, *J. P. Jenkins v. Kingsgate,* the European Court of Justice declared that the 1975 directive was meant "to facilitate the practical application of the principle of equal pay" as outlined in Article 119 of the treaty, and it "in no way alters the content or scope of that principle as defined in the Treaty."[47] No one I interviewed found this pronouncement of the court credible. As already explained, the authors of Article 119 explicitly rejected the ILO equal-value language,[48] and all those involved in formulating the 1975 equal-pay directive believed that they were extending the scope of Article 119 with the "to which equal value is attributed" language. Indeed, the Commission itself said as much in a submission to the court for the earlier *Defrenne* case.[49]

My reading and questioning of U.K. and EC lawyers brought the following explanation for the court's insistence on this fiction.[50] There was considerable controversy after passage of the equal-pay directive about whether the Council of Ministers had had the legal authority to extend by way of a directive the clear language in Article 119 of the treaty. Article 236 of the treaty says that extending the scope of an article requires convening an intergovernmental conference as was done preceding the decision to pass the single European act. By saying that the Council of Ministers had not extended the scope of the treaty – though, in fact, they had – the court, as one law professor told me, "secured the constitutional basis of the directive."

Having thus "secured the constitutional basis of the directive" by ignoring the clear language of the constitution (i.e., the treaty), the court has charged ahead with still other "path-breaking decisions" on the application of the equal-pay directive.[51] The Commission has been unable to get Council of Ministers agreement on a directive shifting the burden of proof in equal-pay cases, but the court's decisions have been so favorable to plaintiffs that much of the proposed directive has now been made superfluous.[52] In one case decided in 1986, *Bilka-Kaufhaus v. Weber Von Hartz,* a department store justified excluding part-time workers from its pension plan because full-time workers entailed lower ancillary costs and were available during the busy late afternoon and Saturday store hours when part-time workers usually refused to work. Thus, the policy was meant to discourage part-time employment. Since women were more likely to be adversely affected by this policy, Weber Von Hartz charged a violation of EC equal-pay law. When preliminary questions were referred to the court, it said that such a policy could in principle be justified, but the burden of proof placed on the employer seemed nearly impossible to meet. All such pay practices must be shown to be "objectively justified," and the means chosen must be both "appropriate" and "necessary" to achieving the objective (in this case discouraging part-time employment).[53] How employers could be expected to show that an appropriate policy that furthers a legitimate commercial objective is also "necessary" to achieve the objective was not discussed.

In the 1989 *HK v. DA (Danfoss)* case female employees carrying out the same work or work of equal value were paid on average 6.85 percent less than male employees in the relevant pay grades. These differences were in part explained by differences in seniority, training, and work schedule flexibility. All of these reasons for differentials the court approved.[54] However, according to the collective agreement, the employer was also allowed to pay more to employees within a grade based on their capacity, their quality and amount of work, and their zeal and sense of initiative.[55] The union complained about the disparity based on sex that resulted from the company's use of this discretion. The court said that though these criteria were neutral from the point of view of sex, they could not be justified by the employer under any circumstances if their use caused disadvantages to women. In the court's view since the criteria were neutral with regard to sex, if when applied they disadvantaged women, the employer must have applied the criteria "in an abusive manner. It is inconceivable that the work carried out by female workers would be generally of a lower quality."[56]

In the United Kingdom an ecstatic *Equal Opportunities Review* called these words "strong stuff indeed." In its view, "there can be no doubt" that the case "makes vulnerable any merit pay or performance assessment system under which there is a statistically significant difference between the ratings of men and women" doing equal work or work of equal value.[57]

Chapter 2 described studies showing that, on average, men consider high pay to be more important to job satisfaction than do women (see Chapter 2, p. 14). This difference in attitude might lead more men than women to approach their work with special zeal if paid under a pay-for-performance plan. Studies have found that, under piecework systems, men earn 10–13 percent more than women in the shoe, furniture, and cotton-weaving industries. As a result, though convinced that discrimination explains part of the overall wage gap, Henry Phelps Brown in a review of the literature finds that "in many employments there are objective reasons for the work of women being of lower net value than that of men."[58] Gary Becker's argument about the energy needed for housework/child care and the relative amount remaining for market work may help explain these findings (see Chapter 2, p. 13).

Although not as directly related to men's more materialistic bent, a study of scientists also suggests that some groups of women may produce less than some groups of men. Jonathan Cole finds that women scientists have IQs at least equal to men's but "produce fewer and less frequently cited papers."[59] This phenomenon occurs as frequently in the better university departments as in the lower-ranked ones and is not explained by marital status. ("Unmarried women scientists published far less than men scientists in all family categories.")[60]

Modern work rarely permits perfectly objective measures of performance. The publication and citation indices do not tell as much as piecework figures do, and the measures available for many other jobs are much worse than those for academics. Still the results from the piecework and academic studies together with the differences between the sexes on the importance they attach to high pay suggest that at least some non-discriminating companies operating a merit pay system might find that, although performance of a single individual could not be predicted, taken as a group men perform slightly better in terms of their quality and amount of work, zeal, and sense of initiative. In *Danfoss* the court declares such results "inconceivable" and declares discriminatory any scheme that produces them. The court will not hear any possible defense of such results. The full effect of this 1989 decision on the use of merit pay or pay-for-performance plans and on EC productivity has yet to be seen. As the *Equal Opportunities Review* noted, however, the decision suggests that any merit pay system that in practice works to the disadvantage of women "should no longer be used."[61]

## THE COUNCIL OF MINISTERS, THE COMMISSION, AND EQUAL-VALUE LEGISLATION

Though the Council of Ministers is considered the most powerful of the EC's institutions, the unelected Commission may have nearly as much power where, as with the equal-value question, it faces a divided Council. The seventeen commissioners are appointed by the member states, with the larger states naming two. The commissioners are usually former politicians, and once appointed by the member states to their four-year terms, they may not be removed unless the European Parliament should vote to dismiss *all* the commissioners. Acting through these commissioners, the Commission has the sole power to initiate legislation and plays the crucial role in redrafting proposals as negotiations take place among the permanent representatives. Two commentators note that the executive (the Commission) does much of the effective legislating, while the presumed legislative body (the Council) has the veto.[62] One of the ways the Commission uses its power of initiative is to bring its favored proposals forward during the Council presidency of states friendly to the proposals. Since the presidency rotates among the states every six months, this tactic is easily employed. Because the president plays the key role in producing compromise proposals and in cajoling members into agreement, this power of timing is quite important.

The Council of Ministers has no consistent, ongoing will of its own. Its members spend most of their working lives preoccupied with policy in their home states, and ministers representing a given state for a given subject area frequently change, as of course does the Council presidency with its six-month term. When they meet, the ministers usually must hurriedly try to reach agreement on many matters in a day or two.

Though at the start of the summer of 1975 negotiations, the Danes and Germans were as concerned about the equal-value language as were the British, the Commission was able to keep them so preoccupied with the supervision provisions that they could not help the British on the definitional question. On three occasions at the crucial Council of Minister's meeting, it seemed that a consensus in favor of the U.K. position might occur. Each time, the Commission intervened to prevent agreement, once jumping in to voice its objection ahead of the member state called on by the president.

In the 1975 U.K. delegation, the principal nonpolitical civil servant, John Rimington, remembers thinking that equal value was "a load of rubbage." He thought that trying to value jobs outside the market was totally subjective. But he also said, "Remember, though, that a civil servant [in this country] learns to suppress" his own views.

The contrast with the Commission's staff could not have been more clear. The civil servants there report to no politically accountable bosses concerned with advancing their government's position. As one interest group notes, they adopt "a much more overt and publicly visible political role":

> They can be heard at consultative meetings openly seeking pressure-group support against recalcitrant national ministries and revealing details of controversial negotiations in a way which would be unthinkable in Whitehall [the principal U.K. government administrative buildings].[63]

In the struggle for equal pay, one Commission lawyer, Marie Jonczy, played a crucial role as an equal-value advocate. She was remembered by John Rimington's deputy, Tim Biddiscombe, as "tenacious" and "a force to be reckoned with"; Rimington himself described her as "a pest . . . who hated any compromise," but also "clever . . . shrewd; [she] could fix the shots." Amidst a divided Council, Jonczy knew what she wanted, and she acknowledged to me that the Commission civil service played a crucial role in influencing the wording of the equal-pay directive. At no stage did Commission civil servants point out the legal and policy pros and cons of extending the deliberately limited scope of Article 119 of the treaty by way of a directive. They were policy partisans.

Commission policy is heavily compartmentalized. Commissioners tend to defer to what their fellow commissioners wish to do in their areas of expertise. The common ethos of the Commission is to advance a strong European-wide policy.[64] The feminist staff took the lead on equal pay fully supported by the social affairs commissioner. This post is usually one of the slots least sought after by commissioners scrambling for a choice assignment. However, since there is frequent contact with feminists and unionists, it usually attracts and is awarded to a commissioner from a left-of-center party.[65] Thus, the tendency for strong proponents of feminist measures to have disproportionate influence on women's issues, noted earlier in connection with the European Parliament and the Economic and Social Committee, also prevails at the Commission.

Indeed, it prevails even at the Council. In most national governments, the labor or social affairs cabinet minister is further left politically than the commerce or industry minister. When contentious domestic issues arise, both sides fight it out in cabinet, and some sort of compromise usually emerges. But the equivalent question in a Council of Ministers session is decided by representatives who are all principally concerned with advancing social policy at home, not, for example, worrying about possible adverse economic consequences of the "social advances." When the Social Affairs Council decides the best compromise solution, the ministers can do so without first listening to the dire warning from the industry or trade ministers who would be present for a similar session at home. There also are no hearings with skeptical witnesses before the ministers are asked to act. All in all, it seems a flawed legislative process.[66]

From my interviews I would judge the civil servants of the European Commission as unusually able and energetic. I suspect they would strongly resist my picturing them as out-of-control bureaucrats. They would point out that the Treaty of Rome makes the Commission the initiator of all Community legislation as well as the body charged with implementing the decisions of the Council. And they would emphasize their more general responsibilities for carrying out the provisions of the treaty. As they frequently put it, the Commission is the "guardian of the treaties."

These arguments notwithstanding, the wisdom of the process is questionable. The influential participants are all inclined to activism. They are essentially unaccountable. And they encounter few skeptics along the way. As noted, it is usually a left-of-center former politician with activist inclinations who heads the Employment, Social Affairs, and Education Directorate. Once in office, he or she is practically unremovable and accountable to no one. Moreover, given the Commission norms of compartmentalization and decentralization, the incumbent has great power to shape policy in the social area. For the most part, the civil service is made up of single-minded partisans of an energetic, interventionist, Community-wide social policy. There are few, if any, cautionary words from that staff about possible negative consequences from intervention. And the civil servants' incantations of the phrase "guardians of the treaties" is the height of cynicism. Even strong advocates of EC social policy acknowledge that the signers of the original treaty did not envision many of the social activities of the EC as "within the Community's scope at all."[67] Moreover, as we have seen, equal value was explicitly rejected when the Article 119 equal-pay wording was agreed to. Yet now, unelected civil servants, discouraged by the Council of Ministers' recent rejections of a proposed directive on the burden of proof in equal-value (and other) cases, argue that, as "the guardian of the Treaty of Rome," the Commission can bypass the Council and take an infringement case before that other pretender to the title "guardian of the treaty," the European Court of Justice.[68]

One should not forget that EC social policy, and in particular equal-value policy, is a tiny part of the total EC. The everyday work of the Community is still mainly concerned with creating a truly common market. Most activity of the EC concerns competition and protection – import levies on produce, fixing prices for wine, and the like. Though some producers in particular countries will lose as the barriers to free trade fall, everyone senses that the Community as a whole will benefit as commerce flows more freely.[69] By resolutely standing for a strong European policy, the Commission and the court advance this widely agreed upon end.

In their treatment of social policy the Commission and the court benefit from the indulgence granted them in the economic area. But there is no reason to think that Community-wide social policy will yield Community-wide benefits as surely as such policy does in the economic realm. Most economists, for example, think that an end to trade barriers will increase Community welfare, but most think that requiring equal value will decrease it. Given the wide differences in legal and administrative systems in the member states, requiring equal value does not even allow all to compete on a "level playing field." Indeed, as the next chapter will argue, the inability to agree on the value of jobs means that even competitors within a single country such as the United Kingdom compete on a much more *unequal* playing field because equal value is the law of the land.

## GOOD TIMES AND THE PASSAGE OF EQUAL-VALUE LEGISLATION

Even the determined and skillful maneuvering of Commission staff would not have been sufficient to make equal value the law of the EC were it not for the fact that the directive was considered at a time when the relatively good economic times of the 1960s and early 1970s were still conditioning policy makers' future expectations. Advocates of women's measures remember with fondness those "heady days" when advances in social policy were relatively uncontroversial.[70] By the time of final passage of the equal-pay directive, increases in unemployment were just beginning to affect the dominant perception that permanent prosperity could be expected regardless of the social policies enacted. As unemployment climbed and persisted, the political climate changed.[71] Two years after advocating strong equal-pay provisions, Ireland was unsuccessfully pleading with the Commission for a special waiver because of its deepening economic crisis.

In my interviews at the EC, I was told that over the course of the next decade, member states and the top levels of the Commission became increasingly concerned about measures that would "hurt small business" or "increase employer costs" or "limit employer flexibility." In bad economic times, governments want to "do only the minimum." Starting in the mid-1970s the European economies began doing much worse than the United States at creating jobs. When I spoke in 1988 to Marie Jonczy, she explained:

> Let's be clear and honest. Things have changed now. The seventies were the best for social policy. . . . Now even women themselves don't dare bring up [equal pay] cases because of [the fear] of unemployment.[72]

M. Fitzgibbon, a man who was the top aide to the social affairs commissioner in 1974–5, told me that the equal-pay directive would never have passed in its enacted form even two years later. None of the knowledgeable people I asked in 1988 thought that the directive could pass in 1988. It was also agreed that the opposition would come from more than just the United Kingdom; although when possible, others preferred to hide behind a Margaret Thatcher veto, in fact the concerns about the economic effects of social measures ran far more widely.

More revealing than the answers to questions about possible passage of the equal-pay directive today are answers to questions about whether the social affairs ministers meeting in 1974 would have passed the directive if they had known how it all would turn out. John Rimington said, "You would not have had a majority then for equal value as it has come out I feel sure." Another observer at the Commission reported: "I am pretty sure that they did not realize what they let themselves in on. The ministers are now more sophisticated, and they try to be sure to check on the implications." Two experienced U.K. observers, both strong proponents of equal value, were in agreement, as one put it, that "it probably wouldn't have been approved then if the politicians had known what they were doing."

Another advocate of equal value has said that member states are now reluctant to pass new legislation meant to advance the status of women because they "realize that legislation, once adopted, must also be implemented."[73] Europe is no longer "a pure abstraction" with no real-world consequences. The goal that Fraser attributed to all the delegations – pass something that requires no action – now seems difficult to realize. And it has become clearer that implementation of social legislation may have broader economic costs. Still, the changed attitude of member states is explained not just by the realization that you "get what you enact," but also by the realization that you sometimes get much more than you think you enact.[74] John Fraser thought the minutes' entry protected the United Kingdom, and Germany thought the fruits of hard bargaining would protect it against Commission charges about inadequate governmental supervision of equal-pay provisions. The Commission showed otherwise.

## CONCLUSION

With a detailed look at equal value in Britain still to come, these conclusions can be offered. Equal value in the EC was passed by a flawed legislative process in which the unelected played the crucial role and partisans of equal value had disproportionate influence. At the time of passage, three of the then nine member states opposed equal value on the merits, and a majority probably would have opposed the policy as it has developed to date. If equal value were not now law in the EC, it is unlikely that it would become law today.

# 6

# Equal pay for work of equal value in the United Kingdom

## THE U.K. EQUAL-VALUE LAW AND THE TRIBUNAL SYSTEM

As explained in Chapter 5, the United Kingdom experience should be of most interest to those who would look to European Community (EC) developments for indications of how a comparable-worth system might work in the United States. This single country has provided more than half of all the equal-value legal cases generated in the Community as a whole; it shares with the United States an adversarial, common-law-based legal system; and it has adopted a firm-centered approach to implementation. Further, unlike Minnesota, Britain applies the law to the private sector.

As in Minnesota, the U.K. experience has been marked by an absence of objective or even agreed-upon criteria for job evaluation and by much wrangling over the relative value of diverse jobs. The process has produced arbitrary and inefficient outcomes, including, once again, a legal requirement that certain employers pay their employees different wages for similar jobs.

The original U.K. Equal Pay Act of 1970 came into full force at the end of 1975. The act required that women (and men) receive equal contractual treatment where they did the same or "broadly similar" work or work that had been given an equal value through job evaluation. Employers were not required to conduct job evaluations if none existed.

From 1970 to 1977 the average weekly earnings of women climbed from 54 percent of men's to 65 percent.[1] For much of this period, an active government incomes policy meant to control wage and price inflation provided for flat-rate pay increases, thus compressing skill differentials. This policy strongly favored the lower paid, including women, so there is some debate about whether the equal-pay policy or the incomes policy explains the greater proportion of the gains for women. However, the most recent research attaches most significance to the Equal Pay Act.[2] There is wide agreement that most of the gains came through the relatively simple act of abolishing the discriminatory "women's rate" in collective agreements with unions.[3]

When the European Court of Justice ruled against the United Kingdom on the equal-value infringement case, new domestic legislation was required. The Thatcher government clearly did not have its heart in the effort. The minister in charge of presenting the proposed regulations indicated his great sympathy for the views of conservative backbenchers who asked what this "rubbish" had to do with the trading purposes that led Britain to join the EC. For their part, the opposition Labour party argued that the government's efforts to amend what the government saw as just a "small gap" in the original legislation left the United Kingdom with a complicated, almost incomprehensible law.[4]

In the government regulations, work of equal value was defined as work that "is, in terms of the demands made on her (for instance, under such headings as effort, skill, and decision), of equal value to that of a man" working for the same employer.[5] This language was seemingly lifted from the definition of job evaluation, which was at the time voluntary, in the Labour government's 1970 act. Thus, the Thatcher government missed any chance (which EC law may or may not have allowed) to somehow link job comparisons to market values, to productivity, or to the needs of employers.[6]

Under the U.K. system, equal-value claims are heard by an industrial tribunal that is meant to provide for hearings that are "quick, cheap, accessible, informal, and expert."[7] Each three-person tribunal is chaired by a lawyer. The other two members are selected by the Department of Employment, one from a list submitted by unions, the other from a list submitted by employers. Tribunal decisions on equal-pay cases may be appealed through three levels – the Employment Appeal Tribunal, the Court of Appeal, and, finally, the House of Lords.

A report by an "independent expert" helps the industrial tribunals to reach a decision. The female plaintiff chooses males in her enterprise whom she believes do work of the same or lesser value than hers, and the independent expert's report either supports or rejects this claim. The independent experts are chosen by the Advisory Conciliation and Arbitration Service from applicants with backgrounds in industrial relations. The experts have enormous discretion since the law gives no guidance as to which evaluation factors should be used.[8] Moreover, the rules of evidence make it nearly impossible at tribunal hearings to challenge the expert on matters of fact in his or her report.[9] In practice tribunals side with the expert's view on the equal-value question in the overwhelming majority of cases.[10]

From 1984 to mid-1990, 5,130 equal pay for work of equal value applications were made. About one-quarter of the total involved just one employer, British Coal, 725 involved Lloyds Bank employees, and 1,500 others involved speech therapists working for various district health authorities. In 1990 the 403 applicants involved only thirty-two employers, the lowest number since 1984. Most of the applications are conciliated, withdrawn, or otherwise disposed of at a preliminary stage. However, tribunals have requested eighty-one reports from independent experts during this six-and-a-half-year period, and around sixty reports have been completed.[11]

## THE INDEPENDENT EXPERTS AT WORK

The philosophy behind traditional job evaluation studies (JESs) in Great Britain was identical to that discussed in Chapter 2. They sought to fill in gaps and "tidy up" the existing wage hierarchies.[12] As Benjamin Roberts, professor of industrial relations at the London School of Economics, told me, "The market is always coming into conflict with job evaluation studies, and businesses always compromise the thing [JES] when it does."[13] In public forums in the United States, comparable-worth proponents disguise the fundamental differences between traditional job evaluation and comparable-worth job evaluation so as to make the latter more politically palatable. In the United Kingdom, equal value is already the law, so this subterfuge is unnecessary. Indeed, proponents there emphasize that the aim of equal value is to "make major changes" in traditional job evaluation and job hierarchies.[14] Though abandonment of the market standard leaves independent experts adrift in a sea of subjectivity, in one sense the expert's job is easier than that of a pay specialist conducting a traditional job evaluation exercise. Whereas the pay specialist must rate all jobs in a job hierarchy, the independent expert need only decide if the female applicant's job is of equal or greater value than that of the male(s) she has chosen to compare herself to.

The most celebrated equal-value case is *Hayward v. Cammell Laird Shipbuilders Ltd.*, which was first filed in 1984 and decided on final appeal in 1988. In this case a female cook claimed that her work was equal to that of a painter, a carpenter, and an installer of insulation around pipework and other metals. The case is famous in part because it raised the issue of whether greater fringe benefits (for the cook) should be seen as compensating for lower pay. The tribunal and two courts of appeal said fringe benefits should be a consideration, but in 1988 the House of Lords reversed, arguing that under British law each "term" of the cook's contract, including pay, must be equal to that of the men doing work of equal value.[15]

A more fundamental reason for the fame of the *Hayward* case is that it was the first to successfully bring a claim comparing radically different occupations.[16] As a case that compares work that is clearly very dissimilar, it thus nicely illustrates an application of the equal-value philosophy. Since the independent expert in the case is considered a "very good expert" with unusual knowledge of equal-value theory,[17] *Hayward v. Cammell Laird* is a good place to begin testing the conclusions of Chapter 4 about how comparable-worth job evaluation is done in practice.

The independent expert in the *Hayward* case, Terry Dillon, worked for years in the research department of a large union. At the time he wrote his *Hayward* report, he was a lecturer in industrial relations at the University College of North Wales. Dillon based his conclusions on three and a half hours of observation on a ship and three hours in a canteen and on submissions and representations from the parties. All jobs were compared by way of a "high," "moderate," or "low" rating on five factors: physical demands, environmental demands, planning and decision-making demands, skill and knowledge demands, and responsibility demands. Dillon rated the painter and carpenter above the cook on responsibility demands because of the use of more valuable tools and materials. All three comparators were ranked below the cook on planning and decision-making demands because the cook's planning decisions were made in the context of a "daily deadline."[18] Dillon's entire analysis and comparisons were made in eight, exceedingly brief, double-spaced pages at the end of which he declared all the jobs of equal value.[19]

Since the number of potentially relevant but excluded factors is huge and because the judgments made about the five included are highly questionable, a critique of the Dillon report could go on at chapter length if space permitted. Another author has noted that Dillon's report "simply ignored many of the most contentious issues," such as the relative costliness of mistakes.[20] For my part, the most questionable part of the report is the treatment of skill and knowledge demands. The entire analysis here consists of 135 words, half of which reject the relevance of one consideration raised by Cammell Laird. The remainder of the analysis is given below:

> In order to reach conclusions about skills and knowledge I have applied a test to determine the level of demand, i.e. whether or not the job holder is in possession of recognised qualifications or training to that level. The applicant and each of the comparators has either the recognised City and Guilds qualification or training to that level of skill and knowledge.[21]

On the basis of this consideration alone, the skill and knowledge demands of all four jobs are ranked equal. The first sentence leaves "that level" completely unexplained. The second sentence suggests that all jobs are equal if they have a recognized city and guilds qualification or equivalent training. This criterion suggests that all successfully completed training programs for any job provide equal amounts of skill and knowledge. Might not the *length* of the training programs matter? To be a fully certified cook requires eighteen months of total education and training, whereas the joiner and painter require four years of off- and on-the-job training. And in any case, what does this *formal* training have to do with a category purported to be comparing skill and knowledge demands on *particular jobholders?* The cook prepares predetermined menus that are repeated in a cycle every six weeks. The tradesmen work on ships that can take four years to build, and no two ships, even of the same type, are exactly the same.[22] The work that has to be carried out varies at each stage of building.

I asked a number of proponents of and skeptics about comparable worth/equal value if they did not think that there was more difference in the capacities and "value" of a Cammell Laird carpenter with two years' experience compared with one with fifteen than there was in the capacities and "value" of a Cammell Laird cook with two years' experience compared with one with fifteen. Everyone I asked agreed that the two carpenters' capacities would probably diverge more than that of the two cooks. This response suggests that the knowledge and skill demands of the carpenter's job make greater "demands" on him.

Cammell Laird had hoped to have an expert of its own testify that the cook's job was not of equal value to those of her comparators. There was a postponement of the hearing, however, and on the date of the rescheduled hearing, the company's expert was unable to appear. In any case, the tribunals, with no firsthand knowledge of their own, typically side with the impartial independent expert in a very high percentage of the cases with multiple experts. Therefore, it is unlikely that the Cammell Laird expert would have made a difference.

The company's lawyer believed Dillon was way off in rating equally the working conditions of the cook and the painter. He would have liked to have been able to present evidence about climbing down "shaky ladders to apply lead-based paint in a fume-filled hold," but the equal-pay regulations did not permit him to do so.[23] In an effort to keep the process quick and efficient, the legislature prohibited the tribunal from hearing evidence challenging the factual basis of the independent expert's report.

The company's lawyer was thus forced to aim his attacks on deficiencies in the report's method of evaluation, on the inadequate time Dillon spent in the shipyard, and the like. These arguments had no effect. While expressing mild displeasure at the fact that the regulations, in effect, transferred to Dillon the tribunal's "primary fact-finding role,"[24] the tribunal nonetheless concluded that the company had not presented evidence sufficient to persuade it to reject Dillon's conclusion that the jobs were of equal value.

In turning from the *Hayward v. Cammell Laird* report to a survey of others, one finds wide variation in the methods used. Most experts have rated factors by a high, medium, or low type of verbal scale as Dillon did, but others have used elaborate quantitative rating schemes. The experts differ on the number of factors used and on the use or absence of subfactors. To a remarkable degree, the extensive commentary on equal value says little about the reports themselves, seemingly taking it for granted that the experts know what they are doing.[25] Cammell Laird's counsel had criticized Dillon's method in the *Hayward* case on the grounds that it "was so simple as to be crude and lacking in precision."[26] However, more elaborate schemes have also been criticized. Indeed, Robin Beddoe has written what I believe to be the only extended criticism of independent expert reports, and he believes that the methods used are not too simple but rather too complex. Beddoe argues that the ranking systems used in several reports try to be too quantitatively precise, and as a result, minor differences in fundamentally similar jobs are made much too important.

Beddoe focuses in particular on *Wells v. Smales*, a case in which the expert found the jobs of some of the fourteen female fish packers equal in value to that of a male laborer, but others not. The *Wells* expert had originally hoped to avoid any numerical values so as to avoid giving "an impression of accuracy which is not justified by the subjective nature of the basic judgments."[27] However, though the fish packers had the same job title, they worked in different departments doing "clearly different types of work." Thus the *Wells* expert found it necessary to give numerical values so as to keep track of the percentage of time that each of the women spent on "a range of individual or separate jobs."[28] The result was a complicated scheme that gave the women differing total scores, such as 26.77225 and 18.268. Though Beddoe criticized this scheme for its artificial precision, he also criticized another expert for inflating male job content by failing to take account of the fact that "a number of the [job] tasks listed were not required on all occasions." Thus, one cannot be sure just what level of precision would please Beddoe, much less other equal-value practitioners.

Beddoe also offers more general criticisms of the experts' work. In a number of cases basic job descriptions did not exist, and the expert had to provide them. Several of these descriptions were too cursory or "seriously flawed" in other ways. Moreover, many of the experts gave no "clear and comprehensive definitions of the factors" used. As a result, the applicants were deprived of the opportunity to question the experts about their factual knowledge of the jobs and about defects in the experts' evaluations of them.

In pondering why some independent experts simply offer scores or conclusions without reasons, Beddoe offers the sensible hypothesis that, by doing so, "they are protecting themselves from challenges." Beddoe, however, credits one expert for providing an explanation for her report's evaluations, thus enabling others to point out the "serious defects" in them. Among these was the fact that the expert in this case had given supervisory credit to a woman applicant under the "judgment and initiative" category, whereas Beddoe and the tribunal concluded that credit for supervision should *also* be given under "training and experience." Beddoe thinks that by providing in the reports more definitions and more details of the reasoning process, others will be able to ascertain "the validity of the independent expert's conclusions." However, he offers no standards for validity, and none exist. And one can be sure that if some expert had pleased Beddoe and the tribunal by counting supervision under two categories, some other consultant would come along to decry this obvious case of double counting.[29]

The inconsistencies in the application of equal value exist at the most fundamental level. For example, when the equal-pay directive mandates equal pay for work to which equal value is attributed, who is meant to be doing the attributing and by whose standards are the relative values to be assessed? A draft of one recent EC document spoke of the long-recognized fact that "the relative value of work carried out by different persons can be measured in terms of the importance of this work to the employer." An alarmed staffer in the Equal Opportunities Unit of the EC thought it "dangerous" and "subjective" to link value so clearly to the employer. He suggested instead emphasizing the "objective" by talking of job content. The final version spoke of measuring "in terms of the importance of the job content to the employer."[30]

It is not clear, however, that this change makes any difference. Most economists would say that in a well-functioning labor market, the value of work is ultimately determined by consumers, but employers act as the intermediaries. The employers seek to pay employees of the desired quality no more than necessary to obtain their labor, but because of competition for labor, they must usually pay their last-hired worker an amount based on the firm's estimate of the revenue which that worker's product adds to the firm.[31] Increased revenues (and profits) are ultimately dependent on whether consumers are happy with the firm's product(s). Thus, whether one talks of measuring the worth of work to employers or of job content to employers, one is talking of market prices or consumer values.

Equal-value proponents strongly resist the tie to the market and thus are delighted that the U.K. law fleshes out the EC language by speaking of equal value "in terms of the demand made on a worker under various headings (for instance effort, skill, decision)."[32] Several proponents argue that this language means that the U.K. law does not permit assessing value in terms of the value of work to employers.[33] When I asked questions about this matter in my interviews, I was told that the value was assessed in terms of "demands on employees," "job content," or "the intrinsic value of the job."

But jobs do not have intrinsic value, and many jobs may make great demands on employees, but be worth relatively little to consumers, employers, or anyone else. Moreover, different employers will surely assign different values to the same jobs. One company may carve out its niche in a market by emphasizing sales and service. It will value good sales and repair personnel and helpful receptionists more than another company in the same line of work whose reputation is based on timely, reliable delivery. The latter company may pay inventory managers relatively more and receptionists, repair, and salespeople relatively less.

There is no consensus on any of these questions internationally or in the United Kingdom.[34] The Confederation of British Industry is persuaded that the law does not permit jobs to be ranked in terms of value to employers, but the Employment Appeal Tribunal describes the current process as one that assesses jobs in terms of "the value of the job to the employer."[35] Somewhat surprisingly, the U.K. Equal Opportunities Commission (EOC) says that good job factor scores are those that reflect a job's "value to the company."[36] One influential local-level application says that equal value is about assessing job factors on the basis of "the value *people* put on them" (emphasis added).[37]

Another embarrassing source of inconsistency and contention is the question of whether "close is good enough." Suppose the applicant's job is found to be of almost equal value to that of the comparator. Should the applicant's pay be made equal to that of the comparator's in such cases? Some independent experts say yes; some, no. Some experts who say yes are overruled by tribunals who say no, and some experts who say no are overruled by tribunals who say yes. Two tribunals have had multiple cases and continue to decide the issue differently. One takes a "broad brush" approach, arguing that greater "demands" on a few factors may not be materially relevant. The other is "astonished" at the broad-brush approach, noting that Parliament's statute said "equal value," not "substantially equal value."[38]

In the fish packers' case briefly discussed earlier, the tribunal overruled its expert and said that even the female fish packer who scored only 79 percent of the male comparator's score held a job equal in value to his. One management consultant has noted that if this principle were generalized, all pay grades would collapse into one since there is rarely a 20 percent pay disparity between them. For example, the highest-ranking fish packer who scored 135 percent of the male comparator's rating could now demand to be paid with a man doing a "135" job, not the "100" job held by the original male comparator. The other thirteen fish packers could then insist, citing the tribunal, that they too be paid at the rate of the highest-rated fish packer.[39]

There is inequity when tribunals reach differing conclusions about

Table 6.1. *Final scores of three independent experts comparing sewing machinists and upholsterers in three different companies*

| | Sewing machinists | Upholsterers |
|---|---|---|
| *White and Others v. Alstons* | 16 | 15½ |
| *Hall and Others v. Frayling* | 58 | 67 |
| *Holden and Others v. Buoyant* | 38 | 44 |

*Source:* Independent experts' reports on the cases.

female applicants with close but not equal scores. The efficiency effects are every bit as important as the inequities resulting from another outcome of equal value in practice: Experts disagree about the relative value of the same jobs in different firms within a single industry. One tabulation of the sixty-four cases that had been referred to independent experts as of mid-1989 showed that though the Smales Company fish packers ultimately were awarded pay equal to that of the male laborers, the expert in the *British Limited* case found packers unequal to laborers, and thus this company's packers got nothing. Similarly, the expert surveying Alstons furniture company found the female machinists there equal to the male upholsterers, but at Frayling Furniture Ltd. and at Buoyant Upholstery, the two different experts assigned the machinists a lower value.[40]

I investigated the furniture cases in more detail, reading all three of the reports of the independent experts, as well as the decision in the one case that was not settled and went to tribunal for a decision. I also spoke to a staff member at the EOC and managers at two of the companies about the cases. It seems that the upholsterers at Frayling Furniture may have had a somewhat more skilled job than those at Alstons, but conclusions among experts about other factors determined the different final outcomes. Moreover, as described in the reports, the sewing and upholstering jobs in the three companies seem quite similar. The experts used somewhat different factors and very different rating schemes. Their final scores are listed in Table 6.1.

At Alstons, the machinists won their case at the tribunal. In the *Holden* case, the applicants withdrew their claim after receiving the unfavorable report from the independent expert. At Frayling, despite the encouraging report of the independent expert, the company decided that it was better to try to settle. They ended up installing new, faster sewing machines while still paying their machinists at the old rate per piece. Spending the money on the machines rather than in fighting the EOC-financed lawyers of their employees seemed the better course. The Frayling machinists thus ended up doing better than those at Buoyant, but not as well as those at Alstons.

Why did the experts disagree in the three furniture cases? One study shows that, from 1980 to 1982, female equal-pay applicants were three times more likely to be successful if there was a woman on the tribunal panel.[41] Correspondingly, one can note that in the one furniture case where the applicants were successful, there were two female members on the tribunal, and the independent expert who determined that the machinists and the upholsterers were of equal value was a woman. In the other two cases, the independent experts were men who found that the machinists were less valuable than upholsterers, and the cases were abandoned before the tribunals reached a decision.[42] One would need a far more elaborate study before making too much of these differences correlated to the sex of the expert and the judges. However, if it turned out that the sexes could never agree on this subject, one would have to wonder about the feasibility and justice of replacing existing pay-setting mechanisms with such government-mandated administrative ones.

If the reports on the furniture companies can be taken at face value, it would seem that the different outcomes stem mainly from very different assessments of the jobs along the responsibility and physical effort dimensions. Though the Alstons expert did note that the upholsterers, at the final stage of manufacturing, had more responsibility for spotting and remedying faults from earlier stages in the process as well as those in their own work, she nonetheless found the two occupations equal on the responsibility dimension. The other two experts both ranked the upholsterers much higher. The upholsterers must take the frames, foam padding, sewn covers, and cushions and put them together in a way that produces a product of high quality. Since the various components are not engineered to fine detail, they must work with them to produce an attractive final product. The difference in the responsibility for the overall appearance of the final product seemed significant to both the Frayling and the Buoyant experts.

For physical effort the Alstons expert did grant the upholsterers one additional point on her five-point scale. However, the two other experts granted them three added points on a ten-point scale (plus another point for "job hazards") in the Frayling case and two points on a five-point scale in the Buoyant case. The upholsterers work with frames that can weigh fifty pounds and with finished products that can weigh a hundred pounds. All work is done in a standing position, leaning forward. Upholsterers must use considerable energy to manipulate the materials so as to create the correct shape and to "hump" and pull with their fingers so as to get the sewn covers on the frame. By comparison, the machinists do their work sitting down, and the worst that the Alstons' expert could say of the work was that it sometimes required the adoption of "awkward postures to manipulate bulky or difficult materials with pulling/pushing/reaching movements."[43]

The Alstons expert did note that she observed two men lifting eighty-eight pound settees by themselves, but she discounted this in her evaluations on physical effort and work hazards since, in her judgment, it was contrary to health and safety recommendations for such weights to be handled by one person. She assessed only what she called "normal" working. My managerial contacts at Alstons and at Frayling, however, assured me that it was in fact quite normal for their workers to lift such weights by themselves. They wanted to make more money under the piecework rates, and despite management's advice, they did not want to slow things up by getting another person to help with the heavy pieces. Both these managers felt strongly that the upholsterers deserved more pay, in part due to their greater responsibility for the final product, but even more because of their far greater physical effort. One noted that the two men in his cushion-filling department earn more than the two women, though all piecework allowances are the same. He also noted that many of the women machinists seemed quite content with minimal output and minimal pay. Many of the women who are single parents, however, worked quite hard.

The other manager was at pains to explain how important piecework was to his business. All U.K. furniture manufacturers who did not pay by piecework had gone out of business. His company had branches in Australia and New Zealand that built the same furniture, but did not pay on piecework. The upholsterers in Britain produced more than three times as many units as those in Australia. Their machinists, spurred on by the piecework rate, also produced more than those in the Pacific, but the difference was much less, about 50 percent more rather than 200+ percent. The female machinists could go only so fast given the capacities of their machines, whereas physical capacity and stamina set the only limit for male upholsterers. So far as he knew, upholsterers of headboards aside, all upholsterers in the United Kingdom were male. He doubted that the average woman, were she to try upholstering, could produce half what the average man could. He also emphasized that there was "no limit, I mean *no* limit" to the exhaustion that some of his men would put up with to earn more money. Since many of the men were now working "beyond what it is reasonable to ask of a man or possible for a woman," he thought it unfair to pay women doing less stressful work as much.

In debate at the pivotal 1974 Council of Ministers meeting in Brussels, John Fraser argued that equal value would not equalize competitive conditions across EC countries because the technique was so imprecise that clerks would be called equal to typists in one country and not equal in another. The technique, eighteen years later, produces results worse than Fraser envisioned. Even in the *same* country, firms can be helped or hampered in an arbitrary way because of the disagreements of experts. In a well-functioning economy, Alstons furniture company will thrive if it keeps costs low and makes a good product. But in the United Kingdom it might not thrive even if it is efficient. Because it was unlucky and drew the wrong expert, it is now legally required to pay its sewing machinists more than its competitors are required to pay theirs.[44]

## SUBJECTIVE JOB EVALUATION AND THE BIAS PROBLEM

In the debate about comparable worth in the United States, proponents realize that the concept is far from solidly established and that opponents of comparable worth charge that the crucial means, job evaluation, is subjective and arbitrary. To counter their opponents, in their public statements proponents usually call job evaluation "objective." In Britain equal value is firmly established in the law, and there has been much experience with its application. Perhaps as a result, one infrequently sees job evaluation described as objective. Instead, one sees complaints by heads of tribunals unhappy with the U.K. regulations for their reliance on "the last refuge of the bewildered and undecided," that is, the independent expert's "pseudoscientific judgment."[45] Or as one union official told me, "There is no such thing as neutral job evaluation. You can get badly screwed, frankly, if you don't pay attention."

In the United Kingdom a majority of proponents as well as opponents seem to acknowledge that job evaluation is subjective. Yet curiously, this acknowledgment does not keep proponents of equal value from constantly warning about the importance of avoiding bias. Quite the contrary. They argue that *because* job evaluation is subjective, it is easy for bias and discrimination to affect outcomes. One expert approvingly quotes an International Labor Organization (ILO) publication which notes that the choice of factors and point values involves many "arbitrary and subjective elements" and that, as a result, it is especially important that one avoid "bias" when making these choices.[46]

Puzzled by these statements, I consulted my dictionary. Among the definitions offered for *subjective* were "characteristic of or belonging to reality as perceived or known as opposed to reality as it is in itself . . . "; "arising from within or belonging strictly to the individual . . . "; "peculiar to a particular individual modified by individual bias and limitations."[47] In other words, to call something subjective is to say that bias is intrinsic and inevitable.

Of the U.K. proponents who acknowledge subjectivity but warn against bias, the most thoughtful is Michael Rubenstein, the editor of the *Equal Opportunities Review*. Though in his book *Equal Pay for Work of Equal Value,* he begins by accepting the proponents' standard position on the issue, as he proceeds, he becomes more and more impatient with his allies' standard remedies. For example, he sees that the usual approach to indirect discrimination – which in this case would mean looking for a job evaluation system that does not have a "disparate impact" on women – makes no sense here. By definition, if the "male jobs" receive higher scores, it must be because there are more factors that men do well on or because of higher weighting for those factors. But any job evaluation scheme that does not have a disparate impact on women would have to have such an impact on men unless, through some miracle, a system were devised that paid men and women exactly the same on average. Rubenstein notes that "women's jobs may receive lower scores because the women are genuinely employed on work requiring less skill, effort and responsibility." Thus, he strongly disagrees with an EOC publication which says that if the predominantly female jobs receive a lot of low scores, "then the set of factors is discriminatory and should be changed."[48] Still, in his book, Rubenstein does give examples for which he believes an inference of discrimination in the choice or weighting of factors would be justified.

When I spoke with Rubenstein, he seemed even more pessimistic than he was in his book about finding standards indicative of biased systems. In his view, the question of how to spot bias in a subjective process was "the single most difficult aspect of this for all of us." He wondered if a system would not have to be "perverse in order to be declared discriminatory in a legal sense."

Even though in principle Rubenstein sees the problem of identifying actionable bias in a subjective process, he wants an equal-value process that in practice leads to major gains in women's wages. Rubenstein's answer to one question at an equal-pay conference suggests that he would be willing to force employers to define their needs and their job evaluation systems in a way that would be sure to lead to wage gains for female employees:

> I think the employers' needs in job evaluation schemes should be defined to include the needs of women who are clearly underpaid. Given the subjectivity of job evaluation, I can tell you it is very easy to do one that will raise the pay of women substantially as professionally and proficiently as those which have resulted in women being low paid.[49]

Other prominent members of the legal community with a strong interest in equal value have come out for precisely the kind of presumption about indirect discrimination that Rubenstein warned against in his book. Anthony Lester, for example, argues that one tribunal searching to see whether a traditionally female attribute or skill was undervalued or a traditionally male attribute overvalued had adopted a "restrictive" view of sex discrimination. Once one considers indirect discrimination, one sees that "the attribute can be completely neutral, but it will be *prima facie* indirectly discriminatory if, in practice, it has an adverse impact on the group of which the claimant is a member."[50] In addition, the EC Commission is now considering possible measures that might rule out some factors as "unacceptably sex biased" and allow others only if they are "balanced by other criteria biased toward the other sex."[51]

Equal-value proponents in Britain are hard at work reminding independent experts and others doing evaluations of the important but traditionally undervalued factors prominent in "women's" jobs. The evaluators are asked to remember that check-out assistants at supermarkets must have the ability to be courteous ("the skills of tact and diplomacy")[52] and that clerk typists must be discreet ("the ability to keep information confidential") and must be able to induce people to tell them what they want (the ability to get "information from others on their needs").[53]

Proponents keep a special eye on how factors are weighted. In their guide to *Job Evaluation Schemes Free of Sex Bias,* the EOC has an elaborate table showing "biased" and "unbiased" weights for a hypothetical evaluation of a fitter and a nurse. The nurse scores better on "complexity of task" and "training," and the corrected "unbiased" weights for these factors go from 7–8 percent to 15 percent. For physical activity and working conditions, where the fitter scores much higher, the "biased" weight of 15 percent for physical activity moves to 10 percent, and for working conditions a 15 percent "biased" weight is corrected to become a 5 percent "unbiased" weight. The only explanation for this advice is a highly debatable assumption about what the organization, which presumably had thought the "biased" factors appropriate, values: "The second set of weights is less biased because it is more likely to reflect the value of these various factors to the organisation as a whole and does not unduly favour characteristics of male as opposed to female work."[54]

As in the United States, the U.K. discussion about unbiased factors and weighting is completely disconnected from markets and supply and demand. The EOC manual for unbiased job evaluation studies has an appendix that lists the factors tending to favor one of the sexes as well as those that are neutral. The factors "strongly" favoring female jobs are "caring," "dexterity," and "typing and keyboard skills." Those strongly favoring male jobs are "heavy lifting," "physical hazards," "spatial ability," and "unpleasant working conditions."[55]

If one asked most people if, pay and other job characteristics being equal, they would rather have a job characterized by heavy lifting, physical hazards, and other unpleasant working conditions or one characterized by caring and dexterity, I would expect an overwhelming preference for the latter.[56] Wage differentials within predominantly male jobs support this expectation. There is clear evidence that predominantly male unskilled jobs characterized by hazards and other disagreeable working conditions pay more than predominantly male unskilled jobs *without* such characteristics.[57] A significant reason why relatively pleasant unskilled jobs often pay less than decidedly unpleasant unskilled jobs is that a somewhat higher wage is needed to get an adequate supply of labor for the latter.[58]

This issue is unexamined in most of the U.K. job evaluation and equal-value literature. Indeed, there is a strong sense in that literature that market considerations are illegitimate. For example, a national study of public-sector manual workers, a study that benefited from the advice of an EOC representative and other "equal-value" consultants, stated:

> The level of skill has nothing to do with the scarcity of skill. For example, there may be many people with the ability to care for young babies but that does not make it any less important as a skill.[59]

The point with respect to infant care is well made, but if we are unwilling to reward highly skills that are relatively scarce in the market, we may see our standard of living tumble quite dramatically since there will no longer be a financial incentive to train for jobs where great scarcities exist.

Despite all the theoretical confusion, the U.K. discussion of bias is also striking in its implicit use of an all-purpose test for a less biased system, namely, an increase in the pay of predominantly female jobs. I have never seen anyone writing on bias in job evaluation identify an underpaid predominantly male job or an overpaid predominantly female one. Similarly, I have never seen a single factor that favors traditionally male jobs described as underweighted or one that favors traditionally female jobs described as overweighted.

Several sources told me that the national study done to reevaluate localities' public-sector, manual workers' salaries was done to try to prevent unpredictable and varying outcomes from multiple equal-value suits. By all accounts EOC and other equal-value consultants strongly supportive of the concept were deeply involved at every stage.[60] One might expect that an evaluator would have been at a loss as to how to fairly rank all the jobs involved with their very different duties. There were home-care helpers, school caretakers, leisure attendants, dining room assistants, and office cleaners, on the one hand, and refuse collectors, grave diggers, roadworkers, and sewer operatives on the other. As noted in Chapter 4, some union leaders in Minnesota think that the physical effort and working environment of many of these "male" jobs have been historically undervalued. The authors of the study done for the British localities were quite sure that the problem was just the reverse. The traditional weighting had emphasized physical effort too much. The study corrected tradition by bringing "equal value considerations to the fore."[61] In other words, its valuation reduced the weight given historically to physical effort and produced the following percentages:[62]

| | |
|---|---|
| Skill | 36 |
| Responsibility | 36 |
| Initiative | 6 |
| Mental Effort | 8 |
| Physical Effort | 8 |
| Working Conditions | 6 |

To declare skill and responsibility to be 72 percent of the total and physical effort and working conditions 14 percent when many of the "male" jobs are unskilled but involve strenuous physical effort and unpleasant working conditions might seem biased against men and was so considered by one female equal-value proponent I interviewed. She thought the manual workers study "overdid it."

As noted later, almost all the commentators on equal value think the tribunal system is unfair to female plaintiffs. But as far as the independent experts are concerned, one might conclude the reverse with as much reason. Just to be chosen to be an expert, one must show knowledge of the "philosophy" behind the equal-value legislation and understand the "ways in which jobs done by women may have come to be undervalued."[63] It is pretty clear that those who think markets get wages right most of the time need not apply. In the United Kingdom, I spoke with a number of people who were convinced that anyone who thinks cafeteria cooks should get pay equal to carpenters or that sewing machinists should get pay equal to upholsterers is blind to the claims of male-dominated jobs, not the reverse. So in Britain, as in Minnesota, it appears that bias in job evaluation is in the eye of the beholder.

## DISAPPOINTMENT REIGNS

The activists, union leaders, academics, and lawyers who care most about the success of equal value take little notice of the problems already discussed such as the absence of any uniform criteria of job evaluation or of similar decisions in similar cases. There is, however, a deep sense of disappointment in results to date. There are three main sources of this discontent. First, though the tribunal system was meant to provide a quick, cheap, and informal process, it has achieved none of these. The experts were meant to report in forty-two days.[64] No expert has ever met this goal. The average report has taken twelve months to complete. The average time from appointment of an expert to tribunal decisions on the equal-value issue has been around seventeen and a half months.[65] Legal representation and appeals are much more common than was anticipated. In my interviews, the tribunal system was described as "remarkably time consuming," "too complicated," "legalistic," and "a mess."

The second line of criticism, though sometimes voiced by the same people, seems to come from the opposite direction. Despite the legalistic procedures, the frequent use of counsel, and the unexpectedly long time taken by the experts on their reports, it is charged that the tribunals are not expert enough on sex discrimination law and that "too little relevant and convincing evidence is being produced to persuade tribunals that discrimination has occurred."[66]

When phrased in this way, so as to indicate a concern with employee cases won, the neutral-sounding attention to expertise and evidence suggests the third and most fundamental problem as seen by most of those who follow and support equal value in the United Kingdom – that is, there are not enough cases, and too few cases are won by women applicants. Advocates had expected far more equal-pay cases than there have been to date and are disappointed with the complainants' success rate.[67] While one editor of the *Equal Opportunities Review* told me that most winnable cases can get EOC help and others get union help, many proponents think the costs, delays, and wrangling in the courts are discouraging applicants nonetheless.

The feeling that there "ought" to be more complainants is no doubt influenced by the fact that macro level gains from equal value are not evident. From 1984 to 1991, the female–male wage ratio closed from 65.5 percent to 69.7 percent, but this gain does not match that in the United States over the same time period (68.9 percent to 73.6 percent), and it is dwarfed by the 11 percent U.K. gain achieved during the seven-year period when equal pay for equal work was being implemented.[68]

Despite the dissatisfaction with results to date, equal-value supporters do not agree on reforms except those of the most innocuous kind, for instance, more money for the EOC or more training in discrimination law for the tribunals. The most extensively discussed radical reform would do away with the role of the independent expert. This reform has been supported by Justice, an all-party, legal-reform group, as well as by the Confederation of British Industry and the Employment Appeal Tribunal.[69] The Confederation of British Industry believes that doing away with a mandatory independent expert would rid the tribunals of an "unacceptable degree of arbitrariness," namely the experts' "highly personal judgment(s)" on a handful of jobs compared without reference to all others in the job hierarchy.[70] The group Justice would give the money saved by eliminating the independent expert to the EOC to help support other applicants.[71] As all three groups see it, the parties could still call their own experts, and the tribunals themselves would take over the role of determining if the jobs were of equal value.

Many supporters of equal value are, however, critical of this proposed reform. They fear that there would not be money for many complainants to afford their own expert witness. They also wonder if the expertise problem would not be accentuated since lawyers, who would not really know what the people actually did on the job, would play a bigger role. In a revealing comment the EOC expresses its fear that without the "independent" expert to give it guidance, the tribunal "may face a difficult choice in the evidence of two experts both of whom appear to be correct."[72]

The proposed reforms that most excite many equal-value proponents are those which would allow job comparisons across firms or which would allow a woman to compare herself with a "hypothetical" male employee.[73] No one in Britain has begun to determine how one should go about comparing secretaries in Company A with laborers in Company B. As was noted, cross-firm comparisons inevitably encounter differing company philosophies, for example, valuing service or repair more than delivery time or vice versa, even when each firm has the same occupations. Hence, when claimants are encouraged to go looking in other companies for "equally valuable" jobs that are unavailable in their own, the problems would be even greater than they are with the existing system.

Given the absence of discussion on implementation, one suspects that the many activist lawyers who support this reform simply assume there is nothing to lose: cross-firm comparisons mean more litigation and thus more money for lawyers and some extra victories for women workers. So too for the proposed reform that would allow a claimant to ask the hypothetical question "What would I have been paid if I had been of the opposite sex?"[74] This reform, supported by one of Britain's foremost equal-value litigators, would no doubt allow for much creative legal speculation. However, the inconsistent results that experience tells us are sure to follow would make the expertise problem loom still larger, a problem that would no doubt be met by still more calls for added training.

## THE EFFECT OF EQUAL VALUE ON INDUSTRIAL RELATIONS AND BUSINESS EFFICIENCY

Equal value has been a boon for U.K. unions. As in the United States, Australia, and elsewhere in the EC, the percentage of employees in unions has been declining there.[75] The Thatcher government's industrial relations laws weakened their power, and the trend to smaller workplaces has made recruitment more difficult. Yet expanding areas in the economy, such as services, have been heavily populated by female workers. By touting equal value and offering to help with claims and negotiations, unions can attract new members. And equal value has, in fact, been a union-led process. In 1989 over 95 percent of the claims filed were backed by unions,[76] and some applicants have also received support from the EOC. Moreover, litigation aside, equal value gives unions a major new weapon to use in negotiations with business. As one proponent has noted, "The potential of these [equal value] cases to disrupt pay structures and so damage workplace harmony is such that personnel managers will usually rather settle than risk an adverse [tribunal] decision."[77] To try to contain things, the companies often claim that the settlements are unrelated to equal value; so it is hard to be sure how much of this behavior occurs.

Though equal value has been good news for unions, it has been bad news for business profits and business efficiency. A business confronting a typical equal-value complaint knows that, if it goes to tribunal, it must pay its costs, whereas the complainant's will usually be paid by the EOC or the union. It also knows that the very fight will harm employee morale. The cases tend to drag on with the company's representatives trying to belittle the responsibility, effort, and other characteristics involved in the complainant's job while her representatives in turn run down the importance of the male comparators' jobs.[78]

Though proponents believe that women are too seldom successful in the cases they bring, the U.K. law in fact gives complainants several important advantages. For example, the law makes it possible for the applicant to compare herself simultaneously with a large number of higher-paid men, and she wins and gets a raise if the expert finds her job equal to any one of them. In one case (*Fleming v. Short Brothers*), the complainants compared themselves to eleven different men doing widely different work.[79] Some of these men worked in a factory requiring a security clearance (which the women did not have) so the women never could have seen at work the men whom they claimed they were equal to. Their union orchestrated their claim.

Clever unions also look for cases in which the woman can claim equality with an atypically overpaid male. For example, in one factory, a comparator chosen was a forklift driver. When the drivers went on strike, the whole assembly line would shut down; so the union had negotiated a good deal for the drivers. Another comparator was an old man in failing health now doing little. The U.K. law as drafted and currently interpreted allows a complainant to choose as a comparator such workers engaged in unusually light work for their jobs.[80] Complainants may also choose as a comparator a male employee who, through error, is paid more than other employees doing his job.[81] The costs of these anomalous comparator cases can be large since all the occupants in the job hierarchy who are paid a salary between that of the complainant and that of the comparators will feel aggrieved and may demand more whenever a woman complainant is successful.

Equal value hit British industry at a time when many companies (e.g., Cammell Laird and Alstons) were losing money and were under great pressure. To try to improve its competitiveness, Cammell Laird let go more than one-half its work force. It also negotiated with its unions an agreement that "provided for complete interchangeability and flexibility within composite groups of various trades with the object of eliminating waiting time and to enable the group to undertake the entire range of tasks required to complete the job."[82] The independent expert in *Hayward v. Cammell Laird* ignored this new agreement, which affected the "male" trades jobs, because he said it was not yet fully implemented. He thought it was his responsibility to assess jobs as they were, not as they might be in the future.[83]

Changes in job duties complicate equal value in many firms, not just at Cammell Laird. The EOC says that delays make it difficult for the experts to do their work because, during the course of the proceedings, "employees may leave or be made redundant . . . or job descriptions may change."[84] This fact, however, shows why the work the experts do is necessarily time-bound and ephemeral. If things are in such flux that they sometimes change during the time it takes to write a report, the equal-value conclusions reached by the experts will often be inadequate two or three years later. The cost to keep everything up to date would thus be quite high.

Facing the threat of a large increase in pay costs if a union can find a single overpaid male, businesses are increasingly turning to the establishment of a job evaluation system as a way out of their predicament. As Michael Rubenstein says:

> The standard pattern has been for organizations which have recognized an equal value problem to commission a job evaluation and then to fiddle about with (or if a union is involved, negotiate over) factor choice, factor weightings, grade

> boundaries, etc. – all with a view to keeping the pain – in terms of the ultimate cost and disruption to existing relativities – under control.[85]

Evaluation systems that employees accept provide protection against suits so long as employers can show that there are no reasonable grounds for believing that their systems discriminate on the grounds of sex.[86] The establishment of job evaluation systems is, however, costly. Consultants must be paid, and employees' time is needed to set the systems up and maintain them. Moreover, studies show that wages usually go up after implementation of a JES.[87]

Firms that use evaluation systems only to avoid equal-value claims obviously think that were it not for the need to protect themselves against such claims, the efficiency costs of the systems exceed the benefits. Thus, from the point of view of economic efficiency it would be best to keep their use completely voluntary so that the market could help decide if firms using them do better than those not using them. The trend toward using job evaluation systems for legal protection is troubling because they can make response to market signals more difficult, and some think they encourage workers to adopt a rigid view of their job's duties. As the Confederation of British Industry has noted, equal value is inducing many firms to adopt job evaluation systems at a time when their desirability is increasingly called into question by changes like those occurring at Cammell Laird:

> All job evaluation schemes depend on specific jobs being identified and defined. What is evaluated are the specific jobs rather than the job holders. However, employers are increasingly seeking to avoid sharp job definitions to enable the contribution of individuals to develop as their potential is realised. Such an approach is often associated with multi-skilling arrangements consequent on the introduction of new technology, greater flexibility in working arrangements and increasing interest in performance-related pay. As Armstrong and Murlis state in their authoritative book *Reward Management:* "More and more, the tasks carried out by individuals will be related to their personal skills and abilities rather than constrained by the parameters of the tasks allocated to job holders. It will no longer be possible to say that you must evaluate the job not the person. . . . "
>
> Job evaluation, as traditionally understood, is changing and it would clearly be against the interests of the long-term competitiveness of businesses, as well as individuals, to seek to buck that trend.[88]

Despite these substantive worries about job evaluation systems, many firms now think they pale beside the risks of being forced to play the "independent expert" lottery. Given their subjective nature and the desire of businesses to pay employees no more than they have to, a skillfully constructed JES is often the easiest method for employers to avoid the potentially high costs of equal value. The other most obvious method is contracting out. Britain's second largest union has charged that "many employers are evading the provisions of the equal value regulations by contracting out services."[89] In the wake of Julie Hayward's victory in the *Cammell Laird* case, the catering trade magazines contained articles predicting that "private catering contractors are likely to win major new accounts at the expense of in-house caterers" since large companies will be seeking "to avoid potential claims by catering staff for pay parity."[90]

Equal value, to date, mainly affects unionized employees, almost all of whom benefit from wages above the nonunionized level. The only immediate result of a successful case is to raise the wage of the directly affected complaining employee(s) still further above nonunion wages. (The law does not permit the employer to achieve equality by cutting the wages of male comparators.) Thus, one would expect to see cases of above-market wages leading to unemployment and contracting out, but not many cases of equal value having an immediately negative effect on the ability to attract labor. There have, however, been a couple of cases where employers have tried to use market forces as a justification for paying "male" jobs more than "female" ones. Tribunals have differed over this use of the U.K. law's provision that allows an employer to avoid paying the equally valued employee equally if the difference in pay is "genuinely due to a material factor which is not the difference of sex."[91]

## CONCLUSION

In the United States comparable worth is extremely controversial, with both interest groups and academics among those strongly opposed. In the United Kingdom, in contrast, there is no fundamental criticism of the concept of equal value. In part, criticism is absent because British business is resigned to it. The Confederation of British Industry realizes that the basic law comes from the EC. Since business in most other countries has not been significantly affected by equal value, the confederation's 1989 report thought it would not be "realistic" to expect a review of the basic Community framework.[92]

I encountered a one-page critique of equal value written by two economists in a free market journal.[93] But most economists seem to know little about the concept. When I interviewed an Oxford labor economist who had written on discrimination, he began by defending equal value as a way to increase the training and talent of women. As we talked, it became clear that he had no idea what the words "equal pay for work of equal value" meant, for example, that it entailed the comparison of the worth of jobs by outside experts. By the end of the interview, he was saying such comparisons could lead to "all sorts of problems." Despite his inclination "to get at discrimination," he thought equal value "perhaps not the best way of proceeding." Economists as well as business would have been more likely to take a critical look at equal value before fundamental legislation had been passed; because the fundamental legislation was passed in EC executive session without full debate in Britain, their effective intervention at that stage was not possible.

The only extensive commentary on equal value that exists comes from the legal community. The labor and discrimination lawyers who do most of the writing are almost all left of center politically. In article after article, they summarize the case law while praising the expansive decisions that help women plaintiffs and criticizing those that hurt them. The writing almost never acknowledges, much less discusses, possible costs of expansive decisions. Thus, the *Equal Opportunities Review* criticized the European Court of Justice for not making Article 119 directly applicable (without further national legislation) in cases where a woman wanted to compare her pay to that of a "hypothetical male worker."[94] On the other hand, the journal gave the court high praise for the (*Danfoss*) decision that made vulnerable all merit pay systems in which women's ratings were lower on average than men's. The journal even urged unions to "immediately examine the impact of such [merit] systems upon their members."[95]

In the U.S. battles over the 1990–1 civil rights legislation, civil rights groups fought for full restoration of the *Griggs v. Duke Power Co.* Supreme Court standard which allowed practices that had a disparate impact on women or minorities only if firms could establish a business necessity for the practices. There is criticism of such a legal standard in the United States from those on the right who think that such a standard places unwarranted constraints on business practices. The EC's *Bilka* decision established such a business necessity standard, but I found no criticism from the right in the U.K. commentary on the case. There was, however, criticism from the left on the grounds that *Bilka* "imposed no obligation upon employers to take account of family responsibilities in organising pension schemes."[96]

Presumably Erika Szyszczak, the author of these words, believes that even documented business necessities should yield to an employer's "obligation" to take account of his employees' "family responsibilities." Like the others who regularly write on equal value, she shows no inclination to see the issues from the point of view of a business executive as well as that of a woman claimant. The criticisms of U.K. law and decisions never extend to those that allow a woman to compare her work to that of an atypical male, one with "much lighter" duties than other males in the job class.[97] Neither in Szyszchak's words nor elsewhere in the U.K. equal-value commentary have I ever encountered a discussion of the efficiency implications of law that requires a firm to pay its sewing machinists more than its competitors pay or of law that may force businesses to abandon their merit pay plans.

One business consultant I spoke with said that the principal problem with British equal-value law is that it is based on "the assumption that all employees are paid what they are as a result of a conscious judgment. Accidents and history [don't exist]. . . . *Every* organization has people whose pay does not equate to the job they are currently doing." This consultant thought business should be able to look beyond the claimant and her chosen comparator to other employees to see if there is systematic discrimination on the basis of all reasonable evidence.

One cannot read through the equal-value cases without seeing many instances of pay anomalies that have nothing to do with discrimination. For example, the independent expert in the *Smales* case was no doubt correct in his conclusion that the fourteen female "fish packers" in fact had very different duties though all had always been paid the same.[98] Since all were women, this anomaly or inequity did not stem from sex discrimination. Businesses must worry about responding to competitors' moves, about assuring supply of raw materials, and about much more besides their pay scales.

But Michael Rubenstein, more aware of business concerns than most U.K. commentators, thinks it insufficient that on balance female employees are treated fairly. He has quarreled with a House of Lords decision that denied equal-pay relief to nurses in an infants' school because their hourly pay was actually equal to that of their male clerical comparators once one considered their shorter work week and more numerous vacation days. In Rubenstein's view, it is not enough that the pay in total seems fair if one considers the matter retrospectively. He would also require clear evidence that the original reason for differences in basic pay was the employer's conscious conclusion that the differences in hours, holidays, and the like made a lower base wage equitable.[99] Again there is not a hint in Rubenstein's position that there may be costs to a bureaucratic requirement that businesses have a paper justification for all their pay decisions – even those that are on balance perfectly fair to their female employees. The time business takes on such matters might, after all, have been spent trying to improve its products or productivity.

An earlier quotation from a Confederation of British Industry publication noted that by emphasizing pay according to job characteristics, job evaluation hindered the beneficial trend toward flexible multiskilling arrangements and payment based on performance. The Thatcher government also criticized the inflexibility of paying according to job evaluation as part of its attack on national pay bargaining. In its view, pay should be based on "profitability, performance, merit and the demand and supply of skills in the local labour market."[100]

Movement in this direction should improve efficiency. It should also improve equity since high, nationally bargained wages lead to high long-term unemployment in many parts of Britain. The OECD and others believe that it is such unemployment in Europe that is "the principal cause of increased inequity in the distribution of income and of social opportunities."[101]

In the United States the involvement of economists in the debate on comparable worth has forced proponents to attend to the argument that by raising women's wages above market levels, comparable worth may cause unemployment. In the United Kingdom this argument is almost never even acknowledged in the literature even though poll data show that fear of unemployment, not concern about low pay, is the main concern of female workers in the EC.[102] Indeed, the literature usually ignores or denies the relevance of economics to equal-value law or decisions. Michael Rubenstein discusses economics a little, but does not so much as hint at the potential for greater unemployment when he declares that paying women less than their assessed value because of labor surpluses "is exploitation and discriminatory."[103] Rubenstein does take the skills shortage problem seriously, stating that "gross inefficiencies" would result if employers could not pay more to attract scarce labor.[104] However, he would require "hard evidence" before allowing employers to pay more to attract scarce labor – evidence not only of a shortage in the male-dominated occupation, but of the necessity "to pay the particular amount more" that the employer did in order to end the shortage.[105]

But how can one meet this strict burden of proof without first showing that the shortage in the predominantly male occupation continued to exist when a series of smaller pay increases were tried over a long period of time? And once this continuing shortage has been shown, how can one be certain that a smaller increment would not suffice six months later without starting the series of increments over the wage for the equally rated female all over again?

In any case, "shortage" is not an absolute term. There are bound to be some applicants for the male-dominated job at the lower wage of the equally valued female-dominated job. Who is to decide if they are sufficiently qualified? And what will we do about the company that finds many minimally qualified male service repair personnel at a lower rate but genuinely believes that it gets its competitive edge by providing above-average service, and thus believes that only a high wage to attract the top technicians will suffice? One suspects that such a company does not stand a prayer, and thus the economy could lose a whole spectrum of companies that do not discriminate and that consumers value.

Regardless, Rubenstein's fundamental distinction – between paying males more than "assessed value" because of shortages and paying females less because of surpluses – breaks down.[106] Even proponents who think that "assessed value" is dependent on something other than the whim of job evaluation experts must acknowledge that values in job evaluation are relative and not bound to absolute dollar figures. Evasion of the principle behind the distinction will thus be very easy. A company legally required to bring all its surplus but equally valued female-dominated classes up to that of its male service technicians could thereafter stop giving raises to all employees. When it starts to lose service technicians, it could give them bonuses, having found a way to transform illegal low pay because of female surpluses into legal extra pay because of labor shortages.

Educated in the United States before moving to England, Rubenstein is the only legal commentator to discuss seriously any of the economic issues that are central to the debate in the United States. In college the typical U.K. lawyer reads the law and studies some jurisprudence. Narrow specialization comes quite early, and lawyers rarely study economics. Also rare among lawyers, two professors note, is knowledge of "the working of the labour market."[107]

Many of the legal commentators on equal value are quite hostile to even the skills shortage exception to the equal pay for equal value requirement.[108] In my interviews, however, I was told that the recent emphasis of political leaders on markets has affected the way that proponents sell their proposals for strengthening equal value. One leading adviser to the EC equal-rights unit laughed as he explained how they now add to their proposals a little something on discrimination as a labor market distortion. Thus, one can now find the arbitrary distortions of market signals that equal value produces defended in terms of the Community's "primary economic function of reducing constraints on the free flow of goods, workers and capital."[109]

Equal value in the United Kingdom has meant wage increases for women in certain occupations in some firms. However, as noted, there is no evidence of an increase in the rate of reduction of the wage gap since equal value was begun. Moreover, proponents are very unhappy about the process to date and are in no agreement about necessary reforms.

It would take a separate, major research effort to even approximate the costs of equal value to the British economy. Aggregate measures of productivity growth or inflation and unemployment are of little help because there have been significant developments affecting these measures that have nothing to do with equal value. For example, the Thatcher government passed labor laws making it much harder for unions to strike. These laws in part explain why there were fewer days lost to strikes in 1990 than in any year since 1963, and, in turn, the decrease in disruptive strikes helps explain why Britain's productivity growth has outpaced gains in the rest of Europe since 1984.[110] The economywide gains from fewer strikes and a trend toward more decentralized pay bargaining swamp the costs of equal value to particular firms. On the other hand, the costs are much greater than simply those incurred due to tribunal decisions on particular cases. Costly settlements are made and job evaluation systems implemented so that firms can avoid the tribunals altogether.[111] Yet matters are more complicated still because there is a shortage of shop workers, typists, and some other female-dominated occupations, and there is wide agreement that some of the pay gains negotiated within an equal-value framework would have been forthcoming anyway because of market pressures.[112]

Despite the absence of hard data, there can be little doubt that equal value is making affected sectors of the U.K. economy work less well. A legal system that has the effect of requiring some employers to pay employees more than their competitors do is going to harm economic efficiency. So, too, will systems that allow complainants to jump many others on the job hierarchy (the *Hayward* decision left Hayward receiving more than her supervisor as well as many other workers) and systems that encourage one group of employees to argue that the job of another group of employees is not very important relative to theirs. The same is true of practices, such as the adoption of job evaluation systems for legal protection reasons, which retard the movement toward multiskilling labor contracts and performance-related pay.

Whatever the costs of equal value to date, they seem likely to mount in the future. Equal value in the United Kingdom has existed only since 1984. The first major case, *Hayward v. Cammell Laird,* completed its succession of appeals only in 1988. After nearly a three-year delay, in 1989 a tribunal awarded an equal-value raise to Lloyds' bank secretaries and typists. If this decision is not overturned on appeal, the sponsoring union figures that the ultimate cost to Lloyds could total nearly $12 million.[113] Moreover, other female employees throughout the banking and finance sector are sure to file cases of their own.

One commentator thinks that the European Court of Justice's *Bilka* and *Danfoss* decisions should lead to an increase in equal-value claims.[114] In any case, parts of the EC Commission and leading U.K. equal-value commentators are eager to provide for changes in the law that will lead to more cases. The efforts to allow cross-industry comparisons and to declare discriminatory existing job evaluation schemes that rate female-dominated jobs or job factors lower than male ones are relevant in this regard. If a Labour government should come into office, it would be much more sympathetic to many of these measures than the Thatcher/Major governments have been.[115]

Aside from the costs in efficiency to firms and consumers, there are the costs of the tribunals themselves and of the appeals to settle the numerous legal questions. Does the employer have the legal right to interview the applicant? No, says the Employment Appeal Tribunal.[116] May the results of a National Health Service evaluation of jobs in England, Scotland, and Wales be applied to counterpart jobs in Northern Ireland without doing a new job evaluation for Northern Ireland? No, says a Northern Ireland tribunal.[117] If some men and many women "warehouse operatives" are employed assembling, checking, and dispatching warehouse orders, and both sexes are paid the same, may women in this job nonetheless claim that their job is equal to that of male warehouse "checker operatives" who unload and check the goods from the vans?

Yes, says the House of Lords, sustaining the opinion of the Court of Appeal that had overturned the contrary view of the Employment Appeals Tribunal and the original industrial tribunal.[118]

The costs to all parties of cases that go all the way to the House of Lords can exceed £100,000 ($190,000). I sat in court as five law lords heard wigged counsel on each side fight out the last-mentioned warehouse case. Each of the chief counsels had two other counsels at his side, and there were numerous other aides at the back benches. The arguments went on for several days. I could not help but wonder why. Both these warehouse jobs are unskilled. So, too, are many of the others that reach tribunal, for instance, the female process operator comparing herself to a male cleaner, the female fish packers and the male laborer, the female stockroom assistant and the male warehouse worker. In these cases, all sides readily admit that both jobs are jobs of "low level skill"[119] or, as one tribunal more delicately put it, "less than semi-skilled."[120] Thus, the comparable-worth proponent's argument that it would be unfair to ask nurses or librarians to retrain for other work in order to receive a decent wage is not applicable. If Sue thinks Fred's got a better deal, why does she not apply for the next opening in his job class?

When I asked one advocate this question, she replied: "Sue doesn't want Fred's job; she wants his pay. That's the inequity she sees. There are no other women in Fred's job."

If the absence of other women is Sue's concern, perhaps she could wait till there are two openings, and then she and Helen can both go over. If we want to break down occupational sex segregation, someone must go first. And unlike equal value, most economists and many others would support the aims of the equal treatment and antiharassment laws that seek to break down occupational discrimination. If enough Sues and Helens shifted, the added supply for the "male" jobs and the reduction in supply for the "female" ones would even tend to equalize wages between the "male" and "female" occupations.

# 7

## Equal pay for work of equal value in Australia

When discussing foreign experience with comparable worth, U.S. proponents turn most often to Australia.[1] Without fail they draw on the work of Australian economist Robert Gregory and various coauthors. Gregory argues that Australian policy has significantly decreased the gap between women's and men's pay without disrupting the economy. Gregory's conclusions are based principally on his examinations of the impact of a 1969 decision of the Australian Conciliation and Arbitration Commission that granted women equal pay for equal work, and of the impact of a 1972 decision that phased in equal pay for work of equal value over a three-year period. By 1975 the pay of women relative to that of men had increased by almost 30 percent, and as Gregory and his colleagues see it, the negative effects were extremely small. In fact, some of their work suggests that negative effects were almost nonexistent.[2] Comparable-worth proponents in the United States note that Australia applied the concept in a dramatic way throughout most of the economy and in a very short time. Since no "economic chaos" resulted, proponents wonder how critics can predict disaster from far more modest U.S. initiatives.[3]

Though proponents treat Gregory's conclusions about comparable-worth practice in Australia as gospel, they are disputed by other economists in Australia and the United States. Moreover, it is acknowledged on all sides that Australian economic performance over recent decades has been poor by most standard measures. A host of economic analysts have linked that poor performance to an unusual centralized wage-setting system, a system that made possible the rapid economywide introduction of large wage increases for female employees. Long before the federal and state Australian wage-setting tribunals were using equal value to boost the wages of predominantly female occupations, they were using concepts such as "comparative wage justice" and "work value" to determine the relative wages of predominantly male jobs such as carpentry and metalworking.

Thus, Australia is a key test. No one would claim that comparable worth meant to help women has been the sole or even primary cause of Australia's weakened economic condition. Indeed, for reasons that will be discussed later, some in Australia doubt that the country actually has had comparable worth as proponents define it. Moreover, as will also be explained, since 1987 Australia has been undergoing radical, decentralizing changes in its historic wage-fixing mechanisms. These changes may well obliterate the Australian model that made possible the rapid reduction in the wage gap in the 1970s. Nevertheless, what Australia unquestionably did have until 1987 and still has to a considerable extent is a system of administered wages motivated by considerations of equity and allowing little room for the interplay of supply and demand. By whatever name, such a system is the essence of comparable-worth schemes in the United States, Britain, and elsewhere, but Australia's variant has existed long enough to have had a significant impact on overall economic performance. Australia thus can provide evidence about the long-term consequences of administered wage systems whatever they may be called and whatever their purpose.

Since the 1972 decision that brought equal value to Australia was itself just a small blip in a decades-long, controversial process by which tribunals have set the wages of almost all employees, one must understand the nature of that general process before turning to equal value per se. Because the process would not be controversial if Australia's economy were performing well, a brief survey of economic performance precedes the discussion of the historic arbitration process.

## AUSTRALIAN ECONOMIC PERFORMANCE

Given a rational economic structure, Australia's economy could be among the healthiest in the world, for the country has ample natural and human resources. Indeed, the Australians think of their nation as the "lucky country." "Extremely well endowed with minerals and pastoral land,"[4] Australia is the world's leading exporter of bauxite, aluminum, wool, and two types of coal. It exports more energy than it imports. Moreover, it is the second-largest zinc producer and the fourth-largest gold producer. These resources support a small population of under 18 million – a population that is educated, politically stable, and placed in a booming region with a desirable climate.[5]

Despite these advantages, both the long- and short-term performance of the Australian economy has been poor. Numbered among the twenty-four members of the Organization for Economic Cooperation and Development (OECD) are the most developed nations of the world including Australia. Only on unemployment has the Australian economy matched OECD or U.S. averages of economic performance since 1973. From 1973 to 1990 Australian unemployment (6.4 percent) was slightly worse than the OECD average (6.2 percent) and slightly better than the U.S. average (6.8 percent). However, Australian inflation was significantly worse (9.7 percent) than the OECD average (7.1 percent) or the U.S. average (6.2 percent) during this period. So too was its international competitiveness. From 1973 to 1990 OECD countries averaged a current balance deficit with other countries of 0.4 percent of the OECD countries' gross domestic product (GDP). The United States enjoyed a balance of payments surplus in most years from 1973 until 1982. From 1982 to 1990 the United States has been in deficit every year with the deficit averaging 2.3 percent of GDP. By comparison Australia has been in deficit every year since 1974, and from 1982 to 1990 their deficit averaged more than twice that of the United States – 4.9 percent of GDP. In 1976 a U.S. dollar was worth 81 Australian cents. In 1990 it was worth 128 Australian cents.[6]

For Australians most discouraging of all are the statistics that measure the standard of living. As late as 1913 Australia had the highest per capita gross domestic product in the world. In 1970 it was seventh among OECD countries. By 1988 it had fallen to thirteenth, more than 30 percent behind the United States, which led OECD countries in both 1970 and 1988.[7]

More recent statistics are, on the whole, even more discouraging. From 1986 to 1990 Australian inflation was twice the OECD average, and its balance of payments deficit as a percentage of GDP was the worst in the OECD.[8] During this period Australia's net external debt as a percentage of GDP climbed from 23.8 to 35.1 percent.[9] In an attempt to deal with the inflation and foreign debt problems, the government has severely restrained demand, leading to the worst recession in sixty years with unemployment climbing over 11 percent by mid-1992. The inflation rate has sunk to below zero.[10] But there has been only modest progress on the balance of payments deficit, which the Australian *Business Review Weekly* calls "shocking . . . for an economy that has suffered such pain."[11] In gross terms the Australian foreign debt is higher than that of Argentina or Mexico, and in per capita terms it is the world's highest.[12] In late 1989 both Moody's and Standard and Poors downgraded Australian long-term sovereign debt from AA1 to AA2.[13]

In 1990 the *Economist* noted that Australia has "one of the most protected manufacturing industries and one of the most parochial, trade-averse economies among the world's advanced nations."[14] Most experts see protection as one of the central causes of poor economic performance.[15]

In the same editorial in which the *Economist* criticized Australian protection, it also supported reforms that it argued would be privately recommended by almost all knowledgeable Australians in business, in government, and in the civil service. The central thrust was less government, but the main focus was not on protection per se, but rather on the labor market. The *Economist* recommended

> the scrapping of a unique system of centralized wage bargaining between government and unions in which managers have no say and in which promised increases in productivity remain imaginary; a revamping of industrial-relations law to let the productive economy breathe free.[16]

The *Economist* suggested that eliminating centralized labor pricing would lead to less protection because Australia has often introduced protective measures in an effort to maintain high tribunal-established wages for low-skilled domestic manufacturing jobs.[17]

A 1991 *Australian Business* commentary begins, "No two words in the Australian political lexicon stimulate greater interest or aggravation than 'industrial relations.' "[18] A 1986 Australian book begins with the words, "No aspect of economic policy is more consistently at the forefront of public debate in Australia than wage fixation."[19] Similarly, in my interviews in Australia the centrality of wage fixation to political and economic fortunes could not have been made more clear. For example, I was told that John Howard, treasurer in the Liberal party government in the late 1970s, acknowledged in retrospect that his government's biggest mistake was not reforming industrial relations law. I was also told that one of the principal reasons for the mid-1980s formation of the Business Council of Australia – made up of chief executives of the largest Australian corporations – was great dissatisfaction with the Australian industrial relations system.[20] The following section outlines that complex system, focusing on the way it sets wages.

## THE AUSTRALIAN WAGE-FIXATION SYSTEM: METHODS AND PRINCIPLES

After a wave of severe strikes in the 1890s, Australian states set up systems of mandatory conciliation and arbitration for intrastate labor disputes. Later, in 1904, the federal government set up a system to handle interstate grievances. In their subsequent work state tribunals have usually followed the awards and principles of the federal tribunal, whose name was recently changed to the Industrial Relations Commission (IRC). The awards made by the federal and state commissions cover about 85 percent of all Australian employees, including most nonunion workers and 42 percent of managers.

Over time industrial relations in Australia became much more highly regulated and much more centralized than was ever intended by the founders of the tribunals. The centralization was defended as necessary to assure the equitable application of consistent principles to varying cases, and to hold back inflationary pressures. Most public attention has been focused on the annual (formerly biannual) national wage cases that have determined the level of general wage increase for the 85 percent of employees covered by awards. There is, however, nothing to prevent a union from seeking additional wages beyond the awards given in the national wage case.[21] Often a union and employers reach agreement either before or after tribunal conciliation, and the tribunal may, if it chooses, register these "consent" awards. If the parties cannot agree, the tribunals arbitrate the disputes and determine whether a wage increase is warranted.[22]

Through the years societal values and proclaimed arbitration principles have influenced the wage-fixation results. The principal societal value has been egalitarianism. The Australian labor movement and Australians generally have a special concern for less well paid workers. For many years awards were granted in terms of a basic wage with margins for skill. During this period the basic wage was adjusted more frequently than the margins for skill, and wages thus became more compressed, as they have at some later times as well.[23]

The longest-lasting principle of wage arbitration was comparative wage justice (CWJ). In its narrowest interpretation this principle required employees in the same occupation (e.g., carpentry) to be paid the same wage, irrespective of their firm's capacity to pay or their locale's cost of living. In the broader sense, however, it came to be felt that CWJ required consistency in the wage differentials between occupations as well as consistency in the pay to all those in a single occupation.

The resulting linkages between various classifications and awards has led J. E. Isaac, professor of economics at the University of Melbourne and a former deputy president of the federal tribunal, to say that CWJ is "conceptually like a national job evaluation system."[24] CWJ is, however, different from the forms of job evaluation that comparable-worth supporters promote because the pay differentials have never been based on a systematic study of job demands such as skill and effort. CWJ compares rates, not jobs.

If not formal job evaluation, what *does* then determine the relative pay rates under CWJ? The best answer seems to be the market rates of years ago compressed somewhat to make them more egalitarian. Justice Kelly, an influential federal judge, noted in 1942 that, "from its inception," the court "has allowed itself to be guided in its assessment of 'fair' wages by the evidence of what reasonable employers of competent labour have found it desirable to pay and what competent workmen have been willing to accept for any particular class of work."[25] These initial market differentials gained a life of their own since it was thought that one courted industrial trouble if "consistency" in the relative rankings of the occupations was not maintained through time. Thus, before long, CWJ came to focus on past relationships. Again I quote Justice Kelly: "A wage fixing authority cannot but pay great regard to wage relationships established by past experience in an industry and in industry in general."[26]

Once the CWJ principle had taken hold, unions knew that if one occupation were successful in a claim to an increase, others could then successfully claim that CWJ required that the increase, as the Australians put it, "flow on" to them as well. Gradually the large Metal Trades Award, which covered many trades and affected many industries, became like a national test case. Parties able to demonstrate an interest in a case before the Commission were granted permission to intervene, and in the 1952 metal trades skill margin case, the tribunal granted permission to intervene to "twenty unions, eight employer associations, eleven state instrumentalities, six major private employers and three state governments."[27]

As one might imagine, a situation in which any granted pay increase sets off a "pay round" where the initial increase leads to increases everywhere has powerful inflationary implications. For this reason, there have been periodic attempts to constrain or suppress the particular skill "anomaly" or other claims that could flow on in this way.[28] As will be explained later, in the late 1980s, a desire to put an emphasis on productivity, not on historic relativities, led to tribunal wage-setting principles that were meant to take the historic concept of CWJ completely off the agenda.

Beyond CWJ there is another long-standing Australian arbitration concept that might be thought to be based on comparable-worth technique, namely, "work value." Some work-value exercises conducted by tribunals do use some of the standard evaluation factors such as skills and responsibility in their judgments. However, there is no attempt to standardize the job factors or characteristics leading to such judgments. One study found at least fifty-four different factors mentioned in judgments over a ten-year period. Among the more unusual were "ability to feel the machine," "public contact standard," "standards and values in the community," and "lack of fear aloft." Work-value judgments usually do no more than summarize the submissions, assert that "everything has been carefully considered," and state "what has been granted."[29] As Clare Burton notes, "The concept [work value] has a circular motion to it and has rarely been applied independently of consideration of other factors, including comparative wage justice, industrial peace, prevailing notions of equity and fairness, and relative bargaining power."[30]

Work-value cases typically involve new jobs or claims that an old job has changed so as to become significantly more demanding, for instance, secretaries using word processors rather than typewriters. Judgments in these cases are sometimes preceded by an examination of jobs by tribunal members, but independent experts are rarely used. Before World War II the tribunals frequently had assessors to help with the technicalities of job analysis, but no more.[31] Instead the tribunals have, until recently, relied on the CWJ principle to help them determine work value.[32]

It is here that Burton and others see the circular process at work. One might have thought that it was a comparison of differing work values that led to the substantive meaning of CWJ. But in fact, work-value exercises frequently proceed by comparing a classification with the money awards given for similar jobs under the historic CWJ understanding of equitable relative wages. The "wage rate so arrived at expresses the work value of a classification; CWJ is the principle underlying the evaluation process which established that value."[33]

In the pivotal 1972 equal-value case, the Commission said that "the value of the work refers to worth in terms of award wage or salary fixation, not worth to the employer."[34] Giving a circular definition in their decision, the Commission in effect says that award wage should be determined by work value, which will be established by reference to award wage and salary fixation. The Commission seems to mean that wages should be established by reference to how it has set wages for similar jobs in the past, that is, by reference to historic relativities that in turn were based in large part on the market wages of years ago. So the high principle that lies behind CWJ – the principle that requires a massive intervention into labor markets – is that current market relativities should not set wages so that market relativities of years ago (compressed a little) may do so.

Concerning first awards for new work the Commission says, "In the making of a first award, the long established principles shall apply, i.e. prima facie the main consideration is the existing rates and conditions."[35] Thus, for new work the current market can rule, but according to the principle of CWJ, thereafter, whatever the relativities were when the new job came into the system shall prevail for evermore.[36]

Only a small kernel of genuine comparable-worth-like technique seems to exist in the traditional Australian wage-setting system. Not job evaluation – but market differentials compressed a little in the name of equality – set the crucial starting points. Moreover, assessment of increases in work value make little, if any, use of job evaluation techniques. But it would seem that increases in work value do reflect judgments about increases in skill, responsibility, and the like. Thus, when an occupation becomes more demanding, it becomes more like higher-paying jobs in the traditional relativity scale and can be awarded a higher wage.

But in practice even this kernel collapses. In fact, the traditional relativities usually reassert themselves. For example, in 1967 a work-value increase granted in the Metal Trades Award was greeted by threats and militancy from other unions, and the Commission soon bowed to the pressure. "Flow-on" wage increases for these other unions were then granted.[37] In 1978 the Commission tried to abandon CWJ and have a pure "work value round" of wage cases in which it would search for employees performing similar work "who are paid dissimilar rates of pay without good reasons." Nevertheless, during 1978–9,

> a work value round rippled through the workforce resulting in similar or identical wage increases. Despite the wording of [the Commission's guidelines] the Commission gave its support to the averaging process which was a major factor in the uniform increases. Further, when formulating the [fourth version of the national wage] guidelines, the bench intimated that an injustice would be done if the work value round was not extended to all sections of the workforce. With Full Bench blessing a restrictive and selective process had been transformed into a mechanism for generalized wage increases in the order of 4 percent.[38]

As one current Commission member told me, many other times in the past the work-value principle has been similarly abused: "One group" in an industry would "make a successful case and get an increase." It would be averaged to all occupations in the industry so the "successful" occupation got no more in percentage terms than others. "The pressure in other sectors would be great [and the increase would flow on to other industries], becoming in effect another wage round."

In the middle to late 1980s the Commission faced a number of new claims for work-value anomalies. The Commission feared another round of inflationary "flow-ons." Moreover, its highest priority was a workplace restructuring exercise aimed at greater productivity. The Commission feared that the work-value cases could use up all the wage increases that were meant to be employed to induce labor's cooperation in the restructuring enterprise. Thus, standards for work-value increases were made extremely tight, and for a time consideration of work-value cases was simply postponed. As one legislative staffer put it, "Work value is an input concept. . . . Supposedly restructuring is looking more at output."

Flow-on problems aside, the work-value principle has not been adhered to in several other ways. Even the *initial* judgments about changes in work value were often less than pure. To understand why requires knowing still another term from the Australian industrial relations lexicon, that is, "overaward." Though many Australian workers are paid at the level determined by a wage tribunal, a growing number of employees covered by the system also receive "overaward" payments.[39] After receiving their award from a tribunal, unions can go to a specific firm and negotiate for such overaward pay. Employers grant such pay most often when labor is scarce or when they cannot afford a strike. ("Their clients say, 'Don't get tough with labor on *my* project.' ")[40] The firm's other employees then threaten a strike if they are not given overawards like those in the occupation where labor is scarce or the union powerful.

A spreading pattern of overawards calls into question "the stature and authority of the Commission's awards."[41] Thus, a number of work-value exercises that led to wage increases have been thinly disguised efforts by the Commission to tidy things up by granting work-value increases that absorbed the overawards. For example, the militancy shown by non–metal trades unions in 1967 was sparked in part by their knowledge that the metal trades' work-value increases were not genuinely caused by changes in the value of the work done by the occupations covered by the Metal Trades Award. "Only 70 of the 330 award classifications were the subject of any examination" in the work-value round of the Metal Trades Award set by the 1967 national wage bench, and "only 26 classifications were examined in any detail." The increases granted "mirrored the pattern of over-award payments submitted at the 1966 national wage case." The whole exercise became an "ill conceived and poorly executed attempt at over-award absorption."[42]

All in all, I found great cynicism about work value in Australia. Michael Angwin, the Business Council of Australia's labor expert said, "There is not much real work value in Australia. It's been power relations I think."[43] A union official stated, "It's a very minor part of the system, ... a device used to fix up an industrial dispute or pressures that come along." Christine Short, an economist who supports comparable worth, said: "Arbitration systems are arbitrary. Decisions are based on the power of the parties. [It's] not about the law or legal principles at all. [It's] about keeping the parties happy."[44] Still another comparable-worth advocate said that it's all about "who shouts the loudest."[45]

Even the comparative-wage principle itself was as much an accommodation to industrial and administrative realities as a firmly held conception of wage justice. As Justice Higgins, the man who first pronounced many of the enduring principles of Australian arbitration, once emphasized, there must be consistency between awards through time, "or else comparisons breed unnecessary restlessness, discontent and industrial trouble."[46] And it would be administratively impossible for the Commission to really do detailed industrial investigations so as to determine how changes in the nature of all occupations through time had changed their value and thus had changed the appropriate meaning of CWJ. Presumably a centralized comparable-worth system would seek to make such a determination, but commentators in Australia seem to agree that it would be impossible even in their small country. CWJ makes things much easier precisely because it makes it unnecessary for the tribunals to examine "the *merits* of each and every case" (emphasis added).[47]

Whatever the reasons for its adoption, CWJ never was a precisely defined concept. "Workers typically compare themselves with the more favourable points of reference."[48] The transport workers union "claims to have been a wage round behind the metal workers for most of the 1980s."[49] And during the 1923–48 period when federal and state tribunals both used the CWJ principle, the "award margins in engineering, butchering, tailoring and engraving" showed "significant differences in rates and movement in rates."[50]

The result has not been "equity" in almost anyone's eyes, including the Commission's. As in Minnesota and the United Kingdom it has not even been possible to pay people the same for doing the *same* work. Thus, in its February 1989 decision the IRC noted that union and other pressures had produced a result such that "there exist in federal awards widespread examples of the prescription of different rates of pay for employees performing the same work." Moreover, "For too long there have existed inequitable relationships among various classifications of employees."[51]

A critic has described the historic philosophy of Australian arbitration not as CWJ, but rather as "doing deals."[52] The Commission adopts some principles and cuts some deals. These make other interests unhappy, so the Commission generates new principles and new deals. Sir Richard Kirby, a past president of the federal Commission, hints at such a philosophy when he states:

> It is important that the Commission should be flexible in approach and that its decisions should not be bound by the legal precedents of previous years but should be framed in the context of their current industrial and economic environment. It is all very well to be able to arrive at a logical and theoretically correct solution... [but unless the interests] accept the solution, its essential validity or correctness is of little importance.[53]

In August 1988 the Commission was unusually tough-minded and announced new principles meant to encourage restructuring and efficiency. It declared that only in "extraordinary circumstances" would it make substantive changes in its principles before sixteen and a half months had passed.[54] Maintaining principles for only sixteen and a half months could seem like resoluteness in a system that had already seen "seven separate wage determination criteria" in the previous seven years.[55]

Wage fixation is always politically hot in Australia, and the effort to appease the unhappy occurs even at the legislative level. The U.S. Wagner Act, which is at the center of U.S. labor relations regulation, has been significantly amended only five times since 1935. The Australian basic labor law has been amended more than sixty times since 1904.[56]

It is not just poor tribunal craftsmanship that leads to impenetrable statements of principle such as the definition of work value offered earlier. Unclear language may puzzle everyone, but at least it does not infuriate anyone; thus it may be serviceable for a time. Christine Short told me that such language "keeps the parties happy and the tribunals in existence. They don't want a [more scientific] job evaluation system." It would allow "no leeway for keeping the peace."[57] Or as Michael Angwin of the Business Council of Australia put it, "vague language" means that their words will not make them "hostages in the future."[58]

## COSTS OF AUSTRALIAN WAGE FIXATION

### *Inflation*

The Australian wage-fixation process is considered one of the principal causes of the Australian economy's problems in recent decades. For one thing, as previously indicated, the CWJ principle with the accompanying flow-on process gives a powerful push for inflation. When the economy starts to build up steam, strong unions exert wage pressure at vulnerable points, or skill shortages lead to a wage breakout in some sectors. Occupations such as transport then demand their CWJ. "Because craft and occupational awards are multiemployer awards operating in many industries, pressure soon emerges in mixed manufacturing to restore relativities between production, clerical and warehousing workers and their craft and occupational colleagues, who number relatively few in manufacturing plants."[59] Soon, with so many being paid beyond the established award rate, the Commission begins to feel irrelevant. Workers in occupations with weak unions and no labor shortages complain that they complied with the Commission's award, but that others who didn't get overawards.[60] The Commission then agrees to a general wage round to catch up with the market. If a recession to wring out the inflation does not ensue, industrial pressures or skill shortages emerge again at the now uniformly higher wage rate, and the process begins all over again.

As recently as 1989, the Business Council of Australia concluded that "conditions continue to exist in Australia – probably to a greater extent than anywhere else in the world – for *sectional* wage pressures to pose a threat of *economy-wide* wage breakout during periods of strong economic growth."[61] The OECD puts it this way: "Australia has largely followed centralized fixing of award (mainly minimum) wages with strong wage–wage links ensuring that increases in one sector quickly flow on elsewhere."[62] In more market-oriented economies when skill or geographic shortages lead wages to rise, the rise in wages is mitigated by the new labor that flows to the skill or area paying top dollar. In Australia, this healthy efficiency-generating and inflation-mitigating response is short circuited. By making the rise in wages a general one, labor's incentive to move to higher-valued uses is dampened considerably, and instead a general inflationary surge is frequently stimulated.

The process can cause even more inflationary havoc than this description suggests because even the sectional wage pressures that start the process appear earlier in Australia than they would without the wage-fixing tribunals. Normally, businesses will hold out against wage increases as long as possible for fear that higher wages for their employees will put them at a competitive disadvantage. In Australia, employers have less incentive to be tough bargainers with employees because they know that their wage increases may soon flow on to their domestic competitors.[63]

## *Unemployment*

As indicated, the Australian unemployment rate was only slightly worse than the OECD average from 1973 to 1990. However, Australia used to have a much better than average record on unemployment. From 1963 to 1970 Australia's unemployment was never above 2.3 percent and was always at least a point below the OECD average. In contrast, from 1973 to 1987 unemployment averaged 6.3 percent, one-tenth of a point above the OECD average.[64] Finding that "flexible wages [downward] allow employment to be maintained" when the economy weakens, the OECD has linked Australia's above-average increases in unemployment to above-average wage rigidity.[65] U.S. economists who have studied Australia also believe that the too rapid increase of real wages relative to the increase in productivity was part of the reason for the rise in unemployment over this period.[66] In 1983 "both the outgoing Liberal government and the incoming Labor government concluded that wage determination was at the heart of the macroeconomic problem." Despite some differences, both developed similar central policies: "A reduction in the level of real wages."[67]

Real wages have declined significantly in recent years,[68] but even before the recent severe recession, Australian unemployment rates were slightly worse than OECD averages. One partial explanation may be an increase in wage compression, that is, equalization, in the middle to late 1980s at the same time as real wages were declining.[69] As already described, Australian egalitarianism has led to consistent efforts to raise wages of workers at the bottom, thus compressing the salary structure. As late as 1988 the federal Commission approved a supplementary payment wage-fixing principle designed "to reduce wage inequalities by reducing differentials."[70] Yet OECD studies find a clear linkage between increased unemployment among the less skilled, on the one hand, and compressed pay scales, on the other.[71]

The tribunals can require that hired, unskilled labor be paid a certain rate, but they cannot require that it be hired or prevent it from being fired. Before 1950 the tribunals gave more weight to economic capacity to pay than they did thereafter.[72] The 1988 national wage case decision did allow for a reduction in *increases* in labor costs under "extreme economic adversity," but applications for such exceptions were to be "rigourously tested."[73]

The OECD believes that the more flexible U.S. labor pricing mechanisms, which allow for concessionary bargaining, help keep and create jobs.[74] Representatives of Australian business look longingly at the U.S. system:

> In the U.S. steel industry in 1983 the United Steel Workers' Union negotiated a $1.25 per hour wage *reduction* across all major plants in the United States. This is hardly a tame cat union, yet because it and its members were involved with the companies in determining what was best for all concerned, this wage reduction was possible. Such a thing is unheard of in Australia. The National Wage Bench, on 23 September 1983, virtually ruled out any exceptions to its general wage increase decision by saying that "the ACTU's [Australian Council of Trade Unions] argument has considerable force. . . . the fundamental basis of a centralised system is uniformity and consistency of treatment."

These Australian business representatives wonder why job-preserving, concessionary bargaining based on market developments should be called the "law of the jungle" by critics of market-sensitive wages.[75]

### *Bad labor relations*

Why have the wage-fixing tribunals so often granted increases that fueled inflation and caused unemployment? Their actions do not seem to stem from an unorthodox, tragically wrong view about the consequences of their policies. The appendix of the 1988 national wage decision, for example, includes statements, like the following, that might have come out of an OECD publication or any other mainstream economic analysis:

> The principal benefits of wage restraint are a lesser rate of inflation, a higher level of economic activity (with more employment and less unemployment), more investment, more rapid economic growth and less difficulty in adjusting the domestic economy to external constraints. Each of these benefits may be pursued by other means. Wage restraint, however, has the unique feature of promoting them all simultaneously.[76]

In the body of its decision, the Commission even said that there "would be significant economic benefits in lower increases" than those it then proceeded to grant.[77]

The Commission agreed to hike wages and thus forsake these significant economic benefits because, as in the past, it believed that "matters of equity and industrial realism" were also important.[78] The Commission decided to forgo higher growth and lower unemployment, inflation, and foreign debt for an increase in wages even though it acknowledged that the increase in money wages it granted might have only a small effect on real (noninflationary) wage growth in the long run. Indeed, if the wage increase dampens productivity growth, as the Commission predicts, it will probably reduce the level of real wages in the long term.[79]

The Commission may have proceeded as it did because it realized that, in the past, commissioners who have refused to give top priority to resolving industrial relations problems (i.e., granting increases) have caused an uproar and have never "sat on a Commission Full Bench again."[80] The Commission would also know that a tougher line might well be ignored by unions and thus would call into question the authority of the Commission. Until the mid-1960s arbitration awards typically contained provisions prohibiting strikes during the lifetime of the agreement. These provisions were of mixed effectiveness, and a large backlog of unpaid fines accumulated in the early 1960s. A systematic union campaign against the "penal clauses" led to their becoming disregarded, and they have remained a dead letter since the late 1960s.[81]

Critics of the Commission believe that it "has encouraged unions in the belief that legal sanctions cannot, should not and will not be taken against unions who do not follow the 'rules of the game.' "[82] All observers agree that the Commission's decisions are now binding on employers, but not on employees. The no-strike clauses are "meaningless,"[83] and sometimes other illegal action (physical intimidation, sabotage) goes unpunished as well.[84]

Tribunal awards were supposed to be a substitute for strikes. The figures, however, show that strikes are much more frequent than in most developed countries though they are typically much shorter.[85] One study ranked Australia fifteenth out of twenty developed countries in days lost per thousand employees from 1978 to 1982, and eleventh from 1983 to 1987.[86] However, Keith Whitfield's text on the Australian labor market notes that there is "a wide body of opinion" that a large number of short strikes are more damaging than a small number of long strikes. In support of this position, Whitfield points to a British Royal Commission study which finds that the first pattern undermines management's confidence and willingness to invest, to "growing evidence" that international perceptions of industrial stability are dependent on the number, not the duration, of strikes, and to some evidence that long strikes are more likely to "provoke attitude change" and more harmony in the future.[87]

In Australia strikes are meant "to warn" rather than "to win." They are often well publicized and accompanied by "veiled threats."[88] The intent is often to tell a tribunal "there will be trouble ahead" unless major demands are met. Many times strikes are used to get a tribunal to give the strikers' case a higher priority on the schedule. Like most bureaucracies, tribunal procedures are slow moving, and there is frequently a considerable backlog of specific disputes. Since "many employees use regular strike action as a means of attracting the attention of the industrial tribunals," one recent study by two labor economists concludes that "the federal industrial relations system appears to promote disputation."[89]

Though the frequency of strikes and illegal industrial action is the most dramatic sign of poor industrial relations in Australia, there are other manifestations as well. First, there are a large number of unions (one recent dock strike involved twenty-three) that often squabble among themselves. Since most arbitration awards are by occupation, employers are usually respondents to many separate awards and involved in frequent demarcation disputes about which union's members should do which work. This makes constructive bargaining and reform of the workplace much more difficult. The OECD and others have observed that the arbitration system evolved in parallel with the union structure, and "one of the system's effects may have been to perpetuate fragmentation, both by granting legal recognition to the existing structure and by shielding it from pressures for change."[90]

By most accounts, industrial relations in Australia are unusually bad. The Australian *Business Review Weekly* notes that government, employers, and unions all want to change the arbitration system – a system that the *Weekly* thinks has "abetted an industrial relations environment that has been based on mistrust, even hostility."[91] One study of the twenty-four OECD countries ranks Australia fifteenth on labor flexibility and on employee productivity, seventeenth on worker motivation, and twentieth on absenteeism and on the impact of job turnover on enterprises.[92] Many observers place much of the blame for this situation on the wage-fixing system. Under the tribunal system, industrial relations have been centralized. Instead of talking seriously with each other, business and labor first stage a ritual confrontation and then talk in legal jargon to a less knowledgeable third party who will decide their fates.[93] From labor's point of view, disputes become a no-lose proposition. If the tribunal sides with them, they get more money; if the tribunal does not, they retain their old wages and can always try to negotiate over-awards with employers. Moreover, "awards are *imposed,* not reached through agreement; thus, Australian unionists lack both U.S. unionists' sense of having participated in making the agreement and their sense of moral obligation to live up to its terms. Arbitration and the no-strike clauses are not viewed as *quid pro quos* as they are in the U.S."[94]

From management's point of view, competence in industrial relations is equated with skill in negotiating the rules and procedures of the tribunals. Industrial relations departments in firms are "forced to develop a remedial rather than preventative orientation."[95]

In Australia issues tend to be taken up one at a time – wages, then overtime, and so forth. "Elaborate tradeoffs and comprehensive reevaluation,"[96] common in the United States, are rare in Australia. Management would like an end to demarcation disputes and a more rapid move to multiskilling, so that workers could perform multiple tasks. Management would also like to eliminate work-load and work-rule abuses, which close some plants at noon every day because, with new machinery, decades old piecework quotas have been met easily by then. New younger members of the work force are interested in flexible work hours and quality of work-life issues. All these sorts of issues are nearly impossible to resolve firm by firm at the central level. The tribunals have rarely touched them. But resolution of these issues may require drastic changes in historic pay rates and methods. That pay has become a tribunal function, often out of the effective control of the firm's employers and employees, means that elaborate tradeoffs to resolve the workplace issues are not possible.[97] Moreover, because business and labor have for so long depended on tribunals to find resolutions to their problems, they confront each other almost as strangers, without the history of exchanging information and developing private relationships common in industrial relations systems that emphasize negotiations.[98]

### *Skilled-labor shortages*

As one might expect, in the typical national wage case, business supports low pay increases, and labor supports high increases; the Commission decides for something in between. But recently, reform-oriented business groups such as the Business Council of Australia have come out for an end to wage ceilings. In the council's view, there should be no such thing as a fixed rate for a job. All depends on the company, its market, its efficiency, its location. Companies in need of scarce labor should be able to pay more to get it. Though a 1983 accord between labor and the government has helped restrain inflation and has led to a reduction in real wages by keeping pay hikes small and uniform, it has done so at the expense of putting "wage relativities between skills, occupations, industries and geographically . . . in a straight-jacket for six years."[99]

During my 1989 visit to Australia I frequently heard stories of skilled tradesmen such as auto mechanics deserting their trade to drive taxis and the like. An Australian Economic Planning Advisory Council paper estimates "wastage from the skilled trades" as "running as high as 6–7 per cent per year."[100] Pay compression helps explain this loss of skilled labor.

Overaward payments currently provide only a partial solution to the problem. Unions complain if the overawards do not go to everyone in the company, whether the person works in an occupation with labor scarcity or not. Complaints have sometimes led commissions to order the withdrawal of "inequitable" overawards. The tribunals themselves dislike overawards, and since 1975, they have opposed rather than ignored them.[101] "Blowouts" of salaries for managers, as occurred in the late 1980s, are especially suspect. The Commission and the government fear the flow-on process. If business gets exceptions for their scarcity problems, unions will want exceptions to reflect their industrial strength.

Pretty soon the Commission will seem irrelevant as market forces effectively set more and more pay rates. The Commission will also be faced with workers who argue that they "abided by Commission awards while others did not. Now we want ours."

To prevent such a process, some unions have encouraged the Commission to issue more "paid rate" awards that set a wage that cannot be lowered or raised. Paid-rate awards already apply in the civil service and in oligopolies such as the auto, airlines, oil, and road transport industries.[102]

The effects of paid-rate awards show in extreme form the labor shortage problems that can result from pay compression and inflexible relative wage rates. For years Qantas Airlines, a government-owned enterprise, has had an exemplary air safety record, and for years its mechanics serviced not only their fleet, but those of many other airlines around the world. No more. Qantas recently turned down a chance to bid on a $73 million service contract on all Nipon aircraft. Indeed, it is now shipping its own aircraft to other airlines – United, Air France, Singapore Airlines, and elsewhere – for servicing. The reason is a shortage of skilled aviation maintenance workers. The Australian industry believes that its wages are $100 a week behind the market, that it is short two thousand skilled maintenance workers, and that it is losing more every month. Qantas cannot pay its mechanics a market wage because the Commission will not allow it. They fear a "wages breakout," as does the government. As one newspaper commentator has noted, the root of the problem is an inflexible wage-fixing system:

> Because of its built-in flow-on potential, the system cannot accommodate a growing export industry and the labour scarcities that are always associated with growth without affecting the entire economy.... The inescapable fact in the Qantas instance is that the United States, France, Ireland, The Netherlands and Singapore can do what we can't and the system must take most of the blame.[103]

Australia could choose to pay Australians the high aircraft mechanic wages, thus inducing more Australians to train for these important, high-paying jobs. Instead, their wage-setting system leads them to pay other nationals these high wages, thereby turning a foreign exchange gain into a foreign exchange loss.

A few months before the *Melbourne Age* reported on Qantas's problems, the *Sydney Morning Herald* wrote of problems the government broadcasting company and government banks were having fending off raids on their executives by private-sector competitors. Special contracts were written to keep some key people, but "employees on award payments" and the secretary of the ACTU were complaining about these increases "outside the wage-fixing guidelines." The government had reluctantly approved the lifting of some pay restrictions to bring salaries more in line with the private sector, but had reined in "Telecom's plans to pay market-related salaries to its top 400 senior executives." The government saw itself as "trying to contain a wages time bomb waiting to explode." Its "biggest problem" was the way the new pay packages were "blowing away traditional relativities."[104]

In Minnesota some localities would have liked to have been able to raise nurses' salaries without raising those of equally or higher rated occupations. Comparable worth made selective wage increases nearly impossible, and they settled for a lower wage and an inefficient number and quality of nurses (see Chapter 4, pp. 100–5). In Australia this result occurs often throughout the economy. As in Minnesota, employers there learn to cope as best they can. For example, I was told that Australian government agencies and universities deal with their computer specialist shortages by hiring people with very minimal qualifications, by saying "work when you want," and "take off all school holidays," and by tolerating "consultant blow outs" in their budget. One U.S.-based computer consultant described how frustrating it was to try to help the Australian utility consortium he advised. They lost good computer people constantly. There was no way to reward the good people without promoting them, and one couldn't promote them without promoting their bosses. He had tried every way he could think of to get performance-based pay – even suggesting that it be absorbed in his consultant charges – but to no avail.

## *Productivity, growth, balance of payments, and administrative costs*

Since 1965 growth in labor productivity in Australia has been well below OECD averages, and in the 1980s Australia has had one of the lowest rates in the OECD. The *Economist* notes:

> Automation in Australia's motor industry is only a third as advanced as in Western Europe....
>
> The damage is greatest in the public sector. When the OECD ran its ruler over the performance of public utilities, it found that their output per worker in

Australia was less than half the average of its 24 members. Since nationalized industries account for more than a quarter of the country's non-housing investment (compared with 10 percent in America and Japan), the inefficiency of the public sector washes right through the rest of the economy.[105]

Though real-wage growth has been held down in recent years, inflation and nominal wage growth has been well above OECD averages. As a result, the federal government's Bureau of Industry Economics finds that "over half the [international] competitiveness gained from the massive depreciations of the Australian dollar in the mid-1980's has been lost through wage growth greater than that of our trading partners."[106] Economist Stephen Miller argues that "a more desirable arrangement than excessive nominal wage growth/currency depreciation would be to secure a circuit-breaking fall in the rate of nominal wage increases [through] a move to a more decentralized wage fixing system."[107]

Earlier sections touch on ways that the tribunal system has helped reduce productivity, growth, and international competitiveness, so the connection need not be illustrated here at length. The Commission's own statement quoted earlier (p. 193) clearly acknowledges that its willingness to grant higher than optimum wages reduces economic growth and makes adjustments to external constraints more difficult. The Qantas situation obviously keeps the firm from optimally allocating its labor, aggravates the balance of payments problem, and retards the development of productivity-enhancing labor skills.[108] The work-rule abuses obviously reduce productivity, and by taking the carrot of more pay out of the company's hands, the Commission makes it much more difficult to end these abuses. The Business Council has collected examples like the following: "Demarcation of work between operators and storemen which were unheard of overseas were normal practice in the Australian production plants that we observed, necessitating double handling, extra forklifts, and more time."[109] The Business Council's research leads it to believe that putting individual enterprises in charge of pay and employee relations could lead to increases in labor productivity of about 25 percent.[110]

Reform is made more difficult because there are always businesses – not just union workers – that gain from anticompetitive measures. It makes little sense for wage rates to be the same in Sydney and in South Australia when the housing and land costs differ markedly. But Sydney-based companies are no more interested in making it possible for competitors in the South to use cheaper labor than unions are interested in seeing nonunion competition in the hinterlands.[111] The tribunals feel they must give up the economic benefits of higher growth and lower inflation, unemployment, and foreign debt because of the need to bend to "industrial realities." They would find those realities less ominous if troublesome unions were confronted by nonunion firms that could pay less for the same job and by other firms willing to pay much more when the job no longer included ridiculous work rules. But if all these changes were allowed, people might begin to ask what function the Commission performs.

Finally, the costs of the wage-setting system must include the costs of the very process itself. Historically, an incremental creep occurred in the number of margins for skill or work value "with different levels of margins being awarded for an increasingly minute grading of skill, determined by reference to an enlarging set of criteria."[112] Employees' time and effort were devoted to trying to show that their work value had gone up or had been improperly classified. One printing press operator would try to show that his job was a little different from that of another operator and was thus worthy of a $.50 an hour increase. From 1930 to 1953 the number of "margins" in the engineering awards went from twenty to fifty-three, and the number of classifications from 154 to 330.[113]

The increase in the complexity of the award structures has led through time to increases in the budgetary costs of the commissions. In 1989–90 the operations of the Australian IRC cost over $25 million per year. State commissions, unions, and businesses have substantial additional costs. In the nurses case to be described about a dozen people testified, and the hearings spread over four days. These hearings led to a decision about appropriate "principles" with decisions on the monetary implications still to come.

## THE TRIBUNALS AND THE 1972 EQUAL-VALUE DECISION

For most of this century Australia symbolized not a country where women workers are paid a wage free of discrimination, but rather one that made wage discrimination against women official policy. From 1919 until 1950 the basic wage for women was set at 54 percent of the male rate, thought to be enough to support a single woman. Women, however, could obtain more when they were in competition with men since it was feared that a very low wage might tempt businesses to fire their men, the "real" family breadwinners, and hire women so as to reduce their wage bills.

During World War II, women regularly got more than 54 percent of the male wage, and in 1950 the arbitration commission raised the basic wage for females to 75 percent of the male rate.[114]

The Australian state tribunals began the reversal of discriminatory policy by adopting an equal pay for equal work standard in the late 1950s and 1960s. Later, in 1969, the federal commission adopted a similar policy, but as in the Australian states, equal pay was not provided for work almost always done by females, but occasionally by males. In 1972 various women's organizations went back to the Commission, saying that only 18 percent of women had received equal pay. They argued for an extension of the 1969 principles, and backed by the enthusiastic support of the newly elected Whitlam (Labor) government, the Commission decided on an "equal pay for work of equal value standard." Award rates were henceforth to be considered without regard to the sex of the employee, and the 1969 equal pay for equal work decision was to be applied to all jobs, even those almost always done by females. In 1974 women's groups and the Whitlam government also successfully pressed the Commission to apply the minimum wage to all adults, not just to males.[115]

The combination of these changes had a dramatic effect in closing the wage gap. From 1971 to 1977 the ratio of female to male weekly award rates rose from 75 percent to 93 percent, and the ratio of actual weekly earnings went from 61 percent to 79 percent.[116] I asked a number of knowledgeable people which policy changes were most significant in explaining these gains. The answer remains unclear, in part because much of the equal-pay implementation was decentralized, with the Commission consenting to what employers and unions agreed to. The most detailed study on this subject is that by Christine Short. She told me that she thought the gains were mainly attributable to the raise in the minimum wage and to the merging of separate male and female rates for jobs where separate rates existed.[117] Other research suggests that comparisons of male- and female-dominated jobs in terms of skill, effort, and the like were not important to the process: "Work value inspections and assessments were rarely conducted" prior to equal-value actions.[118]

Comparable-worth proponents in the United States who refer to the Australian experience usually mention the work of Robert Gregory, a distinguished professor of economics at the Australian National University, and his colleagues on the effect on women's employment of this dramatic increase in women's wages. Proponents say that Gregory finds no negative effect on women's employment, and as Mark Killingsworth has argued, some of Gregory's statements may unintentionally lend themselves to such a misinterpretation.[119] But Gregory, in fact, found that there was a small negative effect on women's employment. A 30 percent increase in women's relative wages led to only a 0.4 percent reduction in female employment relative to male employment. The growth in female employment was reduced by about 1.5 percent, and the female unemployment rate was perhaps 10 percent higher than it would have been had there been no action on women's pay.[120]

Unlike the U.S. equal-pay debate, the Australian literature on the effects of equal pay in Australia frequently cites authors other than Gregory. To be sure, Gregory's work has set the research agenda, but most of the other work has been in some degree critical of his research and conclusions. Gregory's principal antagonist is P. A. McGavin, whose work has grown out of his prize-winning dissertation at the University of Melbourne. McGavin and others make a number of points. First, the unemployment rate for women would have been higher had not the Whitlam government sharply expanded social services spending at the same time that women's wages were going up. Six new ministries were established. Expenditures on education and health "increased massively." Subsidized day care was started. From 1971 to 1975 the percentage of employed persons working for government rose from 22 to 25 percent, and from 1973 to 1977 the number of female hours of full-time employment in "community services" went up by over 27 percent.[121]

The average unemployment figures in the 1970s mask the effect of the wage increases on female unemployment because fairly severe negative effects in the market sector are balanced by this employment growth in community and government services. Between 1973 and 1977 the number of female hours of full-time employment in manufacturing was down by over 16 percent, and in wholesale and retail employment it was down by about 10 percent. McGavin notes that women employed in these areas are generally poorer than women in public or community service employment. He wonders why an egalitarian wage policy should be considered truly egalitarian if it has the practical effect of "depriving those who may be in greatest need from access to wage employment."[122]

Second, Gregory's study tested for the *number* of women employed before and after the wage increases. If instead one looks at the *hours* worked by female workers, the negative effect of the wage increase on women's employment is more substantial. Full-time labor force participation of married women in Australia peaked in 1974 and since has declined. There was, however, a 44 percent increase in part-time employment from 1973 to 1977. This sort of shift does not appear in the United States. It may reflect labor rationing by employers facing a higher wage for female labor and a consequent weakening of employment opportunities for women.[123]

Third, there is good reason to think that unemployment rates in Australia seriously underestimate the number of women who would like to work at the going wage, but cannot find jobs. In his own research, Gregory finds that there are "a large number of females outside the labor force" who "want to work at the going wage." For married women, only 70 percent of those looking for work are in the official labor force. For men the figure is 90 percent. The reason is apparently connected to the Australian unemployment compensation system. Because of an income test, unemployed women whose spouses are fully employed are effectively denied unemployment benefits.[124] Thus, many do not bother looking for work if jobs are not available, and they are not counted as being in the labor force and unemployed.

Responding to McGavin during an interview, Gregory pointed to matters that he thought McGavin underemphasized. First, in 1973 the Whitlam government cut tariffs by 25 percent. Gregory thinks this tariff reduction, together with an appreciation of the Australian dollar, is more important in explaining the rise in unemployment of women in manufacturing than are equal-pay measures. Moreover, even in the private sector, he thought the negative effect on unemployment and employment growth from a large 30 percent pay increase was remarkably small.[125]

Proponents of comparable worth frequently take Gregory's research to show that implementation of comparable worth will not harm the economy. But his research will not bear such an interpretation. He has found that there was only a modest increase in the unemployment rate of women *as compared to that of men* resulting from the equal-pay price hikes. Nevertheless, as Gregory realizes, when labor costs rise, prices rise and demand falls; thus, more unemployment may result, not just for women alone, but for women and men together.[126] Other research suggests that the largest effect of comparable worth on women's employment would be through its effect on *total* employment, not through the *differential* effect on women alone.[127]

As already argued, there is reason to believe that government policies that seek to compress wages lead to more unemployment and lower growth. The equal-pay policies compressed wages. The equal-pay policies also raised wage costs and thus prices directly. From 1963 to 1973 the Australian economy grew at an annual rate of 5.1 percent. The inflation rate was only 3.8 percent; and unemployment, 1.7 percent. From 1973 to 1978 the growth rate was 2.5 percent; inflation, 13.2 percent; and unemployment, 3.6 percent.[128] Caves and Krause note that "Australia's economy was not alone in performing less well during this [latter] period" but also note that "Australians found very little comfort in this because their country has been a net energy exporter and, therefore, the oil price disruptions of the 1970s should have been less damaging to it."[129] The large equal-pay increases were among the factors that led to the poorer performance in the mid-1970s. The Whitlam government itself later reversed its policy of stimulating wage growth because of the effect it saw it was having on unemployment.[130]

## DOES AUSTRALIA HAVE COMPARABLE WORTH?

As indicated at the start of the chapter, most comparable-worth proponents in the United States use Australia as the principal foreign example of the successful implementation of comparable worth. They ask that we follow in the footsteps of the leaders from down under. However, one of the leading texts on the Australian labor market says that comparable worth "has been of considerable importance in the United States but has not yet obtained a mainstream position in Australian wage fixation."[131] Similarly, an Australian Women's Bureau publication says comparable worth was developed overseas and points in particular to U.S. examples that might be useful in the Australian environment.[132]

I asked a number of Australians whether they thought Australia had the functional equivalent of comparable worth. Bob Gregory thought so. J. E. Isaac agreed, as did a unionist with a special interest in women's issues. But Christine Short said no, Australia did not have comparable worth or its equivalent. The noneconomist equal-value proponents I spoke with agreed with Short.

Gregory and others who say that Australia has instituted the equivalent of comparable worth look to aggregate results. Seeing comparable worth as substantial, government-supported pay increases for predominantly female jobs, they think that Australia has achieved comparable worth. They have no great confidence in the job evaluation techniques that supposedly get the job done with more precision elsewhere. Moreover,

Gregory believes that the comparable-worth route to higher female pay is pretty much exhausted in Australia. According to him, no further major gains can be expected because most of what remains of the wage gap does not reflect discrimination. Future gains will have to come through women getting more education and experience and moving into different jobs.

Short believes Australia does not have real comparable worth, and she strongly supports full implementation of the concept. However, she agrees with Gregory that most of the remaining wage gap is not a result of marketplace discrimination, and she would not expect full implementation of comparable worth to have much of an effect on the wage gap.[133]

Noneconomist proponents, on the other hand, told me that implementation of comparable worth could make a major difference for female pay. Several, aware of Gregory's prominence overseas, went out of their way to put him down. Two equal-value proponents in Australia even described Gregory, a professed supporter, as "an opponent of comparable worth." Although she made no reference to Gregory, Joan Ross, at the time assistant director of the Women's Bureau in the Department of Employment, Education, and Training, seemed to speak for the noneconomist proponents when she said that even though the Australian female–male pay ratio may lead the world, "women's wages will [remain] on the agenda until women have the same take-home pay as men."[134] Still another proponent insisted that there was far more than "equal opportunity" yet to do in Australia. Women's jobs were undervalued pretty much across the board. Even a 100 percent female–male pay ratio for full-time workers would not end the problem because the amount of part-time work by women itself reflected underutilization and undervaluation of women's labor. These comparable-worth supporters note that, in fact, even the full-time female–male ratio stood at only 79 percent in 1987, the same ratio that existed in 1977.[135]

As previously explained, the work-value concept in Australia has been frequently distorted in its application because of industrial pressures or fears of flow-on-stimulated inflation if historic relative wages were changed. The comparable-worth supporters in Australia who see no sign of its implementation in their country point to a similar lack of any principled application of equal value in the period after the 1972 decision. Christine Short's detailed investigation concludes that there has been "a notable absence of any work value assessments by the Commission." In only two cases were inspections made by Commission officers, and these did not involve broad comparisons in terms of skill, working conditions, and the like, but rather a simple search for similarity of work content between male and female classifications. Short concludes that although the 1969 decision brought equal pay for the same job and the 1972 decision brought equal pay for similar work, Australia has not addressed the issue of assuring equal pay for dissimilar work that is of equal value.[136] Clare Burton has noted that the fault lies in part with the 1972 ruling itself. The emphasis was on finding comparisons with other female classifications, and it "was also stated that preexisting award relativities may be a relevant factor."[137] The National Pay Equity Coalition concludes that "there has been no attempt to re-assess (or assess for that matter) the value of traditionally female work in relation to the work traditionally performed by males."[138]

In a series of cases throughout the 1980s the ACTU and various women's groups have sought to get the Commission to bring to Australia what they see as real comparable worth. The ACTU believes that an employee's earnings should be based on the "knowledge, skill, effort, responsibility and so on" that the work requires.[139] The National Pay Equity Coalition further emphasizes that the inequities cannot be remedied unless "attention is drawn to the previously unacknowledged job demands [in women's positions] or the fact of their under-valuation."[140] In its submission to the Commission this statement of the coalition is preceded by a series of examples (e.g., responsibility for people, not machines; lifting heavy patients, not heavy objects) meant to highlight the bias in traditional work value/job evaluation. Indeed, the author of the coalition's statement has written a whole book cataloging such bias. The book draws heavily on the U.S. and U.K. literature critically reviewed earlier in the Minnesota and United Kingdom chapters.[141]

The Commission has rejected all pleas that it adopt U.S.-style comparable worth or an expanded understanding of equal value. In 1986 the Commission did determine that nurses had never gotten the post-1972 raise due them. But it insisted that this situation represented "a special and isolated" case.[142] The decision was preceded by strikes of nurses and by subsequent increases granted by state commissions. The state commissions had defended their increases by noting changes in the nature of nursing through time and a nurse shortage as well as by noting equal-value considerations. The federal commission gave a similar smorgasbord of reasons in support of its decision. Thus, the nurses' cases are seen as giving little encouragement to women in other occupations.[143]

Despite the pay increase, the federal nurses' case was especially disappointing to comparable-worth supporters because the federal commission so emphatically rejected the concept. In one amusing section of the decision, its authors noted a definition of comparable worth from a U.S. case that centered on the jobs' being of equal value to the employer. The Commission therefore rejected the position of the women's groups, which was that the 1972 decision proclaiming equal value in effect proclaimed comparable worth. The equal-value decision could not possibly have intended to establish comparable worth, said the Commission, since the 1972 decision explicitly declared that equal value meant value *not* to the employer, but in terms of "award wage or salary fixation." Thus, the Commission's obfuscating language from an earlier decade proved serviceable in allowing them to avoid still another sticky situation in 1986.

The Commission saw that comparable worth could be applied to any classification, male or female,

> with no requirement that the work performed is related or similar. . . . Such an approach would strike at the heart of long accepted methods of wage fixation in this country and would be particularly destructive of the present [restraining] Wage Fixing Principles.[144]

Christine Short has argued that when the pay raise was awarded by the Victorian Commission, first-year nurses were excluded because the Commission feared that granting them a raise would lead to flow-ons. This fear arose because first-year nurses' wages had often been used as benchmarks by other, less skilled hospital employees.[145] But such a distortion of work-value/equal-value results to avoid a problem would not be proof of discrimination. As already argued, a principled application of work value is rare whether the occupation in question is male or female dominated.

The women's groups continue to make their submissions, arguing that the wage-fixing system systematically devalues women's work. With pay discrimination in mind they have called for a "work skills value enquiry to review all aspects of skill evaluation."[146] The Commission firmly rejected this proposal in April of 1991.[147] With the Labor government's support, the Commission has determined that it will not consider claims that the 1972 Equal Pay Principle was improperly applied. Only claims that adjustments were never made at all will be considered.[148] Moreover, the government and the Commission have insisted that all claims be processed as anomalies, not as "straightforward matters of work value."[149] For anomalies the "overriding concept" is that it be an isolated situation that will not lead to general increases in pay.[150]

## REFORMING WAGE FIXATION

Dissatisfaction with wage fixation continues to be at the center of Australian public discussion. In the mid-1980s there were five inquiries into industrial relations in one two-year period.[151] As of the early 1990s every significant party and interest group was calling for broad reform.[152] In 1991–2 the Labor government and the union movement led a successful campaign for extraordinary changes in the Australian wage-fixation system, and the process set under way seems likely to lead to the end of mandatory arbitration and centralized wage setting in the near future.

Facing the severe economic problems already cataloged, the governing Australian Labor party (ALP) has been supporting some fundamental economic changes since 1987. Economists and other observers credit the party for resisting calls for more protection and instead cutting tariffs and moving "to internationalize the economy and require global standards to test local performance."[153]

As balance of payments problems continued, however, it became clear to most parties including the ALP and the ACTU that Australian business could not compete in a tariff-free environment without fundamental changes in its historic wage-fixation system. Although initially opposing moves to firm-level bargaining, the ALP, with strong ACTU support, became supporters of the concept by 1991. The IRC refused to sanction the concept in an April 1991 national wage case, but under extraordinary pressure from business, labor, and the government, it reversed itself in October of that year. In 1992 the Parliament passed ALP-introduced legislation meant to weaken the IRC's ability to disapprove enterprise-level agreements by applying its historic "public interest" test.

Although ACTU leadership has supported enterprise bargaining, individual unions have derailed some deals reached by management and employees.[154] And the ACTU's support for enterprise bargaining has not meant abandonment of its historic support for a centralized system. Together with the Labor government and now the IRC the union movement sees workplace bargaining occurring on top of the centralized foundation that establishes award rates of pay and standards for employment such as for overtime and leave.

All parties to the debate over industrial relations have emphasized the need to "restructure" and increase productivity. The ACTU's principal contribution to this debate has been a proposed "blueprint" or "national framework" determining relative-skill values (and thus pay differentials) across all industries and occupations. The hope is that fixing new and appropriate relativities will encourage skill formation and eliminate inflationary leapfrogging.[155]

The union plan would deal with the productivity problem by having the blueprint incorporate a career/skills ladder. Higher pay for higher skills would encourage the acquisition of skills. The ACTU believes that equivalent levels of skill should be paid equivalently. If one job requires two years of full-time training, it should be paid at the level of other jobs requiring two years of full-time training. The IRC has accepted "in principle" the ACTU blueprint.

The opposition Liberal party and the business community would move even more quickly and more radically than the ALP and ACTU to a decentralized firm-centered industrial relations system. Productivity bargaining at the enterprise level and performance pay comprise the major part of their agenda. The Liberal party and business want enterprise bargaining to be an alternative to the existing award system rather than a marginal add-on.[156] Business cites poll data showing that a majority of Australians now want terms and conditions of work set at the enterprise level and that three-quarters would link pay and performance.[157]

The Liberal party, business, and some independent observers think the ACTU's proposed national skills framework would replace one set of rigidities with another. Since the economy cannot be frozen in time, this new version of comparative wage justice (CWJ) would have the same problems as the old. Scarcities through time would emerge regardless of "top down" commands. Wages would then inevitably break out somewhere and be transmitted elsewhere in accordance with the blueprint.[158]

Critics argue that higher wages must be allowed to encourage people to obtain two years of training where trained workers are scarce, just as lower wages must be allowed to discourage people from beginning training where labor is in surplus. They also fear the pernicious effect of credentialism, "a bureaucratic approach to skilling." In a world where new technologies, products, and forms of work organization constantly appear, only individual enterprises can know what skills will help most. Often no formal courses cover the relevant training. "Rewarding 'qualifications' will skew skill-acquisition away from the informal learning of many relevant, often cutting edge, skills towards the accumulation of 'certificates' whose skill-content may be irrelevant and antiquated for the actual work being done."[159] Critics also note that the ACTU continues to emphasize lifting the wages of those at the bottom, a policy that accentuates the pay-compression problem and one that is hardly designed to encourage the acquisition of skills.

Among women's groups and other advocates of higher women's pay there is enthusiasm for the ACTU's national skills blueprint approach to restructuring. And women have gained from some restructuring awards. A September 1990 IRC decision gave some classifications of day-care workers pay increases ("minimum rates adjustments") over 20 percent as part of the restructuring initiative. Eight levels of qualifications and payment rates were established instead of the previous three. The day-care workers were compared with metal trades' workers not in terms of skill, responsibility, and the like, but in terms of training.[160] Workers in another female-dominated industry group – textiles, clothing, footwear – have obtained smaller (0.6 to 11.1 percent) increases under the minimum-rates adjustment process.[161]

Though women's groups have enthusiastically supported national award restructuring, they have been very concerned about the move toward enterprise-level, decentralized bargaining.[162] Women's groups find firm-level productivity bargaining harmful because the women in most predominantly female jobs have lacked the power to gain overstaffing and undemanding work rules in the first place and thus have little to trade for productivity gains. To make up for ground lost due to productivity bargaining, some women's groups have even asked that productivity gains elsewhere be allowed to flow on to them so as not to *upset* traditional "relativities."[163]

Comparable-worth proponents see gains from award restructuring and losses from decentralized enterprise negotiations, but on balance most of those I spoke with were pessimistic about the future. The union movement supports equal pay for equal value in principle, but many women think its main priority is blue-collar males. An academic advocate put it this way: "Women are less likely to be in unions. Women have restrictions on their time, and they participate less in unions than men." As a result, she thought they would always have less influence.

As with the ACTU, the governing Australian Labor party supports higher pay for women, and in 1991 it set up an Equal Pay Unit in the Department of Industrial Relations. But its priorities are clearly elsewhere. The opposition Liberal party coalition led in political polls throughout most of 1992, and it has made labor market reform its principal issue for the 1993 general election.[164] Some economic commentators agree with the Liberal party view that the ALP is too dependent on union political funding to complete the deregulating reforms that it has begun.[165]

The ALP wants to show otherwise. It strongly supports enterprise bargaining, and when still the government's treasurer, the current prime minister, Paul Keating, said "We are irreversibly moving down a path of greater decentralization in wage bargaining and of less official control."[166] But if the centralized awards do become just a base, it will be the accompanying firm-level bargains that truly determine most wages, and women's gains through marginal adjustments of minimums in the national skills framework will mean little. If, as expected, the Liberal party coalition wins the next election, the centralized system will become even less important than it is becoming under the Labor government. In New Zealand a right-of-center government abolished a wage system like Australia's shortly after taking power in 1991.[167]

The trend toward enterprise bargaining in Australia began as early as 1987 for firms using the IRC's productivity bargaining initiative.[168] But the Commission has not really controlled all the decentralizing forces at work. Though it has discouraged overawards, they increased during the 1980s.[169] The Commission has also tried to control part-time and casual (temporary) employment, but both have increased dramatically in recent years. Judith Sloan, the director of the National Institute of Labour Studies, estimates that over 20 percent of the work force is now employed on a part-time or casual basis, up from 12 percent less than a decade ago. Sloan also finds that the "casualisation" of the work force has grown much faster in Australia than in similar OECD countries.[170]

The economic editor of the *Australian* newspaper, Alan Wood, thinks there is good reason to believe that these trends are explained by employers trying to avoid "rigidities imposed on the labour market by the complex and completely inappropriate structure of award wages and union monopoly practices."[171] A survey of 146 Australian companies conducted by the Business Council of Australia, found that, even at a time of double-digit unemployment, businesses planned continued reductions in their full-time work forces.[172] They intended to rely still more extensively on less regulated consultants and contractors and other forms of temporary or part-time labor.

The Australian work force is becoming increasingly divided between a full-time "privileged" group enjoying high wages and good benefits and a peripheral group of the unemployed or temporary workers with low pay and few benefits. Sloan is among those who think these trends undermine "the legitimacy of the centralized wage-fixing system," which was justified as a means of providing "equitable outcomes for all workers."[173]

The trend toward decentralization is not, however, a simple case of business benefiting at the expense of workers. The president of the ACTU, Martin Ferguson, says that both employers and unions seem "fairly satisfied" with results to date.[174] In one firm workers gained a 2.5 percent pay raise for giving up five-minute wash breaks. In another, meat cutters gained a 25 percent increase in their minimum rate of pay after they agreed to work an hour longer each day and change the historic piecework payment system to one based on a constant unit tally rate. In one paint manufacturing company rigid work demarcations that often required the same tasks to be performed in both the plant and the warehouse have been eliminated, and workers are being trained in several jobs rather than one.[175] This sort of productivity-enhancing multiskilling should mean lower costs for consumers and a reduction in the Australian trade deficit as well as higher profits and wages for companies and their workers.

## CONCLUSION

By some relevant criteria Australia seems a poor test case for comparable worth in action. Formal job evaluation is not of much importance. Moreover, the dramatic wage gains that women achieved in the 1970s seem to owe relatively little to a comparable-worth-like process. Most of the gains occurred by insisting (1) that women be paid equally to men for doing the same or very similar work and (2) that all workers, men and women, be paid a higher minimum wage. In the U.S. context the first of these equates to the already prevalent equal pay for equal work standard and the second to the view that people with relatively *low* skills should be paid more, not to the view that women should be paid more because their *high* skills have been undervalued.

But Australia is a better test case than this analysis suggests. Work value was *meant* to be quite like comparable-worth job evaluation.[176] The fact that over time work value became politicized and technical efforts to measure skill, effort, and the like became much less frequent is relevant to those elsewhere who are trying to assess possible long-term outcomes of wage-setting processes that seek to achieve a non-market-determined form of equity. Moreover, the fact that comparable-worth supporters in Australia think that Australian work value undervalued predominantly female job skills is not unlike the situation in Minnesota where advocates continue to complain about the male bias in the various job evaluation systems. Similarly, in Great Britain many equal-value supporters think that job evaluation factors and weightings are unfair to predominantly female jobs. In any case, the earlier chapters on Minnesota show that prominent practitioners think that comparable worth is fundamentally about raising the salaries of women workers, not about applying job evaluation technique. The following chapter will show that some methodological theorists are in complete agreement.

For most U.S. advocates the really important test for comparable worth is the bottom line. Using that standard, many supporters of comparable worth in Australia say equal value will not be achieved until the wage gap has completely disappeared. But in the United States supporters are willing to acknowledge that only a portion of the wage gap results from discrimination. Thus, it is not surprising that, in the United States, Australia, with its nearly 30 percent wage increase for women in the 1970s and its relatively high ratio of female–male wages, is seen as a success story.

Comparable-worth proponents look at the Australian example and see wage gains and a higher female–male wage ratio. But dismal economic performance has accompanied these changes. When the Whitlam-led Labor party ran for office in 1972, it said its first priority was restoring "genuine full employment." Three years later its treasury announced that the number of unemployed had soared to the highest level since the Great Depression. The Whitlam government itself blamed high wages, which it helped encourage, and the squeeze on profits for the unemployment.[177]

The Australian wage-fixing system has been linked to the economic ills facing the nation. This system made possible the much-discussed gains for women workers. When one remembers that the costs of this system include a substantially lower growth rate, the ostensible gains for women workers fade very quickly. Regardless of their better situation relative to male workers, in terms of real purchasing power female workers are paid much less in Australia than in the United States. In 1913 they were paid more. Australia's lower level of economic growth explains the switch.

Though CWJ, work value, and equal value are norms that are often substantively murky in Australian practice, decisions linked to them are like comparable worth in that they interfere with market wages in a massive way. U.S. comparable-worth proponents will want to argue that their version of wage justice is much different from Australia's, and thus the Australian economic costs would not be reproduced in the United States. For example, proponents say that they are willing to make exceptions for shortages and other economic necessities and that their firm-by-firm method of implementation will avoid centralized wage fixation. We should be skeptical of such assurances. In Minnesota the willingness to make market exceptions is already heavily qualified. And what the authorities will in principle allow may not always be practicable. Minnesota's DOER would have readily approved wage increase exceptions for nurses, and perhaps it would have for computer whizzes in Olmstead County as well. But once a city said that its pay plan would be guided by job evaluation results, it knew its employees would wonder why other equally rated people got more when they did not.

In Australia one hears people say that they understand that companies are having retention problems and need to pay aircraft mechanics more. But then they argue for paying the equally valued women more as well: "Why should we pay more to those who take care of our engines than we pay to those who take care of our children?" Will the "flow on" policy always be resisted in the United States once comparable worth gains a toehold? Australian supporters are no doubt right when they say that women's occupations have far fewer long-standing workplace abuses that can be used to bargain for productivity pay increases. And they are not willing to see the "male" occupations get increases that the "female" occupations do not. Although the desire to defend "female" occupations is understandable, the practical result is to make it much harder to get productivity gains in Australian businesses, and this result reduces the well-being of consumers and workers, female as well as male.

One reason to be skeptical of early assurances of flexible application is the eighty-year history of administered wages in Australia. Until the very recent reforms, that history gives evidence of a system becoming more inflexible and more economically irrational over time. For example, in the early years of arbitration, the commissions allowed lower wages in outlying areas with lower costs of living. For reasons of "industrial justice" this policy was abandoned in 1924.[178] Before 1950, but less often thereafter, the tribunals gave weight to a firm or industry's economic capacity to pay. Originally the awards were minimums. Now they are often maximums as well.[179]

The ACTU and women's groups are concerned about "discriminatory" overawards, and there has been some pressure to extend the paid-rate awards so as to make overawards illegal. I found little understanding of or sympathy for the scarcity reason for wage increases among the comparable-worth proponents I spoke with. When I explained the concerns of U.S. comparable-worth critics by referring to the shortages of qualified math teachers when their pay was set equal to that of English teachers, one proponent asked why mathematical jobs are paid more than verbal ones like being an editor of a magazine. The latter was as difficult and important and "more subtle. The problem is with the market not comparable worth."[180]

As for centralization, it is important to remember that the Australian mandatory arbitration system was no more *meant* to be a centralized wage-fixing apparatus than is comparable worth in the United States. As John Niland has noted, "The origins of the conciliation and arbitration system raised little expectation at the time that the tribunal network would become (or should become) integral to national economic policy making. Yet move to centre stage it did."[181] One sees a similar process occurring in the EC and in Britain. Some influential people make arguments like the following: If the fundamental problem is societal discrimination, it should not matter whether there are male employees in the particular firm where a female worker has a grievance. The current firm-centered approach just encourages evasions of the law through contracting out. Cross-firm comparisons or comparisons with hypothetical male employees would make for better policy.

In Britain inconsistent decisions such as those concerning the furniture companies are bound to accumulate. The only way to avoid ridicule and make equal value at least seem rational and consistent will be to have some central authority establish a common cross-firm policy by fiat.

Despite a stagnant female–male wage ratio at a time when the U.S. ratio has been closing rapidly, leaders of women's groups in Australia remain supportive of a centralized mandatory arbitration system.[182] It may be time for them to rethink this loyalty. In my interviews, I was told by proponents that the IRC has little interest in equal value these days. I was told that women would fare poorly in the productivity exercises that the Commission was pushing. I was told that it was hard to change these unfair practices because women were less active in unions and, more importantly, because equal pay was not even a high priority for women compared to child care and other issues. Joan Ross, the assistant director of the Women's Bureau, went so far as to say that the vast majority of women in Australia would say that they already had equal pay. Another advocate told me the Commission responds to whoever shouts the loudest. There is no reason to think that women, most of whom do not even feel they have a grievance, are going to be shouting the loudest.

Comparable-worth supporters in Australia see the male-dominated unions throwing their monopoly power around and commanding large overawards.[183] They see that these same unions have great influence with the Commission. But they argue that at least the Commission helps the less well organized and gives a nod to egalitarianism after the powerful men achieve most of what they want. The supporters do not see that, in the medium to long term, well-placed unionized males would probably suffer most if the Commission ceased to exist. To give one example, men earn much more overtime than women, and because of tribunals' decisions, in Australia overtime rates must be paid for *all* work on weekends. In a more competitive labor environment, this rule would no longer obtain and overtime pay would not contribute as significantly to the wage gap.

If companies are permitted to pay less to the occupations with the powerful unions, some will pay less, and competitive pressures will reduce the workplace abuses in competing firms even without large productivity bonuses. Threatened strikes would count for less if business leaders could say, "You can threaten all you want, but if we don't change work practices and reduce costs, new company X is going to put us all out of a job."[184]

Since the Australian wage-fixing system is a substantial contributor to the country's slow economic growth, Australian women would probably be doing better in terms of real, absolute income if Australia had never had centralized, mandatory wage arbitration. In the future, they might even have more to gain from the market than from arbitration in terms of relative wages. When the market determines wages, it is not who comes and shouts the loudest in internal union meetings or who threatens most convincingly that counts the most, but rather who has skills in short supply.[185] In Australia, some comparable-worth proponents told me that large private-sector overawards for secretaries showed that discrimination in Australia in award wages was still a problem. Ironically, the market was here being used as a standard of fairness for award wages. These proponents thought the answer to the problem was pressure on the Commission to extend the overaward rates throughout the public and private sectors. The real answer might be eliminating the Commission and the paid-rate awards so that secretaries everywhere can benefit from the scarcity in their skills without the obtrusive bureaucracy. The Commission must always worry about historical relativities, and recently that has meant that first-year nurses are held back so that others in occupations in less short supply do not demand flow-on wages.

Australian news articles have noted shortages of both teachers and nurses, and have asserted that, since 1983, 98 percent of the new jobs created were in the service areas. As for the future, over the next decade "the engine of job growth will be in . . . tourism, finance, community and household services."[186] Women are well represented in these areas. Other things being equal this representation suggests relative labor scarcity and higher wages for women if markets have their way. But they will not if the Commission continues to reign. Through the years it has adopted (and abandoned) many principles, but letting markets price labor services has not been one of them.

# 8

# Conclusion

The main source of support for the comparable-worth movement is the reported wage gap, which proponents see as largely the product of sex discrimination. Chapter 2 explained that empirical studies have reached widely varying conclusions on the importance of discrimination as an explanation for the pay gap. Many opponents of comparable worth think that differences between the sexes in human capital and in the importance the sexes attribute to varying job characteristics explain much more about the wage gap and occupational sex segregation than does discrimination. For example, as explained in Chapter 2, on the average, women have stronger preferences than men for jobs with shorter commutes, more flexible scheduling, and good working conditions, and they more often than men work in jobs with these desired characteristics. Such characteristics can be considered a form of nonmonetary income, and their disproportionate availability in predominantly female jobs means that monetary estimates of the wage gap overstate differences in total compensation for work. In any case opponents believe that even substantial marketplace discrimination need not have a significant effect on the wage gap because of competition for labor among nondiscriminatory firms.

For their part, comparable-worth proponents argue that even supposedly nondiscriminatory factors such as human capital or family responsibilities are themselves tinged with discrimination. Some of this discrimination results from societal forces. Families and schools may raise young women to believe that they are odd if they want to work in scientific fields or in dirty, risky, predominantly male jobs or if they want to devote more energy to their careers than to their families. But proponents believe that much of the discrimination is the fault of employers. For example, employers may give men a human capital advantage by favoring them in management training programs or let their male employees harass women who seek to join good-paying, male-dominated trades.

Both sides have telling points to make in the debate over discrimination in the workplace. Thus, if the argument for comparable worth had only to point to discrimination to make its case, it would be relatively untroubled by this book. Comparable worth, however, is but one of a number of methods meant to combat discrimination. Before adopting it, we should ask if it provides a reliable way of spotting and overcoming discrimination and if the costs associated with it are reasonable.

Comparable worth clearly fails both these tests. It cannot pass the first test because it cannot meet the most basic requirement, that is, providing a reliable way of identifying discrimination. As discussed in Chapter 2, publications of the National Academy of Sciences' National Research Council (NRC) note that comparable worth relies on job evaluation to find discrimination and to provide "objective criteria to value the content and requirements of jobs." Similarly, the bills introduced to mandate comparable worth call for objective analysis of jobs, and some proponents argue that job evaluation systems allow one "to determine to what extent persons in female-dominated jobs are unfairly underpaid" (see Chapter 2, pp. 22–30).

The three cases surveyed here, cases central to the proponents' argument for successful comparable-worth implementation, provide no examples anywhere of objective job evaluation. The guide for local government implementation produced by Minnesota's Department of Employee Relations (DOER) says that job evaluation measures duties against objective criteria, but the guide provides no such criteria. Instead, it lists sixty-six possible criteria and tells localities that they can decide themselves what they value most.

Localities that have turned to the top consulting firms for assistance have never gotten objective job evaluation results though they have often obtained bizarre ones. Police lieutenants have been rated higher than police chiefs; utility and library directors have come out ahead of city managers; workers previously paid equally for doing equal work have been assigned unequal pay for their equal work. The workers who have fared best in the comparable-worth process have not gained because of objective measurement of job value according to objectively determined criteria. Not even the consultants think that their methods are objective. There is no agreement on factors to be included, on how they should be weighed, or even on how factors (such as working conditions) should be measured once decided upon. In Minnesota some of the biggest gainers from job evaluation were those who were prepared, who had articulate, forceful representatives on the committees, and who were skillful and assiduous in filling out the questionnaires.

In the United Kingdom, because of their dispute resolution procedure, there is more reliance on industrial relations experts and less on committees. But the job evaluation results are every bit as arbitrary as in Minnesota. One independent expert suggests that successful completion of different job training programs of varying length is enough to find jobs equal in terms of skill and knowledge. Another expert discounts the lifting of extremely heavy furniture, lifting that regularly occurs on the job, because it seems to her abnormal and contrary to health and safety recommendations. Experts given the relatively narrow task of deciding whether female machinists are as valuable as male upholsterers have been unable to agree. In the United Kingdom there is not even agreement about whether the expert is trying to determine the value of the job to the employer or to someone or something else. Though the real problem lies more with the concept of comparable worth than with the U.K. method of trying to achieve it, the experts' judgments have seemed so arbitrary that both observers sympathetic to business and those sympathetic to women employees are now proposing eliminating the independent experts entirely. Neither these close observers nor others in the United Kingdom think that job evaluation is objective.

There is similarly no claim for objectivity among long-time observers of the Australian methods for determining "comparative wage justice" and "work value." "Work-value" exercises, the element in the Australian system closest to job evaluation, have little technical content. Business, labor, comparable-worth proponents – all are united in thinking that these exercises have a minor role in the politicized wage-fixing system and that they are often a device used to mend an industrial dispute or to obscure a caving in to powerful union pressure.

Chapter 2 quoted critics of comparable worth who argue that the a priori job evaluation systems used to implement the concept are subjective and arbitrary. Subsequent chapters confirm the critics' charge in three of the places proponents see as comparable-worth success stories. How then can U.S. proponents believe that job evaluation is objective? This was one of the principal questions on my mind when, toward the end of my research, I went to the tenth anniversary conference of the National

Committee on Pay Equity (NCPE). At the panel on job evaluation I heard no defense of job evaluation's objectivity and no discussion of efforts or techniques to make job evaluation more objective. The panelists, especially the academics who had been deeply involved with implementing systems in New York and Oregon, emphasized that comparable-worth job evaluation was a matter of politics and power, not of technique. Because there is "no standard, operational, accepted system or definition of equity," each study is a new power struggle with the results determined by political interests and power. "This is not social science . . . this is advocacy. . . . You can manipulate these things; you know, tell me the results you want, and we'll go get it, and if you don't think that's the case, I think you're being extremely naive." So said Margaret Hallock of the University of Oregon.[1]

Strongly supporting Hallock was Ronnie Steinberg of Temple University. "Every detail [of job evaluation] is political." The goal must be to "regain control of job evaluation" at every step from constructing the legislation, to hiring the consultant, to designing the questionnaire and job evaluation system, to setting the standards for wage discrimination and the formula for wage adjustments. If you want a 40 percent raise, "don't pick the system before you know what jobs you're going to do, and make sure that system has in it the factor definitions, the factor complexities, and the factor weights that are going to get you that bottom line." You must "know what you want at the end" before you begin.

One female questioner asked if there were not some way to avoid the "grab someone by the short hairs till they give you what you want" approach. She said she had been in these sorts of negotiations, and it was clear to her audience that she had hated them. She wondered if pay equity advocates should look for some other way, if they should want job evaluation to be a political issue. She hoped there was some way to avoid the "get in there and punch them" approach.

This questioner received no encouragement from the panelists or from those who spoke from the audience. Job evaluation was political and had to be seen as such. If pay equity advocates could do better without it, it could be forgotten. But if they used it, they had to get political – mobilizing people to affect the process and refusing to settle for consultants' assurances that their systems were gender neutral. Instead, proponents should get consultants to show how their systems work in practice, the "before and after" salaries.

After the conference I interviewed Heidi Hartmann, one of the principal authors of the seminal *Women, Work and Wages* published by the NRC of the National Academy of Sciences. In a coauthored introduction to a recent collection of articles, also published by the NRC, Hartmann says that comparable worth generally relies on "the use of objective criteria to value the content and requirements of jobs (job evaluation) in a way that eliminates gender as a compensable factor." She also says that "the logic that would lead one to conclude that comparable worth is a wise social policy requires," among other things, that "the jobs can be objectively evaluated."[2] Yet in an interview Hartmann said that she would "love to have wage boards like in Australia" or boards to set occupational wage ratios so that existing job evaluation could be avoided altogether. When asked specifically about current job evaluation systems, Hartmann said they were "basically a pile of crap." None of the suggestions in *Women, Work and Wages* for improving job evaluations by drawing on developments in social science measurement had been undertaken. According to Hartmann, consultants pushed their "witchcraft" and told clients " 'trust me' "; the "more you look" at the systems, "the worse" they look. "Nevertheless, even with a really crummy system, if applied consistently, you do some good."

Hartmann's last comment points to the belief of many proponents that job evaluation almost inevitably finds that predominantly female jobs receive lower pay per point than do predominantly male jobs. Actually I found the reverse to be the case in several Minnesota localities. Moreover, initial studies in at least four states – Hawaii, Vermont, New Jersey, and Maryland – found no inequities. But the comparable-worth proponents who dominate the task forces are not happy with such conclusions, and they often manage to obtain further analyses. Thus, Maryland evaluators who initially found no discrimination changed their mind after unions objected, and they took another look.[3] Similarly, in New Jersey a systematic study found that state employees rated jobs "quite differently," but that there was no tendency for men to rate predominantly male jobs higher than predominantly female jobs or for women to rate predominantly female jobs higher than predominantly male jobs. There was thus no evidence of evaluator bias. Nor did the study find any tendency for "male" jobs to receive higher pay per point (under the long-established Hay system) than "female" jobs received. Women received only about 70 percent as much as men, but their salary per Hay point was not lower.

As one Hay evaluator told me, there were many very strong advocates of pay equity on the New Jersey Task Force on Equitable Compensation, and they got very upset at these conclusions. The job evaluation system was then revised to emphasize "human relations" more as well as "responsibility for people" and some other factors. The modified job evaluation instrument realigned the internal hierarchy of job titles. As the New Jersey final report explains, "The increase in points for titles dominated by females and minorities met the goals of the Task Force to modify compensable factors to achieve pay equity."[4]

The New Jersey task force report makes clearer than most public documents the real goal of comparable worth – not pay according to objective criteria of job evaluation, but rather more pay for women (and occasionally for minorities). This real goal explains why male-dominated foresters paid well beneath the pay/points line did not at first receive salary increases in Minnesota and why there was talk of a technocratic "twisting" of pay equity whenever males benefited from studies done in localities. Indeed, in all three of the areas I studied proponents equate a less biased evaluation system with one that introduces or weighs more highly factors that favor predominantly female jobs.[5] There are never any exceptions. When a cross section of employees in St. Paul, Minnesota, finds that the male-dominated police are underpaid, politics and an out-of-control committee are said to be at work. Though working conditions are historically rated much lower than other factors in most evaluation systems, the equal-value advisers to the U.K. study of local government manual workers – jobs that include refuse collectors and grave diggers – thought it fair for the weighting of working conditions to be reduced still further.

In the United Kingdom equal value is fairly well established legally. There is little talk there of objective job evaluation. The principal commentators say it is subjective. Equal-value champions warn, however, that the very subjectivity makes it easy for bias to be interjected, and they offer their services in the campaign to spot it and stamp it out.

In Australia almost everyone agrees that work-value studies, which began as attempts to assess systematically the value of jobs, have in fact become thoroughly politicized. But equal-value advocates want to make more gains for women, and they believe American-style comparable worth will be more politically palatable if they emphasize that it is different – that comparable worth involves comparing predominantly female and predominantly male occupations "based on an agreed set of objective non-sexist value criteria."[6]

In the United States – in the Congress, in state government explanatory literature, and in widely circulated publications meant to persuade the uncommitted – advocates emphasize the objectivity of comparable worth. But in interviews and among themselves, those in the know emphasize that it is all subjective and political. At the NCPE tenth anniversary conference where Ronnie Steinberg said that "every detail" of job evaluation was "political," she went on to emphasize strongly the need to "act as if [the details] are technical issues, because you're using it [the system] to get pay equity gains."[7] At another panel an advocate explained that calling job evaluation objective and technical makes it "a motherhood issue."

A Washington lobbyist told me that comparable-worth advocates "want to get the politicians on board before they know what it is." Calling job evaluation objective helps in this regard. So too does linking comparable-worth "a priori" job evaluation to the far different market-sensitive and long-established "policy capturing" job evaluation used by business. So too does telling the politicians that everybody does it. Thus, Australians are told that it is time to adopt the technique long established in the United States, and Americans are told it is time we started to imitate Australian successes. Members of the U.S. Congress are also reminded that "the states are doing it, and they're not bankrupt,"[8] and "somehow the State of Minnesota survived it all, and the morale is much higher."[9]

Nina Rothchild and Claudia Wayne both told me that they thought "comparable worth" and "pay equity" were identical,[10] but both know that "comparable worth" is a far more controversial term. Neither is eager to correct the Minnesota representative who could never support comparable worth, but gladly endorses a pay equity bill, or Congresswoman Morella, who in floor debate chastises opponents who criticize comparable worth, saying that "there is a distinct difference between comparable worth and pay equity."[11]

In the effort to make comparable worth seem uncontroversial, the most important publication has been *Women, Work and Wages.* Constantly mentioned here and abroad, this NRC report "vindicated," according to Eleanor Holmes Norton, "the claim that comparable worth was technically feasible."[12] As noted in Chapter 2, the endorsement in *Women, Work and Wages* of job evaluation was heavily qualified, and it opposed making firms install such systems. Still, the report concluded that job evaluation plans "despite their limitations" provide "a systematic method of comparing jobs to determine whether they are fairly compensated."[13]

When I asked some economist opponents of comparable worth about *Women, Work and Wages* and the NRC more generally, I got an earful. Mark Killingsworth, for example, replied:

> The National Research Council is not respected among economists. [People hear National Academy of Sciences, and they] think, "Gosh, that sounds official." People think it's like the National Institutes of Health. [A colleague] says it should be called the "National Academy of Scientology."

Similarly, June O'Neill said the academy gave the issue respectability, but "on social issues it is terrible. It's very biased, more an advocacy group." Of *Women, Work and Wages* she said, it gives an "exceedingly simplistic, superficial accounting of the [sex wage] differential.... Not very many economists would like that report."

Perhaps the principal intellectual force in the writing of *Women, Work and Wages* was the coeditor Heidi Hartmann. Hartmann currently heads a research organization that is an institutional member of and does work for the NCPE. When I asked Hartmann what school of economics she associated with, she responded, "I've always called myself a radical economist influenced [most] by Marx, the institutionalists, feminists." According to Hartmann, the NRC looked for balance on their research oversight committees. She, however, gave an example in which a scholar had been chosen for an important slot because, though generally moderate to conservative, he had proven surprisingly sympathetic to comparable worth in preliminary conversations. She remembered having great difficulty finding economists for the panel that oversaw *Women, Work and Wages*. Ten to twenty calls were made to get one. In the end two economists were on the fourteen-person panel, one whom she described as a "radical" and a second who had told her he would be abroad and would have to miss all the meetings and who, in fact, did miss almost all of them.

I asked Hartmann why she thought so many economists had turned her down: Was it because they thought comparable worth made no sense? She said, "Maybe." They always explained that they were "too busy," but she thought that this response was typical of what people say when they don't want to do something. Killingsworth and O'Neill thought there were so many rejections because the economists believed the final product would have no credibility, and they feared being used. As O'Neill put it, in these studies, "the in-house staff calls the shots."

On the basis of one long interview I found Heidi Hartmann to be an unusually appealing radical economist – smart, open to argument, and humorous. But she is hardly the person one would choose to write a report meant to reflect the authoritative voice of the best social science on the subject of comparable worth. Yet the imprimatur of the National Academy of Sciences gives her report that status with many nonacademics here and abroad.

Despite the efforts of proponents, comparable worth remains controversial in the United States, and in large part it remains so because of the efforts of professional economists. In academia they are far and away the most numerous among the opponents. Even in the political wars, economists lead the fight against comparable worth.[14] Congressmen Phil Gramm in the Senate and Dick Armey in the House are leading opponents, and both are former economics professors. In 1985, as a first-term representative, Armey decided to make comparable worth his number one priority. He got the bill that included a comparable-worth study for federal employees (a bill that had passed the House in the previous Congress by 413 to 6)[15] taken off the suspension of the rules calendar used for uncontroversial bills assured of quick passage. He lobbied the issue on the floor, trying to see a few representatives before every vote on other issues. Armey told me that he tried to explain why he thought comparable worth represented an unprecedented government administration of a price and was dangerous to the very foundation of our democratic, free-enterprise system. He wrote a series of "Dear Colleague" letters about the issue, had the Chamber of Commerce write also, and arranged for various editorials and talk show appearances. The final vote in favor of the measure in 1985 was 259 to 162,[16] with the minority large enough to sustain a veto.

Economists lead the opposition because they believe that comparable worth will have very large economic costs – most importantly, that it will badly distort labor markets. Well-functioning market economies use rising wages to ameliorate shortages of labor in an occupation or at a particular location and use static or falling wages to reduce surpluses by encouraging exit and discouraging entry. Though proponents of comparable worth doubt that labor markets work in this way, the preceding chapters have discussed how they do so, for example, in the market for nurses. These chapters have also shown how, by holding down wages in the face of shortages, comparable worth or other equity-inspired wage-fixing policies have made it difficult, if not impossible, for Minnesota localities to get the nurses and computer specialists they need and for Qantas in Australia to get enough airplane mechanics to service its own planes, much less to service others' planes. Similarly, these chapters have shown how raising wages in the face of surpluses has jeopardized the jobs of home health aides in Minnesota and of cooks in Minnesota and the United Kingdom.

The stakes here are not small. Comparable-worth studies often think the market gets it very wrong indeed. For example, Washington state's study gave nurses higher points than computer systems analysts though the market paid the analysts 56 percent more; clerical supervisors, more points than chemists though the market paid the chemists 41 percent more; retail clerks, higher points than truck drivers though drivers got 30 percent more.[17]

In 1990 the *New York Times* noted:

> Shortages are growing among some [Washington state government] workers both men and women, with special skills like nursing. More and more to recruit and hold onto these people, the state is granting them special pay increases that violate the guidelines of its program, provoking demands from other workers for similar increases.
>
> State personnel officials... have found serious flaws in the way the program ignores private industry wages.... The free market keeps intruding, in some cases to the greater benefit of female employees than the new program.[18]

Similarly, in Iowa there is concern about the comparable-worth study's recommendation that "almost all people employed in data processing or other computer jobs be reclassified into lower pay grades" at a time "when the state can't pay its data processing people enough to compete with private enterprise."[19]

If applied widely in the public and private sectors, the substantial changes in relative wages recommended in many comparable-worth studies seem certain to lead to surpluses and shortages. Since over time changes in salary affect career decisions, these surpluses and shortages are not likely to be temporary. And since pay rates also affect the location where workers seek jobs, there are also going to be geographic inefficiencies in the distribution of what skills we have. A U.S. company desperate to attract more technical skills so as to develop a product before Sony would be at a severe disadvantage in obtaining personnel if it had to jump through the administrative hoops that companies do in Australia or departments do in Olmstead County, Minnesota.

These problems at the micro level – in particular occupations or industries – will affect overall economic performance. If one changes the basis for pricing labor – more than 73 percent of total business costs[20] – one can expect economywide effects to occur. The Organization for Economic Cooperation and Development (OECD) credits more flexible, market sensitive pricing in labor markets for the relatively good performance of the United States on unemployment in the 1980s.[21] And Chapter 7 shows why most economists and other commentators link Australia's poor performance on economic growth, inflation, industrial relations, and international competitiveness to its wage-fixing system.[22]

The OECD has called "the institutional wage-bargaining process" the

> first major element in the way labour markets work. . . . As with any other market, labour markets need to cope with changes in supply and demand if scarce human resources are to be used as efficiently as possible. If institutional arrangements impede such flexibility, then real incomes can suffer. In particular, higher wages where labour is more productively employed can encourage a more efficient allocation of labour.[23]

The bitter divisions in the comparable-worth debate are in part explainable by differences about a fundamental issue that is never explicitly addressed. By and large, proponents and opponents have a very different understanding of the sources of real income growth for ordinary people. In my interviews, some of the most revealing answers were those to the open-ended question "What factors do you think are most important in explaining why people get paid what they do in this country?" Comparable-worth opponents gave answers such as "supply and demand," "productivity," "skills," "education," "experience," and "working conditions." Among the proponents, those who were also economists often first said "education" and "experience," but then went on to mention characteristics that they saw as signs of relative power, that is, unionization, sex, and race. The proponents who were not economists emphasized power relationships almost exclusively. For example, Claudia Wayne, then executive director of the NCPE, said pay depended mostly on power: "The least powerful are paid the least."[24] Minnesota's Nina Rothchild said pay is "directly proportional to the power wielded in society." Men get more than women, whites more than blacks, union members more than nonunion workers. The more power you have, the more money you have, and the more money you have, the more power you have.[25]

For proponents the route to economic progress for ordinary people is through political action and union muscle. In her keynote speech to the

NCPE tenth anniversary conference Eleanor Holmes Norton emphasized the importance of past legislative successes like the minimum wage and antidiscrimination laws. She then said that "union actions more than any other factor have raised the standard of living in the United States. Never forget how it occurred. Unionization compelled equity. [Unions] forced a bigger share of profits to workers in their industries."[26]

In the plenary session speech that succeeded Norton's, Heidi Hartmann emphasized the importance of Karl Marx's thought, especially his emphasis on class conflict and his belief that workers are coerced to sell their labor power. Like Norton, she thought that worker organization was the most important secret to achieving pay equity.[27] In my interviews a number of other proponents echoed the view that it is laws, "threats," and "organized pressure" that lead to better paid jobs, not "the goodness of employers."

This tough, power-centered view of the world is often mixed with an extremely optimistic non-Marxian view that there need be no significant losers from comparable worth. Most proponents get very upset at any suggestion that it may be necessary to cut or freeze the wages in male-dominated occupations in order to give wage increases to the female-dominated ones. Some oppose cuts and freezes for male-dominated occupations because they realize that such explicit actions would slow the comparable-worth political movement by stimulating male opposition. But many seem to think as well that it should be possible to give female workers more real income without taking it from male workers.

Where is the money to come from? Business profits. Eleanor Holmes Norton told the NCPE tenth anniversary conference that "the surplus income created when women are paid less than they're worth goes to profits, not to the American family."[28] NCPE already knew this, though. One of its slogans in organizing campaigns is "When an employer pays 65 cents for a dollar's worth of work, that employer pockets 35 cents."[29] When I asked Claudia Wayne who gets the dollars that underpaid women don't get, she said, it goes to "profits" since business "won't pay the male workers any more than they need to."[30]

The economists among the proponents jump ship at this point. Heidi Hartmann guesses the money not going to discriminatorily underpaid women probably goes to "favored male workers" and "businesses," and supposes that "some lower prices for consumers are possible here because of cheaper labor."[31] Barbara Bergmann notes that *pre*-tax profits and proprietors' incomes represent only 11 percent of total national income and states that it is unrealistic to expect to get a large part of pay equity adjustment money out of profits. Inevitably, men will have to make do with lower real salaries.[32] If these economists have made any efforts to explain to other proponents that the latter's vision of nearly costless change is impossible, they have so far been largely unpersuasive.

Still, even the economists among the proponents, like Heidi Hartmann, have a profoundly different view of the sources of economic progress than do the vast majority of economists and the critics of comparable worth for whom the economists so often speak. Mainstream economists believe that most gains in real wages come from economic growth, which is far more important for the economic well-being of ordinary people than unionization or political reform. As the liberal economist Alfred Kahn has said, without growth

> liberalism could never have achieved its victories. (The improvement since the 1930s in the material welfare of President Roosevelt's "one third of a nation" has been made possible far, far more by the material progress enjoyed by all three thirds than by the modest redistribution from the top two.)[33]

Though not all of the causes of high productivity growth rates (GNP per employee) are well understood, there is agreement that a crucial element is investment that leads to capital formation. When workers work with better equipment and machinery, they become more productive. Competition in the labor market then causes their real incomes to rise. Investment requires saving, and Americans are near the rear in the developed world in terms of their personal savings rate.[34] Most corporate investment is thus dependent on retained earnings, that is, profits. Since profits are important to investment, which is important to real wage growth, most economists and comparable-worth critics have a much more benign view of profits than do proponents. Indeed, a 1977 report to the OECD by a prominent group of international economists concluded that if investment in the developed world remained low, it might be necessary to reach broad societal consensus on the need for higher profits.[35]

Just as profits enjoy a much better reputation with critics than proponents, so unions suffer from a worse one. Many economists believe that our relative success in reducing both unemployment and inflation during the 1980s stems from "the continued decline in the importance and power of labor unions." Previous U.S. recoveries were cut short by unions negotiating large wage increases and thus stimulating cost-induced inflation.[36] Though unions are seen as helpful to their members, most economists think their gains are made "at the expense of non unionized workers, and not at the expense of earnings on capital."[37] Herbert Stein notes:

> The proportion of nonfarm employees enrolled in unions peaked at about 30 percent in 1955 and has declined since to about 20 percent. . . . During the period of declining unionism, the labor share of the national income increased from 67 percent to 74 percent. This suggests that unions were not essential to improving the condition of labor.[38]

The typical proponents' understanding of both labor markets and the sources of economic progress drastically differs from that of the vast majority of economists. Moreover, the economists I interviewed, both proponents and opponents, agreed that the vast majority of economists would oppose comparable worth. Heidi Hartmann guessed that two-thirds or more of economists would oppose comparable worth. Opponents Randy Filer and June O'Neill thought it would be more like 80–90 percent with most of the remainder unsure rather than supportive.[39] Since it is the business of economists to understand how economies work, the opposition of economists should make one pause before embarking on a brand-new method of pricing labor.

Readers might hear a conservative note in mainstream economists' arguments for economic growth as a means of improving the wages of the ordinary worker rather than for unions or for comparable worth. But a recent poll of academic economists found that 63 percent considered themselves liberal, 20 percent conservative, with the rest middle of the road.[40] Moreover, many of the economists who oppose comparable worth are liberal politically – people like Henry Aaron, Mark Killingsworth, and Victor Fuchs. Aaron is not an all-out opponent since he sees some role for the use of job evaluation studies in court cases on discrimination. But he asks Congress and the courts to avoid neat rules on when comparable worth should be employed, and in court cases where jobs are dissimilar, he would require evidence of discriminatory intent as well as disparate pay before finding for plaintiffs.[41]

As Heidi Hartmann ruefully told me, "I am responsible for Killingsworth." He had a reputation for open-mindedness and had testified for plaintiffs and defendants in discrimination suits in the past. When she asked him to do an NRC paper, she had not expected him to be so opposed to comparable worth. Killingsworth, like Aaron, thinks there is plenty of sex discrimination in the marketplace. He sides with proponents on the discrimination/pay gap issue, but thinks the comparable-worth remedy completely misunderstands labor markets: "Comparable worth does not recommend itself to liberals. Comparable worth is for silly people, not liberal people." Besides the standard economic arguments just listed, Killingsworth adds another: Why arbitrarily "hand out" dollars not needed to attract labor when the money could be "spent on school construction or research for AIDS"?[42]

Victor Fuchs is enormously sympathetic to the contemporary working woman's aspirations. He believes that historically women have been disadvantaged in many ways and that society does put a lower value on women's work. But he thinks that any comprehensive comparable-worth policy

> would seriously jeopardize the market system which is a key element in our material prosperity and our political and social freedoms. At a time when socialist countries such as the Soviet Union and the People's Republic of China are finding it necessary to use markets and market-determined prices to allocate resources, it is alarming that some Americans would seriously urge a major shift in the opposite direction.[43]

For alternative solutions, people like Killingsworth and Aaron recommend more of "the old time religion" – better enforcement of antidiscrimination laws pertaining to hiring and promotion, and in Aaron's case, affirmative action as well.[44] The more conservative Randall Filer also supports the equal-access solution. Filer told me that he thinks that women freely choose predominantly female jobs, whereas Heidi Hartmann thinks they are forced into them. If Hartmann is right, and we go the comparable-worth route, there may be no problem, but if he is right, there will be serious distortions. "Equal access is clearly the better policy." If he is right, the outcome is benign, and if she is right, women will move out of traditionally female occupations, and the result will also be benign.[45]

When I mentioned this argument to an economist proponent, Elaine Sorenson, she said that the equal-access and affirmative action policies had not been very successful since there is about as much occupational segregation by sex now as there used to be. For "young educated women [there has been] a little improvement," but generally things "haven't improved [on occupational segregation] though so much else has." Equal access and affirmative action have not remedied occupational segregation, so there have been insufficient improvements in pay for women's occupations.[46]

But expecting a rapid breakdown of occupational segregation simply assumes what is at issue, that the existing female job selections are mainly the result of discrimination, not free choice. If they are the latter, an end to job segregation is not an appropriate indicator of success.

Noneconomists sometimes link the equal-access solution to what Nina Rothchild calls the "ostrich" proposition:

> Women should switch jobs if they want more pay. The "let them be plumbers" argument, however, overlooks the national statistics showing about 20 million workers would have to switch jobs to equalize wages.
>
> It's preposterous to think 10 million men will voluntarily retrain for women's jobs to earn less.[47]

This argument reveals a serious misunderstanding of how markets work. If women begin to enter the predominantly male occupations, the men there will begin to earn less even if none of them switch to female-dominated jobs. Wages in the male-dominated jobs will decline as the supply of labor increases (just as the wage premium for education has decreased as the number of those educated has increased).[48] In turn, the wages in predominantly female occupations will increase as fewer women enter them, some switch out, and others retire. This reduction in supply leading to a higher wage will benefit all women in the predominantly female occupations, even those who entered their occupations decades before. If equality of wages were viewed as an appropriate policy, it could be achieved via changes in supply and demand if only a fraction of the "10 million" in female-dominated occupations left them for male-dominated occupations.

Many noneconomist proponents dismiss their economist critics as "theorists" who do not understand how the real world of economics works. And as for profits and unions, some would insist that the comparable-worth movement takes no explicit position on profits or unionization. Most proponents would no doubt say that they are all in favor of profits that are not the product of discrimination, and that equitable pay practices, not unionization of the work force, is the goal. Certainly proponents will want to resist any linkage of their plans to poor economic performance elsewhere. They say their system will be flexible. But the evidence in earlier chapters suggests that it will not be. It surely will not countenance paying equally rated female-dominated occupations less because there is a surplus of labor in them.[49] The comparable-worth wage gains for librarians, cooks, and home health aides (but perhaps not the foresters) must be implemented even though the higher pay will mean more unemployment. Though economists might argue about the magnitude of the increase in unemployment, they would see some increase as almost certain.[50]

The advertised flexibility for shortages is even now insufficient to help many Minnesota localities. Earlier chapters relate how the counties "constantly" complain to the Association of Minnesota Counties that comparable worth makes it impossible for them to respond to the market, and that they frequently ask their consultants how they can get their technical people off the line and out of the system. Once the localities have an official job evaluation plan that purports to establish the value of all their jobs, they find that they must either ignore shortages and pay equally rated personnel the same or risk legal suits and bad employee morale.

If the localities did ask more often for exceptions for shortages, they would be likely to encounter great skepticism among comparable-worth proponents. In Minnesota it is made clear that the exception for shortages must be temporary, well documented, and avoid any discriminatory impact on women. In the United Kingdom, where the equal-value policy is more firmly established, the proponents argue for a still tougher line on exceptions for shortages (see Chapter 6, pp. 175–6). In Australia, until an economic crisis brought recent reforms, the system became less flexible through time, and legitimate fears of wage "blowouts" throughout the economy made it extremely difficult to raise pay to meet even severe labor shortages.

The Canadian Human Rights Commission says the "onus is on [the employer] to show that . . . they have done everything they could for a certain period of time to attract people to these jobs and there was nobody available in the market at the rate of pay they were paying."[51] This formulation suggests that, if anyone, even someone with a poor work history, comes through the door and can make some claim to being a computer systems analyst, the firm cannot offer more to try to attract a more skilled analyst.

Real flexibility for shortages is to be expected only if administrators realize that supply and demand, and thus appropriate wages to eliminate scarcity, change frequently and that some businesses have a legitimate need for above-average systems analysts at above-average analyst pay because they are especially important to the survival of their companies. But administrators who really understand how supply and demand work and how firms' needs differ are almost surely going to be skeptical about comparable worth. They will not want to oversee comparable-worth policy, and if they are asked to do it, proponents will complain about those who are too sympathetic to employers being put in charge of keeping tabs on them – the fox guarding the chicken coop. Proponents will understandably want people who believe in comparable worth to administer it. As argued, such believers think either that supply and demand have little effect on wage rates or that wages resulting from the intersection of supply and demand are exploitative. They are unlikely to understand the need for frequent market pressure exceptions to established policy.

Proponents clearly think that critics exaggerate market distortion problems, but this may be because even the most sophisticated of proponents do not seem to fully understand the economics that motivates the critics. For example, during debate before the Civil Rights Commission, Paula England criticized a comparable-worth opponent who said that women were paid less in part because they wanted to be near the phone. She thought that setting wages lower because the employees were women attracted to a phone-based job was discrimination. The women's loyalties to their families should be irrelevant as should their choosing the job freely. The only issue should be skills and contributions to the employer.[52]

But easy access to a phone, air-conditioning, and some other characteristics of office work are going to be attractive to many employees, and other factors being equal, jobs with these benefits are likely to have more applicants than similarly skilled and contributing jobs that do not have them. If comparable worth means employers cannot take account of such factors when setting wages, it means they cannot take account of supply and demand or surpluses and shortages. In that case, comparable worth is likely to disrupt labor markets and cause important inefficiencies.

To be sure, comparable worth in practice will not be as inefficient as it might be because there are lots of ways to evade the intent of the laws without technically violating them. In Minnesota some localities hire a male cook or two to turn an underpaid female-dominated job into a balanced one. To secretaries paid above-market rates, Olmstead County gives new nonsecretarial duties, and to computer systems programmers paid below-market rates it gives either extra time off or a new senior programmer title together with higher pay. Other localities fish for a job evaluation scheme that gives results close to market outcomes, and they change job duties and thus pay if they are unhappy with the results. As Nina Rothchild herself told me, it's "so easy to play games" with the evaluations. Private firms concerned with profits will be forced by competition to search for "friendly" job evaluation schemes. In the United Kingdom firms increasingly adopt such schemes to head off appeals to the industrial tribunals with their "independent experts."

In all three jurisdictions studied there is resort to contracting out as a way of evading the law. In a world of pervasive comparable worth and widespread contracting out one should expect to see an increase in sex-segregated firms to go with the existing sex-segregated occupations. Predominantly male, specialized firms will supply businesses alert to comparable-worth costs with computer, trucking, or engineering services, while largely female firms provide secretaries, cooks, and child-care workers.

Some of these responses, as in Olmstead County, will not result from intentional evasion of the law. They will just represent attempts to get jobs done in bad circumstances. Much of the evasive activity, however, will be conscious and intentional. Legal but deliberately evasive activity will infuriate comparable-worth proponents, who, as in the United Kingdom and Australia, will be disappointed with results and convinced that their hopes for comparable worth will be realized once the loopholes are closed. The following proposals have already come from the leading U.K. experts: Ensure that employers who have shown the need to pay more to overcome shortages have also shown that they have to pay the *particular amount* more that they propose; abandon value to the employer as our standard or at least interpret employers' needs to include the needs of underpaid women; try to deal with the contracting out problem by allowing cross-firm comparisons or comparisons with hypothetical male employees.

Given the indefensible variation in independent experts' decisions on criteria and on results for equivalent cases, the push for common, more centralized standards will be nearly irresistible. But even agreement on criteria and weighting will not yield consistency because, as in the British furniture cases, the experts will disagree about how to measure factors like responsibility and effort. More concern and more well-meaning regulations will follow. In time, as in Australia, academic observers will be able to sit back and marvel that such a seemingly modest reform should have become so central to national economic policy.

Proponents argue that employers will be free to use any nondiscriminatory pay system, and the courts will decide if discrimination has occurred.[53] But inconsistent court decisions will lead to a demand for standards, and this demand will start us groping toward "reforms" like those discussed in the EC and the United Kingdom.

Barbara Bergmann is one of the few comparable-worth supporters willing to acknowledge that some centralized oversight will be needed. She, however, pooh-poohs the opponents of comparable worth who frighten the business community with visions of federal agencies setting wage rates by administrative fiat for every job in the country. Saying that such an inclusive approach would be expensive and unnecessary, she instead proposes:

> An agency might set up minimum wage recommendations for the largest of the typically female occupations – typist, secretary, retail sales clerk, child care workers, teacher, social worker, librarian, nurse. This is the approach taken by Australia, and it has worked effectively to raise women's wages, apparently without adverse economic consequences to the women or to the society generally.

Bergmann's sole source for her praise of Australian results is the ubiquitous Gregory work discussed in Chapter 7. As already argued, however, adverse economic consequences of the Australian approach are manifest. Bergmann then goes on to say:

> Another approach would be for EEOC or the Labor Department to recommend wage ratios for a group of common male and female occupations. For example, the recommendation might be that an employer pay secretaries a certain percent more than that employer pays truck drivers. Such pay patterns could be required of government contractors, along with affirmative action.[54]

But suppose employers cannot get enough truck drivers at the wage ratio deemed appropriate by the federal agency. It is precisely the desire to preserve wage ratios, "comparative wage justice," that has brought such rigidity and poor economic performance to Australia. The commissions cannot accept an exception for the truck drivers (or airplane mechanics) because then the secretaries will want their "fair" wage ratio reestablished, inflation will come, and as with the Whitlam government, high unemployment will follow.

No tinkering can reconcile comparable worth with a market economy. Even if the finest comparable-worth thinkers can succeed in establishing the "appropriate" wage ratios based on skill, effort, and the like, the U.K. Equal Opportunities Commission reminds us that their work may soon be out of date if it is not quickly published (see Chapter 6, p. 169). Technology, jobs, and job duties constantly change. Suppose one establishes that secretaries of average quality deserve 50 percent more than truck drivers of average quality, but at these established rates it is hard to get truck drivers and easy to get secretaries. Companies will soon have to hire ne'er-do-wells as truck drivers and will be able to hire top-notch secretaries who can do more in less time. The average productivity and quality of each will change, and secretaries will "deserve" 80 percent more than truck drivers, not 50 percent. As soon as new comparable-worth wage ratios are established the same process will recur.[55]

Comparable-worth proponents in the United States who cite the 30 percent improvement in the sex wage ratio as a result of equal value in Australia often leave the impression that there were no accompanying costs. In fact, as argued in Chapter 7, the policy of compressed and inflexible wages, which produced what gains there were for female workers, yields a lower growth rate in the standard of living and higher unemployment year after year for both sexes. That policy also holds back some market-driven wage gains for nurses and secretaries because of pay commissions' fears of inflationary "flow ons."

The much-touted smooth functioning and high employee morale produced by the comparable-worth system for state employees in Minnesota provides no more of a testimonial than does Australian experience. The functioning is much less smooth than advertised, and it is not surprising that a policy granting most males above-inflation pay increases and females much higher raises still generated some employee support. Those results are not capable of being generalized to the economy as a whole.

Local Minnesota experience is more instructive. Here, even though comparable worth produced far more pay raises than pay cuts, the process led to much more ill will and bitterness among employees than to good will and improved morale. Local officials were sometimes left with indefensible results, for instance, unequal pay for equal work and an inversion of the job hierarchy. Similar problems have occurred in other states' systems. The vice-president of Iowa's Civil Service Commission calls the Iowa process that produced both unequal pay for equal work and a hierarchy inversion a "nightmare."[56] The pay inversion problems created in Wisconsin have been widespread and have caused "serious morale problems." Some professional employees there have expressed interest in being transferred to "less demanding paraprofessional jobs."[57] In Washington clerk typists 3 are refusing "promotions" to the job of fiscal technician – a job higher in the hierarchy but rated lower and now paid less.[58] In most locations government services deteriorate because when some occupations get a boost from comparable worth, there is less money left for other aspects of services. For example, higher wages mean that libraries have fewer books and schools fewer teacher aides.

In the United States legally mandated comparable worth has come only to units of state and local government. One of the next battlegrounds will be the attempt to bring comparable worth to federal employees. Like comparable worth, the federal pay system has long emphasized internal equity and has based pay on job factors such as skill and responsibility. Comparable-worth proponents want a revised job evaluation system based on different values, on those which will help close the pay gap among the sexes.[59] The Reagan and Bush administrations have proposed very different reforms aimed at a compensation system guided by what local private-sector and government employees receive for similar jobs. Congress has recently agreed to some such locality-based pay reforms.[60]

The push for comparable worth at the federal level is, however, by no means over. Proponents expect new impetus to come from publication in 1993 of a GAO study of bias in the federal government's job evaluation system. Jimmy Carter, Walter Mondale, and Michael Dukakis were comparable-worth supporters, and pay equity is in the 1992 Democratic platform. President-elect Bill Clinton has not yet taken a position on comparable worth.

Clearly, the ultimate goal is legally mandated comparable worth in the private as well as the public sector.[61] That goal could be indirectly achieved if the U.S. Senate were to approve the UN "Convention on the Elimination of All Forms of Discrimination against Women." The Convention, if ratified, would require the United States to guarantee women the right "to equal treatment in respect of work of equal value."[62] President Carter sent the Convention to the Senate shortly before leaving office, but without the support of President Reagan or Bush it has languished in committee there. However, the chairman of the Committee on Foreign Relations, Senator Claiborne Pell (D-R.I.), is a strong supporter, and the Convention may fare better under a Clinton administration and with a Senate containing new female members and others newly sensitive to issues of special concern to women.

Advocates are deeply committed to the goal of advancing comparable worth in both the public and private sectors, and they are well organized. NCPE has legislative and collective bargaining task forces, a speakers' training group, fact sheets, videos, and a public relations firm to help with newspaper editorials. An international network provides advice and support. When I was in Australia, one person I interviewed was on a first-name basis with the principal proponents in Washington, D.C., and in Minnesota; a proponent interviewed in Minnesota was filling out a pay equity questionnaire from New Zealand.

The contrast with the opponents' side is stark. A pay specialist from a Minnesota local government association opposed comparable worth and thought that some economist must have spoken out against the idea because it seemed so antimarket. But she had not found such a person and was not aware of the debate in the journals and in Civil Rights Commission publications. For a time Representative Armey coordinated a small network of opponents. But the Chamber of Commerce and other business groups are preoccupied, opposing mandatory parental leave and other measures that do not distort prices and thus are far less threatening to a market economy and a free enterprise system. To be sure, if a measure that would apply to the private sector should come close to passage, business groups would weigh in strongly. But with comparable worth, even seemingly innocuous measures can become significant. The politicians who first approved wage arbitration in Australia and equal pay in the EC could not have imagined that their modest measures would develop as they have. Moreover, comparable worth has considerable political appeal. A recent poll conducted for NCPE found 77 percent support for a law requiring equal pay for occupations that require the same level of skills and responsibilities even if the occupations are different.[63] And among politicians it is hard to vote against something called "pay equity." In addition, though women have organized to fight on both sides of the debates over abortion and the Equal Rights Amendment, there has been no strong organized women's opposition to comparable worth.[64]

Comparable worth will probably not disappear as a significant political issue until more women oppose it. At least one prominent feminist, Susan Brownmiller, already does.[65] More women will join the opposition if they come to see what I think is likely – that legislative victories would be followed by long-term regrets and disappointment.[66] The Australian experience with an administered wage system suggests that, in the long run, comparable worth would lead to a much more politicized wage-setting system. In Australia, one gets an edge on other workers through strikes, "veiled threats,"[67] "physical intimidation," and "sabotage" aimed at getting the attention of an arbitration commission or a recalcitrant company.[68] With respect to sabotage in 1990 the *Economist* commented on "Australians' immoderate toleration of such high jinks as welding Melbourne's trains to their rails."[69]

Although the strongly egalitarian values of Australians have infused this power-centered system and brought some gains to women, the big winners from the system have been the fitters, transport workers, and other male-dominated unions. The productivity bargaining exercises now underway will reward such unions further if they agree to give up overstaffing, rigid job demarcations, and various other inefficient workplace practices.

There is also reason to doubt that women elsewhere will emerge clear winners from more politicized wage-setting systems. Much research has been conducted on the differences between the sexes in their relative emphasis on desirable aspects of work. The findings show that women put more emphasis than men on friendly relations with management and their co-workers.[70] As might be expected, this emphasis leads women to be less willing than men to support strikes and other militant actions. For example, studies have found that the incidence of strikes is negatively related to the proportion of females in the labor force,[71] and an Australian attitudinal study found that male nurses "were significantly more militant than females."[72]

The studies of attitudes toward job characteristics usually find that men put more emphasis than do women on the money in a job.[73] Broader studies of gender differences usually find that men are more predisposed than are women toward aggression or dominance.[74] These studies all deal with sexual averages, and there are exceptions. Still, if on average men care more about money and tolerate conflict better whereas women are especially concerned about maintaining friendly relations with management and co-workers, there is reason to doubt that women will participate eagerly in and emerge victorious from a process putting a premium on veiled threats and "who shouts the loudest."[75] This is perhaps especially the case for women in the traditionally female caring and helping professions.

Many comparable-worth proponents are of course aware of the evidence showing that women writing their job descriptions are "self-deprecating" whereas men provide "self-enhancing" descriptions of their work. Clare Burton's book explains how the men are constantly "quibbling" over the words used to describe their job, whereas the women "desire not to disturb existing relativities" and seem "content with the symbolic rewards, as against higher pay." Women are found to be less active in union affairs: " 'Even where women were aware of unequal pay, they were reluctant to take action. They feared unpleasantness or negative reactions from fellow workers or management and hostile attitudes on the part of male trade unionists.' "[76] Proponents presumably think that these attitudes, values, and behaviors are changing or can be changed. Yet in my interviews in Minnesota I still encountered female members of job evaluation committees who complained that the male members never did the reading and then dominated the discussions. In a book surveying Oregon's experiences Joan Acker says that women got less than they deserved because, even when they constituted a majority in unions, males dominated the leadership and pushed "harder for increases," while with a few exceptions, "the voices of women workers were silent."[77]

Comparable worth has come to state and local government in the United States in a situation where men have not usually lost income and where female political activists have had disproportionate influence in the choice of consultants and the like. Even so, at the ground level, problems of relative female passivity have caused some setbacks. In the private sector the views of the political activists will count for much less, and men will be more combative since they will more often lose the income that women hope to gain. Without any objective standard for job evaluation, the chances seem remote that women will come out significant winners in the battles that ensue.

And there will be battles with lingering ill will. One prominent academic observer of Australian industrial relations notes that "wages are seen to imprint society's judgment about an individual's worth: deep and abiding rifts emerge over whether one classification should be a dollar a week more than another."[78] No sooner did the nurses obtain their recent gains in Australia than the fire fighters were up in arms, pointing to their shift work and the dangers they face, and demanding a return to their historic relationship vis-à-vis nurses' pay.

People care deeply about their pay, and once pay becomes a political question, it becomes central to politics. In Australia the two big economic events of the year have been the government's presentation of its budget and the start of the national wage case before the IRC. The political parties' policies on wages and their attitudes toward unions have become central to campaigns. In a 1992 Australian Parliament debate, Prime Minister Paul Keating charged that the opposition had been unable to settle on an industrial relations policy in their nine and one-half years in opposition. He concluded by saying, "If you can't run wages, you can't run Australia."[79]

As noted earlier, there were sixty legislative changes in the basic labor law in eighty years, and there were five official inquiries into industrial relations in one recent two-year period. Sydney is the center of Australian commerce and Canberra the home of the national legislature, but the Australian Council of Trade Unions and the two principal organizations representing business (the Business Council of Australia and the Confederation of Australian Industry) are all based in Melbourne – the home of the IRC.

The politicization of such a basic pocketbook issue raises the political stakes and makes political life more contentious. As indicated, the pressures have led the IRC to grant larger wage increases than it thinks wise from the point of view of inflation, unemployment, investment, and growth (see Chapter 7, p. 193). When these economic pains follow the short-term wage gain, political life becomes still more impassioned and unpleasant.

For a number of years most expert observers and most politicians have thought that Australia would profit from more flexible and market-sensitive wages. But proposals for fundamental change are always politically risky. In the long term the economic well-being of most Australian workers will improve if their firms invest more and more wisely, if they and their firms meet the competition to produce high-quality products that consumers want rather than lobby for protection from competition, if their workplace abuses are ended, and if the labor markets that set their wages are more attuned to supply and demand in various occupations. But Australians instead have learned through their historic wage-fixing processes that their wages depend on the wrangling and decisions over ever-changing principles in skyscraper conference rooms overlooking Melbourne. And so it seems, "Once the national [wage] case is decided, virtually all wages and salaries throughout the country are increased accordingly."[80] As the quoted comments of Prime Minister Keating suggest, the government is expected to have a policy for "run[ing] wages."

Contemplating the results of a politicized wage-fixing system in Australia suggests that the political dangers of comparable worth may be as great as the economic ones. Madison and other founders conceived our nation as an extended, commercial republic because such a republic would create wealth but also because commerce encourages a peaceful and industrious citizenry that goes about its private business quietly. Such a political regime serves liberty and democracy and preserves the efficacy of political power by protecting the private sphere and depoliticizing explosive economic issues, such as how much our jobs should pay.[81] Any system that encourages the country's workers to look to government for a higher wage rather than to their own efforts places significant strains on the political system by vastly expanding the scope and responsibility of political power. All the problems of economic distribution *immediately* become political problems and must be treated by parties, legislators, and administrators. Since such issues engage the passions so directly and are not resolvable by objective or neutral criteria, their politicization is likely to lead to cynicism and bitterness all around, as it surely has in Australia. Moreover, given the U.S. nonparliamentary system of government, any policy, once established, will be harder to get rid of than it is in Australia.

The Australian case suggests that, in the long run, women as well as men will be better off without comparable-worth legislation. But surely, at best, it is a mixed bag for women. Why should it be a priority for feminists? This chapter earlier discussed liberal economists who support strong enforcement of antidiscrimination laws pertaining to hiring and promotion (such as Title VII of the Civil Rights Act) but who strongly oppose comparable worth. One reason why I think that more knowledge can change some minds on this issue is that so many comparable-worth supporters do not understand why economists can have such different views on these two matters. Indeed, in Britain legal commentary on the EC's equal-treatment and equal-pay/equal-value directives is similar, and there seems to be no understanding of the fact that most economists would think the potential costs of equal-value legislation are far greater than the costs of Title VII or of the EC's equal-treatment directive.[82]

Laws that forbid discrimination by sex or race in hiring and promotion advance most people's understanding of equity. If they achieve their aim of giving women and minorities with equal or superior talents a fair chance to exercise those talents, they are unlikely to lead to a less productive economy and may lead to a more productive one. If instead, through poor rules or poor applications, Title VII law sometimes puts people with below-average qualifications in some company slots, the costs are not likely to be all that great. But comparable-worth or equal-value laws make it very difficult if not impossible for flexible prices to help reallocate labor from areas of surplus to areas of shortage. And as previously noted, labor is 73 percent of the economy. Comparable worth does not raise wages a little above the market equilibrium for a small sector of the labor force, as the minimum wage does. Instead, it can raise (or lower) relative wages quite substantially for all workers at all levels. As argued in earlier chapters, the results can be very inefficient, and since the results are dependent on arbitrary decisions of experts, committees, and judges, the pattern of pay that results is not even equitable.

Economists pronounce on everything these days. But economic efficiency they actually know something about. Women should not let the small, visible minority of economists who support comparable worth keep them from seriously considering the arguments of the overwhelming majority who would oppose it.[83]

The National Committee on Pay Equity is now trying to get U.S. businesses to adopt comparable worth voluntarily. The committee claims that pay equity will "create high worker morale" and that companies which adopt it will "rapidly outstrip their competitors in productivity and profitability."[84] The committee also claims that some firms are adopting the pay equity policies that it supports. If so, the market will soon tell us whether these firms thrive or suffer, and if NCPE is right and they thrive, other firms will imitate the leaders, and no legislation will be necessary.

Obviously, abandoning mandated comparable worth does not have to mean accepting the status quo with respect to the wage gap and sex segregation in the workplace. When in 1989 I spoke with Robert Gregory about his research, he explained that, since its completion, pay for women in the United States has "suddenly gone whoosh." Normal market processes (including a decrease in the percentage of female workers who are inexperienced), as well as existing antidiscrimination laws, have cut the full-time weekly pay gap from 64.6 percent in 1981 to 74 percent in 1991. This rate of progress is far better than that of Australia (no change) or that of the United Kingdom (a closing of the gap from 65.1 percent to 69.7 percent) over this approximate time frame.[85]

Markets could help women's pay even more if certain barriers to entry were eliminated. For example, state laws could be changed so that legal secretaries could help clients with routine legal documents, and nurses could perform more medical procedures without a doctor's supervision. Such measures would increase demand for secretaries and nurses and raise their salaries. But as argued earlier, shortages in the market seem likely to earn secretaries and nurses above-average wage gains in any case, if comparable worth does not, unintentionally, hold them back. In this regard, these two traditionally female occupations are not atypical. The OECD has found that "to a large extent" women are "strongly concentrated in growing parts of the economy."[86] Whereas in 1960 the female unemployment rate in the United States exceeded that for men by 18 percent, in 1991 the male rate exceeded that for women by 11 percent.[87]

To the extent that discrimination contributes importantly to the wage gap, progress might be faster still if, as Killingsworth and Aaron have urged, enforcement of antidiscrimination laws pertaining to hiring and promotion were strengthened. In addition, public policy might continue to oppose, through education in the schools, stereotypes that could artificially limit the range of young women's occupational choices. As stereotypes become less restricting and women move more frequently into traditionally male occupations, the reduced supply of labor in traditionally female occupations will lead to still higher wages for middle-aged women who may be locked into these jobs.

In the economic realm, aside from the measures just mentioned, one could help working women in ways costing far less than comparable worth by providing for child allowances, by granting a fuller tax deduction for the costs of child care, by restoring the two-earner tax deduction, or by punishing more severely noncustodial parents who ignore their legal obligations. Whether or not such measures are adopted, comparable worth should not be. Predictable and insurmountable problems have occurred wherever it has been tried. To adopt it as public policy would bring us a more acrimonious politics and a much weaker economy. Women – and men – would both be losers.

# Appendix: a note on the research and presentation of findings

Serious research for this book began in early 1988 when I spent six months in Oxford, England. Traveling frequently to London for interviews and spending a week interviewing at the European Community headquarters in Brussels, I conducted seventy-one interviews – twenty-eight in person, the rest by telephone. For the United Kingdom as for my research elsewhere, some of the phone interviews were conducted in succeeding years after my travel had been completed. Thirty of my interviews were with U.K. or EC political/administrative officials having some responsibility for equal value now or in the past. Eighteen were with scholars, and eleven with officials of organizations representing business or employees. Other interviews conducted were with politicians, management consultants, industrial tribunal members, independent experts assisting the tribunals, and people in business. Among my written sources, the *Equal Opportunities Review,* which gives detailed coverage and analysis of developments on equal pay for equal value throughout the United Kingdom and the EC more generally, proved especially helpful.

In the winter and spring of 1989 I turned to Australia. The written sources, both on equal value per se and on the contentious question of wage fixation in Australia, were excellent. After absorbing as much as possible, I traveled to Australia, interviewing in Sydney, Melbourne, and Canberra for two weeks in late March and early April. In all, thirty-two interviews were conducted, sixteen in person. Fourteen of these were with academics, the remainder with government and arbitration commission officials, union and business representatives, politicians, and journalists.

In the late spring, summer, and fall of 1989, I devoted my attention to Minnesota, traveling to that state for a week in June and for two weeks in August. In June 1991 I returned for two additional days of interviewing. On my first visit I discovered the state legislative library's collection of articles on comparable worth from newspapers in and out of Minnesota. These articles, together with Sara Evans and Barbara Nelson's book *Wage Justice,* proved to be invaluable sources for background information on comparable-worth developments in Minnesota. I conducted 101 interviews on comparable worth in Minnesota, 26 in person. Thirty interviews were with state or local administrators. At the local level the interviews were often with the heads of personnel departments or, in the larger cities and counties, the personnel specialists most knowledgeable about comparable worth. Nineteen interviews were with union representatives. Thirty were conducted with nurses, librarians, or their supervisors. Supervisors or representatives of these professionals in the state capital gave me names and numbers of local departments where comparable worth had gone well or poorly, and I discovered new leads from these departments in turn. In the localities I almost always interviewed head librarians or county directors of public health nursing. I often asked these nurses and librarians about experiences elsewhere, and since the professions meet in regional or statewide meetings, I was able to get some sense of the magnitude of problems without interviewing systematically throughout the state. Other groups interviewed in Minnesota included supervisors of data processing departments, management consultants, business and local government representatives, academics, legislators, and arbitrators. I was also able to make use of tapes of state legislative hearings and of floor debates.

In addition to interviews for case studies, I talked in person with thirteen people in Washington, D.C. These were politicians and their staffs, researchers, federal administrators, and representatives of groups supporting or opposing comparable worth. By telephone I interviewed twenty-two additional experts – mainly academics throughout the United States who have written on comparable worth and administrators familiar with comparable-worth implementation in states other than Minnesota.

To encourage candor, no interviews were taped, but extensive notes were taken during the interviews. As soon as practicable thereafter, I reviewed my notes, filling in some gaps while my memory was fresh.

All quotations from written sources are footnoted. All unattributed quotations are from my interviews. Some of those I interviewed asked for anonymity. Most did not. Those who have written on comparable worth or who have played an important role in U.S., or U.K., or Australian comparable-worth developments are identified when they are quoted from my interviews unless anonymity was requested.

# Notes

## 1. *Introduction*

1 *Money Income of Households, Families and Persons in the United States: 1990*, U.S. Government Printing Office, Washington, D.C., 1991, Table 24. This median annual figure is the one highlighted by the National Committee on Pay Equity. See their *Newsnotes* 13, no. 1 (April 1992): Chart A.

2 Minnesota Commission on the Economic Status of Women, *Pay Equity: The Minnesota Experience,* February 1988, pp. 9, 11.

3 Cynthia Goodwin, *Equal Pay Legislation and Implementation: Selected Countries* (Ottawa: Labour Canada, 1984).

4 *New York Times,* July 27, 1989, p. A-1.

5 *St. Paul Pioneer Press Dispatch,* October 20, 1989, p. 8A.

6 On the controversy surrounding the governors' resolution, see *Minneapolis Star & Tribune,* August 1, 1984, p. 13A.

7 Paula England, *Comparable Worth: Theories and Evidence* (New York: De Gruyter, 1982), p. 220; Sara Evans and Barbara Nelson, *Wage Justice: Comparable Worth and the Paradox of Technocratic Reform* (Chicago: University of Chicago, 1989), pp. 69–76.

8 There have been exceptions to the general pattern of partisanship. For example, when he was governor of Washington, former Republican Senator Dan Evans requested the first comparable-worth study of state employees, and he remains strongly supportive of the concept (Sara Evans and Barbara Nelson, *Wage Justice* [Chicago: University of Chicago Press, 1989], pp. 34–5; U.S. Congress, Senate, Subcommittee on Federal Services, Post Office, and Civil Service of the Committee on Governmental Affairs, *Federal Employee Compensation Equity Act of 1987,* hearing, 100th Congress, 1st Session, April 22, 1987, pp. 1–4). So too do some Republican representatives in Congress, especially female ones. In 1984, Maureen Reagan tried hard to persuade her father and the Republican party platform to support comparable worth (*Washington Post,* February 12, 1984, p. A-2). She was not, however, successful.

9 Paul Weiler, "The Wages of Sex: The Uses and Limits of Comparable Worth," *Harvard Law Review* 99 (1986): 1732.

10 Ibid., p. 1754.

11 *New York Times,* November 17, 1984, p. A-15.

12 The bill is reproduced in Jennifer Roback, *A Matter of Choice: A Critique of Comparable Worth by a Skeptical Feminist* (New York: Priority Press, 1986), pp. 51–3. Also see pp. 9–10.

13 *Congressional Record,* House of Representatives, 100th Congress, September 27, 1988, pp. 8430, 8432.

14 *St. Paul Pioneer Press Dispatch,* October 20, 1989, p. 8A.

15 The words are those of Marilyn De Poy, the coordinator for women's rights at the American Federation of State, County, and Municipal Employees, when she spoke on a job evaluation panel at the 10th Anniversary Conference of the National Committee on Pay Equity, October 20, 1989. De Poy's opinion is widely shared among advocates of comparable worth.

16 The importance of the United Kingdom and Australia as test cases is further justified at the start of Chapters 5 and 7.

17 Robert Michael and Heidi Hartmann, "Pay Equity: Assessing the Issues," in Robert Michael, Heidi Hartmann, and Brigid O'Farrell, eds., *Pay Equity: Empirical Inquiries* (Washington, D.C.: National Academy Press, 1989), p. 1.

18 Census Bureau, U.S. Department of Commerce, Current Population Report, Consumer Income, Series P-60, no. 174, Table 24.

## *2. The debate over equal pay for comparable worth*

1 Claudia Goldin reports on one 1940 study of firms hiring office workers which found that 70 percent restricted certain occupations to men only (*Understanding the Gender Gap* [Oxford University Press, 1990], p. 112). See Goldin for other examples of historic discrimination.

2 See Sharon Shepela and Ann Viviano, "Some Psychological Factors Affecting Job Segregation and Wages," in Helen Remick, ed., *Comparable Worth and Wage Discrimination* (Philadelphia: Temple University Press, 1984), pp. 47–58, and Paula England, "Explanations of Job Segregation and the Sex Gap in Pay," in U.S. Commission on Civil Rights, *Comparable Worth: Issue for the 80's,* vol. 1 (Washington, D.C.: U.S. Government Printing Office, 1984), pp. 54–64.

3 Barbara Bergmann, *The Economic Emergence of Women* (New York: Basic, 1986), esp. chaps. 5 and 7.

4 Donald Treiman and Heidi Hartmann, eds., *Women, Work and Wages: Equal Pay for Jobs of Equal Value* (Washington, D.C.: National Academy Press, 1981).

5 Heidi Hartmann in "The Comparable Worth Controversy," *New Perspectives* 17, no. 2 (Spring 1985): 33.

6 Elaine Sorensen, "The Wage Effects of Occupational Sex Composition: A Review and New Findings," in M. Anne Hill and Mark Killingsworth, eds.,

*Comparable Worth: Analyses and Evidence* (Ithaca, N.Y.: Cornell University ILR Press, 1989), p. 57.

7 England, "Explanations of Job Segregation and the Sex Gap in Pay," p. 62.

8 Shepela and Viviano, "Some Psychological Factors Affecting Job Segregation and Wages," p. 47.

9 Treiman and Hartmann, eds., *Women, Work and Wages,* p. 85n.

10 Sorensen, "The Wage Effects of Occupational Sex Composition," reviews the literature and presents new findings. Treiman and Hartmann, eds., *Women, Work and Wages,* contains a nontechnical explanation of the human capital methodology.

11 One of the fuller discussions of the various wage comparisons is in Paul Weiler, "The Wages of Sex: The Uses and Limits of Comparable Worth," *Harvard Law Review* 99 (1986): 1779–82. Later figures are from unpublished 1990 U.S. Bureau of Labor Statistics Current Population Survey Data; June O'Neill "Women and Wages," *American Enterprise* 1, no. 6 (November–December 1990): 26; Robert Rector, "The Pseudo-Science of Comparable Worth," *Heritage Foundation Backgrounder*, no. 635, February 29, 1988; and James P. Smith and Michael Ward, "Women in the Labor Market and in the Family," *Journal of Economic Perspectives* 3 (Winter 1989): 16.

Another factor affecting the wage gap and emphasized by critics of comparable worth is the unanticipated (especially among whites) nature of the recent surge in work force participation by women. When asked in 1968, 29 percent of young white women thought that they would be in the labor force at age 35. In fact more than 60 percent of them are working if married, and the percentage is even higher among the unmarried. See Claudia Goldin, "The Earnings Gap in Historical Perspective," in U.S. Commission on Civil Rights, *Comparable Worth: Issue for the 80's,* vol. 1, p. 18. Since so many of the working women of this generation had not expected to be working, they became less well educated than they otherwise would have, and this has led to lower current wages. One sign that faulty expectations produced inadequate training is the fact that women who in 1968 expected to be in the labor force at age 35 are making 30 percent more than women who had not expected to be and now find that they are (*The Economic Report of the President 1987* [Washington, D.C.: Government Printing Office, 1987], p. 220). That current female teenagers have much higher labor force expectations for the future than did teenagers in 1968 gives some reason for optimism about a further closing of the wage gap in the future. For example, in 1979, 72 percent of white women ages 14–21 intended to work at age 35 (O'Neill, "Women and Wages," p. 29).

12 Kenneth Arrow as quoted in Ronald Ehrenberg and Robert Smith, *Modern Labor Economics* (Glenview, Ill.: Scott, Foresman, 1985), p. 443.

13 Victor Fuchs, *Women's Quest for Economic Equality* (Cambridge, Mass.: Harvard University Press, 1988), p. 36.

14 Ibid., pp. 55–6.

15 Some proponents of comparable worth would not deny that market forces tend to erode discrimination. For example, Paula England only denies that

the forces are strong enough to eliminate discrimination without government intervention ("Explanations of Job Segregation and the Sex Gap in Pay," p. 59).

16 See, e.g., *New York Times,* January 2, 1980, p. D-5; September 2, 1980, p. D-1; February 2, 1980, p. 27; August, 23, 1980, p. 31. See also Organization for Economic Cooperation and Development [OECD], *Economies in Transition: Structural Adjustment in OECD Countries* (Paris: 1989), p. 54.

17 Fuchs, *Women's Quest for Economic Equality,* p. 55. June O'Neill notes that if there is collusion directed at nurses in the hospital industry, it is ineffective since nurses' wages have risen much faster than those of most employees over recent decades ("An Argument Against Comparable Worth," in U.S. Commission on Civil Rights, *Comparable Worth: Issue for the 80's,* vol. 1, p. 183; also see the statistics in note 106). In 1977, 13 percent of women answered affirmatively when asked "Do you feel in anyway discriminated against in your job because you are a woman?" (Goldin, *Understanding the Gender Gap,* p. 208).

Neither Fuchs nor O'Neill would deny the existence of what economists call statistical discrimination. When making personnel decisions, employers never have perfect information about future productivity. They thus use certain rules of thumb, some of which will have a discriminatory effect on many women even though they may not be rooted in employer prejudice. For example, when considering for hiring or promotion qualified women and men, employers will tend to hire the men because on average they are less likely to quit when a new baby joins their family or when their spouse gets an attractive job offer in another city.

In these cases, employers make judgments that penalize those women with above average commitment to their careers. Still, economists have argued that since judgments are being made on estimates of the average productivity of the group as a whole, this sort of discrimination cannot explain the wage gap (Dennis Aigner and Glen Cain, "Statistical Theories of Discrimination in the Labor Market," *Industrial and Labor Relations Review* 30, no. 2 (January 1977): 175–87). Economists also argue that the use of group data as a screening device becomes more costly as the group becomes more diverse. As more women become committed to their careers, employers who use sex as a screening device will make more mistakes. In addition, it can be shown that firms using inappropriate screening devices will have lower profits than those using appropriate screens (see Ehrenberg and Smith, *Modern Labor Economics,* pp. 461–4).

In addition to the job discrimination that has its roots in prejudiced employers, there is discrimination attributable to workers or customers (see ibid., pp. 458–61, and Fuchs, *Women's Quest for Economic Equality,* p. 37).

18 Representative Mary Rose Oakar's complaint is that those who take care of our pets ("dog pound attendants") are usually paid more than those who take care of our children ("child care workers") (*Washington Post,* July 22,

1984, p. F-5). I use a wild animal example here because nonfarm animal caretakers more generally may not be paid more than child-care workers nor are they usually men. In 1990, 60 percent of nonfarm animal caretakers were women, and their median weekly earnings were $228. Prekindergarten and kindergarten teachers were 98 percent women, and their median weekly earnings were $344 (U.S. Department of Labor, Bureau of Labor Statistics, Current Population Survey, 1990 Annual Averages [BLS unpublished tabulation]). Paula England thinks the "bias against female jobs is obvious" when 200 keepers are rated in job evaluation studies more highly than day-care workers. See *Comparable Worth: Theories and Evidence* (New York: De Gruyter, 1992) p. 199.

19 Study by Charles Waldauer discussed in Ellen Frankel Paul, *Equity and Gender: The Comparable Worth Debate* (New Brunswick, N.J.: Transaction, 1989), p. 59.

20 See the literature cited in Mark Aldrich and Robert Buchele, "Where to Look for Comparable Worth," in Hill and Killingsworth, eds., *Comparable Worth: Analyses and Evidence,* pp. 24–5, and Weiler, "The Wages of Sex," pp. 1798–9.

21 Paul, *Equity and Gender,* p. 46, and Solomon Polachek, "Women in the Economy: Perspectives on Gender Inequality" in U.S. Commission on Civil Rights, *Comparable Worth: Issue for the 80's,* vol. 1, p. 40.

22 Fuchs, *Women's Quest for Economic Equality,* p. 140.

23 Carl Hoffman and John Reed, "Sex Discrimination? The XYZ Affair," *Public Interest,* no. 62 (Winter 1981): 34, and Carl and Kathleen Hoffmann, "Does Comparable Worth Obscure the Real Issues?" *Personnel Journal* 66, no. 1 (January 1987): 92.

24 Ehrenberg and Smith, *Modern Labor Economics,* p. 312. Also see Rosalind Rosenberg's testimony in "From the Witness Stand: Previously Unpublished Testimony in the Sex Discrimination Case Against Sears," *Academic Questions,* 1, no. 1 (1987–8): esp. p. 22.

25 Rector, *The Pseudo-Science of Comparable Worth,* p. 6.

26 Arthur Blakemore and Stuart Low, "Sex Differences in Occupational Selection: The Case of College Majors," *Review of Economics and Statistics* 66, no. 1 (Feb. 1984): 157–63. Blakemore and Low also find that expected fertility explains a sizable amount of the male–female differences in college majors. See also June O'Neill, "Role Differentiation and the Gender Gap in Wage Rates," in Laurie Larwood, Ann Stromberg, and Barbara Gutek, *Women and Work,* vol. 1 (Beverly Hills, Calif.: Sage, 1985), p. 70. For contrary evidence, see England, *Comparable Worth,* p. 52.

27 *The Economic Report of the President, 1987,* p. 213.

28 Becker notes that the "same argument explains why students who attend class and do housework have lower hourly earnings than persons not in school when both work the same number of hours and appear to have similar characteristics" (Gary Becker, "Human Capital, Effort, and the Sexual Division of Labor," *Journal of Labor Economics* 3, no. 1, pt. 2 [1985]: S52–3).

Becker does not assume that the sexual division of labor in the family is natural, and he emphasizes that its source may be discrimination. If, for example, women are denied equal access to job training, their productivity in the market place will be lower, and family income will increase if they do more housework than the more highly paid husband, enabling him to do more market work (S35).

Susan Moller Okin, an important feminist theorist, has strong reservations about the way economists such as Becker interpret women's choices within marriage. She seems to agree with Becker, however, that given "unequal sharing of housework . . . the amount of time and energy the wife has left to commit to her wage work is considerably more limited than her husband's" (*Justice, Gender and the Family* [New York: Basic, 1989], pp. 146–59).

29 Carol Kleiman, "Job Segregation by Sex Begins at Home, Study Finds," *Washington Post,* April 21, 1991, p. H-2.

30 Halycone Bohen and Anamaria Viveros-Long, *Balancing Jobs and Family Life,* as quoted in Brigitte Berger, "Comparable Worth at Odds with American Realities," in U.S. Commission on Civil Rights, *Comparable Worth: Issue for the 80's,* vol. 1, p. 69.

31 Randall Filer, "Male–Female Wage Differences: The Importance of Compensating Differentials," *Industrial and Labor Relations Review* 38, no. 3 (April 1985): 427; and idem, "The Role of Personality and Tastes in Determining Occupational Structure," *Industrial and Labor Relations Review* 39, no. 3 (April 1986): 414; Fuchs, *Women's Quest for Economic Equality,* esp. pp. 36, 37, 47, 70; Judith Buber Agassi, *Comparing Work Attitudes of Women and Men* (Lexington, Mass.: Lexington, 1987), esp. pp. 64–6, 97, 101; Philip J. Manhardt, "Job Orientation of Male and Female College Graduates in Business," *Personnel Psychology* 25 (1972): 361–8; Clifford E. Jurgensen, "Job Preferences (What Makes a Job Good or Bad?)," *Journal of Applied Psychology* 63, no. 3 (1978): 267–76; Trudy Ann Cameron, "Some Reflections on Comparable Worth," *Contemporary Policy Issues* 4, no. 2 (April 1986): 33–9; U.S. Office of Personnel Management, *Comparable Worth for Federal Jobs* (Washington, D.C.: U.S. Government Printing Office, 1987), p. 34; Linda Blum, *Between Feminism and Labor: The Significance of the Comparable Worth Movement* (Berkeley and Los Angeles: University of California Press, 1991), pp. 142–7. Paula England thinks "the existing evidence provides no clear answer to the question of whether or not there is a sex difference in the value placed on money." See *Comparable Worth,* pp. 18–19, 35.

32 Kathryn Langwell, "Factors Affecting the Incomes of Men and Women Physicians: Further Explorations," *Journal of Human Resources* 17 (1982): 269–72.

33 Filer, "Male–Female Wage Differences," p. 428.

34 Ibid. Men are also much more likely to be in noisy jobs or jobs requiring lifting. O'Neill, "Role Differentiation and the Gender Gap in Wage Rates," p. 64. Also see Donald Treiman, Heidi Hartmann, and Patricia Roos,

"Assessing Pay Discrimination Using National Data," in Remick, ed., *Comparable Worth and Wage Discrimination* pp. 143–4, and England, *Comparable Worth,* p. 178.

35 Rector, "The Pseudo-Science of Comparable Worth," p. 4. Morton Paglin and Anthony Rufolo, "Heterogeneous Human Capital, Occupational Choice, and Male–Female Earnings Differences," *Journal of Labor Economics* 8, no. 1 (1990): 123–44, find that relatively scarce mathematical reasoning ability (measured by SAT-Math and GRE-Quantitative scores) is a key variable explaining earnings differences. Men and women with high scores on those tests are much more likely to go into the higher paying sciences, but two to five times as many men as women have such scores. Women with high math scores end up with slightly higher starting salaries than men with such scores. Verbal ability on the standardized tests is relatively unimportant in explaining incomes. Paglin and Rufolo find that their model "successfully accounts for the observed male–female differences in earnings."

36 James Smith, "Commentary," in Michael, Hartmann, and O'Farrell, eds., *Pay Equity: Empirical Inquiries*, p. 173.

37 Randall Filer, "Occupational Segregation, Compensating Differentials, and Comparable Worth," in Michael et al., eds., *Pay Equity: Empirical Inquiries,* and Polachek, "Women in the Economy."

38 See, e.g., Fuchs, *Women's Quest for Economic Equality,* p. 55.

39 Margery Turner, Michael Fix, and Raymond Struyk, *Opportunities Denied, Opportunities Diminished: Discrimination in Hiring* (Washington, D.C.: Urban Institute, 1991), p. 1.

40 Richard Epstein, *Forbidden Grounds: The Case Against Employment Discrimination Laws* (Cambridge, Mass.: Harvard University Press, 1992), p. 58.

41 *Washington Post,* April 29, 1992, p. A-16.

42 Robert Michael and Heidi Hartmann, "Pay Equity: Assessing the Issues," in Michael et al., eds., *Pay Equity: Empirical Inquiries,* p. 11. Also see Elaine Sorensen, "The Crowding Hypothesis and Comparable Worth," *Journal of Human Resources* 25 (Winter 1990): 76.

43 For more on the history of U.S. employers' discrimination against married women, see Goldin, *Understanding the Gender Gap,* esp. chap. 5.

44 See *Robinson v. Jacksonville Shipyards,* 760 Fed. Supp. 1486 (1991).

45 Interview with a staff member who asked for anonymity, August 2, 1989. On the floor of the House, Congresswoman Mary Rose Oakar took umbrage at what she took to be a "degrading" suggestion that office work was "easy" (*Congressional Record,* House of Representatives, 100th Congress, September 27, 1988, p. H8439).

46 For proponents who emphasize pay based on worth to the employer, see Ronnie Steinberg, "Identifying Wage Discrimination and Implementing Pay Equity Adjustments," in U.S. Commission on Civil Rights, *Comparable Worth: Issue for the 80's,* vol. 1, p. 99, and Ray Marshall and Beth Paulin, "The Employment and Earnings of Women: The Comparable Worth De-

bate," in ibid., vol. 1, pp. 206–7. For proponents who emphasize pay based on unbiased, gender-neutral criteria, see Nina Rothchild, "Overview of Pay Initiatives, 1974–1984," in ibid., vol. 1, p. 119, and Helen Remick, "Major Issues in *a priori* Applications," in Remick, ed., *Comparable Worth and Wage Discrimination,* p. 99. Heidi Hartmann emphasizes the employer when quoted (at note 5), but (with Robert Michael) she emphasizes objective, gender-neutral criteria in Michael and Hartmann, "Pay Equity: Assessing the Issues," pp. 1–2.

47 See Robert Samuelson, "Working Woman Stymied," *Washington Post,* July 19, 1983, p. D-8.

48 Andrea Beller, "Statement," in U.S. Commission on Civil Rights, *Comparable Worth: Issue for the 80's,* vol. 2, Proceedings, p. 16, and Treiman and Hartmann, eds., *Women, Work and Wages,* p. 23.

49 For a somewhat similar reading of this version of the proponents' position, see Mark Killingsworth, *The Economics of Comparable Worth* (Kalamazoo, Mich.: Upjohn Institute, 1990), p. 46.

50 Comptroller General of the U.S., *Options for Conducting a Pay Equity Study of Federal Pay and Classification Systems* (GGD-85-37) March 1, 1985, p. 47.

51 Comptroller General of the U.S., *Comments on Report on Comparable Worth by the United States Commission on Civil Rights* (GGD-85-59), June 14, 1985, pp. 20–1.

52 Helen Remick, "Major Issues in *a priori* Applications," in Remick, ed., *Comparable Worth and Wage Discrimination,* p. 99. Paula England concludes that "advocates of comparable worth encourage employers in the public and private sectors to use job evaluation for wage setting" (*Comparable Worth: Theories and Evidence,* p. 223; also see p. 190).

53 Lorraine Eyde's survey in U.S. Congress, House, Joint Subcommittee Hearings of the Committee on Post Office and Civil Service, *Pay Equity: Equal Pay for Work of Comparable Value,* 97th Congress, 2nd Session, 1982, pp. 906–9, and David Levine, "Why Comparable Worth Won't Upset the Market Place," *San Francisco Chronicle,* March 7, 1988, p. C–6.

54 Barbara Nelson, "Comparable Worth: A Brief Review of History, Practice and Theory," *Minnesota Law Review* 69, no. 5 (May 1985): 1209.

55 Donald Schwab, "Using Job Evaluation to Obtain Pay Equity," in U.S. Commission on Civil Rights, *Comparable Worth: Issue for the 80's,* vol. 1, p. 87, and Nelson, "Comparable Worth," p. 1209; Sara Evans and Barbara Nelson, *Wage Justice: Comparable Worth and the Paradox of Technocratic Reform* (Chicago: University of Chicago Press, 1989), p. 56.

56 David Treiman, Heidi Hartmann, and Patricia Roos have described a comparable-worth methodology that seeks to find out how much particular firms pay for education, working conditions, substantive complexity, etc. in male-dominated jobs, and then to ensure that the firm pays accordingly for female-dominated jobs ("Assessing Pay Discrimination Using National Data," in Remick, ed., *Comparable Worth and Wage Discrimination,*

pp. 137–54). Paul Weiler ("The Wages of Sex," pp. 1768–71) finds this methodology quite promising. Weiler correctly notes that it would mean analysts need not arbitrarily weight factors in the way that a priori systems do. Nevertheless, the technical problems with this methodology are numerous. The criticism made by Robert Rector (pp. 14–15) would apply. So too would much of that directed at the research to determine how much of the wage gap is explained by "percent female" (see pp. 15–16; also see pp. 16–19 following). (For a fuller discussion of technical problems with this sort of research, see the discussion of job attributes in John Raisian, Michael Ward, Finis Welch, "Pay Equity and Comparable Worth," *Contemporary Policy Issues* 4, no. 2 [April 1986]: 4–20; also see Masanori Hashimoto and Levis Kochin, "A Bias in the Statistical Estimation of the Effects of Discrimination," *Economic Inquiry* 18 [July 1980]: 478–86, and Paglin and Rufolo briefly discussed in note 35).

The political problems would be even greater than the technical because comparable-worth proponents would oppose this (which adopts market values) as would opponents. Treiman and Hartmann, who seemingly first proposed it, have elsewhere made clear that it is not nearly sufficient from their point of view ("Notes on the NAS Study of Equal Pay for Jobs of Equal Value," *Public Personnel Management Journal,* no. 4 [Winter 1983]: 414–16, and Hartmann, "Pay Equity for Women: Wage Discrimination and the Comparable Worth Controversy," in Robert Fullinwider and Claudia Mills, eds., *The Moral Foundations of Civil Rights*, [Totowa, N.J.: Rowman & Littlefield, 1986], pp. 180–3). So too has Ronnie Steinberg, the principal proponent involved with the New York state study that Weiler credits with seemingly having used the policy-capturing model that Weiler finds intellectually credible. (The New York report had just been published as Weiler wrote.) Steinberg ("Identifying Wage Discrimination and Implementing Pay Equity Adjustments," in U.S. Commission on Civil Rights, *Comparable Worth: Issue for the 1980's,* vol. 1) calls the New York approach an "adjusted policy capturing approach" (p. 110). It was "adjusted" in part by including "questions that would be highly related to female-dominated jobs and negatively related to current pay policy" (p. 112). At the NCPE tenth anniversary conference (in remarks made at the Job Evaluation Panel), Steinberg made it clear that she did not like the forms of job evaluation that rely on factors designed by firms to rate traditionally male-dominated jobs. (See also Evans and Nelson, *Wage Justice,* p. 170 and note 17.) Steinberg believes (see Chapter 8) that job evaluation is a political not a technical exercise. Richard Burr (*Are Comparable Worth Systems Truly Comparable?* [St. Louis: Center for the Study of American Business, Washington University, July 1986], pp. 8–9, 11, 14–15) points to evidence suggesting that the New York state study was manipulated to reach a predetermined political outcome.

Whatever the merits of the policy-capturing methodology described by Treiman, Hartmann, Roos, and Weiler, it seems that it has not yet been implemented. Since this book seeks to assess existing systems, no more will be said of it.

57 Senator Daniel Evans (R-Wash.) in U.S. Congress, Senate, Subcommittee on Federal Service, Post Office, and Civil Service of the Committee on Governmental Affairs, *Federal Employee Compensation Equity Act of 1987,* hearing, 100th Congress, April 22, 1987, p. 2 (hereafter *Federal Employee Compensation Equity Act of 1987,* Senate hearing).

58 Representative Patricia Schroeder (D-Colo.), *Congressional Record,* House of Representatives, 100th Congress, September 28, 1988, p. H8569. Also see pp. H8574 and H8996.

59 *Federal Employee Compensation Equity Act of 1987,* Senate hearing, p. 70.

60 Comptroller General for the U.S., *Options for Conducting a Pay Equity Study,* p. 31.

61 Ibid., pp. 32 and 42.

62 Ibid., p. 31.

63 Treiman and Hartmann, eds., *Women, Work and Wages,* p. 94.

64 Ibid., p. 118.

65 Ibid., p. 12. Also see p. 74, where we are told that the use of job evaluation as evidence of discrimination "requires strong assumptions... difficult to satisfy in practice," and p. 95, where we are told that, "under certain circumstances," job evaluation plans may be used to discover discrimination.

66 Ibid., p. 90.

67 Ibid., p. 96.

68 Evans and Nelson, *Wage Justice,* p. 57.

69 Steinberg, "Identifying Wage Discrimination and Implementing Pay Equity Adjustments," pp. 107–8.

70 Michael and Hartmann, "Pay Equity: Assessing the Issues," p. 1. Also see Steinberg, "Identifying Wage Discrimination and Implementing Pay Equity Adjustments," p. 114.

71 Nina Rothchild, "Overview of Pay Initiatives, 1974–1984," in U.S. Commission on Civil Rights, *Comparable Worth: Issue for the 80's,* vol. 1, p. 119.

72 Donald Schwab, "Job Evaluation and Pay Setting: Concepts and Practices," in E. Robert Livernash, ed., *Comparable Worth: Issues and Alternatives* (Washington, D.C.: Equal Employment Advisory Council, 1980), pp. 63 and 68.

73 Charles Fay, "Discussion," in Hill and Killingsworth, eds., *Comparable Worth,* p. 33. Fay further notes that, subjected to greater competition, firms increasingly pay men and women no more than market forces require them to. Also see Herbert Northrup, "Comparable Worth and Realistic Wage Setting," in U.S. Commission on Civil Rights, *Comparable Worth: Issue for the 80's,* vol. 1, pp. 96–7.

74 Comments by Alvin Bellak, Hay Associates, in U.S. Commission on Civil Rights, *Comparable Worth: Issue for the 80's,* vol. 2, pp. 49 and 68. Also see Raisian, Ward, and Welch, "Pay Equity and Comparable Worth," pp. 10–13.

75 See *Federal Employee Compensation Equity Act of 1987,* Senate hearing, p. 28.

76 Rector, *The Pseudo-Science of Comparable Worth,* p. 9. Rector is drawing on Burr, *Are Comparable Worth Systems Truly Comparable?*

77 Willis and Associates did the first study in 1974, Jeanneret and Associates the second in 1983. For a brief discussion of the differences, see *Comparable Worth for Federal Jobs,* p. 41.

78 *Congressional Record,* House of Representatives, 100th Congress, September 29, 1988, p. H8992. Representative Armey confirmed the opponents' thinking on the amendment in an interview August 2, 1989. The differences in study findings are not simply the result of inexperienced evaluators. See Burr, *Are Comparable Worth Systems Truly Comparable?* pp. 18–19; also see Donald Schwab, "Job Evaluation and Pay Setting," pp. 59–61; Aaron and Lougy, *The Comparable Worth Controversy,* p. 29.

79 Burr, *Are Comparable Worth Systems Truly Comparable?* p. 14.

80 Ronald Ehrenberg and Robert Smith, "Comparable Worth in the Public Sector," in David Wise, ed., *Public Sector Payrolls* (Chicago: University of Chicago Press, 1987), p. 279. Also troubling is a finding that, for *men only,* prior to comparable worth, jobs ranking high on the category "mental demands" were paid less than jobs ranking less high. This suggests that the category points were not measuring something significant with any accuracy (June O'Neill, "Effects of Comparable Worth Policy: Evidence from Washington State," *American Economic Association Papers and Proceedings* 79, no. 2 (May 1989): 308).

81 Gerald Pauly, "'Comparable Worth' vs. 'Prevailing Rates,'" in John Matzer, Jr., ed., *Creative Personnel Practices: New Ideas for Local Government* (Washington, D.C.: International City Management Association, 1984), pp. 201–2.

82 *Options for Conducting A Pay Equity Study*, p. 41n.

83 Aaron and Lougy, *The Comparable Worth Controversy,* p. 33. Contrast Ehrenberg and Smith, "Comparable Worth in the Public Sector," p. 257. For a discussion of some other implementation problems, see Walter Oi, "Neglected Women and Other Implications of Comparable Worth," *Contemporary Policy Issues* 4, no. 2 (April 1986): 25.

84 Burr, *Are Comparable Worth Systems Truly Comparable?*, pp. 20 and 22, and Paul, *Equity and Gender,* pp. 54 and 110.

85 *Federal Employee Compensation Act of 1987,* Senate hearing, p. 28.

86 June O'Neill, "The Comparable Worth Controversy: An Interview with Heidi Hartmann and June O'Neill," *New Perspectives* 17, no. 2 (Spring 1985): 32.

87 Paul, *Equity and Gender,* p. 115.

88 *Congressional Record,* House of Representatives, 100th Congress, September 17, 1988, p. H8429. Also see Armey in ibid., September 29, 1988, p. H8991. See Aaron and Lougy, *The Comparable Worth Controversy,* pp. 46–7, on the inability of the courts to resolve the issues.

89 See Jeremy Rapkin, in U.S. Commission on Civil Rights, *Comparable Worth: Issue for the 80's,* vol. 2, p. 122, and Paul, *Equity and Gender,* p. 117.

90 Heidi Hartmann, "The Comparable Worth Controversy," *New Perspectives* 17, no. 2 (Spring 1985): 33. For additional brief comments on oversight, see Barbara Bergmann, *The Economic Emergence of Women* (New York: Basic, 1986), pp. 188–9. See the discussion of Bergmann, Chapter 8, pp. 237–8.

91 An understanding of economic efficiency begins with Pareto optimality. A Pareto optimal allocation is one in which we cannot reallocate resources to improve one person's welfare without impairing at least one other person's welfare. Pareto improvements are those where a change in resource allocation is preferred by one or more members of society and opposed by no one. But obviously such changes are very hard to find. If a single person objects to changing the status quo, then the Pareto improvement criterion gives no unambiguous public policy guidance. The existing situation may be Pareto optimal. But there are a nearly infinite number of noncomparable Pareto optimums, and the concept is of little policy use.

Economically efficient allocations are always Pareto optimal. But if the initial allocation is inefficient, the achievement of economic efficiency does not require that no one be made worse off before a change can be recommended. Economic efficiency requires only that recommended changes use resources in such a way that it would be theoretically possible – assuming costless transfers of income among gainers and losers – to make some better off and no one worse off. Suppose that most people would gain from some change, but some would lose. If the gainers gain enough so that they *could* fully compensate the losers with money or goods and still have an improved situation themselves, the change meets what some economists call the "potential Pareto" criterion and would improve economic efficiency. For more on economic efficiency, see Steven E. Rhoads, *The Economist's View of the World* (Cambridge University Press, 1985), pp. 62–4 and notes.

92 Ehrenberg and Smith, *Modern Labor Economics,* p. 44.

93 The thought that one could pay for wage increases for "female" jobs by drawing on profits is considered in Chapter 8, pp. 229–30.

94 U.S. Office of Personnel Management, *Comparable Worth for Federal Jobs,* p. 47.

95 Rector, *The Pseudo-Science of Comparable Worth,* p. 12.

96 Ehrenberg and Smith, *Modern Labor Economics,* pp. 42 and 31.

97 Mark Killingsworth notes, "Precisely to the extent that it raises pay in predominantly female jobs, comparable worth will make it more expensive to employ workers (male or female) in such jobs without, however, creating additional employment opportunities in either those or other occupations" (*The Economics of Comparable Worth* [Kalamazoo, Mich.: Upjohn Institute, 1990], p. 46). Also see Elaine Sorensen, "Effect of Comparable Worth Policies on Earnings," *Industrial Relations* 26, no. 3 (Fall 1987): 233, and Jennifer Roback, *A Matter of Choice: A Critique of Comparable Worth by a Skeptical Feminist* (New York: Priority Press, 1986), p. 40.

98 Roback, *A Matter of Choice,* p. 40.

99 Ehrenberg and Smith, *Modern Labor Economics,* p. 43. Also see *Structural Adjustment and Economic Performance* (Paris: Organization for Economic

Cooperation and Development [OECD], 1987), pp. 52, 137, 141, and *Economies in Transition: Structural Adjustment in OECD Countries* (Paris: OECD, 1989), p. 52.

100 As Nancy Perlman, former chair of the National Committee on Pay Equity puts it: "The comparable worth issue emphasize[s] the need to design job evaluation systems that are free from sex bias. Systems, if you will, that will pay the orange and the apple equally for giving us the same amount of energy. Systems which will not pay the orange less than the apple because it is not red." Quoted in a statement by Mark Killingsworth, in U.S. Congress, Joint Economic Committee, *Women in the Work Force: Pay Equity,* hearing, 98th Congress, April 10, 1984, p. 95. Also see David Lutes and Nina Rothchild, "Compensation: Pay Equity Loses to Chicken Little and Other Excuses," *Personnel Journal* (October 1986): 124. For a Canadian proponent who compares apples and oranges in terms of vitamins, fiber content, etc., see *Wall Street Journal,* March 9, 1990, p. B-1. Also see Minnesota Commission on the Economic Status of Women, *Pay Equity: The Minnesota Experience,* February 1988, p. 3.

101 For a related argument on the "apples and oranges" example, see Mark Killingsworth, "The Economics of Comparable Worth: Analytical, Empirical and Policy Questions," in Hartmann, ed., *Comparable Worth: New Directions for Research* (Washington, D.C.: National Academy Press, 1985), pp. 94–5.

102 The example, originally Sharon Smith's, is used by Killingsworth in *Women in the Work Force: Pay Equity,* p. 85, and Fuchs, *Women's Quest for Economic Equality,* p. 123, among others.

103 *Economic Report of the President* (Washington, D.C.: U.S. Government Printing Office, 1986), p. 278.

104 June O'Neill, statement, in U.S. Commission on Civil Rights, *Comparable Worth: Issue for the 80's,* vol. 2, pp. 111 and 114; June O'Neill in "The Comparable Worth Controversy," pp. 32–3; Paul, *Equity and Gender,* p. 118; Representative Armey in *Congressional Record,* House of Representatives, 100th Congress, September 27, 1988, p. 8437.

105 Oral comments of Heidi Hartmann at the NCPE tenth anniversary conference, October 21, 1989, and of Joy Ann Grune, former executive director of the NCPE, at the Annual Meeting of the American Political Science Association, September 1986.

106 Though this assurance is often given orally, Bonnie Watkins adds a key proviso for Minnesota: "Pay equity laws allow supply and demand considerations as long as the impact is nondiscriminatory" ("Pay Equity in Action: One State's Perspective," *Complete Lawyer* 3, no. 1 [Winter 1986]: 26). Also see *Minneapolis Star & Tribune,* October 14, 1984, p. D-6.

107 U.S. Office of Personnel Management, *Comparable Worth for Federal Jobs,* pp. 40, 47–8.

108 From 1981 to 1990, the average male real (i.e., adjusted for inflation) wage declined by over 2.8 percent. Registered female nurses' incomes increased by 27.7 percent, female practical nurses by 15.6 percent, female secretaries by 1.4 percent, and female typists by 7.6 percent. Figures for 1990 are

unpublished tabulations from U.S. Department of Labor, Bureau of Labor Statistics, Current Population Survey, 1990. Figures for 1981 are from *Monthly Labor Review,* April 1982. Figures for 1981 are multiplied by 1981–90 inflator of 1.4378 to obtain real-wage changes.

109 Watkins, "Pay Equity in Action," p. 26. This general point was also made by Eleanor Holmes Norton in her keynote speech to the NCPE tenth anniversary conference, October 21, 1989.

110 In U.S. Commission on Civil Rights, *Comparable Worth: Issue for the 80's,* vol. 2, p. 76.

111 Lutes and Rothchild, "Compensation: Pay Equity Loses to Chicken Little and Other Excuses," p. 124. Also see Rothchild's views in *Minneapolis Star & Tribune,* October 14, 1984, p. D-6.

112 Rothchild uses the "wage-fixing" phrase in *Minneapolis Star & Tribune* October 14, 1984, p. D-6.

113 In U.S. Commission on Civil Rights, *Comparable Worth: Issue for the 80's,* vol. 2, p. 97.

114 Fuchs, *Women's Quest for Economic Equality,* p. 123; Roback, *A Matter of Choice,* pp. 36–8; U.S. Office of Personnel Management, *Comparable Worth for Federal Jobs,* p. 42.

115 Robert S. Smith, "Comparable Worth: Limited Coverage and the Exacerbation of Inequality," *Industrial and Labor Relations Review* 41, no. 2 (January 1988): 227–39; Aldrich and Buchele, "Where to Look for Comparable Worth," pp. 26–7.

116 Rector, *The Pseudo-Science of Comparable Worth,* p. 8; Oi, "Neglected Women and Other Implications of Comparable Worth," pp. 26–9; Fuchs, *Women's Quest for Economic Equality,* p. 128; Joyce Jacobsen, "The Economics of Comparable Worth: Theoretical Considerations," in Hill and Killingsworth, eds., *Comparable Worth: Analyses and Evidence,* p. 46.

117 See Roback, *A Matter of Choice,* pp. 34–5. See also Chapter 4, note 45.

118 Between 1981 and 1990, the average male worker's real-wage income was down 2.87 percent. The average female worker's real-wage income was up 8.07 percent. Figures for 1990 are unpublished tabulations from U.S. Department of Labor, Bureau of Labor Statistics, Current Population Survey, 1990. Figures for 1981 are from *Monthly Labor Review,* April 1982. Figures for 1981 are multiplied by 1981–90 inflator of 1.4378 to obtain real-wage changes.

119 June O'Neill, "Effects of Comparable Worth Policy: Evidence from Washington State," *Industrial Relations* 26, no. 3 (Fall 1987): 227–39; Sorensen, "Effect of Comparable Worth Policies on Earnings." Elaine Sorensen, *Wage and Employment Effects of Comparable Worth: The Case of Minnesota* (Washington, D.C.: Urban Institute, March 1990).

120 Killingsworth, *The Economics of Comparable Worth,* chap. 4; Sorensen, *Wage and Employment Effects of Comparable Worth.*

121 Nina Rothchild and Bonnie Watkins, "Pay Equity in Minnesota: The Facts Are In," *Review of Public Personnel Administration* 7, no. 3 (Summer 1987): 16, 26, 28.

122 Ibid., p. 25.

123 Ibid., p. 24.

124 In addition to Rothchild, some of the Minnesota information reported comes from Minnesota Commission on the Economic Status of Women, *Pay Equity: The Minnesota Experience,* esp. p. 15, and Evans and Nelson, *Wage Justice,* esp. pp. 159–61. Rothchild's views are discussed in Chapter 3.

125 Evans and Nelson, *Wage Justice,* p. 173.

126 Ibid., p. 171.

127 Ibid., esp. pp. 171–2.

128 Roback, *A Matter of Choice,* p. 38.

129 Ehrenberg and Smith, "Comparable Worth in the Public Sector," p. 279.

130 P. Beider et al., "Comparable Worth in a General Equilibrium Model of the U.S. Economy," in Ronald Ehrenberg, ed., *Research in Labor Economics,* vol. 9 (Greenwich, Conn.: JAI Press, 1988), pp. 1–52. Reported in Fuchs, *Women's Quest for Economic Equality,* pp. 125–9.

131 Quote from James Medoff, "Comment," in Wise, ed., *Public Sector Payrolls,* p. 289; also see Aldrich and Buchele, *The Economics of Comparable Worth.*

132 Christopher McCrudden, "Comparable Worth: A Common Dilemma," *Yale Journal of International Law* 11, no. 2 (Spring 1986): 435–6.

133 See the discussion of Bob Gregory's work in Chapter 7. Also see Barbara Bergmann, *The Economic Emergence of Women* (New York: Basic, 1986), pp. 189–91; Frances Hutner, *Equal Pay for Comparable Worth* (New York: Praeger, 1986), pp. 38–41. Contrary and less well known assessments of the Australian experience are discussed in Chapter 7.

134 National Committee on Pay Equity, "OPM Comparable Worth/Pay Equity Study Overstates Women's Progress in Federal Workforce," November 3, 1987.

## *3. Implementing comparable worth in Minnesota*

1 Sara Evans and Barbara Nelson, *Wage Justice: Comparable Worth and the Paradox of Technocratic Reform* (Chicago: University of Chicago Press, 1989), pp. 69–76.

2 Quoted in Evans and Nelson, *Wage Justice,* p. 79.

3 Interview with the author, June 15, 1989.

4 Michael Sharpe, "The Minnesota Comparable Worth Statute," *Hamline Journal of Public Law* 6, nos. 1–2 (1985): 26.

5 State of Minnesota, *Journal of the House,* 1982 vol. 4, p. 6922.

6 Sara Evans and Barbara Nelson, "Mandating Local Change in Minnesota: State Required Implementation of Comparable Worth by Local Jurisdictions," in Ronnie Steinberg, ed., *Comparable Worth: A View From the States* (Philadelphia: Temple University Press, forthcoming).

7 Act of Mar. 23, 1982, ch. 634//1–9, 1982 Minnesota Laws 1559–61 (current version at Minnesota Statutes//43A.01, .02, .05, .08, .18 ([1992]).

8 Evans and Nelson, *Wage Justice,* p. 97.

9 Elaine Sorensen, *Wage and Employment Effects of Comparable Worth: The Case of Minnesota* (Washington, D.C.: Urban Institute, March 1990), pp. 14 and 24.

10 Evans and Nelson, *Wage Justice,* p. 99.

11 Ibid., pp. 105 and 117.

12 Nina Rothchild and Bonnie Watkins, "Pay Equity in Minnesota: The Facts Are In," *Review of Public Personnel Administration* 7, no. 3 (Summer 1987): 27.

13 Evans and Nelson, *Wage Justice,* p. 170.

14 See Ibid., pp. 99, 102, 123–4.

15 Ibid., p. 96.

16 Unpublished data supplied by the Compensation Division of DOER show that male employees as well as female employees enjoyed real-wage gains (after adjustment for inflation) during the period when comparable worth was being implemented. It is, of course, impossible to know what might have happened to male or female salaries if comparable worth had never existed. Elaine Sorensen estimates that males were net gainers (those males in female-dominated jobs gained 16.5 percent while others were unaffected; Sorenson, *Wage and Employment Effects of Comparable Worth,* pp. 16–17). In *The Economics of Comparable Worth,* Mark Killingsworth figures men's pay was unchanged relative to the levels that would otherwise have prevailed ([Kalamazoo, Mich.: Upjohn Institute, 1990], p. 129). A later Killingsworth paper making different assumptions calculates significant losses (6.0 percent for women and 9.4 percent for men) of pay in jobs not targeted for comparable-worth raises as compared to levels that otherwise would have prevailed ("Benefits and Costs of Comparable Worth," unpublished paper presented at a symposium on comparable worth at the John Deutsch Institute at Queen's University, Canada, in 1990, pp. 8–9). Also see Evans and Nelson's discussion, which suggests that the comparable-worth years were good times for Minnesota state employees (*Wage Justice,* pp. 97–8).

17 Interview with Nina Rothchild, August 30, 1989; with Bonnie Watkins, June 15, 1989; and phone interview with Faith Zwemke, October 20, 1989.

18 Unpublished statement presented to the DOER negotiations by Peter Lewon, statewide MAPE president on May 25, 1989.

19 This "ballpark" figure came from a MAPE leader and was confirmed by a pay specialist in DOER.

20 Quotes and information on the controversy about raises for the balanced and male classes came from phone conversations with three MAPE representatives, from internal MAPE documents, and from interviews with two DOER employees and one former employee.

21 *Minneapolis Star & Tribune,* June 10, 1985, p. 9A. The *New York Times* (May 31, 1990, p. D-22) reports similar problems in the state of Washington: "The largest group of workers overseen by the state personnel department is its 2,800 clerk-typists. In the past, an ambitious top-level 'clerk-typist 3' who found herself at a career dead end typically sought promotion to the

job of fiscal technician – bookkeeping primarily – where the proportion of women is smaller. That job can then lead to a still bigger promotion to accountant.

With the institution of the comparable-worth program, however, clerk-typists 3 have been refusing the promotion. Their wages have leaped 27 percent, from $15,204 a year to $19,332 while fiscal technicians, awarded fewer points by the job evaluators, have received less. To accept the promotion the typist now has to take a pay cut so many are staying put."

22 Sorensen, *Wage and Employment Effects of Comparable Worth*, p. 24.

23 DOER, "A Guide to Implementing Pay Equity in Local Government" (August 1984), p. 6. The consulting firm of Hubbard and Revo-Cohen, one of the most popular of the consultants among proponents, has also argued that higher wages to overcome critical labor shortages should be permitted ("Final Report for Washington State: Job Classification and Compensation Review," March 31, 1987, p. 80).

24 Evans and Nelson, *Wage Justice*, p. 101.

25 I was told this by her close assistant Bonnie Watkins, among others.

26 Rothchild and Wakings, "Pay Equity in MInnesota," p. 26.

27 Rothchild has said: "In the future, when consulting firms are used, there will be more pressure to allow for broad-based input and to eliminate sources of bias. Such firms will be called on to demonstrate that they can do more than simply mirror the status quo" ("Overview of Pay Initiatives, 1979–1984," in U.S. Commission on Civil Rights, *Comparable Worth: Issue for the 80's*, vol. 1 [Washington, D.C.: U.S. Government Printing Office, 1984], p. 126). Also see Ronnie Steinberg, "Identifying Wage Discrimination and Implementing Pay Equity Adjustments," in U.S. Commission on Civil Rights, *Comparable Worth: Issue for the 80's*, vol. 1, p. 107.

28 At the Syracuse University conference entitled "Pay Equity in Action," March 18, 1989.

29 The analysis in the past two paragraphs draws on interviews with two DOER employees. Also see Ronnie Steinberg, "Identifying Wage Discrimination and Implementing Pay Equity Adjustments," in U.S. Commission on Civil Rights, *Comparable Worth: Issue for the 80's,* vol. 1, pp. 106–7.

30 Rothchild and Watkins, "Pay Equity in Minnesota," p. 21.

31 Interview with Rothchild, August 30, 1989.

32 Sorensen, *Wage and Employment Effects of Comparable Worth*, p. 22.

33 Killingsworth, "Benefits and Costs of Comparable Worth," pp. 9–10. Also see Ronald Ehrenberg, "Empirical Consequences of Comparable Worth," in M. Anne Hill and Mark R. Killingsworth, eds., *Comparable Worth: Analysis and Evidence* (Ithaca, N.Y.: Cornell University Press, 1989), pp. 103–4, and Killingsworth, *The Economics of Comparable Worth*, chap. 4.

34 On passage of the local bill, Evans and Nelson note that, outside the big cities, "even those [local public officials] who followed the legislature closely registered surprise, having expected a voluntary law rather than a mandate" (*Wage Justice*, p. 137).

35 An AFSCME lobbyist told me this in 1989.
36 *Journal of the House*, 1984, p. 9750; *Journal of the Senate*, 1984, p. 6875.
37 For another example of reluctant votes for comparable worth, see the *Minneapolis Star & Tribune*'s report of the meeting of the National Governors' Association, July 31, 1984. Minnesota Governor Rudy Perpich successfully pressed the reluctant governors to go on the record by voting in favor of a resolution supporting pay equity/comparable worth, and all understood that, unlike the Republican incumbent, he was dumped from the association's executive committee in retaliation (August 1, 1984, p. 13A.)
38 Richard Cox, Association of Minnesota Counties, as quoted in *St. Petersburg Times* (Florida), April 15, 1985, p. C-9.
39 See, e.g., Evans and Nelson, "Mandating Local Change in Minnesota"; *Pay Equity: The Minnesota Experience* (Minnesota Commission on the Economic Status of Women, 1986), pp. 17, 28–9.
40 Minnesota Statutes Annotated, Section 471.993.
41 The Watkins statement that included the fact sheet is unpublished. See also Rothchild and Watkins, "Pay Equity in Minnesota," p. 28.
42 Rothchild's words are quoted in *Rochester Post-Bulletin*, October 11, 1986. Watkins voiced similar views in her unpublished remarks at a congressional staff briefing, May 15, 1987.
43 Tape recording of an informal hearing of the Governmental Operations Committee of the Minnesota House of Representatives, October 19, 1989.
44 *Pay Equity: The Minnesota Experience*, p. 19; Minnesota DOER, "Pay Equity in Minnesota Local Governments," January 30, 1986, pp. 8–9 (submitted to Minnesota legislature).
45 Faith Zwemke, "Pay Equity Analysis 100," DOER, December 11, 1989.
46 Rothchild uses this phrase and shows more fully her obvious disappointment at the localities' failure to use job match in a hearing before the Minnesota Senate Governmental Operations Committee, February 23, 1989.
47 The September 1990 DOER "Guide to Implementing Pay Equity in Local Government" listed some criteria that might be used when considering whether jurisdictions not in full compliance with the law had nonetheless made a "good faith" effort. One of these criteria was "If the jurisdiction chose not to use the free job match system, how much money has been spent on outside consultants?" (p. 50).
48 Evans and Nelson, *Wage Justice*, p. 151.
49 County figure was given in testimony by Merry Beckmann of the Association of Minnesota Counties at a public hearing of the Commission on the Economic Status of Women, August 30, 1988 (unpublished minutes of the hearing, p. 3). Also see the association's unpublished poll (Fall 1988, item no. 13). The school districts' figure is from Service Employees International Union, "Minnesota's Local Government Pay Equity Act: Four Years Later," February 1989, p. 3. A survey by the Arthur Young consulting firm of 195 local jurisdictions of all types found that 57 percent used an all-employee line. Twenty-eight percent used the male line. The rest used a balanced-class line, some combination of all three, or some other alternative.

50 Quoted in Evans and Nelson, *Wage Justice,* p. 93. Also see Helen Remick, "Comparable Worth in Washington State," in Rita Mae Kelly and Jane Bayes, *Comparable Worth, Pay Equity and Public Policy* (New York: Greenwood, 1988), pp. 234–5.

51 The Arthur Young consulting firm surveyed 195 local jurisdictions and found that 54 percent used a corridor. The corridor values ranged from 3 percent to 20 percent with the median corridor value at 10 percent on either side of the line ("Pay Equity Survey of Minnesota Jurisdictions," April 1988). (In 1989 the Arthur Young firm became Ernst and Young.) Among those responding to an Association of Minnesota Counties poll, 52 percent of counties used a corridor (Fall 1988, item no. 15).

52 Memorandum from Aviva Breen, executive director, Commission on the Economic Status of Women, to Senator Don Moe, March 16, 1989, p. 3. Also see Rothchild and Watkins, "Pay Equity in Minnesota," p. 27.

53 DOER, "A Guide to Implementing Pay Equity in Local Government" (August 1984), p. 6.

54 Arthur Young and Co., "Pay Equity Survey of Minnesota Jurisdictions," p. 4. A fall 1988 Association of Minnesota Counties poll found that 83 percent of responding counties adjusted all inequitably paid classes, not just female-dominated ones.

55 DOER, "A Guide to Implementing Pay Equity in Local Government," August 1989, p. 5.

56 Breen memorandum to Senator Moe, March 16, 1989, pp. 1 and 2; minutes of the public hearing by the Commission on the Economic Status of Women (August 2, 1988), p. 1; Minnesota Senate Governmental Operations Committee hearing, February 28, 1989.

57 There is no systematic evidence on how pervasive these techniques are. A Service Employees International Union survey of 91 school districts found that 35 percent had proposed a two-tier wage system though only 16 districts had implemented one. The survey found no instance as of 1988 of contracting out of jobs to evade pay equity adjustments, but found that 26 percent of districts had proposed contracting out of jobs during negotiations ("Minnesota, Local Government: Pay Equity Act," February 1989, p. 4). However, in testimony before the Governmental Operations Committee, Minnesota House of Representatives (March 15, 1990), a representative of the Service Employees International Union, Local 284, said that contracting out is "not just hypothetical . . . it's happening." He mentioned the New Alm School District, which contracted out its food service program and openly acknowledged that the costs of comparable worth were a factor. He also discussed a February 1990 legislative audit report which said that "the problem of subcontracting [contracting out] is going to get worse, especially in the food service area." In earlier testimony before the committee (March 8, 1990) a Teamsters' representative spoke at length of his fear of contracting out, and a Hennepin County representative spoke of it as a possible solution to the county's comparable-worth problems. An October 10, 1991, memorandum to clients from Cyrus Smythe and Karen Olsen of Labor Relations

Associates, Inc., noted that "a number of subdivisions have realized considerable economic savings in recent years by subcontracting work to private sector employers" (p. 4).

In my interview (June 1991) with the new commissioner of DOER, Linda Barton, she said that more and more schools are contracting out for food services. She also said that she had been visited by female cooks who asked that she not "make their schools do it [give them raises!]. They will contract us out."

58 See, e.g., Richard Arvey and Katherine Holt, "The Cost of Alternative Comparable Worth Strategies," *Compensation and Benefits Review* 20, no. 5 (September–October 1988): esp. p. 40.

59 This issue came up frequently in my interviews as is suggested by the quotations that follow. Also see Evans and Nelson, *Wage Justice,* p. 153.

60 *Duluth News Tribune and Herald,* January 30, 1987, p. 2A.

61 Evans and Nelson, *Wage Justice,* pp. 142–3.

62 For a late example, see *Minneapolis Star & Tribune,* July 18, 1987, p. 10D.

63 For example, in a long article (in a national personnel journal), they describe the legislation and implementation of both the state and local programs and then say: "The facts about the state's program are clear. No employees had wages reduced or frozen, and no employees were laid off as a result of the pay equity program. There have been no strikes or lawsuits" (Rothchild and Watkins, "Pay Equity in Minnesota," p. 26).

64 For a brief discussion of some lawsuits, see *Minneapolis Star & Tribune,* May 6, 1990, p. 1A; *St. Paul Pioneer Press,* April 14, 1990, p. 7A. Sixty-five of eighty-seven Minneapolis counties responded to an Association of Minnesota counties poll in the fall of 1988, and as of then, seven of the sixty-five had had some legal activity in connection with their comparable-worth plans. I know of no statistics for cities or school districts.

65 Letter from Sam Sivanich, District 6 Commissioner, Board of Hennepin County Commissioners, to Senator Donald Moe, March 21, 1989.

66 See Arvey and Holt, "Cost of Alternative Comparable Worth Strategies," p. 43.

67 Most states with comparable worth seem to have used an all-employee line. Most have also raised male-dominated jobs that fall below their line as well as female-dominated jobs. Thus, local practice in Minnesota was in accord with most practice in the United States even though it brought strong opposition from DOER. The local jurisdictions never made this point to DOER or the legislature because they were unaware of practices elsewhere. Nina Rothchild and Bonnie Watkins were aware of practices elsewhere but did not approve of them. This was just one of many instances in which the proponents' informational advantage proved useful in political skirmishes. See Chapter 8, p. 240.

68 An Association of Minnesota Counties poll of counties (Fall 1988) found that 38 percent of respondents were freezing the pay of at least some jobs paid over the pay line.

69 Minnesota lawyer Frank Madden briefly surveys the results of seventeen

pay equity arbitration cases filed through early 1988. In nine of the seventeen, the localities' position was not upheld and their comparable-worth plans were compromised (unpublished paper, "Legal and Practical Realities of the Pay Equity Act in Minnesota," pp. 11–16).

70 Alan Peterson's letters to Berglin, March 23 and June 12, 1989. Berglin's response, May 25, 1989.

71 Rothchild and Watkins, "Pay Equity in Minnesota," p. 27.

72 Ibid.

73 Evans and Nelson, *Wage Justice,* p. 147.

74 The Metropolitan Airports Commission, using the Control Data methodology used by many counties in Minnesota, found that all employees represented by unions were paid more than their duties warranted (*Minneapolis Star & Tribune,* September 11, 1987, p. 7Bw).

75 Testimony concerning S.F. 488, February 23, 1989.

76 DOER, "A Guide to Implementing Pay Equity in Local Government," August 1984, p. 6.

77 Ibid.

78 David Lutes and Nina Rothchild, "Compensation: Pay Equity Loses to Chicken Little and Other Excuses," *Personnel Journal* 65, no. 10 (October 1986): 127; also see DOER, "A Guide to Implementing Pay Equity in Local Government," p. 9.

79 Letter from Sheryl Le, classification and compensation manager, city of St. Paul, to Senator Donald Moe, chair, Senate Governmental Operations Committee, March 27, 1989.

80 Merry Beckmann, "Third Legislative Strike," *Minnesota Counties* 33, no. 5 (1989): 7.

81 Breen memorandum to Senator Moe, March 16, 1989; *Minneapolis Star & Tribune,* September 11, 1987, p. 7Bw.

82 *Minneapolis Star & Tribune,* October 14, 1984, p. 6D.

83 Rothchild and Watkins, "Pay Equity in Minnesota," p. 19.

84 Helen Remick, "Major Issues in *a priori* Applications," in Remick, ed., *Comparable Worth and Wage Discrimination* (Philadelphia: Temple University Press, 1984), p. 99. Hubbard and Revo-Cohen, one of the most popular of consulting firms among proponents, has called a pay-for-points approach "the most compatible with comparable worth theory" ("Final Report for Washington State: Job Classification and Compensation Review," March 31, 1987, p. 91).

85 The quotation comes from detailed minutes of a public meeting by the Commission on the Economic Status of Women on September 27, 1988. The quoted words are preceded by the words "Rothchild replied" in the commission's minutes. As in the rest of the minutes, quotation marks are not used so the Rothchild words quoted may not be exact. At a Syracuse University pay equity conference (March 18, 1989), I did hear Rothchild complain about local personnel department people who thought that the intent of the law "was to implement job evaluation studies."

86 The complaint about "twisting" the system is Rothchild's at the March 18,

1989, Syracuse University pay equity conference. It is Evans and Nelson who speak of "pay for points" as a new "technocratic" definition of comparable worth ("Comparable Worth: The Paradox of Technocratic Reform," *Feminist Studies* 15, no. 1 [Spring 1989]: 171–92, and *Wage Justice,* pp. 163 and 166).

87 This was the language on "purpose" proposed as an addition to the law by pay equity proponents in December 1989 and adopted with other language in 1990.

88 Rothchild and Watkins, "Pay Equity in Minnesota," p. 119.

89 Nina Rothchild, "Overview of Pay Initiatives, 1974–1984," in U.S. Civil Rights Commission, *Comparable Worth: Issue for the 80's,* vol. 1, p. 119.

90 The University of Minnesota, though fully committed at the top to comparable worth, has felt it necessary to grant increases to male-dominated job classes.

91 Arthur Young and Co., "Pay Equity Survey of Minnesota Jurisdictions," April 1988, p. 4.

92 DOER, "Pay Equity in Minnesota Local Governments" (submitted to Minnesota legislature), January 30, 1986, p. 10.

93 In testimony before the Governmental Operations Committee, Minnesota House of Representatives (March 14, 1990), Faith Zwemke, the Rothchild-appointed pay equity coordinator for DOER, said that despite all the talk about the high costs of pay equity, the latest reports from localities show costs of only about 2 percent of payroll: "These are the numbers the local governments gave us. Straight off their reports."

94 Cited in Evans and Nelson, *Wage Justice,* p. 160.

95 Letter from Sam Sivanich, District 6 Commissioner, Board of Hennepin County Commissioners, to Senator Donald Moe, March 21, 1989, and testimony of Chuck Sprafka, personnel director, Hennepin County, before the Governmental Operations Committee, Minnesota House of Representatives, March 8, 1990. Sprafka explained that Hennepin's big problem concerned 174 plumbers, carpenters, and equipment operators who were ranked with about 2,800 female-dominated jobs (senior clerk typists and other clerical workers). Bringing the 2,800 in female-dominated occupations up to the pay level of the 174 in male-dominated occupations would alone cost $12.3 million. In a sense, then, each of the 174 more highly paid employees would annually be costing Hennepin their salary *plus* $70,689 ($12,300,000 ÷ 174). It was for this reason that Sprafka told the committee that contracting out of the male-dominated jobs would have to be seriously considered.

96 From Linda Barton's testimony before the Senate Governmental Operations Committee (January 30, 1990). Barton was then city manager of Burnsville. She replaced Rothchild as state commissioner of employee relations the following year.

97 Rothchild and Watkins, "Pay Equity in Minnesota," p. 28.

98 Evans and Nelson, *Wage Justice,* pp. 162–3.

99 Minutes of the Annual Business Meeting, Association of Minnesota Counties, January 22, 1985, p. 21.

100 A commissioner in Red Lake County, *Grand Forks Herald,* August 31, 1987.

101 The city manager of Inver Grove Heights, *St. Paul Pioneer Press and Dispatch,* October 2, 1985, pp. 1S–2S.

102 Minnesota Statutes 471.991, subdiv. 5.

103 Proponents thought that they had no chance to pass a law requiring that localities achieve compliance by bringing all women up to the male pay line. Their hope was that this provision would at least ensure that predominantly female occupations were not clustered in the bottom of corridors while predominantly male occupations were clustered in the top.

104 Minnesota Statutes 471.992, subdiv. 1.

105 Minnesota Statutes 471.988 and 471.998, subdiv. 1.

106 From an audio tape of a hearing before the Governmental Operations Committee, Minnesota House of Representatives, March 8, 1990.

107 Ibid.

108 From an audio tape of a hearing before the Governmental Operations Committee, Minnesota House of Representatives, March 15, 1990.

109 Eileen Stein, at the time chair of the NCPE, when introducing Nina Rothchild for a speech at the national committee's annual meeting, December 4, 1987.

110 Evans and Nelson, *Wage Justice,* p. 154.

111 From an audio tape of a hearing before the Governmental Operations Committee, Minnesota House of Representatives, March 14, 1990.

112 Ibid., March 15, 1990.

113 Interview with ex-Senator Moe, June 10, 1991. This explanation for this legislative provision was confirmed in a phone interview with House Chairman Reding (June 11, 1991) and by a Hennepin County personnel expert. In a dialogue with Faith Zwemke during the Senate Governmental Operations Committee hearings (January 30, 1990), Senator Moe said, "To put it bluntly, I think some people fear that your boss is such an advocate that she might not be a completely fair and unbiased judge of the local government's efforts." Zwemke replied, "Well, Mr. Chairman, I'm very glad that my boss is an advocate." Moe is an admirer of Rothchild, calling her (in our interview) a "strong-willed, wonderful woman" and "a good commissioner."

114 From an audio tape of a hearing before the Governmental Operations Committee, Minnesota House of Representatives, March 14, 1990. Well after passage of the 1990 law, former mayor of St. Paul, George Latimer, was defending his sex-neutral approach to pay equity: "It was basic equity. If a guy is working on an undervalued job, why should he be penalized because he is male?" (*St. Paul Pioneer Press,* April 26, 1992, p. 9A).

115 See Aviva Breen's testimony at an informal hearing held at St. Mary's College before the House Governmental Operations Committee, September 14, 1989.

116 From an audio tape of Senate Governmental Operations Committee hearing, January 30, 1990.

117 *New York Times,* October 7, 1989, p. 8.

118 From an audio tape of an informal meeting (at the city of Worthington) of the House Governmental Operations Committee, October 19, 1989.
119 Minutes of the committee, March 15, 1990.
120 Quoted from Faith Zwemke at the March 14, 1990, hearing of the House Governmental Operations Committee. Representative Simoneau in the same committee on March 15 said that, by looking at external comparisons, one was just "taking a snapshot of institutional discrimination in wages."
121 Minnesota Statutes 471.993, subdiv. 1.
122 DOER, *A Guide to Implementing Pay Equity in Local Government* (revised September 1990), pp. 34 and 47.
123 The accepted term in and out of DOER. See the minutes of the DOER Pay Equity Rule Advisory Committee, May 14, 1981, p. 2, and July 1, 1991, p. 2, as well as the letter from Charles Sprafka, Hennepin County, to Administrative Law Judge Allen E. Giles, November 20, 1991.
124 Pay Equity SONAR, chapter 3920, p. 9.
125 Report of the administrative law judge on proposed adoption of DOER Rules Relating to Local Government Pay Equity Compliance, Minnesota Rules, Parts 3920.0100 to 3920.1300 (Office of Administrative Hearings 3–1500–5878–1), December 31, 1991, pp. 24, 29, 22.
126 Ibid., p. 7.
127 For some samples of the strong feelings of localities on this matter, see *Minnesota Star & Tribune,* May 6, 1990, p. 8A.
128 Interview, June 11, 1991.
129 In the summer of 1990, under Rothchild's DOER leadership, Faith Zwemke was not focusing on the law's relatively flexible definition of "equitable compensation relationship." That definition said that, to be equitable, "the compensation for female-dominated classes ... [should] not [be] consistently below the compensation for male-dominated classes of comparable work value." Instead, when speaking to localities, Zwemke quoted from that part of the law which spoke of the requirement "to eliminate sex-based wage disparities." A League of Minnesota *Cities Bulletin* noted: "Zwemke pointed out that the word eliminate is key. It [the law] does not say reduce nor does it say come close. DOER says this means that neither a market exception nor a corridor concept is acceptable if there is an observable trend where females receive less pay than men" (July 13, 1990), p. 1.
130 For example, one section of the Minnesota law (471.993, subdiv. 2) requires that there be a reasonable pay relationship between positions. Reasonable relationship is defined in part as "comparable" compensation "for positions which require comparable skills, effort, responsibility, working conditions and other relevant work-related criteria." For documents hinting at court cases to come, see the unpublished memorandum from Cyrus Smythe and Karen Olsen to clients of their Labor Relations Associates, Inc., October 10, 1991, and the letter of Jeanette Sobania, personnel coordinator of the city of Plymouth, to Faith Zwemke, June 1992.

131 Phone interview with Karen Olsen, consultant to Minnesota localities, June 25, 1992.

132 Though, as previously noted, female-dominated classes were 70 percent or more women, male-dominated classes were 80 percent or more men under the Minnesota law.

133 When I spoke with her about the Fridley scenario, Faith Zwemke said localities should realize that cases like this (where a benign action made a city out of compliance) could occur only if they were settling for the bare minimum four-fifths standard. If they saw the four-fifths as a floor, not as a ceiling, and brought female-dominated classes closer to full equity, this sort of anomaly would not occur (phone interview, June 25, 1992).

## 4. *Job evaluation in Minnesota localities*

1 Minnesota Department of Employee Relations [DOER], "A Guide to Implementing Pay Equity in Local Government," August 1984, pp. 9 and 21.

2 Arthur Young became Ernst and Young in 1989.

3 *Public Administration Times,* June 15, 1984, p. 4.

4 Informal hearing of the Minnesota House Governmental Operations Committee held at St. Mary's College, September 14, 1989.

5 DOER, "Pay Equity in Minnesota Local Governments," January 30, 1986, p. 7 (submitted to Minnesota legislature).

6 Bill Joynes, Golden Valley city manager and chair of the Metropolitan Area Managers Association, as quoted in Sara Evans and Barbara Nelson, *Wage Justice: Comparable Worth and the Paradox of Technocratic Reform* (Chicago: University of Chicago Press, 1989), p. 142.

7 Donald Schwab and Robert Grams, "Sex-Related Errors in Job Evaluation: A Real World Test," *Journal of Applied Psychology* 70, no. 3 (August 1985): 533–9. For other studies, some of which suggest evaluator bias may be present, see Paula England, *Comparable Worth: Theories and Evidence* (New York: De Gruyter, 1992), pp. 200–2, and see citations in Paul Weiler, "The Wages of Sex: The Uses and Limits of Comparable Worth," *Harvard Law Review* 99 (1986): 1767n.

8 See Chapter 8, pp. 222–3.

9 Ronnie Steinberg, "Identifying Wage Discrimination and Implementing Pay Equity Adjustments," in U.S. Commission on Civil Rights, *Comparable Worth: Issue for the 80's,* vol. 1 (Washington, D.C.: U.S. Government Printing Office, 1984), p. 106.

10 DOER, "A Guide to Implementing Pay Equity in Local Government," p. 11.

11 See, e.g., the comments of Minneapolis city council member Joan Niemiec in *Twin Cities Reader,* October 3, 1984, pp. 7–8.

12 Cited in Joan Acker, *Doing Comparable Worth: Gender Class and Pay Equity* (Philadelphia: Temple University Press, 1989), p. 98.

13 Weiler, "The Wages of Sex," p. 1768n.

14 *St. Paul Pioneer Press,* August 5, 1987, pp. 1C–2C.

15 In my interviews proponents of comparable worth described these male-

dominated jobs differently, emphasizing how much time "the cops" spend just driving around and fire fighters spend playing cards and polishing engines. Aviva Breen, executive director of the Commission on the Economic Status of Women, characterized public works employees as "the guys who change the light bulbs in street lights."

16 Even proponents seem to agree that, on average, predominantly male jobs have worse working conditions. See Donald Treiman, Heidi Hartmann, and Patricia Roos, "Assessing Pay Discrimination Using National Data," in Helen Remick, ed., *Comparable Worth and Wage Discrimination* (Philadelphia: Temple University Press, 1984), pp. 143–4; see also Chapter 2, note 34.

17 *Princeton Union Eagle,* February 14, 1984.

18 *Washington Post,* November 22, 1989, p. D-1. Also see the article about a British journalist, " 'a bit of a daredevil,' " who (fresh from Beirut) was killed in El Salvador about the same time as the young Tampa reporter (*Washington Post,* November 18, 1989, p. A-18). More generally, on the importance of heterogeneity of tastes to wage outcomes, see Mark Killingsworth, *The Economics of Comparable Worth* (Kalamazoo, Mich.: Upjohn Institute, 1990), pp. 34–8.

19 Evans and Nelson, *Wage Justice,* p. 105.

20 Nina Rothchild and Bonnie Watkins, "Pay Equity in Minnesota: The Facts Are In," *Review of Public Personnel Administration* 7, no. 3 (Summer 1987): 27.

21 Evans and Nelson, *Wage Justice,* pp. 125, 146–8, 152, 158, 162.

22 A 1990 *Minneapolis Star & Tribune* article (May 6, p. 8A) reported, "Some cities and counties outside the Twin Cities say pay equity has bred so much jealousy and discontent that small-town city halls and county courthouses have become almost impossible to work in." In an October 25, 1989, letter to Representative Richard Jefferson, a Nobles County personnel specialist spoke of "endless headaches with unions and employee groups."

In testimony before the Senate Governmental Operations Committee (February 15, 1990), Plymouth Assistant City Manager Frank Broyles said that implementing pay equity was a "lose–lose proposition. For those you give a pay equity increase to, they say 'thanks, it's not enough, and it's not soon enough.' For those you don't give the pay equity increase to, they say, 'Hey, you don't love us anymore!' We're the ones left dealing with the morale dilemma with our employees, because we are trying to run an operation." See also Linda Barton's comments near the end of Chapter 3. The National Committee on Pay Equity reports (*Newsnotes,* Fall 1991, p. 7) that a report on the first-year experience in Ontario (by SPR Associates) found that there were "negative effects on union–management relationships and morale of employees."

23 DOER, "A Guide to Implementing Pay Equity in Local Government," p. 10.

24 Evans and Nelson, *Wage Justice,* p. 158.

25 Ibid., p. 125. Also see p. 159.

26 Arthur Young and Co., *1988 Pay Equity Survey of Minnesota Jurisdictions,*

April 1988, p. 1. I was also told that 380 out of 435 school boards used committees. An Association of Minnesota Counties survey (Fall 1988) with 65 respondents found that 53 counties used committees, 35 of which combined employees and management.

27 *Faribault Daily News,* May 22, 1987, pp. 1–2.

28 *St. Paul Pioneer Press and Dispatch,* letter to the editor, December 16, 1987, p. 12A.

29 Clare Burton reviews experiments showing that familiarity and experience with a job favorably affect evaluations of it. Clare Burton, Raven Hag, and Gay Thompson, *Women's Worth: Pay Equity and Job Evaluation in Australia* (Canberra: Australian Government Publishing Service, 1987), pp. 4–6.

30 In San Jose, California, a female member of that city's evaluation committee remembered that "all the women were saying: 'We're going to make sure that the women's jobs get more points than any others.' Even though a lot of people will tell you: 'Oh no, we were really unbiased!' But we weren't. We were fighting like anything for the women's jobs.... We fought and fought and fought" (as quoted in Linda Blum, *Between Feminism and Labor: The Significance of the Comparable Worth Movement* [Berkeley and Los Angeles: University of California Press, 1991], pp. 79–80).

31 *St. Paul Pioneer Press and Dispatch,* January 21, 1987, pp. 1C–2C.

32 *Rochester Post-Bulletin,* April 7, 1987, p. 4B.

33 Quoted words are from an interview, but also see *Brainerd Daily Dispatch,* January 22, 1986, p. 8A.

34 *Plymouth Post,* January 3, 1985, p. 1.

35 *Brooklyn Center Post,* July 10, 1986, pp. 1–2.

36 From a tape of an informal hearing of the Minnesota House Governmental Operations Committee at St. Mary's College, September 14, 1989.

37 DOER, "A Guide to Implementing Pay Equity in Local Government," p. 9.

38 *Brooklyn Center Post,* July 10, 1986, pp. 1–2; *Qualle v. County of Beltrami,* 422 N.W.2d 291 (Mn. Ct. App. 1988).

39 On St. Paul, see *Minneapolis Star & Tribune,* December 11, 1986, p. 5B, and Evans and Nelson, *Wage Justice,* p. 157. On Minneapolis, see the minutes of the public hearings of the Commission on the Economic Status of Women, August 2, 1988, pp. 7–8, and August 30, 1988, pp. 5–6.

40 E.g., see Donald Treiman and Heidi Hartmann, eds., *Women, Work and Wages* (Washington, D.C.: National Academy Press, 1981), pp. 1–2.

41 For a discussion of *Lemons v. City and County of Denver,* 620 F.2d 228 (10th Cir. 1980), and other cases involving nurses, see Susan Gluck Mezey, *In Pursuit of Equality: Women, Public Policy, and the Federal Courts* (New York: St. Martin's, 1992), pp. 101–6.

42 The American Library Association (ALA) can provide those interested with bibliographies, packets of resource materials, recommended policy language to be adopted by local libraries, a 106-page "Action Manual" that includes detailed instructions on how to conduct your own JES, and an index of pay

equity videotapes and bumper stickers. The ALA has had programs on pay equity at every one of its annual conferences since 1979.

43 The *Fargo Forum* (December 22, 1985, p. D-10) reports that three female library media specialists working for the Moorhead School District were above the pay equity corridor and that their pay was to be held down in the future.

44 Memorandum dated March 16, 1989, with reference to bill S.F. 488. Unfortunately, 1990 census data that would enable one to compare 1980 and 1990 librarian salaries in Minnesota and in the nation as a whole are not yet available. Librarians have also done very well in the Ontario, Canada, process. The *Wall Street Journal* reports: "When the provincial government finally announced its own plan last week, the biggest boost went to 39 librarians. Their wages will be raised $7 an hour to match those of engineers, whose work it found to be of equal value" (March 9, 1990, p. B-7).

45 In San Jose the librarians were apparently equally as skillful. Extensive research was done on the Hay system, and supervising and budgetary responsibilities were emphasized in librarian job descriptions because these were emphasized in the Hay scheme. (Instead of " 'I help people get books' the librarians would put down: 'I'm responsible for a $1.5 million book collection.' ")

Linda Blum reports: "The librarians were so successful in this aspect of the study that other groups were resentful. One engineering technician, a woman who had switched to this male-dominated job category, told me that she felt personnel ought to have looked at 'what people *really* do, and not at how they describe what they do. Because some people are just better at describing. . . . Librarians are in the word business anyway.' She also commented that the technicians had just taken the whole study 'very casually,' while the librarians obviously had not" (*Between Feminism and Labor,* p. 76).

46 See, e.g., Frank Levy, Arnold Meltsner, and Aaron Wildavsky, *Urban Outcomes* (Berkeley and Los Angeles: University of California Press, 1974), chap. 3. Nationally, 60.8 percent of public library operating expenses go to personnel. "Public Libraries in 44 States and D.C.," National Center for Educational Statistics working paper, U.S. Department of Education (November 1989).

47 For example, this shift of funds occurred in the city of Gilbert.

48 See the discussion of overpayment and the specific example of societal losses from overpayment of New York city sanitation workers in Chapter 2 (pp. 31–2). It would not be economically inefficient to raise salaries substantially for a position where there are dozens of applicants at the original, lower wage, if the applicants at the original, lower wage were of low quality. In my interviews with head librarians, I received no indication that, prior to comparable worth, there were problems with the quality of librarians or applicants. To the contrary, the concern was that existing librarians of such demonstrable quality should be paid so poorly and that qualified applicants

with degrees and experience should have to settle for even more poorly paid trainee or clerical positions while waiting for a real librarian slot to open up.

49 I have been unable to find data that might confirm or contradict the clear impression I have received from my interviews: that raises for public-sector nurses in Minnesota have not kept up with those for private-sector nurses during the comparable-worth era. My search did uncover Chris Mahonney, a nurse and faculty member at St. Cloud State. An active member of the Minnesota Nurses Association, Mahonney conducts most of her research on nursing issues. She thought she was quite familiar with the pay for Minnesota nurses and was confident that the increases in the private sector had been greater in recent years. Mahonney thought that the primary cause was a general tendency for the public sector to be slower to change pay, with comparable worth being a secondary reason.

50 *Washington Post,* July 17, 1988, p. A-9.

51 *Minneapolis Star & Tribune,* August 16, 1989, p. 10.

52 Two other public health nursing directors said an opening had produced only one applicant. The contrast with those hiring librarians was striking.

53 Informal hearing of Minnesota House Governmental Operations Committee in the city of Worthington, October 19, 1989. The quotes are those of the director of public health nursing for Nobles and Rock counties. Other counties where I was told public-sector nursing salaries trailed that of the private sector, in part because of comparable worth, were Morrison, Todd, Wilken, and Olmstead. These counties are in the central and southern portions of the state. In Washington state there are also reported shortages of nurses because the comparable-worth pay guidelines are below market levels (*New York Times,* May 31, 1990, p. D-22).

54 The public health nursing director of Todd County thought that a lawsuit against the comparable-worth plan (filed in another department) made it hard for the county board to increase nurses' salaries. In testimony before the Minnesota House Governmental Operations Committee, a Teamsters Union leader pointedly noted that three nurses in Wadina County had received, for market reasons, more pay than their job evaluation points warranted. He insisted on similar negotiating flexibility for his union members (March 8, 1990).

Some counties do pay nurses more for market reasons, even if it takes them well above the line (e.g., Aitkin and Hennepin). Hennepin increased nurses' salaries by 29 percent from 1989 to 1991. Public-sector nurses' salaries are now competitive with those in the private sector and "way above" the line. Turnover has "dropped tremendously" (interview with a Hennepin personnel specialist, June 18, 1991).

55 Quoted words are from Joy Ann Grune, "Pay Equity Is a Necessary Remedy for Wage Discrimination," in U.S. Commission on Civil Rights, *Comparable Worth: Issue for the 80's,* vol. 1, p. 169.

56 Ehrenberg and Smith, *Modern Labor Economics,* pp. 45–6.

57 June O'Neill, "An Argument Against Comparable Worth," in U.S. Com-

mission on Civil Rights, *Comparable Worth: Issue for the 80's,* vol. 1, p. 183.

58 U.S. Office of Personnel Management, *Comparable Worth for Federal Jobs* (Washington, D.C.: U.S. Government Printing Office, September 1987), pp. 32–3.

59 Based on U.S. Department of Labor, Bureau of Labor Statistics, Current Population Survey, 1990, unpublished tabulations, and *Monthly Labor Review* (April 1982) for 1981 figures. (I multiplied 1981 figures by the 1981–90 inflator of 1.4378 to obtain real-wage changes.)

60 There is no Bureau of Labor Statistics figure for skilled blue-collar craft workers per se. The figure for "precision production craft and repair" is used as the closest approximation. Figures for professionals and other workers are from the Current Population Survey, 1990, unpublished tabulations.

61 In saying this, I do not mean to take sides in the debate among opponents of comparable worth as to whether nurses' salaries would be even higher were it not for the collusive behavior of the hospital industry or the tough cost-containment policies of the federal government. I simply argue that whatever the effect of these attempts to hold costs down, they have clearly not been sufficient to keep nurses' wages from rising as shortages have arisen. On the debate, see the statement of Mark Killingsworth in U.S. Congress, Joint Economic Committee, *Women in the Work Force: Pay Equity,* hearing, 98th Congress, April 10, 1984, esp. p. 113, and O'Neill, "An Argument Against Comparable Worth," p. 183.

62 See, e.g., the comments of Representative Oakar in *Congressional Record,* House of Representatives, 100th Congress, September 29, 1988, p. 8994, and those of Barbara Curtis, from the board of directors of the American Nurses Association, in U.S. Congress, Senate, Subcommittee on Federal Services, Post Office, and Civil Service of the Committee on Governmental Affairs, *Federal Employee Compensation Equity Act of 1987,* hearing, 100th Congress, April 22, 1987, pp. 21–2.

63 The *Washington Post* (December 17, 1989, p. A-10) reports a 50 percent increase for the 1989–90 academic year after sharp declines in the previous four years. Of freshmen entering college in 1990, 3.8 percent expressed interest in a career in nursing, compared to 2.7 percent in 1989, and 2.2 percent in 1987 (Alexander Astin, William Korn, and Ellyne Berz, *The American Freshman: National Norms for 1990* [Higher Education Research Institute, Graduate School of Education, University of California, Los Angeles, December 1990], p. 6).

64 Among many other news articles, see *St. Paul Pioneer Press and Dispatch,* February 27, 1987, p. 12, and *Minneapolis Star & Tribune,* May 1, 1987, p. 1B, and May 13, 1987, p. 7B.

65 Among many other news articles, see *St. Paul Pioneer Press,* August 5, 1987, pp. 1C–2C, and *Minneapolis Star & Tribune,* August 19, 1987, p. 7B.

66 From a talk given at the "Pay Equity in Action" conference, Syracuse University, March 17, 1989.

67 Interview with the author, June 1, 1989.

68 Sara Evans and Barbara Nelson, "Comparable Worth for Public Employees: Implementing a New Wage Policy in Minnesota," in Rita Mae Kelly and Jane Bayes, eds., *Comparable Worth, Pay Equity and Public Policy* (New York: Greenwood, 1988), p. 206.

69 Evans and Nelson, *Wage Justice*, pp. 151 and 159.

70 Briefly mentioned in *Minneapolis Star & Tribune* (St. Paul edition), November 14, 1987, p. 1B.

71 The Minneapolis study was later redone, and police have not received pay equity raises in Minneapolis.

72 Evans and Nelson, *Wage Justice*, Table 6.1.

73 For one example of public praise for police for their willingness to do important dangerous work, see *Washington Post*, October 22, 1989, p. C-6.

74 See note 41 and Chapter 2, pp. 31–2.

75 For another example, see the discussion in Ehrenberg and Smith, *Modern Labor Economics*, p. 43.

76 Rothchild and Watkins, "Pay Equity in Minnesota," p. 24.

77 There was essentially no change in the inflation-adjusted real wage of the average worker from 1981 to 1990. During that period secretaries gained 1.4 percent, typists 7.6 percent, bookkeepers 5.0 percent, file clerks 2.0 percent. Figures are based on U.S. Bureau of Labor Statistics unpublished tabulations from the Current Population Survey, 1990, and *Monthly Labor Review* (April 1982) for 1981 figures. I multiplied 1981 figures by the 1981–90 inflator of 1.4378 to obtain real wage changes.

78 The quotation is from an interview, but see Minnesota House Governmental Operations Committee, informal hearing at College of St. Mary's, September 14, 1989, for other evidence of such constituent complaints. In a June 1991 interview, the new commissioner of DOER, Linda Barton, recalled her tenure as city manager of Burnsville when businesses used to complain about the city stealing their secretaries. She remembered that the Chamber of Commerce decided not to get involved because of fear that it could lead to a new law applying comparable worth to the private sector. A 1992 state auditor's study found that, in St. Paul's government, a secretary's average pay was $35,842 compared with $21,510 in private industry (reported in *St. Paul Pioneer Press*, April 26, 1992, p. 10A).

79 For more on contracting out, see Chapter 3, note 57.

80 Deborah Swenson-Klatt and Margaret Boyer, *Eliminating Sex-Based Wage Disparities: Pay Equity and Minnesota's Child Care and Education Employees*, Child Care Workers Alliance pamphlet, April 1991, esp. pp. 8, 17. Also see the minutes of the hearings before the Commission on the Economic Status of Women, August 2, 1988, p. 3, and September 27, 1988, pp. 1–2, for a discussion of dilemmas faced by the child-care facility at the University of Minnesota.

81 *Rochester Post-Bulletin*, October 11, 1986, p. 1A.

82 An anonymous reader of an earlier draft of this book here asked if I think such customer discrimination should be allowed, noting that restaurants

cannot refuse to hire black waiters because they think customers will go elsewhere. It is not clear to me why my reader thinks consumers here have discriminatory tastes. It seems quite unlikely that consumers would be willing to pay more for day-care workers or home health-care providers if they were men, not women.

83 *Rochester Post-Bulletin,* October 11, 1986, p. 1A.

84 Hearing of the Minnesota Senate Governmental Operations Committee, February 28, 1989.

85 Bonnie Watkins, "Pay Equity in Action," *Compleat Lawyer* 3, no. 1 (Winter 1986): 26.

86 *Rochester Post-Bulletin* (Rochester, Minn.), October 11, 1986, p. 1A.

87 This example shows that the views of the local officials who say comparable worth buys nothing for the public should be qualified. In time it should buy higher-quality employees who will be capable of doing more demanding work. Since the more demanding work is not additionally compensated, this added benefit comes only when comparable-worth principles are violated.

88 Faith Zwemke, pay equity coordinator, Minnesota DOER, *Pay Equity Analysis 100,* December 11, 1989, p. 2.

89 The fact that some localities were blending male- and female-dominated classes into a balanced class so as to make inequities disappear was mentioned in a meeting of the Pay Equity Advisory Committee (minutes, May 24, 1991); it is also noted in Cyrus Smythe and Karen Olsen's memorandum to clients of Labor Relations Associates, Inc., October 10, 1991, p. 3.

90 Aviva Breen, letter to Senator Moe on S.F. 488, March 16, 1989, p. 4; minutes of the hearing before the Commission on the Economic Status of Women, August 2, 1988, p. 7.

91 See Minnesota House Bill 959, introduced March 7, 1991. For a discussion of the extent of contracting out, see Chapter 3, note 56.

92 DOER, "A Guide to Implementing Pay Equity in Local Government," pp. 9 and 21.

93 *Minnesota Daily,* April 11, 1985, pp. 4 and 11.

94 *Wall Street Journal,* May 10, 1985, p. 27.

95 In testimony before the U.S. Commission on Civil Rights, Nina Rothchild emphasized the Princeton experience and said that Zwemke and the city administrator had developed a job evaluation system "which everybody thought was fair" (*Comparable Worth: Issue for the 80's,* vol. 2, p. 74).

96 Rothchild and Watkins, "Pay Equity in Minnesota," pp. 26–7.

97 See, e.g., Sara Evans and Barbara Nelson, "Comparable Worth: The Paradox of Technocratic Reform," *Feminist Studies* 15, no. 1 (Spring 1989): 185, and *Wage Justice,* p. 105.

98 See Jennifer Roback, *A Matter of Choice: A Critique of Comparable Worth by A Skeptical Feminist* (New York: Priority Press, 1986), p. 42.

99 Evans and Nelson, *Wage Justice,* p. 100.

100 All redistributive schemes interfere with market prices to some degree, but low-income tax credits or a negative income tax would do so to a much

less degree than would comparable worth. See Edgar Browning and Jacquelene Browning, *Public Finance and the Price System* (New York: Macmillan, 1987), chaps. 8 and 9, for a discussion of taxes and welfare costs. A 1978 survey of 211 randomly selected economists asks their reaction to thirty statements. The most striking areas of concerns involved the opposition to government "interference with the price mechanism and exchange" (J. R. Kearl, Clayne Pope, Gordon Whiting, and Larry Wimmer, "What Economists Think," *American Economic Review: Papers and Proceedings* 69 [May 1979]: 34).

101 *Washington Post,* December 29, 1990, p. A-18.

102 Organization for Economic Cooperation and Development, *Structural Adjustment and Economic Performance* (Paris: OECD, 1987), p. 144.

103 Reasons why males could come to dominate comparable-worth processes in the long run are explored in Chapter 8.

### *5. Equal pay for work of equal value in the European Community*

1 Christopher McCrudden, "Comparable Worth: A Common Dilemma," *Yale Journal of International Law* 11, no. 2 (Spring 1986):397.

2 Ibid., p. 436.

3 Ibid., p. 410.

4 F. von Prondzynski, *Network of Experts on the Implementation of the Equality Directives: Final Consolidated Report, 1987,* Commission of the European Communities, V/1087/88-EN, May 1988, p. 18.

5 I explain later why, within the EC, I focus on the United Kingdom in my discussion here. However, the reader should not be left to wonder if the Irish case was omitted because it was going much better than the British. The Irish have avoided the worst of the delays in the British system, but only through the use of a system so informal that the Irish Employment Equality Agency has recommended a significant tightening up of procedural rules covering matters such as the Labor Court's investigative approach and rules of evidence so that the individual right of the complaining employee is not lost sight of. Moreover, the "equality officers" who do the actual comparing of jobs not infrequently use "a highly subjective approach, lacking precision" ("Equal Opportunity in Ireland," *Equal Opportunities Review,* no. 9 [September–October 1986]: 12–18).

6 Commission of the European Community, *Community Law and Women,* Supplement no. 25, Women of Europe, X152/87-EN, pp. 23–4.

7 F. von Prondzynski, *Implementation of the Equality Directives,* Commission of the European Communities, V/1511/86-EN, July 1986, p. 24.

8 Ibid., p. 26. Also see McCrudden, "Comparable Worth: A Common Dilemma," p. 432.

9 The *Economist* notes that Italians "delight in legalisms and the law (there are more lawyers in Rome alone than in the whole of France)," but Italians also believe "it is enough to pass laws; there is no need to implement them" ("Survey Italy," May 26, 1990, p. 20). Elizabeth Vallance and Elizabeth

Davies say the following about another EC country: "By comparison with other member states, Greece is fairly progressive in giving full legal rights to women workers and in complying with EC law. Yet the actual situation of the Greek woman worker is amongst the worst in the Community" (*Women of Europe: Women MEP's and Equality Policy* [Cambridge University Press, 1986], p. 104).

10 Vallance and Davies, *Women of Europe,* p. 100.

11 *Equal Opportunities Review,* no. 7 (May–June 1986): 16.

12 Janice Bellace, "A Foreign Perspective," in E. Robert Livernash, ed., *Comparable Worth: Issues and Alternatives* (Washington, D.C.: Equal Employment Advisory Council, 1980), pp. 140–1.

13 The EC was first called the European Economic Community (EEC). Since 1967 when Euratom and the European Coal and Steel Community were merged with the EEC, it has usually been called the "European Community," though the abbreviation "EEC" is still seen frequently (Dick Leonard, *Pocket Guide to the European Community* [Oxford: Blackwell Publisher, 1988], p. 3).

14 Articles 117 and 118, Treaty of Rome, U.N. Treaty Series V. 298, pp. 61–2.

15 "Equal Pay," *Common Market,* 2 N.Y. (April 4, 1962): 66. Also see Vallance and Davies, *Women of Europe,* p. 73.

16 Commission of the European Community, *How Fares Equal Pay?: A Report of Progress in the Community: Summary,* Background Report ISEC/138/79, February 22, 1979, p. 1. The Commission later found that the differences among the EC countries on female pay were not as significant as the French had thought. Hans Smit and Peter Herzog, *The Law of the European Economic Community,* vol. 3 (New York: Bender, 1988), p. 3-761.

17 McCrudden, "Comparable Worth: A Common Dilemma," p. 399; Doreen Collins, *Social Policy of the European Community* (New York: Wiley, 1975), p. 85; B. A. Hepple, *Equal Pay and the Industrial Tribunals* (London: Sweet & Maxwell, 1984), p. 9; W. B. Creighton, *Working Women and the Law* (London: Mansell, 1979), pp. 110–11.

18 Article 119, Treaty of Rome, U.N. Treaty Series V. 298, p. 62.

19 European Economic Community [EEC], *Fifth General Report – 1962,* pp. 185–6; "Equal Pay," pp. 65–7; Collins, *Social Policy of the European Community,* pp. 84–9.

20 Collins, *Social Policy of the European Community,* p. 87; "Equal Pay," p. 66.

21 *Social Exposé 1968,* par. 29, p. 240, as quoted in Collins, *Social Policy of the European Community,* p. 88.

22 Commission of the European Community, Proposal for a *Council Directive* on the principle of equal pay, COM(73) 1927, November 14, 1973; Amended proposal for a *Council Directive* on the principle of equal pay, COM(74) 1010, July 3, 1974.

23 In the 1980s, the European Parliament gained the power to amend certain legislation. The member states of the EC have agreed to expand the powers

of Parliament further in the 1990s. Still, a 1982 poll found that only 7 percent of U.K. respondents could name their European parliamentary representatives (Vallance and Davies, *Women of Europe,* p. 7).

24 This interventionist tilt is particularly evident in the staff of the Committee's social section, one member of which told me that he saw his job as "peeling off the enlightened business representatives from the hard-liners" so as to get section support for "progressive" social policy. Also see Vallance and Davies, *Women of Europe,* pp. 79 and 85.

25 European Parliament, *Working Documents,* 1974–5, Report on the Proposal for a Directive on Equal Pay (Doc. 262/73), Doc. 21/74, April 22, 1974; Economic and Social Committee, Section for Social Questions, on Proposed Equal Pay Directive, April 16, 1974.

26 European Communities, the Council, meeting on June 27, 1974, of the Working Party on Social Questions, 1327/74 (Soc. 150) July 8, 1974, p. 6.

27 European Communities, the Council, *Results of Decisions,* R 3228/74 (Soc. 260), December 3, 1974; European Communities, the Council, *Note,* meeting on June 27, 1974, of the Working Party on Social Questions, 1327/74 (Soc. 150), July 8, 1974.

28 European Communities, the Council, *Note,* meeting on July 9, 1974, of the Working Party on Social Questions, 1422/74 (Soc. 163) August 6, 1974, p. 3. The Commission referred to a resolution dated December 30, 1961. The closest that resolution came to calling for equal value was not very close: "The member states further recognize that any practices of systematic downgrading of women workers shall be incompatible with the principle of equal remuneration when different qualification rules are adopted for men and women or when criteria in job evaluation for the classification of workers are used which are not related to the objective conditions in which the work is done" (Council decision entitled "Equal Remuneration for Equal Work as Between Men and Women Workers," December 30, 1961 [Bulletin of the EEC, no. 1, 1962]).

29 The Council, *Results of Decisions,* December 3, 1974.

30 Ibid.

31 Ibid.

32 Ibid.

33 Council of the European Communities, *Press Release,* 320th meeting of the Council, Social Affairs, December 17, 1974.

34 John Fraser, interview with the author, June 14, 1988.

35 *Hansard* (House of Commons) *Parliamentary Debates,* vol. 795, 1970, February 9, 1970, pp. 915–16. On job evaluation, Castle quoted ILO Convention 100 as follows: "Where such action will assist in giving effect to the provisions of this Convention, measures shall be taken to promote objective appraisal of jobs on the basis of the work to be performed."

36 Ibid.

37 The analysis is based in part on interviews with three people in the United Kingdom who were representatives to the EC in 1974 and with John Fraser. Quotations are from Fraser.

38 The facts and quotations are based on the transcript of the 320th meeting of the Council, Social Affairs, December 17, 1974.

39 Memorandum of the permanent representatives committee, January 31, 1975.

40 Commission of the European Community, *The Commission Moves on Discrimination Against Women,* ISEC/B16/79, April 20, 1979.

41 Also see Commission of the European Community, *How Fares Equal Pay?* ISEC/B8/79, February 22, 1979; McCrudden, "Comparable Worth: A Common Dilemma," p. 410. Von Prondzynski, *Network of Experts on the Implementation of the Equality Directives,* p. 18.

42 Commission of the European Community, *How Fares Equal Pay?* pp. 1 and 3.

43 *Commission of the European Community v. United Kingdom of Great Britain and Northern Ireland,* Case 61/81, July 6, 1982, in *Equality in Law Between Men and Women: Textbook* (LouVain-la-Neuve, 1987), pp. 313–28.

44 Anthony Lester, "The Sex Discrimination Legislation and Employment Practices," Equal Opportunities Commission for Northern Ireland, in *Equality in Employment,* 1986, pp. 13–15; *Equal Opportunities Review,* no. 29 (January–February 1990): 43; Chris Docksey, "Overview of European Action and Perspectives on Equal Value," remarks at the Equal Opportunity Commission of Northern Ireland conference entitled "Equal Pay for Work of Equal Value," November 10, 1989, Conference report, pp. 6–9.

45 John Usher, "European Community Equality Law: Legal Instruments and Judicial Remedies," in Christopher McCrudden, ed., *Women, Employment and European Equality Law* (London: Eclipse, 1987), p. 171; Lester, "The Sex Discrimination Legislation and Employment Practices," p. 13. For sharp criticism of the court for its extratextual decisions on the direct applicability of directives, see Hjalte Rasmussen, *On Law and Policy in the European Court of Justice* (Dordrecht: Nijhoff, 1986), p. 12. In June of 1988, John Rimington, the U.K. permanent representative to the Social Affairs Council, told me that the U.K. delegation surely would have fought harder for their position on the equal-value language if they had known that the equal-pay directive would be found directly applicable.

46 *Defrenne v. Sabena,* Case 43/75, April 4, 1976, in *Equality in Law,* pp. 135–62.

47 *Jenkins v. Kingsgate,* Case 96/80, March 31, 1981, in *Equality in Law,* p. 248.

48 See p. 129. The French text of the treaty does not connote equal value any more than does the English version. See Paul Davies and Mark Freedland, *Labor Law: Text and Materials* (London: Weidenfeld Nicolson, 1984), p. 381.

49 See *Equality in Law,* p. 149.

50 For two very brief discussions, see Hepple, *Equal Pay and the Industrial Tribunals,* p. 10; Davies and Freedland, *Labor Law,* p. 381.

51 Docksey, "Overview of European Action and Perspectives on Equal Value," p. 6.

52 See the views of Christopher Docksey, at the time the legal coordinator with the Equal Opportunities Unit of the EC, ibid., pp. 6–7, and also "EEC Law on Indirectly Discriminatory Pay Criteria," *Equal Opportunities Review,* no. 29 (January–February 1990): 43.

53 *Bilka-Kaufhaus v. Weber von Hartz,* 170/84, *Industrial Relations Law Reports* 15 (1986): 317.

54 A later 1991 case (*Nimz v. Freie und Hansestadt Hamburg*) disallows certain seniority payments that have an indirectly discriminatory effect on women (*Equal Opportunities Review,* no. 38 [July–August 1991]: 36).

55 "EEC Law," pp. 41 and 43.

56 *Handels-OG Kontorfunktionaerernes Forbund i Danmark v. Dansk Arbejdsgiverforening* (acting for Danfoss), *Industrial Relations Law Reports* 18 (1989): 536.

57 "E.E.C. Law," p. 43.

58 Henry Phelps Brown, *The Inequality of Pay* (Oxford University Press, 1978), p. 158. Also see pp. 155–7. For supporting evidence from the nineteenth century, see Claudia Goldin, *Understanding the Gender Gap: An Economic History of American Women* (Oxford University Press, 1990), p. 104. Also see the discussion of male upholsterers and cushion fillers in Chapter 6, pp. 157–60. For evidence that women on average dislike incentive pay systems more than do men, see Judith Agassi, *Comparing the Work Attitudes of Women and Men* (Lexington, Mass.: Lexington, 1982), p. 57.

59 Jonathan Cole, *Fair Science: Women in the Scientific Community* (New York: Free Press, 1979), p. 68. Later work by Cole and Harriet Zuckerman finds that men who received their Ph.D.s in six scientific fields in 1969–70 published, on average, 11.2 papers, while women who received Ph.D.s in the same fields at the same time have published 6.4 ("The Productivity Puzzle: Persistence and Change in Patterns of Publication of Men and Women Scientists," in Marjorie Steinkamp and Martin Maehr, eds., *Advances in Motivation and Achievement: Women in Science,* vol. 2 [Greenwich, Conn.: JAI, 1984], p. 224).

60 Cole, *Fair Science,* p. 66.

61 *Equal Opportunities Review,* no. 29 (July–August 1990): 21. In a letter to the author commenting on an earlier draft, Michael Rubenstein argues that, in *Danfoss,* the European Court of Justice did not prohibit direct pay-for-performance plans like piecework. Though the case before it was clearly not a piecework case, the Court's sweeping language would seem to incorporate piecework schemes. Tess Gill, a barrister and member of the Advisory Board of the *Equal Opportunities Review,* notes that, under *Danfoss,* "no justification is available" for a pay-for-performance plan using sex-neutral criteria that in practice is disadvantageous to women (*Equal Opportunities Review,* no. 39 [September–October 1991]: 23). Piecework would appear to be a sex-neutral criterion. Gill urges unions

to examine all bonus schemes, merit pay, and pay-for-performance plans with *Danfoss* in mind.

In any case, as already mentioned, piecework is relatively unimportant in modern economies, and most pay-for-performance plans do not operate with measures as objective as piecework. But if the lure of more money has, on average, more effect on men than on women under piecework schemes, it may well have more effect under less objective merit or performance pay schemes as well. Though the differences may be small, as they were in *Danfoss,* they may lead to statistically significant differences in pay for men and women in many companies. By calling such outcomes inconceivable in a fairly administered system and allowing no defense of such outcomes, the principles of *Danfoss* could ultimately undermine merit pay plans throughout the EC.

In the course of my research, I encountered signs that money is relatively more important to men than to women in the U.S. nursing profession. In an early interview, I was told that the high and rapidly increasing salaries of nurse anesthetists were causing major financial problems for Hennepin County, Minnesota. I could not understand this since I assumed that this nursing specialty was overwhelmingly female like the profession as a whole. It turned out that I was incorrect. Although only about 6 percent of nurses are men, over 41 percent of nurse anesthetists are men. In 1988 the average registered nurse working full time was paid $28,383, whereas the average full-time nurse anesthetist was paid $47,717. (Figures are from the U.S. Department of Health and Human Services unpublished data based on a 1988 national sample survey of registered nurses. In a 1991 survey of nurse anesthetists conducted by the American Association of Nurse Anesthetists, respondents working full time reported salaries that averaged $77,569.) In Hennepin County nurse anesthetists were a balanced not a female-dominated class, and since Hennepin used a balanced-class line as their standard, the high salaries of nurse anesthetists were leading to raises for other occupations that were below the line.

I later spoke with three nurse anesthetists and several other nurses about why men were apparently so much more likely to aim for this extremely high-paying branch of nursing. Most respondents thought it was largely because it paid well. One said "almost every man I knew in nursing school" wanted to become a nurse anesthetist. The women students would say they got into nursing because they wanted "to work with people." This same woman reported: "I'd find [the anesthetist's job] boring. You have no contact with patients. The patient is unconscious and you're just administering drugs." The responses I received lend support to studies which show that, on average, a job's pay is more important to men than to women and the interpersonal aspects of the job are more important to women than to men (see Chapter 2, p. 14).

62 Vallance and Davies, *Women of Europe,* p. 34. Neil Nugent observes the following about the Commission and Council powers: "The Council's

legislative capacity is heavily dependent on the willingness and ability of the Commission to put proposals before it. The Council cannot initiate and draft legislation itself. Furthermore, if the Council wishes to amend a Commission proposal, Article 149 of the EC Treaty states that it can only do so either with the Commission's agreement of [*sic*] by acting unanimously if the Commission disagrees. If neither of these two routes are open, the Council must accept the Commission's proposal as it stands, reject it, or refer it back to the Commission for reconsideration and resubmission at a later date" (*The Government and Politics of the European Community* [London: Macmillan Press, 1989], p. 67).

Margaret Thatcher and many other Conservative party politicians in Britain have long thought the Commission has too much power, especially on social policy. Nicholas Ridley had to resign from Thatcher's government in 1990 because of intemperate remarks about the EC that included his condemnation of its "breath-taking arrogance" and his charge that it was run by "17 unelected reject politicians" (*Daily Progress* [Charlottesville, Va.], July 15, 1990, p. D-6). More recently, Thatcher's successor, John Major, has said that he will not ask the British Parliament to approve the Maastricht Treaty on European union until strict limits are placed on the power of European Community bureaucrats (*Washington Post,* September 25, 1992, p. A-27). Also see *Washington Post,* October 31, 1988, p. A-13, and "The Dark Side of 1992," *Forbes,* January 22, 1990, pp. 85–9.

63 Rights of Women, "The EEC and Women – A Case Study of British and European Legislation on Equal Pay," Paper presented at the Conference of PSA Women and Politics Groups, Bedford College, September 27, 1980, pp. 3–4, as quoted in Elizabeth Meehan, *Women's Rights at Work* (London: Macmillan Press, 1985), p. 170. Also see Vallance and Davies, *Women of Europe,* pp. 105 and 118.

64 Vallance and Davies, *Women of Europe,* p. 105; Rasmussen, *On Law and Policy in the European Court of Justice,* p. 3. Also see *Economist,* July 28, 1990, p. 60.

65 The Commission directorate is currently headed by Ms. Vasso Papandreou, formerly a Greek Socialist party politician. In the *Economist*'s words, she has been "vigorously" pushing a new social charter (June 30, 1990, p. 24). As part of a five-year (1991–5) action program on equal opportunities for women and men, the Commission plans to issue a memorandum "to define the scope and content of equal pay for work of equal value" (*Equal Opportunities Review,* no. 36 [March–April 1991]: 24).

Prior to Papandreou, the commissioner for social affairs, employment, education, and training was a member of the Spanish Socialist Workers' party, Manuel Marin (1986–8). Other recent social affairs commissioners from left-of-center parties were Ivor Richard (British Labour – 1982–4) and Henk Vredeling (Netherlands PvdA-labor/Social Democratic – 1976–80). The only other commissioners since passage of the equal pay directive have been from Ireland: Peter Sutherland (Fine Gael party – 1985) and Patrick

John Hillery (Fianna Fial party – 1972–6). The Irish parties are difficult to classify ideologically. Hillery, however, served as an Irish governmental minister in the 1950s and 1960s, a period during which his party expanded social programs rapidly in areas such as unemployment insurance and aid to poor families.

66 For criticism of the process from a somewhat different perspective, see "All Aboard," *Economist,* May 5, 1990, pp. 13–14. Also see Michael Elliott, "Little Denmark's Big No," *Washington Post,* June 7, 1992, p. C-1.

67 Vallance and Davies, *Women of Europe,* p. 19; McCrudden, ed., *Women, Employment and European Equality Law,* p. xi.

68 Docksey, "Overview of European Action and Perspectives on Equal Value," p. 7.

69 See Paolo Cecchini, *The European Challenge, 1992: The Benefits of a Single Market* (Aldershot; Gower, 1988), and "All Aboard," *Economist,* May 5, 1990, pp. 13–14.

70 "Heady days" is from Vallance and Davies, *Women of Europe,* p. 87.

71 McCrudden, "Comparable Worth: A Common Dilemma," p. 406.

72 In June of 1990, unemployment of European women was running about 5 percent above that of European men (*Economist,* June 30, 1991, p. 21).

73 Isabelle Prondzynski, "European Initiatives on Equal Opportunities for Men and Women," in *Equality in Employment* (Belfast: Equal Opportunities Commission for Northern Ireland, 1986), p. 9.

74 See Rasmussen, *On Law and Policy in the European Court of Justice,* for the court's role in bringing about this realization.

## 6. *Equal pay for work of equal value in the United Kingdom*

1 United Kingdom, Department of Employment, *New Earnings Survey,* as cited in R. G. Gregory, A. Daly, V. Ho, "A Tale of Two Countries: Equal Pay for Women in Australia and Britain," Australian National University, Centre for Economic Policy Research, Discussion paper no. 147, August 1986.

2 A. Zabalza and Z. Tzannatos, *Women and Equal Pay: The Effects of Legislation* (Cambridge University Press, 1985). For a discussion of alternative views, also see Michael Rubenstein, *Equal Pay for Work of Equal Value* (London: Macmillan Press, 1984), pp. 40–1.

3 Zabalza and Tzannatos, *Women and Equal Pay,* pp. 104–5; P. L. Davies, "European Equality Legislation, U.K. Legislative Policy and Industrial Relations," in Christopher McCrudden, ed., *Women, Employment and European Equality Law* (London: Eclipse, 1987), pp. 44–5.

4 Quotations from *Hansard* (House of Commons) *Parliamentary Debates,* July 20, 1983, p. 480. Also see pp. 477–96, and February 1, 1984, pp. 359–77.

5 B. A. Hepple, *Equal Pay and the Industrial Tribunals* (London: Sweet & Maxwell, 1984), p. 16.

6 Ibid., p. 19.

7 Linda Dickens, "Unfair Dismissal Applications and the Industrial Tribunal System," *Industrial Relations Journal* 9, no. 4 (1978–9): 4.

8 Erika Szyszczak, "The Equal Pay Directive and U.K. Law," in McCrudden, ed., *Women, Employment and European Equality Law,* p. 67; Anthony Lester, "Equal Pay and Equal Treatment Without Sex Discrimination: Community and United Kingdom Law," in *Equality in Law Between Men and Women in the European Community,* vol. 2 (Brussels: Louvain-la-Neuve, 1986), p. 416; Hepple, *Equal Pay and the Industrial Tribunals,* p. 19.

9 Lester, "Equal Pay and Equal Treatment Without Sex Discrimination," p. 424.

10 Based on data provided by the *Equal Opportunities Review* (no. 38 [July–August 1991]: 16–23), I calculate that, as of May 1991, tribunals' decisions have followed independent experts' recommendations in twenty-three of the twenty-nine cases that have proceeded through the tribunal stage. In one case the tribunal simply reversed the experts' conclusions, in two cases reports were rejected, and in three other cases the tribunals disagreed with the experts on some applicants' claims, but not on others.

11 *Equal Opportunities Review,* no. 38 (July–August 1991): 12–30. The number of applicants may have picked up again in early 1991. See ibid., no. 42 (March–April 1992): 33.

12 Trade Union Research Unit (Oxford), "Job Evaluation and 'Equal Value' – Similarities and Differences," Technical note no. 104, December 1987, pp. 1 and 5.

13 Phone interview, June 23, 1988.

14 "Job Evaluation and 'Equal Value' – Similarities and Differences," pp. 1 and 5.

15 *Hayward v. Cammell Laird Shipbuilders, Ltd.* (1988), vol. 2, All England Law Reports.

16 *Times* (London), May 6, 1988, pp. 1–2.

17 This is the view of an Advisory Conciliation and Arbitration Service staff member who works closely with the experts.

18 "*J. A. Hayward v. Cammell Laird Shipbuilders,* Report of the Independent Expert," Case no. 5979/84, p. 35.

19 Though the independent expert's submitted report had thirty-seven pages and one page of notes, the first twenty-nine pages consisted of a short four-page introduction and then twenty-five pages that simply summarized and quoted from the submissions of the two parties.

20 Steven Willborn, *A Secretary and a Cook: Challenging Women's Wages in the Courts of the United States and Great Britain* (Ithaca, N.Y.: Cornell University, ILR Press, 1989), pp. 43–5.

21 "*Hayward v. Cammell Laird,* Report of the Independent Expert," p. 36.

22 Ibid., pp. 9 and 16. It is also worth noting that though the union was supporting the Hayward claim, it had earlier ratified the national agreement that classifies cooks as unskilled (*Equal Opportunities Review,* no. 1 [May–June 1985]: 8).

23 Quoted from Willborn, *A Secretary and a Cook,* p. 47. Much of this and the previous paragraph draws heavily on Willborn.

24 Decision on the Industrial Tribunals Case no. 5979/84, between J. A. Hayward and Cammell Laird Shipbuilders Limited, Liverpool, October 4, 1984, p. 5.

25 Even the *Financial Times,* which one might expect to be more skeptical, has said, "Those on the ground seem to have little difficulty agreeing what in practice constitutes work of 'equal value' " (May 6, 1988), a position contradicted by a subsequent letter to the *Financial Times* from a management consultant (May 11, 1988, p. 23) as well as by what follows here.

26 Decision on the Industrial Tribunals Case no. 5979/84, between Hayward and Cammell Laird, p. 8.

27 *Equal Opportunities Review,* no. 2 (July–August 1985): 31.

28 Ibid., p. 30.

29 All Beddoe quotations are from "Independent Experts," *Equal Opportunities Review,* no. 6 (March–April 1986): 13–16. See the Equal Opportunities Commission's (EOC) complaints about double counting when it seems to benefit male workers (*Job Evaluation Schemes Free of Sex Bias: Revised Edition,* EOC 125R/7–5K/09/85, p. 8).

30 F. von Prondzynski, *Network of Experts on the Implementation of the Equality Directives: Final Consolidated Report, 1987,* Commission of the European Community, V1087/88-EN, p. 19.

31 For a fuller discussion of employers' demand for labor, see Ronald Ehrenberg and Robert Smith, *Modern Labor Economics* (Glenview, Ill.: Scott, Foresman, 1985), chaps. 2 and 3.

32 W. B. Creighton, *Working Women and the Law* (London: Mansoll, 1979), p. 114.

33 Lester, "Equal Pay and Equal Treatment Without Sex Discrimination," p. 416, and in my interviews.

34 Department of Employment, Education, and Training, Women's Bureau, *Pay Equity: A Survey of 7 OECD Countries,* Information Paper no. 5 (Canberra: Australian Government Publishing Service, 1987), pp. 18–19.

35 Confederation of British Industry, "Equal Pay for Work of Equal Value" (London: November 1989), p. 18; and, for the EAT, the case of *Aldridge v. Telecommunications plc* (Sept. 26, 1989), *Equal Opportunities Review,* no. 29 (January–February 1990): 45.

36 EOC, *Job Evaluation Schemes Free of Sex Bias,* p. 9.

37 National Joint Council for Local Authorities' Services, "Manual Workers: Review of Grading Structure, Assimilation and Assessment," August 1987, p. 6.

38 The different approaches are discussed in *Equal Opportunities Review,* no. 26 (July–August 1989): 25, and no. 18 (March–April 1988): 16–17. Excerpts from the contending tribunals' opinions are in ibid., no. 2 (July–August 1985): 26–30, and no. 6 (March–April 1986): 27–33. Also see ibid., no. 38 (July–August 1991): 30. Not every case of tribunal inconsistency is

cataloged here. For example, Christopher McCrudden notes that several tribunals have disagreed about whether "the fact that the relevant men and women are in different collective bargaining units or separate pay structures may constitute a justification for a variation in pay between them" ("Between Legality and Reality: The Implementation of Equal Pay for Work of Equal Value in Great Britain," *International Review of Comparative Public Policy* 3 [1991]: 190).

39 The management consultant's views are in P.A. Personnel Services, "Equal Pay: The Precedents, Problems and Priorities" (London: 1985), pp. 8–9.

40 *Equal Opportunities Review,* no. 26 (July–August 1989): 14–20.

41 Alice Leonard, *Judging Inequality: The Effectiveness of the Industrial Tribunal System in Sex Discrimination and Equal Pay Cases* (London: Cobden Trust, 1987), p. 122.

42 One of these independent experts (for Holden) was Terry Dillon, who sided with the cook in the *Hayward v. Cammell Laird* case.

43 "*Mrs. Rita White and others v. Alstons (Colchester) LTD*, Case nos. 9188/85/LN/A and 22 others: Report By the Independent Expert," September 1986, p. 13. The other reports and the tribunal decision were in "Report of Independent Expert, Case No. 24611/84 and 24614/84, *Whitmore and Alcock v. Frayling Furniture LTD,*" May 14, 1985; "Case No. 33292/84 *Mrs. Brenda Holden and others (Applicants) v. ABF Limited-Buoyant Upholstery Division (Respondents)* – Report of The Independent Expert"; Decision of the Industrial Tribunal, *Mrs. R. White v. Alstons (Colchester) Limited,* 09188/85/LN/A (November 1986).

44 The differences among independent experts in valuing jobs were matched by the employee–management panels which examined jobs more or less like committees had in Minnesota. Fearing equal-value lawsuits, the National Joint Council for Local Authorities' Services had ten panels equally balanced between management and unions and men and women look at the same jobs. The "Coordinating Panel" found that "there were some differences in interpretation between panels and there appeared to be an inconsistent pattern to the results which could not be explained simply or without further analysis" ("Manual Workers," Appendix C. p. 3). Eventually the inconsistencies were explained away by assuming (the jobs were not rechecked) that the same titles in different locations must have had different duties. On another (university) study, an EOC staffer told me that he was unsure what to do about the fact that one of his three panels consistently rated some jobs much higher on responsibility than the other two did.

45 *Equal Opportunities Review,* no. 13 (May–June 1987): 13.

46 Hepple, *Equal Pay and the Industrial Tribunals,* p. 19; also see Rubenstein, *Equal Pay for Work of Equal Value,* p. 31; EOC, *Job Evaluation Schemes Free of Sex Bias: Revised Edition,* p. 10.

47 *Webster's 3rd New International Dictionary* (Merriam, 1961), pp. 2275–6. The relevant *Compact Oxford English Dictionary* definitions are similar: "Relating to the thinking subject, proceeding from or taking place within the subject; having its source in the mind" and "Pertaining to or peculiar

to an individual subject or his mental operations; depending upon one's individuality; personal, individual" (Oxford University Press, 1971), p. 3121.

48 Rubenstein, *Equal Pay for Work of Equal Value,* p. 93.

49 EOC for Northern Ireland, *Equality in Employment: Conference Report 10: Making It Work for Men and Women,* 1986, p. 29.

50 Lester, "Equal Pay and Equal Treatment Without Sex Discrimination," p. 417; Bob Hepple, "The Judicial Process in Claims for Equal Pay and Equal Treatment in the United Kingdom," in McCrudden, ed., *Women, Employment and European Equality Law,* p. 155.

51 Chris Docksey, "Overview of European Action and Perspectives on Equal Value," in *Equal Pay for Work of Equal Value: Conference Report,* EOC for Northern Ireland, November 10, 1989, Mimeographed, p. 8.

52 National Joint Council for Local Authorities' Services, "Manual Workers," p. B-9.

53 Rubenstein, *Equal Pay for Work of Equal Value,* p. 97.

54 EOC, *Job Evaluation Schemes Free of Sex Bias,* p. 11.

55 Ibid., pp. 20–1.

56 Biacna Beccalli notes that feminist union members in Italy have been divided on the question of access to low-level traditionally male jobs. They have questioned "the prospect of an 'equality' that was full of disadvantage" with many wondering, "why should women struggle to get into heavy, dirty and risky jobs?" ("Italy: Working Class Militancy, Feminism and Trade Union Politics," *Radical America,* no. 5 [1984]: 47).

57 Martin Bailey, *Measuring the Benefits of Life Saving* (Washington, D.C.: American Enterprise Institute, 1979), and W. Kip Viscusi, *Employment Hazards: An Investigation of Market Performance* (Cambridge, Mass.: Harvard University Press, 1979).

58 A number of comparable-worth supporters seem to think exactly the reverse should occur – that somehow, all else being equal, the most satisfying and enjoyable jobs should also pay more. A San Jose librarian says: " 'I *don't* want to leave librarianship to make an adequate salary in some field that pays more money but is . . . is. . . . *Why* is that [field] more financially rewarding and less emotionally satisfying, less intellectually satisfying? The only explanation I could come up with finally was because it's [library work is] run by *women* and that's why it's not valued' " (quoted in Linda Blum, *Between Feminism and Labor: The Significance of the Comparable Worth Movement* [Berkeley and Los Angeles: University of California Press, 1991], p. 65). Similarly, a Hofstra University executive secretary participating in a comparable-worth strike readily agrees that plenty of qualified people will take the job at the wage she scorns because it's a good job. The *New York Times* quotes Lois Rabarge as saying: "I really love my job. It's challenging and wonderful. It's just the pay" (October 17, 1989, p. B-1).

In the United States both general carpentry and precision woodworking (cabinetmaking, furniture and wood finishing, etc.) are predominantly male occupations, so sex discrimination presumably does not affect their relative pay. Though the two occupations use some of the same skills, I think most people would say that the woodworker job is more skilled and also more intellectually and emotionally satisfying. On the other hand, the general carpentry job is usually accompanied by more physical hazards and other unpleasant working conditions. In 1990 precision woodworkers' median weekly earnings were $356, while general carpenters made $412 (U.S. Department of Labor, Bureau of Labor Statistics, *Current Population Survey,* 1990, unpublished tabulations). This result would probably surprise comparable-worth proponents though most economists, aware that enjoyable jobs attract applicants and less enjoyable ones face reduced supply, would find it unexceptional.

59 National Joint Council for Local Authorities' Services, "Manual Workers," p. B-10.

60 Ibid., pp. C-1, C-11, C-13.

61 Ibid., p. C-9.

62 Ibid.

63 *Equal Opportunities Review,* no. 24 (March–April 1989): 17.

64 EOC, *Equal Pay: Making It Work,* EOC 274/3K (Manchester, 1989), p. 15.

65 *Equal Opportunities Review,* no. 38 (July–August 1991): 12 and 26.

66 Leonard, *Judging Inequality,* p. 68; also see Hepple, "The Judicial Process in Claims for Equal Pay and Equal Treatment in the United Kingdom," pp. 144–7, 157–8; McCrudden, "Between Legality and Reality," pp. 209–13.

67 Leonard, *Judging Inequality,* pp. 119–120; *Equal Opportunities Review,* no. 30 (March–April 1990): 3; interviews. In her analysis of the 1980–2 cases, Leonard finds that *equal-pay* claimants succeed only 29 percent of the time. However, my calculations based on data provided by the *Equal Opportunities Review* (no. 38 [July/August 1991]: 16–23), show that, as of May 1991, applicants had won sixteen of the twenty-four *equal-value* cases referred to independent experts and decided by tribunals. In three additional cases, some applicants' claims were upheld and some were dismissed.

68 United Kingdom, Department of Employment, *New Earnings Survey,* 1991 (April of 1984 and 1991), Table 15, pp. A-15.1–A-15.2. U.K. figures are averages for full-time adults not affected by absence. U.S. figures are from Bureau of Labor Statistics, unpublished data. U.S. figures are usual weekly earnings of full-time wage and salary workers.

69 See *Equal Opportunities Review,* no. 32 (July–August 1990): 11–12.

70 Confederation of British Industry, "Equal Pay for Work of Equal Value," p. 25.

71 *Equal Opportunities Review,* no. 18 (March–April 1988): 3–4; on the Employment Appeal Tribunal, see ibid., no. 28 (November–December 1989): 2–3.

72 EOC, *Equal Pay: Making It Work,* p. 14; also see *Equal Opportunities Review,* no. 29 (January–February 1990): 45. Some have proposed expanding the role of the independent expert. See McCrudden's discussion in "Between Legality and Reality," p. 206.

73 For a brief written discussion, see F. von Prondzynski, Commission of the European Community, *Implementation of the Equality Directives,* V/1511/86 EN (July 1986), p. 3; Szyszczak, "The Equal Pay Directive and U.K. Law," pp. 64–5. McCrudden, "Between Legality and Reality," p. 211.
74 Anthony Lester, "The Sex Discrimination Legislation and Employment Practices," in EOC for Northern Ireland, *Equality in Employment,* p. 13.
75 *Yearbook Australia, 1989,* no. 72, Australian Bureau of Statistics, Canberra, p. 205; *Economist,* June 23, 1990, p. 61.
76 *Equal Opportunities Review,* no. 32 (July–August 1990): 12.
77 Bob Hepple, "The Judicial Process in Claims for Equal Pay and Equal Treatment in the United Kingdom," p. 151.
78 This effort to attack the importance of the other side's jobs is clearly seen in some of the experts' reports when they discuss the statements received from the contending parties.
79 P.A. Personnel Services, *Equal Pay: The Precedents, Problems and Priorities,* p. 10.
80 *Equal Opportunities Review,* no. 26 (July–August 1989): 12; also see no. 38 (July–August 1991): 14–15.
81 Some courts of appeal have recently expressed concern about the effects of these anomalous comparator cases, but to date the law is as stated (*Equal Opportunities Review,* no. 38 [July–August 1991]: 14–15). At least one firm has, however, defended itself against an anomalous comparator claim by using the genuine material factor defense (see p. 171). (*Equal Opportunities Review,* no. 38 [July–August 1991]: 26).
82 "Equal Value Claim Succeeds," *Industrial Relations Legal Information Bulletin* 269 (November 20, 1984): 12.
83 Decision on the Industrial Tribunals Case no. 5979/84 between J. A. Hayward and Cammell Laird Shipbuilders, Limited.
84 EOC, *Equal Pay,* p. 11.
85 "The Practical Implications of Equal Value for Employers and Trade Unions," remarks at the EOC of Northern Ireland conference entitled "Equal Pay for Work of Equal Value," November 10, 1989, Conference report, p. 23. For discussion of a report that documents the spread of job evaluation, see *Equal Opportunities Review,* no. 37 (May–June 1991): 22. Also see McCrudden, "Between Legality and Reality," p. 208.
86 *Equal Opportunities Review,* no. 26 (July–August 1989): 13.
87 In one study an increase in payroll costs was seen to occur for 83 percent of employers. Moreover, employees' representatives were as likely to think that job evaluation studies increased disagreements about pay differentials as to think that they decreased them (Abby Ghobadian and Michael White, *Job Evaluation and Equal Pay,* Research Paper no. 58, U.K. Department of Employment, 1986).
88 Confederation of British Industry, "Equal Pay for Work of Equal Value," p. 24. In sections seemingly relevant to the comparable-worth debate, an OECD report clearly links the growth in European unemployment to balky responses to changes in supply and demand and to a decline in "mobility

between occupations." With an eye to further growth prospects, it argues that "the effective implementation of new production technologies depends on the internal mobility and flexibility of the labour force, and especially on the willingness of employees to alter their skill base and work practices several times in the course of working life" (*Structural Adjustment and Economic Performance* [Paris, 1987], pp. 135 and 141).

89 *Equal Opportunities Review,* no. 14 (July–August 1987): 3.

90 *Caterer and Hotelkeeper,* May 12, 1988, p. 6. On contracting out, also see McCrudden, "Between Legality and Reality," p. 201.

91 See Christopher McCrudden, "Comparable Worth: A Common Dilemma," *Yale Journal of International Law* 11, no. 2 (Spring 1986): 425–7; "Equal Pay for Work of Equal Value, 1" *Income Data Services Brief* 367 (February 1988): 7–8. Most uses of the "material factor" defense have involved matters such as collective bargaining, employer errors, grading differences, and other matters having nothing to do with market forces defenses (see *Equal Opportunities Review,* no. 32 [July–August 1990]: 20–21). The EOC and most legal commentators/proponents would like to see the scope for this defense narrowed (see ibid. no. 35 [January–February 1991]: 14, and the citation for n. 106 following).

92 Rubenstein, *Equal Pay for Work of Equal Value,* p. 9.

93 Forrest Capie and Geoffrey Wood, "The Folly of Comparable Worth," *Economic Affairs* 7, no. 5 (June–July 1987): 46.

94 *Equal Opportunities Review,* no. 7 (May–June, 1986): 17. The case discussed was *Macarthys, Ltd. v. Smith* (1980).

95 Ibid., no. 29 (January–February 1990): 43. Also see McCrudden, ed., *Women, Employment and European Equality Law,* e.g., pp. 182 and 184.

96 Szyszczak, "The Equal Pay Directive and U.K. Law," in McCrudden, ed., *Women, Employment and European Equality Law,* p. 59.

97 *Equal Opportunities Review,* no. 26 (July–August 1989): 12.

98 Ibid., no. 2 (July–August 1985): 24–33.

99 Ibid., no. 24 (March–April 1989): 40, and no. 26 (July–August 1989): 21. Rubenstein told me that he writes all the unsigned equal-value commentary in this publication, and in our interview he confirmed his support of the position I attribute to him.

100 "Changing Labour Market – More Flexibility," unpublished lecture by Kenneth Clarke, paymaster general and employment minister, delivered at the City University and Business School, February 11, 1987. The speech is summarized in *Financial Times,* February 12, 1987, p. 1. For a discussion of increasing decentralization in U.K. pay negotiations and greater efforts to relate pay to company, plant, and individual performance, see *Economist,* September 7, 1991, p. 56.

101 OECD views as summarized in *International Herald Tribune,* February 29, 1988, p. 5.

102 "Survey of European Women in Paid Employment," Commission of the European Community, IP (84) 436, December 6, 1984, p. 2.

103 Rubenstein, "Equal Pay and Equal Value – The Lessons So Far," in *Equality in Employment*, EOC for Northern Ireland, p. 25.
104 Ibid., p. 143.
105 *Equal Opportunities Review*, no. 5 (January–February 1986): 13.
106 Rubenstein, *Equal Pay for Work of Equal Value*, pp. 145, 163–4. This distinction is also frequently made by proponents in the United States.
107 Paul Davies and Mark Freedland, *Labor Law: Text and Materials* (London: Weidenfeld Nicolson, 1984), p. 387.
108 Lester, "Equal Pay and Equal Treatment Without Sex Discrimination," pp. 409, 419, 420; Commission of the European Community, *Implementation of the Equality Directives*, p. 39; Elizabeth Meehan, *Women's Rights at Work* (London: Macmillan Press, 1985), p. 120.
109 Christopher McCrudden, "Women, Employment and European Equality Law: Some Tentative Conclusions and Issues for the Future," in McCrudden, ed., *Women, Employment and European Equality Law*, p. 185.
110 *Washington Post*, October 6, 1991, p. H-1; *Economist*, April 13, 1991, p. 54, and September 7, 1991, pp. 56–7.
111 *Equal Opportunities Review*, no. 32 (July–August 1990): 12–13. See also note 84.
112 *Economist*, October 27, 1990, p. 62, and *Equal Opportunities Review*, no. 34 (November–December 1990): 25. Also from a 1991 phone interview with Dr. Ann Robinson, Institute of Directors, London.
113 *Equal Opportunities Review*, no. 32 (July–August 1990): 12. For a brief discussion of some pay gains for women and costs to business, see McCrudden, "Between Legality and Reality," pp. 200–3.
114 Tess Gill, "Making Equal Pay Defences Transparent," *Equal Opportunities Review*, no. 33 (September–October 1990): 48.
115 In the 1992 election, the Labour party pledged, if elected, to change the equal-value law to allow both cross-firm comparisons and comparisons with what a hypothetical male would have been paid (*Equal Opportunities Review*, no. 42 [March–April 1992]: 12).
116 Ibid., no. 24 (March–April 1989): 45.
117 Ibid., no. 26 (July–August 1989): 20.
118 *Times* (London), July 1, 1988, p. 1.
119 *Equal Opportunities Review*, no. 26 (July–August 1989): 25.
120 Ibid., no. 2 (July–August 1985): 27.

### *7. Equal pay for work of equal value in Australia*

1 See Frances Hutner, *Equal Pay for Comparable Worth: The Working Women's Issue of the Eighties* (New York: Praeger, 1986), pp. 38–41; Donald Treiman and Heidi Hartmann, eds., *Women, Work and Wages: Equal Pay for Jobs of Equal Value* (Washington, D.C.: National Academy Press, 1981), p. 67n; Eleanor Holmes Norton testimony before the Com-

mittee on Post Office and Civil Service, 1983, p. 44, as quoted by Mark Killingsworth, in U.S. Congress, Joint Economic Committee, *Women in the Work Force: Pay Equity,* hearing 98 Congress, April 10, 1984, p. 107; Sara Evans and Barbara Nelson, *Wage Justice: Comparable Worth and the Paradox of Technocratic Reform* (Chicago: University of Chicago Press, 1989), pp. 53–4; Barbara Bergmann, *The Economic Emergence of Women* (New York: Basic, 1986), pp. 189–91; Ronnie Steinberg, " 'A Want of Harmony': Perspectives on Wage Discrimination and Comparable Worth," in Helen Remick, ed., *Comparable Worth and Wage Discrimination* (Philadelphia: Temple University Press, 1984), p. 4n. The Australian experience is even raised before state task forces on pay equity – for example, by a representative of the League of Women Voters testifying in New Jersey (New Jersey Task Force on Equitable Compensation, *Interim Report: Six Months of Progress,* June 1, 1985, p. 14).

2 See Killingsworth, *Women in the Workforce,* pp. 105–9.

3 Hutner, *Equal Pay for Comparable Worth,* p. 41.

4 Richard Caves and Lawrence Krause, "Introduction," in Caves and Krause, eds., *The Australian Economy: A View from the North* (Washington: Brookings Institution, 1984), pp. 1 and 2.

5 *Economist,* March 3, 1990, p. 16, and the special Australian insert to the *Economist,* May 6, 1989, p. 18. Caves and Krause, "Introduction," p. 3.

6 Unemployment, inflation, and international trade figures are based on my summary calculations of data provided in *OECD Economic Outlook* 49 (July 1991): 185, 191, 195, 196.

7 Caves and Krause, "Introduction," pp. 4–5; *Economist,* February 3, 1990, p. 34; U.S. Bureau of the Census, *Statistical Abstract of the United States: 1991,* 111th ed. (Washington, D.C.: 1982), Table no. 1450. Despite its continued leadership, since 1970 the United States has also lost significant ground to the average OECD country in terms of GDP per capita. However, as two Australian economists note, there has been a general tendency for OECD per capita income levels to converge since 1950. For the most part, though, the rich countries have remained rich while the poorer countries closed the gap. "Australia, by contrast, started as a rich country in 1950 and ended as only average by 1985" (P. J. Drake and J. P. Nieuwenhuysen, *Economic Growth for Australia* [Oxford University Press, 1988], p. 4). This book was sponsored by the Committee for Economic Development of Australia.

8 Based on data in *OECD Economic Outlook* 49 (July 1981): 185 and 195.

9 *Economist,* March 16, 1991, p. 29.

10 Ibid., August 22, 1992, p. 87.

11 Ibid., June 7, 1991, p. 25. Though the 1991 balance of payments deficit is much improved over that of 1990, the figure is still the second highest in over two decades. Cf. Ibid., December 14, 1991, p. 112, and *OECD Economic Outlook* 49 (July 1991): 194.

12 *Economist,* March 3, 1990, p. 14, and March 31, 1990, p. 31.

13 *OECD Economic Surveys: Australia* (1990), p. 108.

14 *Economist,* March 3, 1990, p. 16.
15 See, e.g., Lawrence Krause, "Australia's Comparative Advantage in International Trade," in Caves and Krause, eds., *The Australian Economy,* pp. 286–92.
16 *Economist,* March 3, 1990, p. 14.
17 Drake and Nieuwenhuysen share the *Economist*'s perspective: "Historically, the growth of trade protection in Australia is very closely linked with labor market regulation" (*Economic Growth For Australia,* p. 12). "As Professor Heinz Arndt notes, 'Tariff protection was increasingly given to any manufacturer who could demonstrate that he was managing his plant reasonably competently but could not compete with imports while conforming to minimum wage and working conditions laid down by the arbitration authorities' " (p. 60). For additional commentary discussing the connection between protection and the Australian wage system, see Caves and Krause, "Conclusions," pp. 396–7, 401; OECD, *Structural Adjustment and Economic Performance* (Paris, 1987), pp. 130 and 149 (n. 74), *Weekend Australian,* April 8–9, 1989, p. 29. Recently the government has relaxed some protectionist measures.
18 *Australian Business,* March 21, 1991, p. 36.
19 John Niland, "Introduction," in Niland, ed., *Wage Fixation in Australia* (Sydney: Allen & Unwin, 1986), p. xiii.
20 It is perhaps also significant that the longest chapter in the 1990 OECD economic survey of Australia is entitled "Industrial Relations Reform and the Labour Market."
21 "Awards" are documents setting out the legally binding terms and conditions of employment.
22 This survey draws in particular on two articles in *Industrial Relations* (27, no. 2 [Spring 1988]), George Strauss, "Australian Labor Relations Through American Eyes," pp. 131–48, and Keith Whitfield, "The Australian Wage System and Its Labor Market Effects," pp. 149–65.
23 J. E. Isaac, "The Meaning and Significance of Comparative Wage Justice," in Niland, ed., *Wage Fixation in Australia,* p. 91; Strauss, "Australian Labor Relations Through American Eyes," p. 133.
24 Isaac, "The Meaning and Significance of Comparative Wage Justice," p. 90.
25 As quoted in ibid., p. 86.
26 See ibid. generally on comparative wage justice, esp. pp. 86–90. Under the historic Australian system, wage relativities tended to stay the same or reassert themselves when changed, but long-term changes in relativities did occur and there were, as well, inconsistent applications of the CWJ principle.
27 David Plowman, "Developments in Australian Wage Determination, 1953–83: The Institutional Dimension," in Niland, ed., *Wage Fixation in Australia,* p. 19.
28 Ibid., pp. 18–19; Isaac, "The Meaning and Significance of Comparative Wage Justice," p. 90; Whitfield, "The Australian Wage System and Its Labor Market Effects," p. 153.
29 J. Hutson, *Six Wage Concepts* (Sydney: Amalgamated Engineering Union,

1971), p. 215, as quoted in Clare Burton, *Work Value, Comparable Worth or Pay Equity? A Discussion of the Australian Situation,* September 1987, prepared for a presentation to the National Committee on Pay Equity, Washington, D.C., October 15, 1987.

30 Burton, *Work Value, Comparable Worth or Pay Equity?* p. 5.

31 Isaac, "The Meaning and Significance of Comparative Wage Justice," p. 85.

32 Keith Whitfield, *The Australian Labour Market* (New York: Harper & Row, 1987), p. 169; Isaac, "The Meaning and Significance of Comparative Wage Justice," p. 85.

33 Isaac, "The Meaning and Significance of Comparative Wage Justice," p. 87. Also see Plowman, "Developments in Australian Wage Determination, 1953–83," p. 18.

34 Australian Conciliation and Arbitration Commission [ACAC], *Private Hospitals' and Doctors' Nurses (ACT) Award, 1972,* as quoted in the *Applications by the Royal Australian Nursing Federation and the Hospital Employees Federation of Australia to Vary the 1972 Award.* Decision, February 18, 1986, p. 2.

35 Australian Conciliation and Arbitration Commission, *National Wage Case: Reasons for Decision,* August, 1988, p. 16.

36 In fact, over time, relative wages did sometimes change. See note 26 and pp. 187–8.

37 Plowman, "Developments in Australian Wage Determination, 1953–83," pp. 20–1.

38 Ibid., pp. 34–5. Also see P. A. McGavin, *Wages & Whitlam: The Wages Policy of the Whitlam Government* (Oxford University Press, 1987), p. 67.

39 About 76 percent of businesses pay some overawards; 57 percent of companies report increases in overaward payments during the 1980s. *Australian Business,* April 3, 1991, p. 24.

40 Interview with a Confederation of Australian Industry staff member, March 1989.

41 Plowman, "Developments in Australian Wage Determination, 1953–83," p. 20.

42 Ibid., p. 21. Also see pp. 34–5, and Isaac, "The Meaning and Significance of Comparative Wage Justice," p. 90.

43 Interview with the author, April 5, 1989.

44 Phone interview with the author, April 4, 1989.

45 Interview with the author, March 28, 1989.

46 Quoted in Isaac, "The Meaning and Significance of Comparative Wage Justice," p. 90.

47 Whitfield, *The Australian Labour Market,* p. 179; Isaac, "The Meaning and Significance of Comparative Wage Justice," p. 89; P. P. McGuinness, *The Case Against the Arbitration Commission* (St. Leonards: Centre for Independent Studies, 1985), p. 10; Strauss, "Australian Labor Relations Through American Eyes," p. 142.

48 Niland, "Introduction," p. xv.

49 *Melbourne Age,* April 5, 1989, p. 14.
50 Isaac, "The Meaning and Significance of Comparative Wage Justice," p. 96.
51 Australian Industrial Relations Commission, *February 1989 Review: Reasons For Decision,* Print H82000, p. 6.
52 Gerald Henderson, "The Industrial Relations Club," *Quadrant* 27, no. 9 (September 1983): 24.
53 As quoted in Whitfield, "The Australian Wage System and Its Labor Market Effects," p. 150.
54 Australian Conciliation and Arbitration Commission, *National Wage Case: Reasons for Decision,* August, 1988, p. 8.
55 "A New Set of Wage Determination Principles?" *Australian Quarterly* 60, no. 2 (Winter 1988): 166.
56 Daniel Mitchell, "The Australian Labor Market," in Caves and Krause, eds., *The Australian Economy,* p. 170.
57 Phone interview with the author, April 4, 1989.
58 Interview with the author, April 5, 1989.
59 *Business Council Bulletin* (February 1989): 6.
60 Interview with a member of the federal Commission, March 1989.
61 *Business Council Bulletin* (February 1989): 4.
62 *OECD Economic Surveys: Australia* (1990), p. 46. Writing in the *Australian,* Alan Wood reports: "The spread of awards and unions across industries makes it impossible to contain wage rises negotiated in one sector or industry. . . . Over-award payments conceded by one industry or employer 'in the field' (that is outside the national wage case framework) tend to spread rapidly, lifting the rate of wage increase to economically inappropriate levels and in a way that has generally been difficult for the arbitral authorities or the government to check" ("Industrial Roulette with the Future at Stake," April 9, 1991), p. 11. Also see "Wage System Has Outlived Its Usefulness," *Australian,* editorial, April 17, 1991, n.p. For further evidence of economists who see the Commission furthering inflation, see Caves and Krause, "Conclusion," pp. 392–3; McGavin, *Wages and Whitlam,* p. 67.
63 The OECD makes this point in the following way: "Employer resistance to wage increases may have been weakened by the multifirm nature of many awards. Since any award increases will affect all firms covered by the award, the competitive position of the individual firm is not affected" (*OECD Economic Surveys: Australia* [1990], p. 46; also see p. 79, and Strauss, "Australian Labor Relations Through American Eyes," p. 146).
64 My calculations are from data provided in *OECD Economic Outlook* 49 (July 1991): 193; OECD, *Labor Force Statistics, 1969–1989* (Paris: OECD, 1991), p. 32; *OECD Economic Outlook* 21 (July 1977): 29.
65 OECD, *Economies in Transition* (Paris, 1989), pp. 45 and 46.
66 Caves and Krause, "Introduction," pp. 15–16.
67 Mitchell, "The Australian Labor Market," in Caves and Krause, eds., *The Australian Economy,* p. 146.
68 *OECD Economic Surveys: Australia* (1990), p. 21.

69 Ibid., p. 8. Also see the interview with David Hale, chief economist and first vice-president of Kemper Financial Services in Chicago, in (Australian) *Financial Review,* May 21, 1991, p. 12.

70 As summarized in Department of Employment, Education and Training, Women's Bureau, *Pay Equity: A Survey of 7 OECD Countries,* Information Paper no. 5 (Canberra: Australian Government Publishing Service, 1987), p. 53. Also see Labour Research Centre (for the National Women's Consultative Council), *Pay Equity for Women in Australia* (Canberra: Australian Government Publishing Service, 1990), pp. 42–5.

71 OECD, *Structural Adjustment and Economic Performance,* p. 138; also see *OECD Economic Surveys: Australia,* 1990, p. 76.

72 Isaac, "The Meaning and Significance of Comparative Wage Justice," pp. 87 and 89.

73 Australian Conciliation and Arbitration Commission [ACAC], *National Wage Case: Reasons for Decision,* August 1988, p. 17.

74 Though wage compression is meant to improve equity, the OECD thinks that it may do the reverse since it leads to long-term unemployment and such unemployment "is the principal cause of increased inequity in the distribution of income and of social opportunities" (*International Herald Tribune,* February 29, 1988, p. 5). The OECD argues that, when wages are compressed, the unemployed are unable "to offer their labour for low wages as a path to higher wage jobs.... Lower wages are to some extent a 'bond' (or deposit) employees pay to show what they can do in order to compete for higher earnings in years to come; and the existence of jobs at low pay will be of particular importance to workers with few certified skills, since employers bear an obvious risk in recruiting them – a risk which the payment of a lower wage may offset" (OECD, *Structural Adjustment and Economic Performance,* p. 137).

75 W. J. Brown and L. G. Rowe, "Employers and the Push for Decentralized Wage Setting," in Niland, ed., *Wage Fixation in Australia,* pp. 136–7. Similarly, Drake and Nieuwenhuysen note that "the uniformity engendered by the arbitration system makes difficult... the downward flexibility possible in United States plant bargaining.... sustained wage cuts for employees have been negotiated in order to stave off plant closure. It is hard to envisage this outcome in the Australian system." Drake and Nieuwenhuysen also note that award rates that "form the first and major base of total earnings" impose nationwide, rates that "do not reflect local economic capacity to pay.... It would indeed be remarkable if the arbitration Commissioners could produce rates appropriate economically to such an enormous range of situations" (*Economic Growth for Australia,* pp. 62–3).

76 ACAC, *National Wage Case: Reasons for Decision,* August, 1988, p. 42.

77 Ibid., p. 3.

78 Ibid.

79 Ibid., p. 42.

80 Henderson, "The Industrial Relations Club," p. 24.

81 OECD, *Structural Adjustment and Economic Performance,* p. 149, n. 75;

McGuinness, *The Case Against the Arbitration Committee*, pp. 8, 27–8; Henderson, "The Industrial Relations Club," p. 24.

82 McGuinness, *The Case Against the Arbitration Commission*, p. 28.

83 Strauss, "Australian Labor Relations Through American Eyes," p. 137.

84 McGuiness, *The Case Against the Arbitration Commission*, pp. 27–8; Henderson, "The Industrial Relations Club," p. 24; *Economist*, March 3, 1990, p. 14.

85 *Business Review Weekly*, August 16, 1991, p. 26; Mitchell, "The Australian Labor Market," pp. 172–3; and Whitfield, *The Australian Labour Market*, p. 183.

86 *Business Review Weekly*, August 16, 1991, p. 26. There is some disagreement as to why Australia's strike record has recently improved. Many observers credit the "accord" over wages and other policy between the Labor government and labor unions (see *OECD Economic Surveys: Australia* [1990], p. 21, and the views of the government as found in *Business Review Weekly*, August 16, 1991, pp. 34 and 38). Others point to the more effective legal remedies that employers have had to deal with destructive strikes over the last decade ("Wage System has Outlived Its Usefulness," n.p.).

87 Whitfield, *The Australian Labour Market*, p. 184. Whitfield surveys the literature and explains the views of dissenters.

88 Strauss, "Australian Labor Relations Through American Eyes," pp. 137 and 145; also see McGuinness, *The Case Against the Arbitration Commission*, p. 19.

89 The quotes are from *Australian Business* (May 16, 1990, p. 34), summarizing some of the "findings" of a recent report by Robert Drago and Mark Wooden. For a recent example of the use of industrial action/threats against the [illegible]'s earlier attention to a claim, see *Financial Review*, June 11, 1991, p. 16. New Zealand has a similar form of arbitration and a similar pattern of strike activity (Whitfield, *The Australian Labour Market*, p. 185).

90 OECD, *Structural Adjustment and Economic Performance*, p. 130; McGuinness, *The Case Against the Arbitration Commission*, p. 7. Also see *OECD Economic Surveys: Australia* (1980), p. 62.

91 August 16, 1991, p. 26.

92 *Australian Business* (March 21, 1990, p. 22) citing the findings of the Swiss-based World Economic Forum's *World Competitiveness Report*.

93 [illegible] think that the criticisms of those who say that the system creates "delay and undue complexity" and encourages "antagonism" and an "unhelpful adversary procedure" are well founded (*Economic Outlook for Australia*, p. [illegible]. See also OECD *Economic Surveys: Australia* (1990), pp. 59 and 62.

94 Strauss, "Australian Labor Relations Through American Eyes," p. 145.

95 Brown and Rowe, "Employers and the Push for Decentralized Wage Setting," p. 133.

96 Strauss, "Australian Labor Relations Through American Eyes," p. 142.

97 John Freebairn links the problem to the arbitration system in the following way: "Because of the centralized wage setting system, whereby gains in

national productivity are distributed nearly equally across the entire workforce, there are limited opportunities for rewarding workers at the enterprise level with higher wages or changes in work conditions for higher enterprise level activity" (quoted in Drake and Nieuwenhuysen, *Economic Growth for Australia,* p. 61).

98 This paragraph draws heavily on Mitchell, "The Australian Labor Market," esp. pp. 172–5, 191–2. The *Melbourne Age* reports that, in 1989, the Liberal party's industrial relations spokesman said there is "no doubt that the 'overcentralized' nature of the wage-fixing system" is "the most important barrier to improvement of working relations between employers and employees" (April 6, 1989, p. 5). For examples of workplace abuses see Drake and Nieuwenhuysen, *Economic Growth for Australia,* p. 97.

99 *Business Council Bulletin,* February 1989, p. 4.

100 Paper no. 32, 1988, p. 22, as cited in M. Keating and G. Dixon, *Making Economic Policy in Australia, 1983–1988* (Melbourne: Longman Chesire, 1988), p. 32.

101 David Plowman, "Award Restructuring: Possibilities and Portents," *Economic and Labour Relations Review* 1, no. 1 (1990): 35.

102 *Melbourne Age,* April 5, 1989, p. 14.

103 *Weekend Australian,* April 8–9, 1989, p. 32.

104 *Sydney Morning Herald,* December 3, 1988, p. 36. Also see Public Service Commission, Senior Executive Staffing Unit, *The State of the Australian Public Service,* Reports to the Heads of Management Meeting, Canberra, April 19, 1989 (Canberra: Australian Government Publishing Service, 1989), p. 2.

105 *Economist,* March 16, 1991, pp. 29–30. Also see January 26, 1991, p. 34.

106 Conclusions summarized in *Australian Business,* March 21, 1990, p. 22.

107 In ibid.

108 See OECD, *Structural Adjustment and Economic Performance,* p. 140, on the relationship of well-functioning labor markets to productivity.

109 *Business Council Bulletin,* April 1989, p. 28. See the discussion of the connection between demarcation squabbles and the wage arbitration system in the earlier section entitled "Bad Labor Relations." Also see Keating and Dixon, *Making Economic Policy in Australia,* pp. 28–9.

110 Ibid.

111 McGuinness, *The Case Against the Arbitration Commission,* pp. 9 and 25; Brown and Rowe, "Employers and the Push for Decentralized Wage Setting," pp. 125–32.

112 Plowman, "Developments in Australian Wage Determination, 1953–83," p. 18.

113 Ibid., p. 18. Also see Keating and Dixon, *Making Economic Policy in Australia,* p. 28.

114 Christine Short, "Equal Pay – What Happened?" *Journal of Industrial Relations* 28, no. 3 (September 1986): 315–17; Carol O'Donnell and Philippa Hall, *Getting Equal: Labour Market Regulation and Women's Work*

(London: Allen & Unwin, 1988), pp. 48–9; Department of Employment, Education, and Training, *Pay Equity,* pp. 6 and 26.

115 Short, "Equal Pay – What Happened?" p. 318; O'Donnell and Hall, *Getting Equal,* p. 54; space prohibits consideration of equal-pay/value developments at the state level, which often preceded federal initiatives. See McGavin, *Wages and Whitlam,* pp. 107–10.

116 *National Pay Equity Coalition Submission to the 1988 National Wage Case,* June 16, 1988, pp. 32 and 43. Isaac, "The Meaning and Significance of Comparative Wage Justice," p. 93.

117 See Short, "Equal Pay – What Happened?," esp. p. 320; also see R. G. Gregory, et al., "Women's Pay in Australia, Great Britain, and the United States: The Role of Laws, Regulations, and Human Capital," in R. Michael, H. Hartmann, B. O'Farrell, eds., *Pay Equity: Empirical Inquiries* (Washington, D.C.: National Academy Press, 1989), p. 239. Gregory focuses on the same two factors and his assessment is only slightly different. An ACTU unionist showed me tables showing separate male and female rates in 1971 for many occupations even including child-care workers, so simply merging rates could have done a great deal.

118 *National Pay Equity Coalition Submission to the 1988 National Wage Case,* June 16, 1988, p. 2. This submission goes on to note that work-value assessments were carried out by the Commission in only two of the cases brought before the Commonwealth Arbitration Commission between 1972 and 1980. In those two cases, "the focus of the assessment was on the similarity of job content in various classifications rather than on the value of the work."

119 See Killingsworth in *Women in the Work Force: Pay Equity,* pp. 106–7, for examples of such statements by proponents and of Gregory's misinterpreted statements. Also see Killingsworth, *The Economics of Comparable Worth* (Kalamazoo, Mich.: Upjohn, 1990), pp. 244–9, where he argues that Gregory's regression analysis showed "negative, statistically significant and rather large effects on female relative employment growth."

120 R. G. Gregory and R. C. Duncan, "Segmented Labor Market Theories and the Australian Experience of Equal Pay for Women," *Journal of Post Keynesian Economics* 3, no. 3 (1981): 403–28; idem, "Equal Pay for Women: A Reply," 22 (June 1983): 60–4; Killingsworth, in *Women in the Work Force: Pay Equity,* p. 106.

Killingsworth's subsequent research using a time series model and simulation finds that secular trends, government wage indexation policy, and other factors explain much of the relative wage gains for women that are usually attributed to equal value and that, in fact, the equal-value policy itself raised women's relative wages only about 9.8 percent by late 1975 and caused a substantial 5.2 percent loss in women's employment relative to men's at that time. Killingsworth also finds that though the equal-value policy got women higher wages more quickly, they were not, by 1986, receiving higher wages than they would have in the absence of the policy

(*The Economics of Comparable Worth,* pp. 250–65, 279–81). Killingsworth's analysis is criticized in R. E. Gregory and A. Daly, "Can Economic Theory Explain Why Australian Women Are So Well Paid Relative to Their United States Counterparts?" *The International Review of Comparative Public Policy* 81 (1991): 81–128.

121 Mitchell, "The Australian Labor Market," p. 130; McGavin, *Wages and Whitlam,* p. 121.

122 McGavin, *Wages and Whitlam,* p. 122.

123 Mitchell, "The Australian Labor Market," p. 134; McGavin, *Wages and Whitlam,* pp. 115–16; R. G. Gregory, P. McMahon, and B. Whittingham, "Women in the Australian Labor Force: Trends, Causes, and Consequences," *Journal of Labor Economics* 3, no. 1, pt. 2 (January 1985): 294–5.

124 Henry Aaron, "Social Welfare in Australia," in Caves and Krause, eds., *The Australian Economy,* pp. 366–7. On this point the OECD has noted that the restricted coverage of Australian unemployment benefits has led women to be much less likely to register with the Commonwealth Employment Service (CES). For example, "In July 1982, 37.2 per cent of women who were looking for work were not registered with the CES compared to 19.7 per cent of unemployed men" (*The Integration of Women into the Economy* [Paris, 1985], p. 22).

125 For Gregory and Duncan's short written reply to McGavin, see "Equal Pay for Women: A Reply," *Australian Economic Papers* 22 (June 1983): 60–4; also see Lawrence Krause, "Australia's Comparative Advantage in International Trade," in Caves and Krause, eds., *The Australian Economy,* p. 290; for other short discussions of the Gregory–McGavin findings, see Whitfield, *The Australian Labour Market,* pp. 124–7, and Sandra Eccles, "The Role of Women in the Australian Labour Market: A Survey of the Literature," *Journal of Industrial Relations* 24 (September 1982): 330–1.

126 Gregory made this very clear in my interview. Also see Gregory et al., "Women's Pay in Australia, Great Britain and the United States," pp. 237–9, and Killingsworth, in *Women in the Work Force: Pay Equity Hearing,* p. 103.

127 Killingsworth, in *Women in the Work Force: Pay Equity,* p. 102.

128 Caves and Krause, "Introduction," p. 3.

129 Ibid.

130 McGavin, *Wages and Whitlam;* cf. pp. 1, 60, 62, 150.

131 Whitfield, *The Australian Labour Market,* p. 136.

132 Ursula Doyle, "Times Up," address to a conference entitled "Equal Pay and Economic Justice for Women," September 13, 1985 (DOER, Women's Bureau, 1985), pp. 4–6. Also see ACAC, *Private Hospitals' and Doctors' Nurses (ACT) Award, 1972,* Transcript of proceedings, December 12, 1985, pp. 68–70.

133 Short, "Equal Pay–What Happened?" p. 332.

134 Dr. Meridith Burgmann, a Labor member of Parliament and member of the National Pay Equity Coalition, has said, "I believe . . . that until we get

a wage gender gap of 0.0 per cent then we have an unfair society" (*Australian,* October 17, 1991).

135 *National Pay Equity Coalition Submission to the 1988 National Wage Case,* p. 32.

136 Short, "Equal Pay – What Happened?" pp. 324–9.

137 Burton, *Work Value, Comparable Worth or Pay Equity?* p. 11.

138 *National Pay Equity Coalition Submission to the 1988 National Wage Case,* p. 9.

139 Quoted in ibid., p. 10.

140 Ibid., p. 18.

141 Clare Burton, *Women's Worth: Pay Equity and Job Evaluation in Australia* (Canberra: Australian Government Publishing Service, 1987). Also see Labour Research Centre, *Pay Equity for Women in Australia,* p. 57.

142 Quoted in *National Pay Equity Coalition Submission to the 1988 National Wage Case,* p. 12.

143 Ibid., pp. 22–4; Short, "Equal Pay – What Happened?" pp. 330–1; Department of Employment, Education, and Training, *Pay Equity: A Survey,* pp. 50–2.

144 ACAC, *Private Hospitals' and Doctors' Nurses (ACT) Award, 1972: Decision,* February 18, 1986 (Print G2250), p. 6.

145 Short, "Equal Pay – What Happened?" p. 331.

146 ACAC, *National Wage Case, April 1991,* Print J7400, p. 56.

147 Ibid.

148 ACAC, *Private Hospitals' and Doctors' Nurses (ACT) Award, 1972: Decision* (1986), pp. 4 and 7.

149 Department of Employment, Education and Training, *Pay Equity: A Survey,* p. 50.

150 ACAC, *National Wage Case, August 1988: Reasons for Decision* (Dec. Print H 4000), p. 15.

151 Brown and Rowe, "Employers and the Push for Decentralized Wage Setting," p. 135.

152 *Business Review Weekly,* August 16, 1991, p. 26.

153 Editorial, *Weekend Australian,* February 22–3, 1992, p. 28.

154 *Weekend Australian,* March 14–15, 1992, p. 10.

155 ACTU, *Blueprint for Changing Awards and Agreements,* February 1989.

156 Peter McLaughlin, "Enterprise Bargaining: Making Australia Competitive," *Economic and Labor Relations Review* 1, no. 1 (1990): 65.

157 *Business Council Bulletin,* April 1989, p. 30; also see the special insert on Australia in the *Economist,* May 6, 1989, p. 8; Peter Reith, Member of Parliament, *Paper No. 2 – Award Restructuring,* January 1989. As recently as 1981, however, 61 percent of Australians favored arbitration over private collective bargaining for setting wages (Mitchell, "The Australian Labor Market," p. 160).

158 Peter Reith, *Paper No. 2 – Award Restructuring; Business Council Bulletin,* February 1989, p. 6; *Melbourne Age,* April 5, 1989, p. 14. On the connection between the new union-led "blueprint" reform and the old dis-

credited comparative wage justice, see David Plowman, "Award Restructuring: Possibilities and Portents," esp. pp. 22–4, 33–4.

159 See Richard Blandy and Susan Hancock, "The Australian Labour Market, September 1988," *Australian Bulletin of Labour* 14, no. 4 (September 1988): 540–1. Business support for specific skill training and other in-house approaches and opposition to the national skill frameworks approach comes through in a Business Council of Australia report based on a survey of business: *Workforce 2000* (see discussions in *Weekend Australian,* July 11–12, 1991, p. 8, and July 18–19, 1990, p. 50). The head of the Equal Pay Unit in thc Australian Department of Industrial Relations, Dr. Kathy MacDermott, told me that recently "technical colleges are putting in courses everywhere" (phone interview August 26, 1992). This is presumably because of IRC support for the ACTU idea that increased training should bring more pay.

160 Australian Industrial Relations Commission, Industrial Relations Act, 1988, Child Care Industry (Australian Capital Territory), Award 1985; Child Care Industry (Northern Territory), Award 1986; Child Care Workers/Health and Welfare Services, September 14, 1990, Print J4316.

161 Department of Industrial Relations, *Equal Pay Unit Newsletter,* October 1991, p. 5.

162 See, e.g., D. H. Plowman, "The 1991 National Wage Case: An Industrial Relations Perspective," *Economic and Labour Relations Review* 2, no. 1 (1991): 25. Department of Industrial Relations, *Women in Restructured Awards,* 1990, p. 7.

163 *National Pay Equity Coalition Submission to the 1988 National Wage Case,* p. 4.

164 See *Weekend Australian,* May 23–4, 1992, p. 4. Others outside the Liberal party also see labor market reform as the key election issue. See ibid., May 30–1, 1991, p. 24, and March 7–8, 1992, p. 23.

165 See Alan Wood, "Wages and the Price of Neglect," *Weekend Australian,* May 30–1, 1992, p. 24.

166 *Weekend Australian,* April 20–1, 1991, p. 10.

167 Ibid., April 4–5, 1992, p. 15.

168 Ibid., March 14–15, 1992, p. 10.

169 Tim Blue, "Institute Ponders Its Future after Veto," *Australian Business,* April 3, 1991, p. 24.

170 Discussed in *Weekend Australian,* July 18–19, 1992, pp. 4 and 17.

171 Ibid., July 11–12, 1992, p. 18. Also see July 18–19, 1992, pp. 4 and 17.

172 Discussed in ibid., July 11–12, 1992, p. 8.

173 Ibid., July 18–19, 1992, p. 4. Also see p. 18.

174 Ibid., March 14–15, 1992, p. 10.

175 Enterprise bargaining examples are from ibid., February 22–3, 1992, p. 8, and March 14–15, 1992, pp. 10–11.

176 In arguing for the relevance of Australian experience to the comparable-worth debate, Mark Killingsworth puts the matter as follows: "Australian work value determinations generally *include* the same factors typically

considered in most comparable worth job evaluations in the U.S. (skill, effort, responsibility and working conditions) and generally *exclude* the same factors that are usually excluded from consideration in comparable worth job evaluations in the U.S. (i.e., market considerations such as the profitability of individual employers)" (*The Economics of Comparable Worth,* p. 239).

177 McGavin, *Wages and Whitlam,* pp. 1, 54, 150.

178 Confederation of Australian Industry, *National Wage Fixation in Australia (1907 to 1978): An Historical Overview,* January 1979, pp. 15–16.

179 *Weekend Australian,* April 8–9, 1989, p. 32.

180 Chapter 2, note 35, is relevant here.

181 Niland, "Introduction," p. xv.

182 For recent written evidence of this, see Labour Research Centre, *Pay Equity for Women in Australia,* p. 57.

183 The recent report of the Labour Research Centre for the National Women's Consultative Council finds that one reason men earn more than women is "the importance of higher unionization and militancy among traditionally male occupations" (*Pay Equity for Women in Australia,* p. 36).

184 For evidence of how the threat of competition has increased the willingness of U.S. public-sector unions to consider work reforms, see Urban Institute, *Policy and Research Report,* Winter 1988, p. 9.

185 Of course, strategically placed unions that threaten strikes may also make income gains, but in the long run, competition from nonunion firms will reduce the power of such unions, if laws and institutions make such competition possible. See OECD, *Structural Adjustment and Economic Performance* (Paris, 1987), pp. 143–5, for a discussion of the ways in which the existence of a sizeable nonunion sector can discipline collective bargaining.

186 *Weekend Australian,* May 30–1, 1992, p. 26. *Sydney Morning Herald,* April 1, 1989, p. 13; *Melbourne Age,* April 4, 1989, p. 11. More generally, in OECD countries women "to a large extent" are "strongly concentrated in growing parts of the economy" (OECD, *The Integration of Women Into the Economy,* p. 54).

## *8. Conclusion*

1 With the one exception in note 7, all quotations from the National Committee on Pay Equity (NCPE) tenth anniversary conference program evaluation panel are taken from a tape of the panel sent to me by NCPE staff.

2 Robert Michael and Heidi Hartmann, "Pay Equity: Assessing the Issues," in Robert Michael, Heidi Hartmann, and Brigid O'Farrell, eds., *Pay Equity: Empirical Inquiries* (Washington, D.C.: National Academy Press, 1989), pp. 1–2.

3 Ellen Paul, *Equity and Gender* (New Brunswick, N.J.: Transaction, 1989), pp. 109–10.

4 Quoted passages are from State of New Jersey, *Interim Report – Six Months*

*of Progress by the Task Force on Equitable Compensation,* June 1, 1985, p. 21, and *The Task Force on Equitable Compensation: Final Report,* November 30, 1987, pp. 18 and 30. The Iowa Oversight Committee also "modified the factor weights twice after examining their impact on the final results" (Peter Orazem and Peter Mattila, "Comparable Worth and the Structure of Earnings: The Iowa Case," in Michael, Hartmann, and O'Farrell, eds., *Pay Equity: Empirical Inquiries,* p. 180).

5 On the tendency to equate bias-free evaluations with those that increase wages in women's jobs, see Mark Killingsworth, "The Economics of Comparable Worth: A Comment on Hartmann," in Robert Fullinwider and Claudia Mills, eds., *The Moral Foundations of Civil Rights* (Totowa, N.J.: Rowman & Littlefield, 1986), p. 190.

6 Australian Conciliation and Arbitration Commission [ACAC], *Private Hospitals' and Doctors' Nurses (ACT) Award, 1972: Applications by the Royal Australian Nurses Federation to Vary Re Rates of Pay and Wage Rates,* December 12, 1985, p. 91. Also see the unpublished *National Pay Equity Coalition Submission to the 1988 National Wage Case,* June 16, 1988, p. 9.

7 This Steinberg quotation comes from my notes taken at the panel session, not from the NCPE tape of the session. The first side of the tape ended in the midst of Steinberg's remarks. At the beginning of the second side the tape is blank for several minutes, and thereafter the quality of the sound is much poorer. My notes show that it was during the period of the blank tape that Steinberg made the remarks quoted here. There was apparently a technical problem with the tape. The tape shows my notes to be generally accurate. In my notes I place the words quoted in text in quotation marks, a notational device that I use to show that I am quite sure of the accuracy of the words I have in my notes.

8 Interview with a staff member for Congressional Caucus on Women's Issues, August 2, 1989.

9 Congresswoman Mary Rose Oakar in *Federal Pay Equity Act of 1984,* Hearing before the Subcommittee on Compensation and Employee Benefits of the Committee on Post Office and Civil Service on HR 4599 and HR 5092, July 17, 1984, 98th Congress, 2d Session, p. 132.

10 Rothchild says this in print (with Bonnie Watkins) in "Pay Equity in Minnesota: The Facts Are In," *Review of Public Personnel Administration* 7, no. 3 (Summer 1987): 18.

11 *Congressional Record,* 100th Congress, House of Representatives, September 28, 1988, p. 8570. Also see Morella on September 27, 1988, p. H 8438.

12 Keynote speech to the NCPE tenth anniversary conference, October 21, 1989. Linda Blum notes that the National Academy of Sciences report "expressed a clear, expert consensus in favor of comparable worth that is often seen as definitive. The report, therefore, provides local activists and nonexperts with the legitimation or authority they may need to bring pay equity into the political arena" (*Between Feminism and Labor: The Significance of the Comparable Worth Movement* [Berkeley and Los Angeles: University of California Press, 1991], p. 52). *Women, Work and Wages* is called a

"classic" study in Sara Evans and Barbara Nelson, *Wage Justice: Comparable Worth and the Paradox of Technocratic Reform* (Chicago: University of Chicago Press, 1989), p. 38, and its association with the "prestigious" National Academy of Sciences' National Research Council (NRC) is noted in Michael Rubenstein's book *Equal Pay for Work of Equal Value* published in England (London: Macmillan Press, 1984), p. 15. The NRC study was distributed to every member of the New Jersey Task Force on Equitable Compensation.

13 Donald Treiman and Heidi Hartmann, eds., *Women, Work and Wages: Equal Pay for Jobs of Equal Value* (Washington, D.C.: National Academy Press, 1981), p. 81.

14 Paula England says, "The politics of comparable worth features business groups and academic economists opposing the concept" (*Comparable Worth: Theories and Evidence* [New York: De Gruyter, 1992], p. 222).

15 *Congressional Quarterly Almanac* (Washington, D.C., 1985), p. 82-H.

16 Ibid. (1986), p. 100-H.

17 June O'Neill, "An Argument Against Comparable Worth," in U.S. Commission on Civil Rights, *Comparable Worth: Issue for the 80's,* vol. 1 (Washington, D.C.: U.S. Government Printing Office, 1984), p. 184.

18 *New York Times,* May 31, 1990, p. D-12.

19 Tim Witosky, "Nurses Stand to Gain under Comparable Worth," *Des Moines Register,* May 16, 1984, n.p.

20 *Economic Report of the President* (Washington, D.C.: U.S. Government Printing Office, 1986), p. 278.

21 See *Structural Adjustment and Economic Performance* (Paris: Organization For Economic Cooperation and Development [OECD], 1987), pp. 135–44, and *Economies in Transition: Structural Adjustment in OECD Countries,* (Paris, OECD: 1989), pp. 43 and 54.

22 There are, of course, other causes of Australia's poor performance. But, as argued in Chapter 7, many, such as tariff protection, have their roots in a desire to preserve the wages/incomes granted by the wage-setting tribunals.

23 *Economies in Transition,* p. 52. Though these general comments are obviously relevant to Australia, the OECD is not specifically discussing Australia in the section I quote from.

24 Interview with the author, October 26, 1989.

25 Interview with the author, August 30, 1989; also see Evans and Nelson, *Wage Justice,* p. 69.

26 Speech, delivered October 21, 1989.

27 Ibid.

28 Ibid.

29 NCPE, *Grassroots Action Kit* (Washington, D.C., 1988), p. 25.

30 Interview with the author, October 26, 1989.

31 Interview with the author, October 27, 1989.

32 Barbara Bergmann, *The Economic Emergence of Women* (New York: Basic, 1986), pp. 195–7.

33 Alfred Kahn, "America's Democrats: Can Liberalism Survive Inflation?"

*Economist,* March 7, 1981, p. 22. Neither Kahn nor the economists quoted on profits and unions in succeeding paragraphs are discussing comparable worth per se.

34 *OECD Economic Outlook* 45 (June 1989): 183.

35 Paul McCracken et al., *Towards Full Employment and Price Stability* (Paris: OECD, 1977).

36 Robert M. Dunn, Jr., "Don't Knock Reaganomics: Luck and Policy Produced a Winning Record on Jobs and Prices," *Washington Post,* July 24, 1988, p. C-5.

37 Harry Johnson and Peter Mieszkowski, "The Effects of Unionization on the Distribution of Income: A General Equilibrium Approach," *Quarterly Journal of Economics* 84 (November 1970): 560. For more on economists' views on equity and growth, see Steven Rhoads, *The Economist's View of the World: Government, Markets and Public Policy* (Cambridge University Press, 1985), chap. 6.

38 Herbert Stein, "The U.S. Economy: A Visitor's Guide," *American Enterprise* 1, no. 4 (July–August 1990): 12.

39 Interview with the author, Heidi Hartmann, October 27, 1989; phone interviews with the author, Randall Filer, November 3, 1989, and June O'Neill, 1986 (my notes do not give an exact date for this phone call).

40 "Politics of the Professoriate," *American Enterprise* 2, no. 4 (July–August 1991): 87.

41 Henry Aaron and Cameron Lougy, *The Comparable Worth Controversy* (Washington, D.C.: Brookings Institution, 1986), pp. 49–50.

42 Interview with the author, November 1989.

43 Victor Fuchs, *Women's Quest for Economic Equality* (Cambridge, Mass.: Harvard University Press, 1988), p. 146.

44 Killingsworth in U.S. Congress, Joint Economic Committee, *Women in the Work Force: Pay Equity,* hearing, April 10, 1984, p. 87, and Aaron and Lougy, *The Comparable Worth Controversy,* p. 50.

45 Phone interview with the author, November 3, 1989.

46 Phone interview with the author, November 21, 1989.

47 David Lutes and Nina Rothchild, "Compensation: Pay Equity Loses to Chicken Little and Other Excuses," *Personnel Journal* 65, no. 10 (October 1986): 126.

48 Claudia Goldin, "The Earnings Gap in Historical Perspective," in U.S. Commission on Civil Rights, *Comparable Worth: Issue for the 80's,* vol. 1, pp. 13–14.

49 I argued before that, without too much difficulty, businesses would be able to turn an illicit situation where "female" jobs are paid less because there is a surplus of labor into a legal situation, where "male" jobs are paid more to overcome a shortage of labor (see Chapter 6, p. 175).

50 As long as the demand curve for labor slopes downward, some unemployment will result when the wages of predominantly female occupations rise above market equilibrium. Even Gregory and other economists who support

comparable worth do not doubt that the demand curve slopes downward. At the higher wage, some employers somewhere will hire fewer people. This unemployment effect has not been hypothetical for some home health aides in Minnesota and in Australia.

51 As quoted in Frances Hutner, *Equal Pay for Comparable Worth* (New York: Praeger, 1986), p. 46. Also see p. 54.

52 See U.S. Commission on Civil Rights, *Comparable Worth: Issue for the 80's,* vol. 2, pp. 35 and 44.

53 Ray Marshall and Beth Paulin, "The Employment and Earnings of Women: The Comparable Worth Debate," in ibid., vol. 1, p. 207. See Jeremy Rabkin's powerful rebuttal, "Comparable Worth as Civil Rights Policy: Potentials for Disaster," in ibid., vol. 1, p. 191n.

54 Bergmann, *The Economic Emergence of Women,* pp. 188–9.

55 Ehrenberg and Smith use a similar example to show that "it is difficult to 'trick the market.' In the face of changing relative demand conditions, either wage differentials for the two types of professors [computer science and English] must be allowed to arise or quality differentials will arise. In neither case, however, can comparable worth be achieved. Put another way, the value of a job cannot be determined independently of market conditions" (*Modern Labor Economics* [Glenview, Ill.: Scott, Foresman, 1985], p. 476).

56 Hugh Winebrenner, "The Implementation of Comparable Worth in Iowa," in Rita Mae Kelly and Jane Bayes, eds., *Comparable Worth, Pay Equity, and Public Policy* (New York: Greenwood, 1988), p. 221.

57 Memorandum from John Tries, secretary, Department of Employment Relations, State of Wisconsin, to co-chairpersons and members of the Joint Committee on Employment Relations, January 21, 1988.

58 *New York Times,* May 31, 1990, p. D-22. In Canada there have also been examples of hierarchy inversions: "At the University of Toronto... pay equity changes will leave some accountants earning less than the clerks they supervise" (*Wall Street Journal,* March 9, 1990, p. B-7).

59 Discussed in *Comparable Worth for Federal Jobs,* U.S. Office of Personnel Management, OPM Doc. 149-40-3 (Washington, D.C.: U.S. Government Printing Office, 1987), pp. 49–53.

60 *Washington Post,* October 18, 1990, p. A-1, October 25, 1990, p. A-5. These reforms are to go into effect in 1994 (see July 14, 1992, p. A-11).

61 Congresswoman Mary Rose Oakar in *Equal Employment Opportunity Commission's Handling of Pay Equity Cases,* Hearings before the House Subcommittee on Manpower and Housing of the Government Operations Committee, February 29, 1984, p. 8. Also see Paul, *Equity and Gender,* p. 88; Jennifer Roback, *A Matter of Choice* (New York: Priority Press, 1986), p. 15; Rabkin, "Comparable Worth as Civil Rights Policy: Potentials for Disaster," in U.S. Commission on Civil Rights, *Comparable Worth: Issue for the 80's,* vol. 1, p. 188; Senate Bill S-5, 99th Congress, 1st Session; House Bill H.R. 5092, 98th Congress, 2d Session.

62 United Nations General Assembly, Thirty-fourth session, Agenda item 75, A/RES/34/180, January 22, 1980. For discussion, see *Convention on the Elimination of All Forms of Discrimination against Women,* Hearing before the Senate Committee on Foreign Relations, 101st Congress, August 2, 1990.

63 National Committee on Pay Equity, *Newsnotes,* April 1992, p. 1.

64 Phyllis Schlafly and the Eagle Forum have opposed comparable worth but have not stimulated much grassroots concern. See Blum, *Between Feminism and Labor,* pp. 195–6; also see Evans and Nelson, *Wage Justice,* p. 64; Jane Mansbridge, *Why We Lost the ERA* (Chicago: University of Chicago Press, 1986), pp. 18 and 36.

65 See Dinesh D'Souza, "The New Feminist Revolt," *Policy Review,* no. 35 (Winter 1986): 49.

66 On this theme, see Rabkin, "Comparable Worth as Civil Rights Policy," pp. 193–4.

67 George Strauss, "Australian Labor Relations Through American Eyes," *Industrial Relations* 20, no. 2 (Spring 1988): 137.

68 P. P. McGuinness, *The Case Against the Arbitration Commission,* Centre for Independent Studies Occasional Paper no. 11 (St. Leonards: 1985), p. 27.

69 *Economist,* March 3, 1990, p. 14.

70 Judith Agassi, *Comparing the Work Attitudes of Women and Men* (Lexington, Mass.: Lexington, 1982), pp. 61–7; Michael Murray and Tom Atkinson ("Gender Differences in Correlates of Job Satisfaction," *Canadian Journal of Behavioral Science* 13, no. 1, [1981]: 44–52) report that most studies find "that men attach greater importance to extrinsic features of the job, i.e., pay and security, and to features such as advancement, self-determination or autonomy, and accomplishment or achievement. The most consistent finding for women is the greater importance they place on social aspects of the job and relations with supervisors and company, with some suggestions of the importance of interesting and varied work" (p. 49). Murray and Atkinson's findings differ from this consensus in important ways but not with regard to the importance that women attach to social relations on the job. Also see sources in Chapter 2, note 31.

71 Cynthia Gramm, "The Determinants of Strike Incidence and Severity," *Industrial and Labor Relations Review* 39, no. 3 (April 1986): 369 and 374.

72 Heather Gardner and Brigid McCoppin, "The Politicization of Australian Nurses: Victoria, 1984–1986," *Politics* 22, no. 1 (May 1987): 30.

73 Agassi, *Comparing the Work Attitudes of Women and Men,* pp. 61–7.

74 Winfred Gallagher, "Sex and Hormones," *Atlantic Monthly* 261, no. 3 (March 1988): 77–82; Cynthia Gorney, "Boys Just Want to Have Guns," *Washington Post,* August 4, 1985, p. G–1.

75 There is also reason to doubt that women will like the process itself, a process that produces "rotten" labor relations (*Economist,* March 3, 1990, p. 16).

76 Clare Burton (with Raven Hag and Gay Thompson), *Women's Worth: Pay*

*Equity and Job Evaluation in Australia* (Canberra: Australian Government Printing Service, 1987), pp. 98, 108–9. At the end Burton is quoting Mandy Snell, "The Equal Pay and Sex Discrimination Acts: Their Impact in the Workplace," *Feminist Review* no. 1 (1979): 43–4. Also see Helen Remick, who notes that women tend to use "weaker verbs" ("Major Issues in a priori Applications," in Remick, ed., *Comparable Worth and Wage Discrimination* [Philadelphia: Temple University Press, 1984], p. 107). On women's dislike of confrontation, see Marilyn Loden, "Feminine Leadership," *Vital Speeches of the Day* 52 (May 15, 1986): 473, and Elizabeth Vallance and Elizabeth Davies, *Women of Europe: Women MEPs and Equality Policy* (Cambridge University Press, 1986), p. 8.

77 Joan Acker, *Doing Comparable Worth: Gender, Class and Pay Equity* (Philadelphia: Temple University Press, 1989), pp. 148–9. Though these sex-related tendencies may or may not be changeable, some of them have been present since early childhood. Studies of three- and four-year-old nursery school children have found that girls make more "clear calls," i.e., "requests for contact or signs of affiliation," whereas boys "make almost all the harsh noises (barks, growls and roars)." Boys also uttered more "commands and expletives, and used more abrupt phrases such as 'look at me' " (Diane McGuinness, "How Schools Discriminate Against Boys," *Human Nature* 2, no. 2 [February 1979]: 84 and 87). Boys and girls alike paid attention when a boy cried no, but "a similar prohibition from a girl tended to have little effect on the boy she was playing with" (Gorney, "Boys Just Want to Have Guns," p. G–3).

78 John Niland, "Introduction," in Niland, ed., *Wage Fixation in Australia* (London: Allen & Unwin, 1986) p. xv. A 1991 report to the Ontario, Canada, Pay Equity Commission finds that the Ontario experience has produced "negative effects on union–management relationships and morale of employees" (National Committee on Pay Equity, *Newsletter* [Fall 1991]: 7).

79 Debate during question time in the Australian House of Representatives, July 24, 1992, as seen on C-SPAN I, July 18, 1992.

80 Strauss, "Australian Labor Relations Through American Eyes," p. 141.

81 On protecting the private sphere and preventing sharp economic divisions, see Marc Plattner, "American Democracy and the Acquisitive Spirit," in Robert Goldwin and William Schambra, eds., *How Capitalistic Is the Constitution?* (Washington, D.C.: American Enterprise Institute, 1982), pp. 1–21.

82 Cf. the treatment of Title VII and comparable worth in Aaron and Lougy, *The Comparable Worth Controversy*, pp. 49–51; Mark Killingsworth, *The Economics of Comparable Worth* (Kalamazoo, Mich.: Upjohn Institute, 1990), pp. 282–3; and Ronald Ehrenberg and Robert Smith, *Modern Labor Economics* (Glenview, Ill.: Scott, Foresman, 1985), chap. 14. Richard Epstein, a libertarian law professor and follower of the law and economics school of law, opposes both Title VII and comparable worth. He says, however, that though Title VII is "misconceived, so much more is the notion

of comparable worth" (*Forbidden Ground: The Case Against Employment Discrimination Laws* [Cambridge, Mass.: Harvard University Press, 1992], p. 282). Also see note 83.

83 I use the phrase "would oppose" because many economists may know too little of comparable worth to have an opinion. See Chapter 6, p. 172. But as Arthur Okun has said, "Controls and constraints on prices and wages" is at the heart of economists' "non-agenda for government" (*The Political Economy of Prosperity* [Washington, D.C.: Brookings Institution, 1970], p. 6). Also see the survey mentioned in Chapter 4, note 100, and note 14, this chapter.

84 National Committee on Pay Equity, *Pay Equity Makes Good Business Sense,* undated pamphlet, p. 6.

85 From 1981 to 1991 the pay gap for full-time Australian workers *decreased* from 80 to 81 percent. From 1981 to 1990, however, the pay gap *increased* from 80 to 78.8 percent. The recent improvement is thought to be primarily the result of reduced overtime by men in the severe recession. From May 1991 to May 1992 the pay gap again increased from 81 to 79.8 percent (Australian Bureau of Statistics [ABS], Average Weekly Earnings, States and Australia, Catalogue no. 6302.0 for May 1992 and May 1991, *National Pay Equity Coalition Submission to the 1988 National Wage Case,* June 16, 1988, Exhibit 1 [using Australian Bureau of Statistics data]). U.K. data is from Department of Employment, *New Earnings Survey,* April 1991, Table 15, pp. A15.1–A15.2. U.S. data is for *median* weekly earnings in 1981 and 1991. Australian and U.K. data are for *average* weekly earnings. Average earnings for the United States are not available for 1981 or earlier years. However, median (74.0 percent) and average earnings (73.6 percent) pay gaps are quite similar in 1991 and other recent years (U.S. Bureau of Statistics unpublished data). Since full-time men work more hours per week than full-time women, a fairer pay gap measure is earnings per hour. In terms of earnings per hour worked the gap closed from 64 percent in 1979 to 74 percent in 1988 (U.S. Department of Labor, *Facts on Working Women,* no. 90–3 [October 1990], p. 1). I do not have later earnings per hour figures, but from 1988 to 1991 the median weekly earnings gap closed almost 4 points so the U.S. hourly wage gap is probably now close to 78 percent.

86 OECD, *The Integration of Women into the Economy* (Paris: 1985), p. 22. Also see June O'Neill's conclusion that, during the 1980s, "changes in market demand for different types of skills were generally more favorable to women than men" ("Women and Wages," *American Enterprise* 1, no. 6 [November–December 1990]: 26).

87 Calculated from figures given in the *Statistical Abstract of the U.S., 1991,* Table 386, and Bureau of Labor Statistics, *Employment and Earnings,* January 1992, Table 39, p. 208.

# Index